THE STORY OF OLD SARATOGA

THE BURGOYNE CAMPAIGN
TO WHICH IS ADDED
NEW YORK'S SHARE IN THE REVOLUTION

John Henry Brandow, M.A.
Sometime Pastor of the (Dutch) Reformed Church of Schuylerville, N.Y.
and member of the New York State Historical Association

SECOND EDITION

HERITAGE BOOKS
2010

HERITAGE BOOKS
AN IMPRINT OF HERITAGE BOOKS, INC.

Books, CDs, and more—Worldwide

For our listing of thousands of titles see our website
at
www.HeritageBooks.com

A Facsimile Reprint
Published 2010 by
HERITAGE BOOKS, INC.
Publishing Division
100 Railroad Ave. #104
Westminster, Maryland 21157

Copyright © 1919 John Henry Brandow

— Publisher's Notice —

We have elected ot omit unnecessary blank pages in the beginning of this book. As a result, this book begins with page v. We would like to assure our readers that no original text has been omitted.

In reprints such as this, it is often not possible to remove blemishes from the original. We feel the contents of this book warrant its reissue despite these blemishes and hope you will agree and read it with pleasure.

International Standard Book Numbers
Paperbound: 978-0-7884-1510-4
Clothbound: 978-0-7884-8391-2

THE STORY OF OLD SARATOGA

DEDICATION

*To the
Patriotic Societies
in the United States
and to all Americans who revere
the characters and cherish
the heroic deeds
of their
forebears
I dedicate this book*

THE SARATOGA MONUMENT

Erected by the Saratoga Monument Association to commemorate the Surrender of Burgoyne's Army to Gen. Gates, October 17, 1777, the grand finale of one of the fifteen decisive battles of the world. It stands on the site of Burgoyne's fortified camp, on the hill overlooking the place of his surrender. The corner stone was laid with civic and military ceremonies, October 17, 1877, and completed in June, 1883.

Height, 155 feet; Base, 40 feet square; 184 steps lead up to the last windows, which command an enchanting view of from ten to eighty miles in all directions.

PREFACE

This book, like many another, is a growth from a small beginning; the outcome of a brief sketch made for another purpose. The author never dreamed that he would be guilty of perpetrating a book. When he began the aforesaid sketch he supposed that the history of the locality had been thoroughly written up and that nothing of interest could be found which had not repeatedly been spread before the interested public.

This surmise was certainly true of the Burgoyne campaign with its battles and auspicious ending which occurred within the bounds of Old Saratoga. All of this had become well threshed straw before we began our task; hence, we have been able to add but a little to what has already appeared in print concerning it, except a few anecdotes of a personal nature. We can claim nothing more with respect to that decisive campaign in the great struggle of the fathers for independence than that we have redrawn the picture from the view point of the "Heights of Saratoga," and have put into the scene a series of details which heretofore had appeared only as scattered and disjointed fragments.

Our excuse for the book is this: While hunting for Colonial or ante-Revolutionary data relative to the history of this locality we discovered that there was very much more to it than had yet appeared in any form accessible to the public; and, what is more to the point, we found that this is the only locality, worthy of it, in the valley between New York City and Plattsburg, whose Colonial history had not been carefully explored and written up. With this in mind we resolved to dig down and get at the roots of its history; so we have diligently examined everything we could hear of or find that would throw any light on that shadowy epoch in Old Saratoga's story; and we trust that those who are interested in such matters will agree with us that we have been measurably paid for the trouble. In the meantime we believe we have also discovered several important historic sites, together with the name of the one local annalist, the anonymous Sexagenary, which had long been lost.

It is a pity that there had not been more chroniclers to record the many interesting incidents which must have occurred here, particularly during the period of King George's war, and yet more is the pity that many of the records that were made have been lost. Still, as it is, we feel that we can assert without fear of successful contradiction that outside the cities of New York and Albany, Old Saratoga is the most interesting historic locality in New York State, and New York was the battle ground of America in Revolutionary and Colonial days. But notwithstanding the fact that this is the scene of so many events, tragic, thrilling, and heroic, in their character; events far reaching and superlatively beneficent in their effects on our civilization, Saratoga is a name that has been made little of by American writers, and is seldom used to conjure with in speech or story.

We have in this work kept the military history separate from the civil in the belief that the average reader will find it less confusing, and hence more satisfactory, than any attempt at mixing the two together, and yet we confess that the line of demarkation between the civil and the military is sometimes pretty hazy.

That we have been enabled to carry this work to completion grateful acknowledgments are due, first, to the many interested citizens of Schuylerville, without whose encouragement we would not have dared to embark on such a venture; to Mr. W. L. Stone, the accomplished Revolutionary historian, and to Gen. J. Watts De Peyster, military critic and prolific author, for valuable facts and suggestions; to Miss Fanny Schuyler, for the loan of Schuyler manuscripts and for criticising a portion of the work; to Mr. W. B. Melius, the erudite keeper of the Albany County records, for help in our search for data; to Mr. Hugh Hastings, State Historian, and Henry Harmon Noble, his efficient assistant, for their hearty encouragement, timely suggestions and valuable hints concerning historic manuscripts preserved in the State Library; and to Mr. Arnold J. F. van Laer, State Archivist, for invaluable assistance in deciphering some of the ancient manuscripts under his care.

We are also especially obligated to Mr. C. W. Mayhew of Schuylerville for the free use of his library, rich in historic works; to Miss Anna Hill for generously typewriting a large portion of the manuscript; to Mrs. John H. Lowber and Mrs. Jane Marshall for courteously permitting a careful examination of their historic homes, and for interesting facts connected therewith.

We also feel deeply indebted to Rev. F. C. Scoville of Greenwich, N. Y., for valuable assistance in our search for the author of the Sexagenary.

SCHUYLERVILLE. N. Y., *Dec. 15, 1900.*

PREFACE TO THE SECOND EDITION

ABOUT the time the first edition of this work was exhausted the author received notice from the Chief of the School Libraries Division of The University of New York that he had placed the story of Old Saratoga on the list of supplementary readings for our public schools. Naturally pleased by such a gracious testimony to the value of the work the author decided to publish a new edition. Before doing so, however, he resolved to make a second and somewhat more extended research among original sources for data concerning the early history of this locality. The result was the discovery of many facts which, though not of prime importance, yet, at least, are interesting and illuminating; and furthermore, by them gaps in the story have been filled, and many questions that before were puzzling have been answered.

This edition being designed for a wider constituency will omit several chapters and a number of paragraphs which appeared in the first edition. Our reasons for this are 1st: Because such annals of this locality as are of Statewide interest, and really important, have to do almost exclusively with its Colonial and Revolutionary history. Much of the latter has heretofore been inaccessible to our people, while the modern history is less interesting, and is also within easy reach of the curious.* Because of this much of the matter relating to modern Schuylerville, etc., we have left out. 2d. We have done this because room was needed for the new and important material above referred to. 3d. Because we are publish-

---

* Such should read the first edition of this work.

ing in this new edition four chapters on New York's Share in the Revolution. These contain a series of important facts which never before have we seen collated, and which, we believe, should be made accessible to the youth in our public schools.

The author is painfully aware that these chapters do not fit well in this volume, but they are not bulky enough for a separate book, and he flatters himself that they contain facts well worth placing before such New Yorkers as are interested in the history of their own State.

In the preparation of this second edition the author feels himself specially obligated to Rev. H. D. B. Mulford, D. D., sometime Professor of English Language and Literature in Rutgers College, Sherman Williams, Chief of the School Libraries of the University of New York, A. W. Risley, Professor of History in the New York State College for Teachers, and James Sullivan, Director of Division of Archives and History for the University of the State of New York, for their valuable criticisms, and many wise and helpful suggestions, generously given.

ALBANY, N. Y., FEB. 15th, 1919.

CONTENTS

BOOK I

MILITARY HISTORY

CHAPTER I
Discovery and Discoverers of the valley between New York Bay and Canada.

CHAPTER II
Saratoga. Origin of the name. Old Indian trails. Hostile forays from both sides of the line.

CHAPTER III
Destruction of Schenectady and return blows.

CHAPTER IV
First settlement at Old Saratoga. Queen Anne's War. Nicholson's expeditions against Canada.

CHAPTER V
King George's War. Building of the forts.

CHAPTER VI
Destruction of Saratoga. A word about the captives.

CHAPTER VII
Fort Clinton. Discovery of its site. Its fate.

CHAPTER VIII
The French and Indian War.

CHAPTER IX
The Revolution. Causes of the war. First period of the Burgoyne campaign.

CHAPTER X
Second period of Burgoyne campaign. Indian atrocities. Oriskany and Bennington. Schuyler superseded by Gates. Movements of hostile armies.

xvii

CHAPTER XI
First battle of Saratoga. Results.

CHAPTER XII
Second battle of Saratoga.

CHAPTER XIII
Third period of campaign. Burgoyne retreats.

CHAPTER XIV
Burgoyne surrounded and besieged. Woes of the besieged.

CHAPTER XV
Terms and description of Burgoyne's surrender. Saratoga a decisive battle, why?

CHAPTER XVI
General Gates, his behavior after the surrender. The Conway cabal. Conditions at Saratoga.

CHAPTER XVII
Dark days of the Revolution.

CHAPTER XVIII
1781 at Saratoga. Generals Stark and Lord Sterling in command at.

CHAPTER XIX
Anecdotes connected with the Revolution.

CHAPTER XX
Anecdotes continued.

CHAPTER XXI
War of 1812 and the Civil War.

BOOK II

CIVIL HISTORY

CHAPTER I
Saratoga. Significance of the name. First settlers. Resettlement after the massacre.

CHAPTER II
The first permanent settlers.

CHAPTER III
Revolutionary trials of the citizens.

CHAPTER IV
About the several Schuyler mansions and their occupants.

CHAPTER V
Mansion No. 3 built in record time. Visits of Washington.

CHAPTER VI
Mansion No. 3 continued. Its later occupants.

CHAPTER VII
About William Duer, and Colonel James Livingston.

CHAPTER VIII
A historic church. Reorganization and settlement of Saratoga after the Revolution. Partition of the township.

CHAPTER IX
Growth of villages. Advent of the canal, its effect. The coming of railroads.

CHAPTER X
The Saratoga monument, the building of it, etc.

BOOK III

NEW YORK'S SHARE IN THE REVOLUTION

CHAPTER I
New York unfairly dealt with in most histories. Some things that differentiated her from New England. Some of her contributions to our civilization.

CHAPTER II
Causes of the Revolution. Some of New York's contributions toward independence, and her early sufferings. The Boston port bill.

CHAPTER III
Certain reflections on preceding events, and their outcome.

CHAPTER IV
The war in New York. New York's strategic importance. Importance of Lexington and Concord compared with some other battles. New York's contributions and sacrifices compared with other states.

CHAPTER V
The treaty of peace with England. John Jay's part in it. A word about Gouverneur Morris and Gen. Philip Schuyler.

CHAPTER VI
Origin and adoption of the Federal Constitution. New York's share in the launching of the government of the United States.

GUIDES to the battlefield and historic Saratoga, or Schuylerville, with maps.

INTRODUCTION

It would be impossible to write an intelligible narrative of Old Saratoga, now Schuylerville, without sketching the broader field of history of which it forms a part. As well attempt a satisfactory description of a two-mile section of the majestic Hudson that flows before it without telling whence the river rises and whither its gleaming waters go. Old Saratoga is but one link in a chain of marvellous story. We must at least catch a glimpse of the whole chain or we shall never come to appreciate this one golden link.

That the place now called Schuylerville has become historic is due neither to the size of the town, to the famous deeds of its inhabitants, nor to the fact that someone whom the world calls specially great was born here. It was well known to two great nations while yet it was a howling wilderness, and it had obtained worldwide renown before any one had yet dreamed of the village of Schuylerville. Its place in history is due mainly to its location. Here, in military language, was one of the few strategic points in the great Hudson valley. Whoever held these points held the whole valley, and whoever held this valley could hold the continent.

How is that? you may ask. Well, take a good map of New York State and you will notice that an extraordinary depression or valley extends from the river St. Lawrence, in Canada, directly south to New York bay. This valley is the result of some mighty convulsion in nature, which rent the mountains asunder, leaving this chasm between the ranges, to be further hollowed out and smoothed down by the action of those giant rivers of ice, the glaciers. The highest point of the divide, or watershed, in this depression is between Fort Edward and Fort Ann, and this is only 147 feet above sea level. This elevation is remarkably slight in a distance of 350 miles, especially when one considers the mountain ranges between which the valley runs. With the exception of some twenty miles this whole distance between New York and Montreal was navigable for small craft before the dams were built in the Hudson.

Besides this valley running north and south, another depression, starting from Schenectady, stretches westward and cleaves the great Appalachian mountain range in twain, forming an open gateway toward the setting sun. Through this runs the Mohawk.

Scan your map of North America closely from the Gulf of St. Lawrence to Florida and you will learn to your surprise, mayhap, that from the Gulf of St. Lawrence to the Gulf of Mexico there is no other wide-open portal except the Mohawk, to the west, through those mighty barriers which the great Appalachian range has thrown across the pathway to the imperial domain of the Mississippi valley. Thus, if you have a military eye, you can readily see that, before the days of railroads, whoever held the Hudson valley held the key to the continent from the east.

Turn to your map of New York State again and you will notice that the country where dwelt the Iroquois is drained by the St. Lawrence through the Black, the Seneca and the Genesee rivers; by New York bay through the Mohawk and Hudson rivers; by Delaware bay through the Delaware river; by Chesapeake bay through the Susquehanna river, and by the Gulf of Mexico through the Allegheny and Ohio rivers.

Those old "Romans of the West," the Five Nations or

Iroquois, somehow discovered the strategic value of their position and took advantage of it. Having formed a civil confederacy, and then uniting their military forces, they became a menace and a terror to all their neighbors. The trails leading up and down these various rivers they transformed into warpaths. Ere long their fierce warwhoop was heard westward to the Mississippi, northward to the Saguenay, and southward to the great gulf, and from everywhere they returned as conquerors, proudly bringing with them those spoils so dear to the savage heart, scalps and captives. These conquests were completed by the year 1715 when they brought back the Tuscaroras from the Carolinas, and admitted them into their confederacy. After that they were called the Six Nations.

The Adirondack region, including the Champlain and Hudson valleys, as far south as the old district of Saratoga extended, was reckoned specially desirable as a possession, and had long been disputed territory between the Algonquins of the north and the Iroquois. Long before the white man set eyes on this region it was known to the red man as "the dark and bloody ground." Against all opponents, the indomitable courage and persistency of the fierce Iroquois had quite won the day when the white man appeared on the scene as a new contestant for the valuable prize. When he entered the field, he was destined to add some still darker chapters to its already bloody history.

BOOK I

MILITARY HISTORY

CHAPTER I

Discovery of this Valley

OUR first introduction to these natural pathways leading northward and westward is connected with the meeting of a party of whites and Indians drifting south from Canada on discovery intent, and a party of painted Iroquois hastening north, on war and pillage bent. The leader of the party from the north was Samuel de Champlain, the founder of Quebec, and the first French Governor of Canada. The Algonquins had told him of a wonderful inland sea that stretched far southward into the land of the terrible Iroquois. He became curious to see it, and so in the spring of 1609, with two white companions and 60 native warriors with their canoes, he started on the eventful voyage. They reached the lake July 4th and paddled south leisurely, till they arrived in the vicinity of Ticonderoga, where in the night they met the party of two hundred Iroquois painted and plumed for war. Immediately on the discovery of the approaching enemy the Iroquois hastened ashore to fortify themselves. The Algonquins lined up their canoes just beyond arrow shot and having mutually agreed to wait till morning for the fight, they spent the night in jeering one another, and boasting what terrible things each would do to the other at the break of day. At daylight the Algonquins went ashore and quickly advanced for the deadly grapple. Because of their superior numbers and position the Iroquois felt confident of victory, but the sudden apparition of three strangely-dressed men with white faces, a thing never before dreamed of by them, together with the thunder of their arquebuses and the terrible execution they wrought, quickly decided the day, and the Iroquois fled precipitately, not pleased with their first experience of the white man. Champlain came no farther, but the beautiful lake which he had discovered and described, fittingly bears his honored name.

It is worthy of note that this is the first known appearance of a white man within the borders of northern New York, and that too through the northern gateway. And Champlain's contest with those Indians was the first recorded battle on the soil of this State, and on a spot which afterwards was the scene of many bloody conflicts.

Six weeks after this event, by a strange coincidence, Hendrick Hudson, an Englishman, commanding a Dutch ship, sailed into the splendid harbor now known as New York bay, and laying his course due north entered what he fondly hoped would prove to be the much looked for passage to the East Indies, but which turned out to be only a river, yet a river far more beautiful than any his eyes had ever beheld. Wishing to learn the character and size of his great find, he worked his way as far north as Troy or Cohoes. Then he returned to report his discovery. He, too, was honored by having his name affixed to the southern portion of this marvellous valley and its noble river. Five years thereafter a trading post was established 150 miles north of New York bay, and which for fifty-five years bore the name of Fort Orange, after the noble house whose sons had successfully led the Netherlands in their eighty years' fight for liberty against Spain. But a hundred miles of this valley from Troy to Crown Point was as yet *terra incognita* to the white man, and it remained so for one-third of a century.

During all this time the Iroquois of Central New York had refrained from war against the north; but they by no means forgot their humiliating defeat at the hands of the white men who were the allies of their ancient foes in Canada. For thirty-three years they had nursed their wrath and drilled themselves in warfare with other tribes, to the west and south, when in the spring of 1642, after having become possessed of fire-arms and practiced in their use, they decided that the time had come to blot out their disgrace in the blood of the Algonquins and French. And had it not been for the timely arrival of some French troops the Canadian settlements would have been utterly exterminated.

Among their captives on that foray was a noble Jesuit priest, Father Isaac Jogues, who in company with several helpers and converts were returning, with their canoes loaded with supplies, to a mission already established among the Hurons in the distant west. He, with two assistants, Couture and Goupil, and a number of Hurons, were horribly tortured; then they were bound and headed south for the Mohawk country. It was about the 1st of September when they arrived at that bold promontory jutting out into Lake Champlain, which has since become famous as Ticonderoga. Rounding this they turned west where soon they were stopped by the churning rapids and chiming falls of a goodly stream, the outlet of another lake. Here the Indians landed, shouldered their canoes, followed up the stream, and soon with their captives launched forth upon the crystal waters of Andiatarocte (Lake George). Here, for the first time since the dawn of creation, eyes, that could appreciate, looked upon the rare beauty of that "fair Naiad of the ancient wilderness," Lac St. Sacrament, as it was christened four years later by Father Jogues.

These savage warriors, with their hapless victims,

duly landed where now stands that handsome hostelry, the Fort William Henry Hotel, and straightway plunged into the dusky woods and followed the ancient war trail. This trail led from Lake George to the bend in the Hudson a few miles west of Glens Falls, thence southwestward till it struck the Mohawk in the vicinity of Amsterdam. Arrived at their castles, the captives were again ferociously tortured for the entertainment of savage women and children. Finally Goupil was murdered. Couture having struck the fancy of the Indians by some act of skill or bravery, was adopted into the tribe. Father Jogues lived for months in daily expectation of being murdered. The latter was given to an old Indian as a slave and performed for him the most menial tasks. In the following March he accompanied his master on his spring fishing trip. They repaired to a lake four days distant. On reasonable grounds this is supposed to have been Lake Saratoga. If so Father Jogues was the first white man who ever gazed upon the placid surface of that beautiful sheet of water.

About the 1st of August, 1643, he accompanied a party of Indians on a fishing trip down the Hudson about twenty miles below Albany. Before the main body was ready to leave he secured permission to return with a few Indians who were going up the river in a canoe. At Albany he was very kindly treated by the Dutch who urged him to escape, they having previously made a fruitless attempt to ransom him. Finally he concluded to make the attempt, slipped away from his custodians, and secreted himself. But the Indians made such an ado about it, that to pacify them Megapolensis, the good Dutch Dominie, or clergyman, and Arendt Van Curler, the subsequent founder of Schenectady, collected enough goods to ransom him. The Albany Dutchmen then gave him free passage to France. At New York Gov. Kieft exchanged his squalid and savage dress for a good suit of Dutch cloth and placed him aboard a small vessel bound for his home. On his arrival there he was received as one risen from the dead, for they had heard of his capture. He at once became an object of curiosity and reverence. He was summoned to court and Queen Anne of Austria kissed his mutilated hands.

Soon he returned to Canada. In 1646 he was ordered by his superior to go to the Mohawk country on an embassage of peace for the government. He with Sieur Bourdon, an engineer, and two Algonquin Indians started about the middle of May, laden with rich gifts for the Mohawks to confirm the peace. They reached Lake George on the eve of the feast of Corpus Christi. From this fact he named it Lac St. Sacrament, a name which was retained for more than a hundred years. From Lake George they took the trail to the Hudson, where, being greatly fatigued by their loads of gifts, they borrowed some canoes from an Iroquois fishing party and descended the Hudson, passing Old Saratoga to Fort Orange. Here the Dutchmen, to whose sacrifices he owed his life, heartily welcomed and entertained him. After a few days he left them for the Mohawk council where he was received with grudging courtesy.

His mission having ended successfully, he started for home, but with the determination to return and found a mission among the Mohawks. With this purpose in mind he left behind a small chest containing a few trinkets and necessaries. But the Indians were persuaded that it harbored some malignant spirits that would work mischief among them. And indeed there was sickness in the village that summer, and the caterpillars ate their corn. All this was of course laid to the evil spirits left in that box. Hence, when Father Jogues returned, there was a case against him. He was foully murdered on the 18th of October, 1646. "Thus," as Parkman says, "died Isaac Jogues, one of the purest examples of Roman Catholic virtue which this Western continent has seen."[1] (The shrine at Auriesville is erected on the traditional site of his martyrdom.)

Thus, when Father Jogues reached Albany in 1646 the whole of the Champlain-Hudson valley had been traversed by the white man. It is also interesting to note that he and Sieur Bourdon were the first to see the site of Schuylerville.

The reader will recall the fact that New York and Albany had been occupied as trading posts since 1614, and the latter had been permanently settled or colonized since 1623.

---
[1] See Parkman's Jesuits in North America.

CHAPTER II

SARATOGA—ORIGIN OF THE NAME, THE OLD INDIAN TRAILS—FIRST EXPEDITION FROM CANADA INTO THE MOHAWK COUNTRY UNDER COURCELLE AND DE TRACY

To most people outside the boundaries of this county the name Saratoga is coupled always and only with the great watering place, twelve miles west of the Hudson, whose medicinal waters gush forth "for the healing of the nations," whereas its adoption there was a long afterthought. Indeed, the name as applied first to a river district, and later to a definite locality, was known to white men for scores of years before the springs were discovered. Saratoga is an Indian word, and was used by the red men as the name of a favorite hunting and fishing ground, including the eastern section of the present county of Saratoga. It was written in the original Saratoga Patent as Ochserantongue, or Sarachtogie. This Patent took in land on both sides of the Hudson from Mechanicville north to near Fort Miller. Later the name was given to the settlement on the south side of the Fishkill creek, across from Schuylerville. Within a radius of, say, four miles of Schuylerville this region is still called by its inhabitants Old Saratoga. Indeed, the name as applied to a river district was known to white men for a hundred years before the springs were discovered.

As has already been intimated, Schuylerville, or old Saratoga, owes its historic importance to its geographical location. In colonial days it was regarded by military men as an important strategic position. From this point important lateral trails diverged from the main one, which ran like a great trunk line up and down the Hudson valley. These lateral trails started here because at this point two large streams empty into the Hudson; the Battenkill (or Di-an-on-de-howa, in Indian) from the east, and the Fishcreek from the west. The one afforded easy access to the Connecticut valley, while the other offered ready passage from the north and east over into the valley of the Mohawk. In short, here was a sort of Indian "four corners."

Two trails led from the north or Champlain valley into the Mohawk valley. One started at Ticonderoga, passed through Lake George, thence across country, passing the Hudson not far west from Glens Falls, thence through the towns of Moreau and Wilton turning west through the pass south of Mt. McGregor at Stile's Tavern, over near Lake Desolation, southwest through Galway, thence into the Mohawk valley a little west of Amsterdam. This was called the Kayadrosseras trail[1] The other started at Whitehall, thence to Fort Edward and down the Hudson to Schuylerville, up the Fishcreek to Saratoga lake, thence up the Kayadrosseras river to the Mourningkill, thence over a carry into Ballston lake, over another carry into Eelplace creek (or Alplaus), and down this into the Mohawk river. This was called the Saratoga trail. If on their expeditions to the north the Mohawk Indians chose to build their canoes at home before starting, they came down the Saratoga trail because it was a waterway. If they decided to build their canoes at the head of the lake, then they took the Kayadrosseras trail overland, for it was shorter.

These trails were already ancient and warworn before the white man appeared on the scene. He promptly appropriated them to his own use for purposes not only of warfare but for commerce.

---

[2] Sylvester's Hist. of Saratoga County. Edition of 1878, p. 32.

Courcelle's Expedition against the Iroquois.

This region was frequently seen and traversed by the white man years before the name Saratoga appeared in printer's ink, or official correspondence. For years prior to 1666, bands from the Five Nations, or Iroquois, had harassed the French settlements in Canada, at Montreal, Three Rivers and Quebec, murdering and carrying the settlers into captivity. Finally a full regiment of French soldiers was sent to their defense. The French governor, Samuel de Remi Sieur de Courcelle, impatient of delay after they came, started out with a force of 600 men and a number of Algonquin Indians as guides to wreak vengeance on the hated savages. Equipped with snow shoes, and with provisions loaded on toboggans drawn by mastiff dogs, they started from Quebec on October 29, 1665. Slowly and laboriously they made their way south over frozen lakes and the wilderness of snow till they arrived at the Hudson about February 1st, 1666. Their Indian guides failing them on account of too much "fire-water," they missed the Kayadrosseras trail, their intended route, and took the Saratoga trail instead. This brought them down to the mouth of the Fishcreek at Schuylerville, up which they went to Saratoga lake and so on. The 9th of February they discovered to their chagrin that instead of being near the Mohawk castles, or palisaded forts, they were within two miles of the Dutch trading post at Schenectady. Here they fell into an ambush set by the Mohawk Indians and lost eleven men. The Indians fled and gave the alarm. Nearly exhausted from cold and exposure, but receiving some timely succor from the Dutch, they abandoned the enterprise, and hastily retreated by the way they came, down through Old Saratoga and up the Hudson and Lake Champlain.[3] That trip of some 700 miles over a frozen desert, void of

---

[3] Documents relating to Colonial Hist. of N. Y. Vol. III, pp. 118, 126.

human habitation, in the teeth of howling blizzards and biting cold, was an achievement never excelled before that day.

De Tracy's Expedition. Stung to madness by the murder, that summer, of Sieur Chazy, a favorite captain in the regiment, at the hands of these same Iroquois, a new expedition was organized. In October of the same year, 1666, under the efficient leadership of the Marquis de Tracy, a force of 1,300 men and two cannons started on their mission of vengeance. They came with boats instead of toboggans and snow shoes, and as their flotilla of at least 250 canoes and bateaux swept over the crystal waters of Lac St. Sacrament, (Lake George) it formed the first of those splendid military pageants which were destined to render forever famous that pellucid gem of the old wilderness. This force took the Kayadrosseras trail and plunged boldly into the woods, reaching the Mohawk in due time, where they succeeded in utterly destroying the strongholds of the Indians and laying waste their fields, yet capturing and killing but few of their wily foes. Then with a vast deal of flourish and gusto, de Tracy caused a cross to be erected, the arms of France elevated on a pole, and a high sounding proclamation read, declaring all this territory to belong to His Majesty, the King of France, by the right of conquest. Then they went home by the way they came without the loss of a man.[4]

Descent of the Iroquois upon Canada. After de Tracy's punishment of the Mohawks they kept shy of the Canadians for more than twenty years. The peace then conquered would have doubtless continued indefinitely had not Canada been most unfortunate in one of her governors. Denonville, greedy for trade and

---
[4] Documents relating to Colonial Hist. of N. Y. Vol. IX, pp. 56, 79.

THE STORY OF OLD SARATOGA 11

the extension of the French dominions, tried to woo the Iroquois from their English allegiance. Failing in this he trespassed on their territories, attacked some of the villages of the Senecas, and killed and captured a number of their people. This roused the slumbering hate of the whole Confederacy, and war to the death was declared. Their forces having assembled, they paddled down the Mohawk river in their bark canoes, passed the little frontier village of Schenectady, and landed at Alplaus creek about the 1st of August, 1689. They had decided upon the Saratoga trail. A flotilla of about 250 canoes filled with 1,300 plumed and painted warriors, the fiercest in the new world, must have been a stirring sight as they debouched from the Kayadrosseras and floated out upon the tranquil bosom of Saratoga lake. It was a fit forerunner of the showy regattas seen on the same waters 200 years later.[5] And again when they glided into Fishcreek, lined with tamaracks, and embowered with birches and maples and oaks, festooned with the wild grape and clematis vines, could we have stood that day, behind some bushy screen, say at Stafford's Bridge, we would have witnessed a splendid pageant of over a mile in length. They swept down the crooked and tortuous Fishcreek to the modern village of Victory, whence they carried their canoes down the south side to the Hudson, and then lustily paddled north on their bloody mission. Their descent upon the settlements about Montreal was as a thunderbolt out of a clear sky. This was the most dreadful blow sustained, the most terrible event recorded in Canadian history. The buildings of the settlers were burned, their garnered harvests destroyed, between three and four hundred citizens and soldiers[6] were butchered, and 130 were brought back to be tortured for the enter-

---
[5] Sylvester's Saratoga County Hist., p. 34.
[6] Documents relating to Colonial Hist. of N. Y. Vol. IX, pp. 431, 434.

tainment of those left at home, or to supply their savage feasts with unusual and dainty meats. The Indians returned, most of them, as they had gone, by the Saratoga trail. The ancient forest then standing here, echoed that day to the sighs of those hapless captives, and the soil of old Saratoga was moistened with their tears, as they toiled up the carry from the river to the smooth water of Fishcreek above Victory. That was one procession at Schuylerville which none of us, I fancy, would care to have beheld, unless prepared to rescue the unfortunate victims.

CHAPTER III

DESTRUCTION OF SCHENECTADY AND RETALIATION

THE above mentioned descent of the Iroquois upon Canada, though wholly an affair of their own, proved to be coincident with the outbreak of war between France and England, which, of course, would surely involve their colonies. This war grew out of the English Revolution of 1688, which dethroned James II of England and enthroned, in his place, William and Mary of Holland. France proposed to replace King James on his throne.

Count de Frontenac was sent over by the French in October, 1689, to displace the impolitic Denonville. He resolved to be the first to strike a blow in that war on this side the water, and accordingly, fitted out three expeditions, one from Quebec against Maine, the second from Three Rivers against New Hampshire and the third from Montreal against Albany.

The force designed for Albany numbered 210 men, ninety-six of whom were Indians, under the command of two Canadian officers, Sieur la Moyne de St. Helene and Lieut. Daillebout de Mantet. Forgetful of the experience of de Courcelle, twenty-three years before, they, like him, started out in the dead of winter. Having reached the head of Lake Champlain, near Ticonderoga, they halted and held a council. The Indians, under the lead of Chief Kryn, a converted Mohawk, who had moved to Canada and of whose people about 60 had been murdered by the Iroquois in their late foray, demanded to know whither they were bound. De St. Helene replied that he wished to surprise and take Fort Orange (Albany). The Indians remembering the defeats which the French had lately sustained, strongly objected and said: "Since when have the French become so brave?" Still undecided they continued their march for eight days, toward Albany, till they came to the parting of the ways here at Old Saratoga,[1] (Schuylerville). On their own motion the Indians left the Hudson here, turned to the right, and took the trail leading toward Schenectady, and the French followed after without serious protest. A thaw had set in and they waded through snow and slush that were knee deep. It must have been dreadfully exhausting work, for it took them nine days to make the trip from Schuylerville to Schenectady, a distance of thirty-seven miles by the route they took. But just before they reached their goal one of those sudden and extreme changes occurred, so common to our winters in this latitude. A blizzard came howling down from the northwest, which chilled them to the marrow. They had intended to defer the attack till about two o'clock a. m., on February 10th, but they were forced to proceed at once or perish from the cold. They afterward said, had they been attacked at that time, or had they met with resistance when they attacked, they would have been forced to surrender, so benumbed were they by the cold. There was no need, however, for delay on their part, for they could not have imagined better arrangements for their reception than they found.

The Revolution in England naturally created two parties; those who sided with and those who sided against the dethroned King James. These parties were duplicated in the colonies. There were many here who were intensely loyal to James, as well as many who were eager to swear allegiance to William and Mary. Of course, this caused trouble and divisions throughout the realm.

After the sudden departure of Lieut. Governor Nichol-

---

[1] Documents relating to Colonial Hist. of N. Y. Vol. IX, p. 466.

son one Jacob Leisler had been appointed by the Committee of Safety of New York city as Governor *ad interim,* he to hold office until the arrival of the official soon to be appointed by King William. Leisler's claim to the office was readily allowed by the common people, to which class he belonged, but he was repudiated by the aristocrats, and the Patroons, or great landholders. Hence, out of this difference, there arose two political factions in the Province called the Aristocratic and the Democratic parties.

Schenectady and Albany had already become very jealous of each other because of a strong rivalry for the fur trade with the Indians to the west. Hence anything that Albany favored Schenectady was quite sure to frown upon, and *vice versa.* Therefore since the Aristocrats, who at this time ruled in Albany, opposed Leisler, Schenectady could be depended on to favor him.

Connecticut, like New York, fearing an attack from Canada, had sent one Capt. Bull with 87 men to aid in the defense of this frontier. He arrived in Albany November 25th, 1689, with the understanding that his troops were to be supported by, and under the direction of, the Albanians. On the 29th, Lieut. Talmadge, with 24 of the Connecticut men was sent over to garrison the fort at Schenectady. But controlled mainly by their prejudices the Schenectady people refused to aid in the support of these men who had come to defend them, 1st, because they had been procured through the mediation of the Aristocrats, and 2nd, because they felt that Connecticut ought to provide for her own soldiery, she being equally with New York menaced by the danger from the north. There was however a small minority of anti Leislerites, or Aristocrats, in Schenectady.

These were greatly encouraged in their opposition by the coming of the soldiers. The result was that the quarrel between the factions became so heated that neither would do a thing for the town's protection though they well knew that a state of war already existed between France and England. The two gates of the little town fronting east and west were left wide open and a dummy sentinel made of snow, in mockery of the idle troops quartered within the town, stood guard before the western portal.

Everybody, even the soldiers, were sleeping in fancied security. A body of Mohawk Indians had been engaged by the Albany authorities to scout to the north, but the love of the fireside proved more alluring than the charms of fire-water and Dutch gold, and so they had lingered at or near Schenectady.

Guided by some captured squaws, the Canadians crossed the Mohawk on the ice and appeared before the western gate. Silently, as if shod with wool, they glided in and posted themselves next the palisades that surrounded the village. Then the hideous warwhoop was raised, and before the stupefied inhabitants could realize what it all meant, the work of destruction and butchery was under way. For two hours hell was let loose in Schenectady while Satan and his imps held high carnival. It would be useless to attempt a description of the horrors crowded into that brief space. Suffice it to say that at the end of it sixty men, women and children lay stark in death, horribly mutilated, or roasting in the flames of their former homes. Among the victims were Hendrick Meese Vrooman and his son Bartel Vrooman, the latter the first settler of Old Saratoga. Between eighty and ninety were reserved as prisoners while a few escaped in their night robes, and with bare feet, carried the dreadful tale to Albany, seventeen miles away.

After refreshing themselves a little, the victors started on their retreat, the following morning. Leaving behind the old men, the women and children, and retaining twenty-seven of the younger men and boys as prisoners, they hastened away, taking the Kayadrosseras trail toward Canada. But they were not allowed to return unmolested. They were chased to Lake Champlain and eighteen of their number killed or captured by a band of Mohawk Indians.[2]

Winthrop's Expedition. The fight was now on in dead earnest, for the colonists could not allow so cruel a deed to go unavenged.

The authorities at Albany on the 26th of March, 1690, ordered Capt. Jacob de Warm to proceed to Crown Point with a party of twelve English and twenty Indians to watch the motions of the enemy. On the 30th, Capt. Abram Schuyler was sent to Otter Creek, Vt., which was the usual starting point for forays into Massachusetts, with nine men and a party of Indians to do like service at that point.

Massachusetts, Plymouth, Connecticut, New York and Maryland resolved upon an invasion of Canada. Each agreed to furnish its quota of troops. Fitz John Winthrop of Connecticut was commissioned major-general to lead the expedition. The troops from Massachusetts and Plymouth did not materialize. Winthrop brought 135 of those promised by Connecticut, Maryland sent fifty, New York furnished 150 men besides 180 Indians. 515 men was not a very formidable array to be led by a major-general.

On the 30th of July, 1690, the Yankees with the Dutch troops assembled from this colony set out from Albany and camped the first night at the Flatts, the old Schuyler homestead. August 1st they marched to the Stillwater,

---
[2] Documents relating to Colonial Hist. of N. Y. Vol. IX, p. 466.

"soe named," says Winthrop, "for that the water passeth soe slowly as not to be discerned."

"August 2d," continued the journal of Winthrop, "we martched forwards and quartered this night at a place called Saratogo, about 50 English miles from Albany, where is a blockhouse and some of the Dutch soldiers."[3] The site of this blockhouse is a matter of conjecture. Certainly it was on the west side of the river for the army marched on that side. It was as certainly on the south side of Fishcreek, for the first settlement was made there, and the creek would be one of its defences against the north. It probably stood on the ground afterward occupied by Forts Saratoga and Clinton.

It was here that Winthrop established his depot of supplies, for on August 7th he says, "I sent 30 horse under Ensigne Thomlinson to Saratogo for more provition." Thus, in this, the first of many expeditions against Canada, Saratoga (Schuylerville) looms up as an important point. "At the great carrying place [Fort Edward] we overtook the Dutch companyes carrying their canoes and provition about 12 miles [to Fort Anne]; very bad and difficult passing. This hardship the Burghers and Dutch soldiers performed vigorously and without any repining which made me think noe thing would be difficult for them to perform."

The little army got no nearer Canada than Whitehall, through lack of canoes and provision, and because of sickness among the troops. This according to Winthrop. But Capt. Johannes Schuyler of Albany, only twenty-three years old, commanding those Dutch troops that Winthrop was moved to praise so highly because of their superior efficiency, was clearly dissatisfied that the expedition should be abandoned without an attempt to strike a blow. And this not alone because of its depressing

---

[3] Documents relating to Colonial Hist. of N. Y. Vol. IV, pp. 194, 195.

effect upon the colonists, but he greatly feared the effect of failure upon the Indians who were just then wavering in their allegiance between the French who were so belligerent and the English who showed so little fight. He therefore resolved that as for his single self he would not return to Albany without an effort to bring back something to show for all the trouble. He applied to Gen. Winthrop for permission to go forward. Winthrop cheerfully granted it and commissioned him captain for the venture.[4]

At once he called for volunteers; twenty-nine whites and 120 Indians responded. Loading their canoes with sufficient provision, they cut loose for the north. The first day out he met Capt. Sanders Glen from Schenectady, with his company, who had been posted in advance. Here he recruited 13 white men and 125 Indians. August 13th, they surprised La Prarie, south of Montreal, killed a number of the inhabitants, took many prisoners, did great damage to property and returned with but little loss to themselves. This was the first armed force that ever penetrated Canada from the English colonies. They reached Albany on the 31st of August, only eleven days after Winthrop and his hundreds had sheepishly crept back. This Johannes Schuyler was the grand-father of General Phillip Schuyler.

Expedition of 1691. The success of Johannes Schuyler's raid seemed to whet the appetite of the Albany Dutchman, and also of the Indians, for more experience of like flavor. Hence on June 21, 1691, another expedition started from Albany, this time led by Pieter Schuyler, brother of Johannes, the hero of the campaign of '90. They started with 120 whites, and sixty river Indians (Catskills and Schagticokes). The first night

---
[4] Documents relating to Colonial Hist. of N. Y. Vol. IV, p. 196.

they camped at Stillwater. "On the 24th," says Schuyler's Journal, "we marched to Saraghtoga, 16 miles distant, and camped about 2 of the clock afternoone."

"June 26th. We continued at Saraghtoga; foul weather, where we were joined by 15 Mohawks commanded by one Schayavanhoendere." These Mohawks came over by the Saratoga trail from Schenectady and were from a party of ninety-five or more, which later joined the expedition at Ticonderoga.

Pieter Schuyler [5] followed the tracks of his brother of the year before, fought and won two battles in one day, August 1st; killed many of the enemy, paralyzed the plans of Frontenac for that year, and returned with a goodly number of prisoners and much glory. But what was of much more consequence at the time, they had won for their fighting qualities the high esteem and firm allegiance of the Iroquois. The French account of these actions declares that Schuyler's party was practically annihilated. Schuyler reports thirty-seven of his men captured and killed, and twenty-five wounded, out of a force of 260.[6]

The French admitted in their report to the home government, that these battles were the "most obstinate ever fought in Canada," and that after the battle in the woods they could not pursue, the "men able to march being sent to the fort for assistance to carry off the wounded."

John Nelson, an English gentleman taken prisoner by the French, arrived at Quebec about the time when the news of Schuyler's expedition was received. In his memorial to the English government on the state of the colonies, he says: "In an action performed by one Skyler

---

[5] This Peter Schuyler was the first Mayor of Albany, and gained unbounded influence over the Indians, by whom he was called Quider, pronounced Keeder, which was as near as they could speak the name of Peter.

[6] Documents relating to Colonial Hist. of N. Y. Vol. III, pp. 781-795, 800.

of Albanie, whilst I arrived at Quebec in the year 1691, when he made one of the most vigorous and glorious attempts that hath been known in these parts, with great slaughter on the enemie's part, and losse on his own, in which if he had not been discovered by an accident, it is very probable he had become master of Monreall. I have heard the thing reported so much in his honor by the French, that had the like been done by any of theire nation, he could never missed of an acknowledgment and reward from the court, tho I do not hear of anything amongst us hath been done for him."[7]

There is nothing in the records to indicate that the home government ever took any notice of these most heroic deeds performed by the Schuylers at a very critical juncture in our colonial history. It is acknowledged by all who are familiar with the situation in 1690-1 that those two successes preserved the friendship of the Iroquois, at a time when their friendship was absolutely essential to England's hold on New York, and New York was the key to the situation. Bancroft styles Pieter Schuyler "the Washington of his times."

The French get even with the Mohawks. For the next year and a half the Iroquois, especially the Mohawks, so harassed the Canadian settlers that Count de Frontenac determined to exterminate them utterly. Collecting a force of 625 French and Indians he started for them in January, 1693. The party endured the usual hardships, but no cold could chill their ardor, nor blizzard beat them back, so determined were they upon vengeance. They took the Kayadrosseras trail from Lake George, reached the Mohawk valley and took the Indians wholly by surprise. They stormed and destroyed all their towns save one, which was several miles back from

---

[7] Documents relating to Colonial Hist. of N. Y. Vol. IV, p. 209.

the river, captured over 300 prisoners, had a grand jubilation and started back with their booty.[8] But most of their prisoners escaped or were rescued before they reached Canada.

Fortunately for New York, the peace of Ryswick in 1697 put an end to King William's war. In fact, the war had proved especially costly to Albany county, comprising as it then did all the northern settlements in the colony of New York. It is interesting at this day to read the comparative census of the years 1689 and 1698. In 1689 Albany county had 2,016 white inhabitants. At the end of the war in 1698, 567 were missing. That left but 1,449 with which to begin the 18th century. The Indians lost more than half their number. In 1689 they had 2,800 warriors, in 1698 only 1,320. It was about time for all concerned to bury the hatchet.

---

[8] Documents relating to Colonial Hist. of N. Y. Vol. IX, pp. 649-656; also Vol. IV, pp. 173, 180.

CHAPTER IV

FIRST SETTLEMENT OF OLD SARATOGA—QUEEN ANNE'S WAR—NICHOLSON'S EXPEDITIONS AGAINST CANADA

COINCIDENT with the time that King William's war was threatening to involve the colonies the records refer to Saratoga as a settlement already in existence. E. g. in the Journal of the Albany Convention (of Magistrates) appear the following entries:

"Ye 1st day of Sept. 1689.

"Harme Janse Van Bommel brings news yt our Indians have taken 5 Praying Canida Indians upon ye Lake who were bound hither to do mischeeffe, & yt several french were seen upon ye Lake. Upon which Capt. Wendel & 6 men were ordered to goe to Sarachtoga to examine sd Indians & to make enquiry of affairs there.[1]"

A stockaded fort was then ordered to be built about the house of Bartel (Bartolomeus) Vrooman. Parties of men with Schaghticoke Indians were kept there during the autumn of 1689 to protect the settlers and patrol the country to the north.

From Col. Romer's report,[2] in 1698, we learn that "the farms and fort built at Saratoga, in Leisler's time, have been entirely ruined by the late war, since which time they have never been thought of, and the settlers have never thought of returning thither." He suggests the building of a fort to protect possible settlers. It is probable that these first settlers had left the place for the winter of 1689-90 else they would have been discovered and the fact of their capture would have appeared in

---
[1] Documentary History, N. Y., pp. 87, 89.
[2] Documents relating to Colonial Hist. of N. Y. Vol. IV, p. 441.

the French report of the expedition against Schenectady in 1690.

The next we hear of Saratoga as a military post is in the report of the governor, Lord Cornbury, dated September 24, 1702. There among other recommendations he says: "I propose there should be a stockadoed fort at Saractoga, a place six and twenty miles above the Half Moon upon Hudson's River *and is the farthest settlement we have.*"[3]

Again in his report of June 30, 1703, he is about to set to work on the fort, for he says: "There are but few families there yet, and these will desert their habitations if they are not protected."

Meanwhile war had again broken out between France and England, known in England as the war of the Spanish succession. In this war the French and Indians seemed to wreak their vengeance specially on the New England settlements; for example, Deerfield, Mass., was destroyed in 1704, and Haverhill in 1708. Why New York escaped was not known to the settlers at the time, but subsequently it was learned that the Iroquois and their Roman Catholic relatives in Canada had made a treaty not to molest each other's domain in that war.

One Congreve reported, in 1704, that most of the forts on the northern frontier were out of order, among which was the fort of 1689 at old Saratoga.[4]

The many outrages from Canada, at last impelled the colonists of Massachusetts, Connecticut, New York and New Jersey to unite for an invasion of Canada. A fleet was to attack Quebec while a formidable army of 1,500 was to reduce Montreal. This force assembled at Albany and got under way the fore part of June, 1709. The main body had been preceded by a force of 300

---

[3] Documents relating to Colonial Hist. of N. Y. Vol. IV, p. 969.
[4] Documents relating to Colonial Hist. of N. Y. Vol. IV, p. 1128.

Dutchmen from Albany and vicinity under Col. Peter Schuyler. First this pioneer force built a stockade fort at Stillwater, which Schuyler called Fort Ingoldsby, after the governor; then they moved up to Saratoga and built a similar fort on the east side of the river, evidently to guard the ford which crossed just below the island over which the bridge and highway to Greenwich now pass.

The next was built at the Great Carrying place (Fort Edward), which he named Fort Nicholson, and the next at the forks of Wood creek, which he called at first Queens' Fort, but later Fort Anne in honor of the reigning English sovereign.

Moreover Colonel Schuyler and his pioneers built the first military road in this country of which we have record. This road began here at Old Saratoga, at the ford no doubt, on the east side of the river and ran up that side of the stream to Fort Edward, thence to Wood creek. It had to be cut most of the way through the primeval forest. The road to Fort Edward has no doubt been practically the same ever since.

This army was under the command of General Francis Nicholson, who, Governor Hunter declared, had never seen an army in the open field.[5] This was the first time the red-coated British regular appeared on the scene and trod this old war-worn trail which was so soon to become familiar tramping-ground to him.

Gen. Nicholson marched bravely up, garrisoned the several forts which had been built for him and then, like Micawber, sat down at Fort Anne and waited for something to turn up. The first thing that turned up was a malignant disease in his camp by which he lost more men than if he had hastened forward and fought a disastrous battle with the French. The next thing that did not

---
[5] Documents relating to Colonial Hist. of N. Y. Vol. V, p. 451.

turn up was the British fleet, which had been promised to co-operate with him on the St. Lawrence. In the midst of such calamities what was there left for brave men like him and his army to do but to turn their backs upon Canada and march down the hill again to Albany? Which thing they did.

In 1711 another campaign was organized for the conquest of Canada. The plan was a duplicate of the previous one, with this difference that the force which marched up through Old Saratoga was about twice as formidable, numbering nearly 3,000 regulars, colonists and Indians. This time they selected the Lake George route instead of the one through Fort Anne and Whitehall, evidently because it was the healthier. This was wise, but the redoubtable Gen. Nicholson had no sooner reached Lake George than he heard that the fleet on which he depended for support had been scattered by the winds and wrecked. At once he threw up his hands in despair, burned forts Anne and Nicholson and marched back ingloriously. Thus the third attempt at conquering Canada failed, mainly through the inefficiency of its leaders. Had either John, or Peter Schuyler been at the head of the expedition we feel sure that that army would have been heard from in Canada, but no New York Dutchman could hope for any worthy recognition from either Old or New England. The fort at Saratoga was thus left the uttermost military post of the colony facing the ever frowning north.

The treaty of Utrecht between France and England put the finale on Queen Anne's war.

CHAPTER V

KING GEORGE'S WAR—THE BUILDING OF THE FORTS

IN all the early histories of New York much is made of the sack and massacre of Schenectady in 1690, and that of Cherry valley in 1778, while little or nothing is said of the equally tragic fate of Old Saratoga in 1745. One is led to wonder why that event should have received from the historians such scant courtesy. The only reasons for it that suggest themselves to the writer are first: That most of the people who made up the village at that time were doubtless illiterate. None of the survivors nor any of their friends was possessed of sufficient literary ability, or interest in the event to write up a worthy account of the fate of this frontier village. Apparently the only one present who could have done it, died bravely fighting for his honor and his home, and "dead men tell no tales." That was Capt. Philip Schuyler, uncle of the general.

A second reason which suggests itself is the existence of fiercest political dissension between the people and their governors, which largely absorbed the thought and time of the thinkers. About the only detailed accounts that we possess of the massacre are found in the reports given by the French of their exploit.

In order to a better appreciation of that event it will be well to glance at such fragments of history as have been preserved relating to the planting and growth of the settlement at Old Saratoga.

As we have seen, the first settlers were obliged tc abandon the place at the time of King William's war in 1689-'97. Just when the settlers ventured back the record saith not, but there were a few families here in 1703 as we have already learned.

During the long peace which followed Queen Anne's war the little settlement at Saratoga developed gradually under the fostering care of the enterprising Schuylers. The settlers by no means confined themselves to the west side of the river, but cleared for themselves many a broad acre of those rich bottom lands on the east side. There too, substantial homes were reared, and no doubt one of the houses on that side was built in blockhouse style for their common defence, and called The Fort. Where it was located we know not.

The French and the English of those days were very anxious to extend the sphere of their influence in the great American wilderness, just as they now are doing in Asia and Africa. The French looked with covetous eyes upon the colony of New York especially, for they had already discovered that whoever held New York could have it all. Hence we are not surprised at seeing them attempt to move their frontiers as far south as the elastic treaty of Utrecht and the patience of the English would permit. In 1731 they determined to appropriate that natural stronghold, Crown Point, to themselves.[1] Brooking no delay, they began to fortify it, first by a stockade, then soon by a substantial stone work which they called Fort St. Frederic. Quite a town grew up around it numbering 1,500, it is said. This was a menace to both the New York and New England colonists, who viewed the movement with deepest apprehension and chagrin. The ease with which France could now invade New York from Canada retarded the settlement of those fertile regions to the north of Albany. After this no one who could appreciate the situation would deliberately put himself under the

---

[1] Documents relating to Colonial Hist of N. Y. Vol. VIII, p. 345.

shadow of such a threat. As a counter move they should have fortified Ticonderoga, but political strife and jealousies between the several governors and their legislatures seemed to paralyze every effort looking toward the public safety and welfare.

The building of this fort together with the constant efforts to win over the Six Nations and steal away the fur trade greatly exasperated the colonists. And whenever the relations between France and England became especially strained the New Yorkers would think about their defenses toward the north.

One of those crises occurred in 1721, when the authorities decided to delay no longer in building a fort at Saratoga for the defense of the northern frontier. This was erected in the months of September and October of that year under the superintendency of Philip Livingston.

The bill of items presented by Livingston for the building of this fort, with many receipts from the workmen, are still preserved in the archives at Albany. The document is a fine specimen of penmanship. The bill as rendered amounted to 153£ 11s. 4d. Johannes Schuyler, proprietor of the first sawmills erected here, furnished much of the material for the above mentioned fort.[2]

Captain William Helling [3] was the first commandant of this fort; whether he had any successors does not appear.

Another crisis occurred in 1739. As a result of this one, Lieut.-Governor Clarke reporting to the Lords of Trade in London, says that he had persuaded the Assembly to make provisions for building several forts, among the rest, one at "Sarachtoga;" but as no appropriation for this fort appears in the Act to which the governor refers we are left in the dark as to when it was begun

---

[2] N. Y. Colonial MSS. Vol. LXIV, pp. 39, 40.
[3] Ibid., p. 45.

or finished; but subsequent events make it evident that the fort was really built at that time. For example, Governor Clinton, reporting to the Lords of Trade June 5, 1744, says, he is about to send "a party of troops to the fort at Saratoga for the defense of that place."[4] A few years later we see the Assembly squaring its accounts with a large number of individuals for work done in 1745 in rebuilding this fort.[5] Since the old records say that the effective life of those wooden forts was only five to seven years, this "rebuilding" would indicate that there was a fort built here at least as early as 1739. The fort as rebuilt in the winter and spring of 1745 was square with a blockhouse on each corner.[6]

The long peace of thirty-one years was broken in 1744 by France declaring war against England. In fact pretty much all Europe was involved in that war. It started with a quarrel between rival claimants to the Austrian throne. The chief competitors for the prize were the noted Maria Theresa, daughter of the late Emperor Charles VI., and Charles Albert, Elector of Bavaria. England sided with Maria Theresa while France took the part of Charles. It was called in Europe the War of the Austrian Succession, but it is usually set down by Americans as King George's war. The representatives of the two belligerent nations on this continent cared precious little about who should sit on the Austrian throne, but they did care very much about who should hold the sceptre over the imperial domain of this continent, and for this they were ready to fight.

---
[4] Documents relating to Colonial Hist. of N. Y. Vol. VI, p. 255.
[5] Documents relating to Colonial Hist. of N. Y. Vol. VI, p. 648.
[6] A block house was built of heavy logs, with the second story projecting over the first about two feet, and pierced for small arms and, some times, cannon. In a fort these block houses were connected by palisades of logs set in the ground and extending from 10 to 12 feet above ground. A gallery was built inside the palisades and high enough from the ground to enable a sentinel to walk about and look over.

In this war the English struck the first blow.. Early in 1745 an expedition was organized against Louisburg, a stronghold of the French on Cape Breton island. The French had spent fully $5,000,000 and thirty years of labor on the fortifications there, and it was called by them the Gibraltar of America. Each of the New England colonies furnished its quota of troops, while New York appropriated 5,000£ in aid of the expedition. The campaign was entirely successful; Louisburg fell and great was the rejoicing in both Old and New England. New England troops did about all the fighting, but the Old England officers and troops got most of the rewards.

The French forces at that time in Canada were not very numerous, but with what they had they must avenge such a disaster as best they could. Where should they strike? Why, of course, where they could do the most harm with the forces they had, and that "where" lay through the open gateway of the Champlain and Hudson valleys.

CHAPTER VI

Destruction of Saratoga

The governor of Canada planned an expedition in the fall of that same year, 1745, with the design of striking the New England settlements along the Connecticut river.

The forces were put under the control of M. Marin. It consisted of 280 French and 229 Indians, in all 509. The chaplain was the Abbe Francois Picquet, who afterward became famous as the founder of the Mission La Presentation at Ogdensburg, N. Y.

They started from Montreal the 4th of November and arrived at Fort St. Frederick (Crown Point) the 13th.

In the council convened at Fort St. Frederick the Indians held, that it was too late in the season to go over the mountains into the Connecticut valley. Then, the Abbe Picquet, displaying a map of the Hudson, pointed out Saratoga among other places as worthy of capture. The map showed thirty-one houses and two forts, (one on each side of the river no doubt). After much expostulation and argument M. Marin concluded to yield to the wishes of the Indians, and so the doom of fair Saratoga was sealed.

Embarking again they paddled south for a distance, then left their canoes and took up their march along the north shore of South Bay, thence over the Fort Anne Mountains heading for Fort Edward. They lost their way, however, and spent several days wandering about before they got out of the woods. At last on the morning of the 27th of November they struck the Hudson near the house of John H. Lydius, a bold trader who had dared to establish himself so far away from his white neighbors. His was a large house built on the site of old Fort Nicholson, (Fort Edward). Here they captured a boy and hired man, Lydius and his family having retired to Albany for the winter. In a house near by, the Indians found three men; all these together with two Schaghticoke Indians, captured the day before, they placed in the Lydius house under a guard of twenty men. Then the men, having received absolution from the priest, who remained behind, hastened on, taking the old military road built by Peter Schuyler in 1709. Marin went ahead down the river with a few men in canoes to find a suitable fording place. On the way, the Indians captured six or seven men in a house near the road. They were sent to keep company with the other captives at Lydius'. About four and a half miles from Saratoga the army met a man and his wife returning from Schuyler's Mills with some bags of flour. After some parley the man and woman were given to Atagaronche, a chief, while the French appropriated the flour and horses. As the woman started for Lydius' she said, in hopes of frightening them off: "You are going to Saratoga, but you will find 200 men in the fort waiting to give you a warm reception." This did not disturb them, for the two Schaghticokes, above mentioned, had told them that the fort was empty.

The place selected for a crossing was evidently a little below the State dam, at Northumberland, for it was south of Fort Miller where the man and woman were captured, and in describing the crossing the journal of the expedition says: "Happily we found ourselves near an island and a waterfall, whose sound mingled with the noise we made in crossing the river." The island mentioned is doubtless the one just below the railroad bridge at Thompson's Mills.

It was about midnight before they got across. Then

says the journal: "The night was very cold, and had it not been for a little fire, which the bed of a creek sheltered by two hillocks enabled us to make, some would have run the risk of freezing their feet, as we all had wet feet." The *"creek"* mentioned is evidently the little stream that crosses the highway perhaps twenty rods south of the residence of Mr. E. W. Towne, and about five rods south of a road which turns up the hill to the west. The "hillocks" are either the steep banks of the creek, or the steep wooded hill back of Mr. Towne's, and the bare hill back of Mr. D. A. Bullard's farm buildings. The first theory is doubtless preferable.

While the main body was thus trying to thaw itself out and make itself comfortable, M. Beauvais was sent forward with a scout to make a reconnaissance of the doomed hamlet.

A generation had passed since this ancient war-path had been pressed by hostile feet. Most of the inhabitants of the sleeping village knew not what war and pillage meant except from hearsay. One need not stretch his imagination to form a pretty correct picture of Old Saratoga as it looked on the 27th of November, 1745.

Here were at least thirty dwellings with their usual outbuildings, barns, granaries, pens, etc.; four mills, a blacksmith shop, perhaps a store of general merchandise, and the frowning fort, made up the material portion of this primitive hamlet. These buildings were all strung like beads on a single narrow, lane-like road running north and south for perhaps a half mile above and one mile below Fishcreek. There was no bridge across the creek at that time. It was forded a few rods above the present canal aqueduct. The only brick house in the place was owned and occupied by Philip Schuyler, uncle of Gen. Philip Schuyler; this was located twenty rods directly east of the present mansion. This house was designed for defense, being pierced above and below for small arms. The original road ran east of that house. The fort stood a half mile below the creek on the flats. Most of the houses were about and below the fort. The fort, though much had been done on it, was still in bad repair, so much so that the troops claimed that they could not stay there with comfort or safety. Instead of there being 200 in the garrison, as the woman told the Frenchmen, there had been only ten privates stationed there in charge of one Sergeant Convers, who in turn had gone over to Schenectady, leaving a corporal in command. Governor Clinton had left it optional with the Lieutenant of the company whether the men should remain or withdraw. Their stay was to depend on the treatment they should receive at the hands of the Indian Commissioners, who seemed to be the source of supplies and repairs. The little garrison withdrew only a short time before the attack, and reported at Albany. It is a wonder that the settlers did not follow them, as they must have known that they were liable to an attack at any time from the north. But thirty years of peace seem to have lulled their fears to sleep.

The settlement had evidently enjoyed a prosperous season. The barns, the granaries, and the cellars were full to repletion; many goodly stacks of hay and grain nestled close to the buildings. Herds of sleek cattle and plump sheep lay in their comfortable stalls; great piles of lumber were awaiting shipment to the markets below, and the mills were grinding and sawing night and day, seemingly rushed with orders. " The evening meal had been eaten; the mother had sung her lullaby over the cradle; the fires were all ' raked up ' on the hearthstone, and all had gone to rest," save a few men at the sawmill.

" Boast not thyself of to-morrow, for thou knowest not what a day may bring forth," is an oracle that was tragically, yes luridly, illustrated in the fate of Saratoga on the morning of November 28, 1745. For, owing to the wariness of the invaders its people had not received the least intimation that that morning should not be just as peaceful as any that preceded it.

On the return of M. Beauvais from below with his report, Marin gave orders for the advance and attack. From this point let the journal of the French adjutant be our guide.[1]

"The Nipissing and Abenakis followed the eastern shore of the river under the lead of Messrs. de Courtemanche and Niverville with a few French volunteers." to look after the settlement on that side.

"November 28. On the return of Beauvais we began to move quietly, and in good order with all the officers at their posts. We marched through the woods about a league along a very good road and then came to the houses. When we reached the first one M. Marin ordered me to detail four Frenchmen and ten Indians to go and surround it, but did not permit them to attack it until daybreak, which was the time when we were all to make the attack together. We had not gone more than an eighth of a league when they fired a gun and uttered their death yells, rushing to the assault. The Abenakis, [on the east side], who until then had awaited the signal, took upon themselves to make the attack, and from that time it was not possible to exercise any control. However, we went on to the edge of the wood in good order. M. de Beauvais having told M. Marin that we were discovered, he directed us to follow him. We passed a very rapid river [Fish creek], for which we were not prepared, and came to a sawmill, which

---

[1] This journal was found in the archives at Quebec after its capture by Wolfe in 1759. It was placed in the hands of Col. Philip Schuyler, as the one most interested.

two men (a negro and a Dutchman), were running, and in which there was a large fire. M. de St. Ours and M. Marin's son were disputing the possession of the negro with an Indian, although another Indian said that it was Marin who had captured him. His father, with whom I was, told him this was not the time to dispute about prisoners, and that it was necessary to go on and take others. A large party attacked a blacksmith's house on this side of the river [creek], when a native unfortunately killed a child twelve or fourteen years old. It was doubtless the darkness of the night and the fear of the river that separated us.

"Coming out of the mill we went to the house of a man named Philip Schuyler, a brave man, who would not have been seriously incommoded if he had only had a dozen men as valiant as himself. M. Beauvais, who knew and liked him, entered the house first, and, giving his name, asked him to give himself up, saying that no harm would be done him. The other replied that he was a dog, and that he would kill him. In fact, he fired his gun. Beauvais repeated the request to surrender, to which Philip replied by several shots. Finally Beauvais, being exposed to his fire, shot and killed him. We immediately entered and all was quickly pillaged. This house was of brick, pierced with loop-holes to the ground floor. The Indians had told us that it was a sort of guard house where there were soldiers. In fact, I found there more than twenty-five pounds of powder, but no soldiers. We made some of the servants prisoners, and it was said that some people were burned who had taken refuge in the cellar.

"We burned no more houses before reaching the fort, as this was the last. We had captured everybody, and had no longer any cause to fear lest anyone should go and warn the fort of our approach. It was at quite a considerable distance from the houses where we had been. We found no one in it. We admired its construction. It was regularly built, and some thought one hundred men would have been able to defend it against 500. I asked M. Marin if he wished to place a detachment there? He replied that he was going to set fire to it, and then told me I might go and do my best. This permission gave several of us the pleasure of taking some prisoners, and it did not take us long to get possession of all the houses below the fort, breaking the windows and doors in order to get at the people inside. However, everyone surrendered very peaceably. We had never counted on the facility with which all the houses were taken and the pillage accomplished. We set fire to everything good and useful; for instance, more than 10,000 planks and joists, four fine mills, and all the barns and stables, some of which were filled with animals. The people who were in the fields were in great part killed by French and Indians. In short, according to our estimation, the Dutch will not repair the damage we caused short of 200 marks. The barns were full of wheat, Indian corn and other grains. The number of prisoners amounted to 109, and about a dozen were killed and burned in the houses. Our achievement would have been much more widely known and glorious, if all the merchants of Saratoga had not left their country houses, and gone to spend the winter at Albany; and, I may add, had we met with more resistance.

"The work was complete at 8 a. m., when M. Marin issued orders for the retreat. On our return we reached Fort St. Frederic, December 3d, and Montreal, December 7th."[2]

Such is the French account of that deed of savagery.

---

[2] Documents relating to Colonial Hist of N. Y. Vol. X, p. 76; also G. W. Schuyler's Colonial Hist. of N. Y. Vol. II.

The chronicler, apparently somewhat ashamed of their work, strives to paint the barbarities of that night in as light a shade as they will bear. The number of prisoners given is no doubt correct, because he was in a position to know, but the number mentioned as butchered is palpably incorrect. The savages, greatly exasperated over the recent execution of seven of their braves by the English, would not be content with ten or a dozen scalps. Nor could any individual in that party possibly know how many perished. It was night and they were concerned only to do their work of destruction as quickly as possible and retire. Governor Clinton gives the number killed as thirty. This is doubtless much nearer the truth. Only one family escaped by flight.[3]

Thus what we saw to be a busy, thriving hamlet on the 27th of November was a scene of blackened ruins and an utter solitude on the 28th. The prisoners, men, women and children, many of them half clothed and barefooted, were collected, bound together and headed toward the frowning north, doomed to a fate which, to many of them, was worse by far than death. Some died in prisons. A few were ransomed from the Indians and returned, but most of them never saw the old home-land again.

A thrill of horror ran through the colonies as the news of this catastrophe spread. A storm of indignation broke over the heads of the governor, the Assembly, and on everyone who could, in any way, be held responsible for the defenseless condition of this frontier post.

Captain John Rutherford, who commanded the company from which the men were detailed to garrison the fort, demanded a court of inquiry, which was granted. The men swore that the fort was neither habitable nor

---

[3] Documents relating to Colonial Hist. of N. Y. Vol. VI, p. 288; Vol. X, p. 39.

defensible; that there was no well for water, nor oven for baking bread. Lieutenant Blood testified that Governor Clinton had given him orders to withdraw unless the Indian Commissioners should repair and equip it as they had promised. They failed to do so, and therefore he had withdrawn the men as per orders.

There is little doubt but that the men exaggerated the facts considerably, as they probably found it dull business doing garrison duty at such an out-of-the-way place, and naturally wanted to get away, and keep away.

That the fort was untenable is disproved by the testimony of the Frenchmen above quoted. They thought it to be admirably built, and that 100 men could hold it against 500.

The only English account of the massacre at Saratoga which has been preserved, aside from Governor Clinton's brief report to the Lords of Trade appears in a letter to Sir William Johnson. It is dated

Albany, Nov. 28, 1745.

Sr.

I have received your favor of the 23d instant &c. The bearer hereof In obedience to your Request therein shall herein give you as brief and true account of that unfortunate Affair which happened on the 17th[4] [O. S.] Instant at Saraghtogue — as I am Every Other Night & day on the watch, and my houses full of people soe That I cannot be at Large herein—Viz: at Break of Day or one hour or two before Day a Number of 400 french & 200 Indians appeared and did Besett all the houses there, Burnt and Destroyed all that came Before them. Left only one Sawmill standing which stood a little out

---

[4] The English at this time used the old style of reckoning, which was eleven days behind that of the French, who used the new style. The English dated the massacre of Saratoga, November 17th; the French November 28th.

their way it seems; took along with them such Booty as they thought fit & kilt and took Captives 100 or 101 persons, Black and white. I guess the Black most all prisoners, and the number of them exceeds the number of the white. The unfortunate Capt. Philip Schuyler was kilt in this Barbarous action, they say certain true; hoped He may Rather Be prisoner, the Latter is not Believed.[5]

               Sr,
               Your friend; well wisher
               & Very Humble Servant
               ROBT. SANDERS.

The Assembly severely blamed the governor for withdrawing the garrison. Instead of doing that, he should have reinforced the post with some of the many idle troops camped below Albany, where they were of no use to anybody. Once at the fort they could have repaired it speedily, dug a well, and built an oven as a matter of agreeable employment and exercise.

The truth is that the Governor and the Assembly were both to blame; for each was more anxious to spite the other than to care for the public interests.

The secret of this animosity was that Clinton, like his predecessors, was an absolutist, very jealous of the King's, and especially his own, prerogatives. On the other hand the Assembly, as representing the people, who were largely Dutch trained to republicanism before they emigrated, was equally jealous of its rights and liberties, and would neither be cajoled nor bullied into giving up a single privilege it had gained, but constantly pressed for more. The struggle for liberty and independence and the drill for self-government in these colonies began long years before the Revolutionary war. The Dutch of

---
[5] Johnson MSS. Vol. XXIII, p. 18.

New York and the Pilgrims of New England had tasted the sweets of civil and religious liberty, and self-government in Holland, before they came here, and they were not disposed to yield them up at the beck and call of despotic governors who did not believe that colonial subjects had any rights which they were bound to respect.

SOME EXPERIENCES OF THE SARATOGIANS IN CAPTIVITY

Up to the time of the publication of the first edition of this work we had been unable to find the names of the residents of the original Saratoga; none of those who were among the victims of the massacre, or the names of any who had been carried captive to Canada. The only name recorded by M. Marin, who led the attack, was that of Philip Schuyler who perished in his house as already recorded.

Since then we have discovered several Journals that were kept by certain New England men who were companions in distress, at Quebec, of a number of the Saratoga captives. Among these were Nehemiah How whose Journal is published in Drake's Indian Captivities, Norton's Redeemed Captive, and Capt. Wm. Pote's Journal. Wm. Pote was a sea captain. From these Journals we have gleaned the following facts: Nehemiah How says a Dutchman captured at Saratoga told him that 50 whites and 60 negroes were taken during that raid. This quite agrees with M. Marin's report of 109 taken. Only 25 of the prisoners reached Quebec. and they were sent there in instalments from Dec. 11th, 1745 to Feb. 22, 1746. The rest were distributed among the Indians. Only two entire families seem to have been taken to Quebec. These were Jacob Quackenbush and wife and three children, Isaac, Rachel and Martha. Gratus Vander Vericke, (Vander Werken, a name still common in this region) his father and mother aged respectively 75 and 72. They had been compelled to walk most of the way to the places of their captivity. The father had already been a prisoner at Quebec in Queen Anne's war. These old people were also the parents of Mrs. Quackenbush. Besides there were Lawrence Platter, a German, Andrew Hanes, (probably Hans) a Dutchman, and James Price, a lad. There is also mentioned a nameless woman whom Capt. Pote says " had her husband killed when taken & had 6 Children in ye hands of ye Savages. She expects to stay here till a peace by Reason of the fact her children Cannot be Exchanged. She lives with a Gentleman in town In a Genteel hansom manner & I believe will content her self to Live hear all ye days of her life."

During the late fall of 1746 a fever, contagious and deadly in its nature, broke out in the prison, and this together with very unsanitary conditions resulted in a great mortality. On Nov. 18th 1746 Andrew Hans died, Dec. 1st, following, Gratus Vander Vericke died, ae 30. Dec. 7th Martha Quackenbush died, ae 12. On the 26th of April 1747 both Jacob Quackenbush and his son Isaac died. Mrs. Quackenbush was also seized with the disease but recovered. Capt. Pote says one rough box was used for carrying out all the dead. What they did with them he never learned but the same box was quickly returned for a fresh corpse.

James Price, released from prison, went to live with a Roman Catholic priest named Father Tonnancourt. At some point on the way north from Saratoga Rachel Quackenbush was separated from her parents and compelled to go and live with the Indians. Their village was on the south side of the St. Lawrence. One night the following summer she secured a canoe and paddled across the river to Three Rivers. From thence she stealthily worked her way toward Quebec assisted by some kindly disposed French people. There she was received into the family of a well-to-do gentlemen where she was kindly treated. After a time she was taken to the prison to see her mother. The mother of course was overjoyed to see her long lost daughter, for Rachel was now all that was left her. But who can measure the anguish of that mother's heart when she found that Rachel would have nothing to do with her, but had decided to remain with her newly found friends. Nor would the gentleman with whom she was staying accept the terms offered by sympathetic friends for her ransom. The explanation for this unnatural conduct as given in the journal is that she had abjured the Protestant faith and accepted Catholicism. But here is another possible explanation which offers itself: Perhaps that mother had not been, in the days gone by, as wise and kind in the treatment of her daughter as she should have been. Rachel was said to be 16 by one journalist, and 18 by another.

Another fact connected with this captivity, and learned from Drake's Indian Wars, p. 87, is that the owners of the negro slaves offered to redeem them from their Indian captors, but the negroes utterly refused to go back preferring the larger liberty allowed by their new masters to the exacting drudgery enforced by their old white owners.

CHAPTER VII

Fort Clinton — Its Site — Its Fate

IMMEDIATELY after the destruction of Saratoga Colonel Schuyler (cousin of the general) suggested to the governor that the fort be rebuilt. The governor and council took the matter under advisement at once. As a result, Clinton ordered it to be rebuilt immediately, trusting that the Assembly would furnish the means with alacrity.[1] The Assembly appropriated to this purpose 150£ ($750) on the 24th of December, 1745; a sum wholly inadequate, as this sixth fort in the series was to be considerably larger than the one destroyed. The work was started, and much of that winter was apparently spent in the work of reconstruction. In March it was ready for occupancy and was named Fort Clinton after the governor, but great difficulty was found in getting the militia up to garrison it.

A garrison was evidently secured however, at an early date; for the Provincial Council received a letter from the commandant of that fort, Jacob Ten Eycke, dated May 10th, 1746, in which he says: "The garrison is uneasy and desires to be relieved, and the enemy is constantly passing and repassing in great companies, and there are scarce men enough here to hold the fort."[2] William Smith, in his history of New York, says, 30 men made up the garrison here in May, 1746.

A party of Indians hovering about Saratoga in July, of that year, reported to the French that there were 300 at the fort. Still another party reported to the French that no person went outside the fort except in parties of

---
[1] Minutes of Council in MSS. Vol. XXI, p. 66.
[2] Council Minutes, Vol. 21, p. 93.

thirty. This was about August first of that year, 1746.[3]

Early in September a band of fourteen Abenaki Indians, headed by Sieur de Montigny, who had been detached by M. Rigaud, after his attack on Fort Massachusetts,[4] came over this way to keep an eye on Saratoga, and learn more about the rumored English expedition against Crown Point. One day they caught a party of twenty soldiers outside the fort, escorting a wagon loaded with clay for making a chimney. They fell upon them, took four prisoners, killed and scalped four; the rest, some of whom were badly wounded, threw themselves precipitately into the fort.

About October 23 a scouting party of thirty-three Indians and four Frenchmen, under M. Repentigny, hovering about the road somewhere between Saratoga and Waterford, heard a great noise through the woods toward the river. The Indian chief skulked down to the road to see what was up and discovered a great train of wagons escorted by several hundred troops bound for Fort Clinton. There were a few carriages in the cavalcade occupied by finely-dressed officers. The enemy stationed themselves near the road in a thicket and waited their chance. Seeing a couple of carts somewhat separated from the rest they pounced upon the drivers, killed both of them, scalped one, and scattered in the woods before any one could come to the rescue.[5]

This was no doubt the New York militia, under the command of Captain Henry Livingston, who was commandant of the fort from November, 1746, till March, 1747. The wagons were loaded with ammunition and camp belongings, provisions, etc.

---

[3] Documents relating to Colonial Hist. of N. Y. Vol. X, p. 59.

[4] Fort Massachusetts was located at Williamstown, Mass. Its site is marked by a liberty pole and can be seen from the train a little way east of the B. & M. Station.

[5] Documents relating to Colonial Hist. of N. Y. Vol. X, p. 75.

THE STORY OF OLD SARATOGA 47

In December, '46, a French and Indian scouting party observed the fort [no doubt from the top of some trees on the high ground toward Victory], and reported that it was twice as large as the old one; that the English had a large storehouse erected near the fort, and that the garrison numbered perhaps 300.[6]

Early in April, '47, Lieutenant Herbin at the head of a party of thirty French and Indians struck a blow near Saratoga. They fell upon a detachment of twenty-five on their way to Albany, killed six of them, captured four, and the remaining fifteen threw away their muskets and took to flight. These prisoners reported some interesting facts concerning Fort Clinton, viz: That there were twelve cannon at the fort, six eighteen-pounders and six eight-pounders; that 100 bateaux had been built for the proposed expedition against Crown Point; that a great sickness had prevailed that winter at Albany and was still raging there and at Saratoga, where a great many of the soldiers had died.[7] A letter was found in the pocket of the commanding officer, who was killed, written by Commandant Livingston. This letter declares that "all the soldiers are ill; the garrison is in a miserable condition; no more than a hundred men are fit for duty; and we are in want of every succor, and then adds: "Were we killed in this expedition against Canada it would have been an honor to us; that the fort is in the worst condition imaginable, and I pity the men who are to succeed us."

It was in the mind of Gov. Clinton to erect a strong fortified camp of stone at Fort Edward capable of housing a garrison of 500. But the provincial Assembly, Clinton afterward concurring, thought it wiser to use

[7] Documents relating to Colonial Hist. of N. Y. Vol. X. pp. 93, 96.
[6] Ibid. p. 89.

the money for erecting a chain of block houses from the frontier of Mass. to Saratoga, thence to the westward.

In a message to the Assembly dated April 4th 1747 Clinton says among other things: "The Forces did March for the Carrying Place [Ft. Edward] but by the unexpected Interruption in the Provisions for the Men, who were to cover the Works while they were erecting, and to defend the place after it was erected, this work (though in my opinion) was absolutely necessary, was laid aside, and the officers who had the Command, were by the Cold Weather, which came on, forced to take up with the old Fort at Saratoga, only enlarging it and making new Defenses to it. Then too, by all the Information which I had of that Place, it is the most disadvantageously situated that anything of the kind could be, as it cannot serve for any of the Purposes, which I had in view by the fortified Camp at the Carrying Place, and is so overlooked by Hills and covered with Woods, that the skulking Parties of the Enemy can discover every motion in the Fort by the lowness of its situation and the watery swamps around it. It has always been unhealthful and has brought on a continued sickness in every Garrison that has been placed in it."

The Assembly in its reply says that the expense connected with a fort at the Great Carrying place, as of the other expenses of the war, were to be met by the several Colonies and not by New York alone, which was unable to bear, unassisted, a burden in which all were equally interested. And about the Fort at Saratoga they say: "As to the Fort at Saratoga we can say little about it, the placing of it being within the Governor's province at the time it was first built, and was afterwards rebuilt by your Excellencie's Directions." According to their statements much or most of the money raised for the public good and defense had somehow disappeared with little or nothing to show for it.⁸ That is a specimen of what we in this year of grace call "grafting."

Clinton's response to the long and unanswerable reply of the Assembly was its forced adjournment till June. He would also tell the King all about their naughty behavior.

Verily, when two mother hens spend their time fighting each other (as did Gov. Clinton ⁹ and the Assembly) the chickens are pretty sure to suffer.

Capt. Livingston was succeeded by Colonel Peter Schuyler who came up from New Jersey with his Regiment. But apparently Capt. Livingston did not at once withdraw, for with a part of his men, he stayed till in April. On March 9th 1747 Col. Schuyler reported 386 men present & fit for duty, & 75 deserters.

Early in the spring of 1747, the enemy again appeared at Saratoga ready for the season's campaign. For the records say that on April 7th, as Captain Trent with Lieut. Proctor's party went out of the fort and started north along the river, passing the ruins of Capt. Philip Schuyler's house, intending to cross Fish creek, they were ambushed by 60 French and Indians who killed 8 men and wounded several others. Trent and Proctor rallied their men and bravely fought the enemy for an hour. Captain Livingston on learning the nature of the contest dispatched Capt. Bradt with a company who succeeded in crossing to the north side of the creek. The enemy thus threatened in their rear hastily withdrew leaving behind considerable plunder and one wounded Frenchman.¹⁰

---

⁸ Journal of the Gen'l Assembly of New York, pp. 146 and 152.

⁹ This Gov. Clinton was the father of Sir Henry Clinton who succeeded Gen. Howe at New York in the Revolution, and a kinsman of George Clinton, first Governor of New York State.

¹⁰ Drake's French and Indian Wars, p. 142.

Chew's Exploit. In the early part of June 1747 Sir Wm. Johnson (then Col.) was advised that the French, with their Indian allies were again showing themselves in the vicinity of Fort Clinton.

On the 16th of the same month he was also informed by a war party of Schoharies, just returned from an unsuccessful foray, of the approach on Lake Champlain of a fleet of 300 canoes and admonished to be on his guard against surprise. A runner was at once dispatched to Fort Clinton with this intelligence. Immediately Capt. Chew was ordered forth with a detachment of a hundred men to patrol the country between that post and the head of Lake Champlain. Falling in with the enemy, or quite probably being ambushed, 15 of his men were killed and 47 more, including himself, were captured. It appears that La Corne St. Luc was the leader of this advanced party of French and Indians. He on meeting with and being attacked by Chew at once fell back on the larger force which succeeded in entrapping the eager but unsuspecting English.[11]

La Corne St. Luc's Expedition Against Fort Clinton, 1747. Immediately after this encounter with Capt. Chew the French and Indians returned to Fort St. Frederick to repair damages and replenish their stores. Capt. Chew with his fellow prisoners were at once sent to Quebec.

The energetic leader, St. Luc, pining for a speedy repetition of similar exploits prevailed upon M. Regaud de Vaudreuil, Commandant at Fort St. Frederick, to detach 20 Frenchmen and 200 Indians of the various tribes, and place them under his command, then he would make an immediate and resolute attempt at the reduction of Fort Clinton. The journal of that expedition is worth the reading, so we give it here:

---
[11] Stone's Life of Johnson. Vol. I, p. 279.

"June 23d. Started from Fort St. Frederic at midnight for Sarastau to endeavor to find an opportunity to strike some good blow on the English or Dutch garrison at Fort Klincton, as they called it.

"26th. Left his canoes and slept near the river of Orange [Hudson], which he crossed, the first in a little pirogue. Had five canoes made of elm bark. Left Messrs. de Carqueville and St. Ours to cross their men. All were over at two o'clock in the afternoon.

"28th. At early dawn the Abenakis told him he was exposing his men very much, and they wished to form an ambuscade on a little island in front of the fort, in order to try and break somebody's head. He told them they must go to the fort.

"He sent Sieur de Carqueville with seven Indians of the Saut and Nepissings, to see what was going on at the fort. They reported that some forty or fifty English were fishing in a little river [the Fish creek], which falls into that of Orange, on this side of the fort. He sent Sieur de Carqueville, a Nepissing, and an Abenaki to examine where the fort could be approached. M. de St. Luc said he should give his gun, a double-barreled one, to the first who would take a prisoner, and told them that after the first volley they should charge axe in hand. He said the same thing to the French. Sieur de Carqueville arrived, and said the English had retired into the fort. I sent M. de St. Ours to see where the river [Fishcreek] could be crossed, and to watch the movements of the fort. He returned to say that he had found a good place; that several Englishmen were out walking. They crossed the river [creek] and spent the remainder of the day watching the enemy.

"29. They all crossed half a league above [Victory Mills], though the Abenakis were opposed to it. Waited all day to see if any person would come out. Sent twenty men on the road to Orange [Albany], who returned under the supposition that they were discovered, passing near the fort. Made a feint to induce them to come out. He demanded of the chiefs six of their swiftest and bravest men; commanded them to lie in ambush, on the banks of the river, within eight paces of the fort at daybreak, to fire on those who should come out of the fort, and to try and take a scalp, and if the fort returned their fire to pretend to be wounded and exhibit some difficulty in getting off so as to induce the enemy to leave the fort. Those in ambush neither saw any person nor heard any noise; they came to say they thought they were discovered. The chiefs assembled around the officers and said that they must retreat; that they were surrounded by 400 men who had just come out of the fort. These gentlemen told them that it was not the custom of the French to retire without fighting, when so near the enemy and that they were able to defend themselves against this number of men, should they be so bold as to come and attack them.

They sent out the six scouts to lie in ambush at their appointed place, and to pass the night on their arms. He commanded the French and Indians to discharge their pieces in case a large number of people came out and to let them return the fire, and then to rush on them axe in hand, which was done.

"30th. Those who lay in ambush fired on two Englishmen who came out of the fort at the break of day on the 30th, and who came towards them. The fort made a movement to come against our scouts who withdrew. About a hundred and twenty men came out in order of battle, headed by two Lieutenants and four or five other officers. They made towards our people, in order to get nearer to them by making a wheel. They halted at the spot where our scouts had abandoned one of their muskets and a tomahawk. [Another account says they were lured some distance from the fort.] De St. Luc arose and discharged his piece, crying to all his men to fire; some did so, and the enemy fired back, and the fort let fly some grape, which spread consternation among the Indians and Canadians, as it was followed by two other discharges of cannon ball. Our men then rushed on them, axe in hand, and routed the enemy, who they pursued within thirty *toises* [about 200 feet] of the fort, fighting [Another account says St. Luc surrounded them][12] Some threw themselves into the river and were killed by blows of the hatchet, and by gunshots. Forty prisoners were taken and twenty-eight scalps. The number of those drowned could not be ascertained. One lieutenant, who commanded, with four or five other officers, were killed and one lieutenant was taken prisoner. Only one Iroquois of the Saut was killed, he was attacked by three Englishmen; five were slightly wounded.

"The attack being finished, Sieur de St. Luc collected the arms and withdrew his men. He remained with three Frenchmen and as many Indians, watching the enemy's movements. About 150 men, as well as they could judge, came out of the fort, without daring to advance. Of the 120 or 130 who might have been in the sortie from the fort, some twenty or twenty-five only appeared to have re-entered it."

The above quotation is given at length chiefly that the interested reader might have the data from which to form his own opinion as to the location of Fort Clinton. It has been a bone of historic contention for many years. Some writers, taking their cue from the description given by the Swedish traveller Kalm, have placed it on a hill

---

[12] Documents relating to Colonial Hist. of N. Y. Vol. X, p. 112.

east of the Hudson.[13] Others insist that it was located north of the Fishcreek on or near the site of Fort Hardy.

After a careful analysis of the above journal the present writer ventures to claim that the movements of the French described, and the conditions revealed therein, warrant the assertion that Fort Clinton, like the blockhouse of 1689, and the two wooden forts which succeeded it (of 1739 and 1745) were all of them located on the west side of the Hudson, south of Fishcreek, and near the bank of the river.

A landmark or two mentioned in St. Luc's Journal, together with a statement of locality found in Marin's account of his destruction of the fort in 1745, suggested to the writer where he ought to look for the site of old Forts Saratoga and Clinton. Soon after this, in a conversation with a citizen of Schuylerville, whose father for many years owned the river flats in that locality, that gentleman told of remains of a former occupancy, still to be seen, and of many relics found on the site in question, such as lead balls, grape shot, cannon balls, brass buttons, inkstands, etc., which, said he, led his father to believe it must have been the location of a fort or barracks.

This very interesting historic spot is about half a mile below Fishcreek on the river flats. There, on personal inspection, the writer found scattered over the ground a little higher than the rest, many brick-bats and rough

---

[13] " Saratoga has been a fort built of wood by the English to stop the attacks of French Indians upon the English inhabitants in these parts, and to serve as a rampart to Albany. It is situated on a hill on the east side of the River Hudson, and is built of thick posts, driven in the ground, close to each other, after the manner of palisades, forming a square, the length of whose sides was within the reach of a musket shot. At each corner are the houses of the officers and within the palisades are the barracks, all of timber. The English themselves set fire to it in 1747, not being able to defend themselves against the attacks of the French and their Indians."— *Peter Kalm's Travels. Vol. II, p. 287.*

stones which had no doubt formed part of the "twenty chimneys" and fire-places in the old fort. The space over which these fragments are scattered is about 225 feet square. Loads of them have been dumped over the bank, doubtless to get rid of them. On a later visit the writer's attention was called to what appeared to be sections of heavy stone walls embedded in the bank 100 feet or more below the dumping place, and which recent freshets had exposed; for the river is rapidly cutting away the banks here. There, plainly visible, were some foundations of the old fire-places, three in a row, together with a stratum of broken brick, stone and charred wood about sixteen inches below the surface. In laying them the builders had dug three feet below the surface. Many thin brick of the old Holland pattern lay about mingled with the stone that had tumbled down. About 100 feet north of these we discovered another foundation which had been partially disclosed by an enterprising woodchuck. We also picked up many old hand-made nails in the charred wood embedded in the steep bank. Another person found in the same place an English half-penny dated 1736.

A careful reading of Kalm's account leads one to conclude that despite the fact that the fort, seen by him, had been set on fire, much of it was yet standing, else he could not have given so detailed a description of its construction; whereas, the French account declares that nothing remained of Fort Clinton but twenty chimneys.

Moreover Kalm's fort was square, whereas, Fort Clinton was oblong according to French measurements. The fort described by Kalm was doubtless the one built by Philip Livingston in 1721, and kept in repair as a refuge for the people on the east side of the river. Kalm evidently did not inspect the west bank of the river, and hence did not see the remains of Fort Clinton. In a speech at Albany in 1754 King Hendrick chides the English for having burned their "forts at Saratoga," which leaves room for Kalm's fort in addition to Fort Clinton. Recall also the two forts marked on Father Picquet's map in connection with Marin's expedition against Saratoga.[14]

As a decisive proof that Fort Clinton was not on a hill but on low ground we would recall Gov. Clinton's criticism of the location of this work, quoted on a preceding page. There he finds fault with the "lowness of its situation," that it is "so overlooked by hills that the skulking parties of the enemy can discover every motion within the fort." He also calls attention to "the watery swamps around it, which has always made it unhealthful to the garrisons placed in it." Some of those "water swamps" still remain to the west and south of the site we discovered.

The following letter written to Sir William Johnson the day after the attack is of so interesting a character and in certain particulars tallies so closely with the French account that we insert it:

"Saratog, Saturday night, June 20th, [O. S.]
July 1st. [N. S.] 1747

"I wrote you last night which was giving you an account of the unhappy ingagement we had yesterday with the French, and have thought proper to write you again this evening for the following Reasons. This morning,

---

[14] On invitation of the writer, Messrs. Samuel Wells, William S. Ostrander, George R. Salisbury and W. E. Bennett, prominent lawyers in Schuylerville, went down and looked the ground over carefully. He thereupon read to them the above journals, and his conclusions therefrom, when they agreed that the spot answers all the conditions, and the remains and relics which have been discovered here, confirm the fact that this must be the site of those two Colonial forts known as Saratoga and Fort Clinton. Forts Clinton and Hardy alone, of the eight or more that were erected here, received a name; the others, each in its time, were always spoken of as the block house, or "fort at Saratoga."

at ten of the clock, A French Indian Came running towards the Garrison, and made all the signs of a distressed person, fired off his Piece, laid it down, and came up to the Garrison, and Desired to be admitted; which was granted, and has made the following discourse, to wit: He says he came out of Crown pt under the command of one Monjr Laicore [La Corne St. Luc] who is commander in Chief of the whole party which consists of Twelve Companies. And since [then] he has Tould us he has Four Thousand French and Indians. And he further tells us that Monsr Lacore went up to the place of Rendesvous, which is The Great Carrying Place, [Fort Edward] after the engagement with Mr. Chews, who with the rest of the prisoners are sent to Crown pt. Monsr Lacore has left Monsr Lagud [Laquel] as commanding officer of 300 men who are constantly seen in the woods Round the Garrison, and he says his desire is to intercept all parties coming from Albany; And that Monsr Lacorn is expected down from ye Carrying Place with the rest of the forces under his command this Evening, and are determined to stay here until they can have several Guns, Provisions &c. that they have sent for to Crown pt. as thinking it impossible to reduce this place without them, tho he says they have got hand-grenades, Cohorns, shovels & spades, & fire-arrows in order to fire the Block Houses, which that party attempted to do that fired upon the Rounds [sentries] from under the Bank. The person appointed to perform the same had a Blankit carryed before him that we should not Discover the fyer upon the point of the arrows. They not finding [the] thing according to their mind thought it best to come the next night and undermine ye Blokhouse No. 1, which they understood the Maggazine was in. But now I have rendered it impossible by Levelling ye Bank, and am in such a posture of Defense which will render it impossible to take ye Garrison with small arms, or anything else they have with them.[15]

Here the letter ends, apparently unfinished, and is without signature. This officer, who was evidently Col. Peter Schuyler of N. J., displays a good deal of pluck and resolution after the severe losses of the day before, and, despite the threatening disclosures of the Indian, says not a word about reinforcements. The letter written the day before, describing the attack has been lost.

Peter Kalm, the noted Swedish naturalist, passed up through here on a tour of exploration just two years after this famous attack on Fort Clinton. He tells the story of it in his book as he had heard it from the lips of participants on both sides, and since it throws some new light on the situation here at the time we give it herewith.

"I shall only mention one out of many artful tricks which were played here [at Saratoga], and which both the English and the French who were present here at that time told me repeatedly. A party of French with their Indians, concealed themselves one night in a thicket near the fort. In the morning some of the Indians, as they had previously determined, went to have a nearer view of the fort. The English fired upon them as soon as they saw them at a distance; the Indians pretended to be wounded, fell down, got up again, ran a little way and dropped again. Above half the garrison rushed out to take them prisoners; but as soon as they were come up with them, the French and the remaining Indians came out of the bushes, betwixt the fortress and the English, surrounded them and took them prisoners. Those who remained in the fort had hardly time to shut the gates, nor could they fire upon the enemy, because they equally exposed their countrymen to danger, and

---

[15] Sir William Johnson's MSS. Vol. XXIII, p. 44.

they were vexed to see their enemies take and carry them off before their eyes, and under their cannon. There was an island in the river near Saratoga much better situated for a fortification."[16]

The last garrison that served in Fort Clinton was made up of New Jersey troops under Colonel Peter Schuyler, already mentioned. These troops seem to have fared worse at the hands of the public than any of their predecessors. Governor Clinton insisted that the New York Assembly should provide for them; but the Assembly refused on the ground that since this was a general war, and all the colonies alike interested in the defense of the frontiers, it was the duty of each colony to subsist its own troops, wherever they were on service.

During the latter part of the summer of 1747 the Assembly becoming apprehensive that the garrison would desert because of lack of subsistence, apprised Governor Clinton of the facts, and asked that a sufficient number of the forces recently levied in New York for the proposed expedition against Canada be sent to garrison the fort at Saratoga, or that a hundred of the regulars be sent up, assuring him that they had an abundance of provision for their own troops.[17]

The first outburst of the much dreaded mutiny occurred apparently the latter part of August. But Col. Schuyler was enabled to suppress it for the time being by advancing to the men, from his own private resources, sufficient money for their present maintenance. For this he was reprimanded by both Gov. Clinton, and President Hamilton of N. J. because it would tend to increase discontent among the other soldiers, and encourage mutinies.[18]

---
[16] Kalm's Travels in North America. Vol. II, pp. 289, 290.
[17] Documents relating to Colonial Hist. of N. Y. Vol. VI, p. 618.
[18] Colonel Peter Schuyler was clearly a man whose military enthusiasm could not be easily damped. For we read that in 1755 he was in command

60 THE STORY OF OLD SARATOGA

Finally the storm, which for sometime had been brewing, broke in September of that year, when the majority of the garrison resolved to right their wrongs in their own way. So on the morning of the 20th, at the word of their leaders, they shouldered their muskets and started for Albany. The official account of the incident is still preserved in manuscript, which we shall herewith put in type, for the first time, and as one reads it he is constrained to wish that the soldier's side of the story had also been preserved.

This letter was addressed to Governor George Clinton then in New York city.

"Albany, Sept. 22d, 1747.
"Sir:

"On the 20th inst. deserted from the garrison of Fort Clinton (after the provision arrived there and the party had come away) [Provisions were finally sent from Albany on the 18th, but evidently too late] about 220 of the troops under Coll Schuyler's command and left him with about forty men. I immediately summoned a council of war, who join with me in the opinion, as there were not a sufficient number of men able to go to Saraghtoga without leaving the City and Quarters, with the sick entirely defenseless, that the cannon and other warlike stores belonging to His Majesty ought (comfortable [to] the Paragraff of your Excellencie's letter of the 10th instant) to be brought away to Albany. I have accordingly ordered a Detatched party from the whole, except your Excellency's Company who go down by the Douw [name of a sloop perhaps], for that service with horses, car-

---

of a N. J. regiment at the battle of Lake George. Again in 1756 he was there with his regiment and was among the prisoners surrendered to Montcalm. He was released from Quebec in Oct. 1757, but while in confinement had from his own resources contributed largely to the support and comfort of his fellow prisoners. Again he offered his services and was in the final campaign which resulted in the capture of Quebec.

riages, &c, as is necessary for that purpose, [and] which are just marched. The Mayor and Corporation this morning applied to me to request that I would, if possible, prolong the time of removing the artillery, &c, till the Return of an Express they now send down with the utmost dispatch, with one of their Aldermen to apply to your Excelency and Assembly, that a Provition may be made for maintaining that Garrison, which they are convinced cannot be by the new Levies in their present situation. I have consented to it provided the Corporation would be at the expense of keeping the horses and workmen so many days longer than otherwise would be necessary, which they have agreed to; Especial as they assure me it will occation most of the Inhabitants of this City deserting it, and be a further predjudice to us in regard to our Interest with the Indians. I have therefore wrote to Coll. Schuyler to this purpose and have desired him to prolong the time of the preparation as will be necessary for removing; as Corking batteaux, &c., and that I would send your Excel'cy's commands up the Instant the Express returns, which beg may be as soon as possible; for I can have no dependence on the present Garrison, nor is there well men enough to relieve it.

"I have, however, advised Coll. [Peter] Schuyler if he finds he cannot maintain the Garrison till he hears from me, and it is your Excel'cy's Orders that the artillery, Stores, &c., belonging to His Majesty be all brought down to Albany. I take this opportunity of writing, and as I have but a quarter of an hour's notice hope you will forgive the hurry I am obliged to write with,[19] I am

    Sir, Your Excel'cy's Most
     Obliged & Humble Serv't,
      J. ROBERTS [Colonel]"[20]

---

[19] N. Y. Colonial Mss. Vol. LXXVI.
[20] Col. John Roberts was commandant at Albany in 1746-'47.

On the receipt of this letter, Sept. 26th, Clinton immediately convened his council, laid the communication before them, and asked their advice. The council, which was wholly subservient to the governor, advised the abandonment and burning of Fort Clinton, and the saving of as much of the timber as could be used in the construction of a new fort at Stillwater.

Accordingly the governor, despite the pleas and protests of the Albany delegation, sent up orders to burn the fort and remove the cannon, stores, etc. On the 14th of October following he laid before the council the aforesaid orders together with a statement that the fort was in ashes, and that the cannon, etc., were removed to Stillwater.[21] But there was no fort built at Stillwater to take its place.

Fort Clinton was dismantled and the torch applied October 6th, 1747, when the men, we may suppose with alacrity, turned their backs on the whole business, and left Saratoga to its pristine solitude, to savage beasts and the still more savage men from the north. The governor said in excuse for his orders that he had learned that the only persons interested in having a fort there were the Schuylers, and a few others who wanted it as a protection for their wheat fields.[22] When he made this statement he seems to have forgotten those Commissioners who came to plead, in behalf of Albany and English prestige with the Indians, that the fort be preserved and regarrisoned, and also that he himself had favored constructing a battlemented work at Fort Edward. Hence the act of the governor smacks far more strongly of personal spite than of solicitude for the public treasury and the public safety.

At the end of November, 1747, Sieur de Villiers, at the

---
[21] Council Minutes. Vol. XXI.
[22] Documents relating to Colonial Hist. of N. Y. Vol. VI, p. 630.

head of a troop of seventy Indians and French, while out on a foray, visited Saratoga and was greatly surprised to find Fort Clinton in ashes. He describes it as about 135x150 feet in size; that twenty chimneys were still standing; and that the well had been polluted.[23]

Thus Old Saratoga and her forts seem to have been doomed to hard luck, judging from the records. No story of heroic deeds done by the garrisons, has been preserved, if they were ever performed. Their neglected and half-starved condition seems to have sapped their energies, and quenched their fighting spirit.

That the Albany people were right in their contention with the governor that the destruction of Fort Clinton would hurt the standing of the English with the Six Nations is evidenced by the following.

In a General Colonial Council, held at Albany, in July, 1754, to confer with the Indians, and endeavor to retain their allegiance, King Hendrick, the great sachem of the Mohawks, in his speech said this among other things:

" 'Tis your fault, brethren, that we are not strengthened by conquest; for we would have gone and taken Crown Point, but you hindered us. We had concluded to go and take it, but we were told that it was too late, and that the ice would not bear us; instead of this you burnt your own forts at Saratoga, and ran away from them, *which was a shame and a scandal to you.* Look about your country and see! you have no fortifications, no, not even to this city. 'Tis but a step from Canada hither, and the French may easily come and turn you out of your doors.[24]

From the beginning of the war there had been much talk about and preparation for the conquest of Canada. The colony of New York spent £70,000 ($350,000.) on

---
[23] Documents relating to Colonial Hist. of N. Y. Vol. X, pp. 147, 148.
[24] Documents relating to Colonial Hist. of N. Y. Vol. VI, p. 870.

5

it; but it all evaporated in talk and preparation instead of actual performance.

Massachusetts, Connecticut, New Jersey, Pennsylvania, and Maryland were all to help, but only a few troops ever assembled at Albany. After the fall of Louisburg an army of 3,000, well equipped and led could have marched from end to end of Canada without serious opposition; for she had only a few troops at that time with which to defend herself. But jealousy and inefficiency then ruled in the seats of authority in these colonies, and so nothing was accomplished.

"In union there is strength;" but first get your "union."

The treaty of peace signed at Aix-la-Chapelle, in May, 1748, put an end to King George's war and gave the colonists a breathing spell, but not for long.

CHAPTER VIII

THE FRENCH AND INDIAN WAR

THERE could be no permanent peace on this continent so long as both the French and English laid claim to all the vast territory west of the Alleghany mountains, and so long as their representatives here were each straining every nerve to make good that claim. The war which afterwards became general in Europe and was known there as the Seven Years War, began here in 1754 with a blow struck for English sovereignty in western Pennsylvania by a detachment led by a young man, with an old man's head on his shoulders. That young fellow bore a name afterward to become famous. It was George Washington, and at the time he was only twenty-two years old.

England had begun to realize the value of her possessions here, and she decided to do more for her colonies now than she had in the last war. Three separate expeditions against the French were to be organized: one led by General Braddock, against Fort Du Quesne; one by Governor Shirley, of Massachusetts, against Niagara, and the third, directed against the very vitals of French power in Canada, must of necessity take the ancient war trail up the Hudson against Crown Point, and Quebec, if possible.

The latter was entrusted to the command of William Johnson, then a colonel of militia, and a great favorite with the home authorities. The army was made up of five thousand provincials from the neighboring colonies, and collected at that ancient rendezvous of councils, and armies, Albany. There too, that brave old Mohawk Sachem, King Hendrick, assembled his dusky warriors.

Early in July six hundred pioneers went forward to clear the path to Lac St. Sacrament [Lake George,] and build at the Great Carrying place a fort. This they called Fort Lyman, in honor of the brave General who was leader of the party. Soon afterwards Johnson renamed it Fort Edward, in honor of the Duke of York and brother of George III. On the 8th of August, General Johnson, as he was now called, started from Albany, and the whole war-like procession passed through Old Saratoga about three days thereafter.

Since Saratoga figured so little in the war of 1754-'60, we shall give but a brief resumé of the thrilling events of that period, referring the reader, to the many excellent histories that describe them. So far as can be learned very few people had ventured to settle at old Saratoga after the close of King George's war in 1748. The unusually fertile soil with the promise of big crops had evidently drawn a few of the more venturesome hither, but the terror of the massacre of '45 was still like a nightmare resting heavily on most spirits. Hence, when the news of a probable rupture, between France and England, came in 1753, Saratoga was again abandoned.[1]

Johnson's mission was the reduction of Ticonderoga and Crown Point. He reached Lac St. Sacrament in due time, and at once took the liberty to rechristen it Lake George, in honor of his sovereign, and, as he said, "an assertion of his king's right of dominion there." Having reached there he showed no anxiety about proceeding farther. The French were more aggressive, and since their foe did not come to them they would go to him and attack him on his own ground. Baron Dieskau marched around by South Bay and Fort Edward and attacked Johnson on the 8th of September. John-

---
[1] N. Y. His. Soc. Mag. Vol. III, p. 142.

son was able to beat him off, yet with great loss to both sides. Johnson failed to follow up his victory, while the scare of it was on the enemy, and spent his time building a fort at the south end of the lake instead of taking the one at the north end, which he was sent to do, and which he might have done, had he been a Baron Dieskau. He named it Fort William Henry. "I found," he said, "a wilderness, never was house or fort erected here before." So that campaign failed of its object, but it gave the provincials a higher and truer notion of their own fighting qualities. Philip Schuyler took a hand in the battle of Lake George as a captain of the Albany County Militia. While nothing specially belligerent occurred at Old Saratoga during the French and Indian war, yet the Johnson Mss. contain a few items which throw some light on the material conditions here at that time.

General Johnson, on his march to Lake George, found the roads in a most wretched state. After the battle we find him taking steps to repair them, and improve the means of communication with Albany. In his letters and orders concerning these we find that Saratoga figures quite prominently. Early in October, 200 men were set to work on the road between Albany and Saratoga; a large number were also set to similar work between Saratoga and Fort Edward on the east side. His soul was mightily vexed at the tardy manner in which his orders about these roads were obeyed, and at the way in which the soldiers "sojered." As Saratoga was the point where the supply trains crossed the river, much attention had to be given to the ways and means of the crossing. It appears that the point where his army crossed on the advance was not the best possible; for in a report to Governor Hardy, dated, Camp Lake George, 7th October, 1755, he says among other things:

"Mr. Wraxall informs me that at the north end of an Island, opposite the House of Killaen DeRidder's, if the Bank on the west side is dug away & a waggon passage made, the Ford of the River is not above Horse knee High,[2] whereas through the usual Ford, [below the island] unless the wagons are uncommonly high the water generally comes into the wagons by which means the Provisions have been often damaged."[3]

Again as the river could be forded only at low water, provision had to be made for crossing at high water, and also for defending the passage against an enemy. A large scow boat was therefore built for ferrying the wagons, etc., over the Hudson. This ferry-boat was built near the house of one Hans Steerhart on the west side of the river at Saratoga. A picked company of fifty men from a Massachusetts regiment was posted here, during the fall of 1755, to guard the supplies and the crossing, and to help the wagoners, etc., to pass the ford.[4]

Campaign of 1756. Another expedition was planned the next year with the same objective, but under a different commander. This time it was led by General John Winslow. He started from Albany, about the first of June, with a force of 5,000 men. He built a fort at Stillwater, and honored it with his own name. But, he like so many of his predecessors, marched up the hill and then marched down again, with nothing accomplished. It is to be presumed, however, that the General and his warriors bold had a pleasant summer outing on Lake George,

---

[2] The river bank has been greatly worn away on the west side at this point, but remains of the old dug-way are still visible, and stock yet pass down it for water. From this point the ford passed to the north end of the island, thence north-east to where the line fence between Robert Coffin's farm and Walsh's reaches the river.

[4] Johnson's Mss. Vol. ——, p. 45.

[3] Johnson's Mss. Vol. III, pp. 131, 158.

at the public expense. Philip Schuyler, disgusted with the inaction and incapacity of the leaders, left the service at the end of this campaign, but afterward served in the quartermaster's department under Col. John Bradstreet. With him he saw active service, and was in several hotly contested fights. All of this proved a good schooling for the future general.

Campaign of 1757. The next campaign against Crown Point was under the leadership of the most spiritless, sneaking poltroon that had yet led the soldiery of these colonies to inaction and disgrace, General Daniel Webb.

The efficient and stirring Montcalm, leader of the French forces, organized an expedition the same year against Fort William Henry. He was before it with 6,000 men, 2,000 of whom were Indians, by the 2d of August. The fort was defended by two thousand two hundred men under Colonel Monroe. Webb, with an army of four or five thousand, was at Fort Edward doing nothing. And when called upon for help virtually refused to give it, and traitorously allowed Fort William Henry to be besieged and captured without lifting a finger to give it succor. For example, Sir William Johnson, having obtained Webb's reluctant consent, started with a body of provincials and Putnam's rangers for the relief of Monroe, when, after proceeding a few miles Webb sent an aide and ordered him back.

Webb was clearly a coward. On hearing of the fall of Fort William Henry, he at once sent his own baggage to a place of safety far down the Hudson, and would have ordered a retreat to the Highlands had it not been for the timely arrival of young Lord Howe, who succeeded in assuring him that he was in no immediate danger. And Lord Loudoun, the commander-in-chief in America for that year, and who, if possible, was a bigger coward than Webb, was utterly paralyzed by the news, and grimly proposed to encamp his army of twelve or fifteen thousand men on Long Island " for the defense of the Continent"! The French could not possibly have mustered over seven thousand men in all Canada at the time.

It was during this campaign that an incident of some local interest occurred on the east side of the river opposite Saratoga. It is related by the Sexagenary, whose father was one of a body of wagoners returning from a trip to Fort Edward. He says: "The main body of wagoners returned by the west side of the river, but my father and his friends kept on the east side, and when they reached the Battenkill, they discovered on crossing the bed of the creek the wet print of a moccasin upon one of the rocks. They were confident from this circumstance that hostile Indians were near them, and that one must have passed that way but a few minutes before. To go back seemed as dangerous as to go forward. They therefore pushed on towards the river [at the ford] but had scarcely reached its bank when the distinct report of a musket in their rear brought with it the confirmation of their fears. When this firing was heard, a detachment from an escort guarding the wagoners on the west side came across to ascertain the cause. On searching, they found in a garden belonging to a Mr. De Ruyter [De Ridder] the body of a dead man, still warm and apparently shot while in the act of weeding, and then scalped."

It was during this year, 1757, that the authorities again decided to adorn Old Saratoga with another fort. It was built on the north side of Fish creek in the angle made by it with the river, and named Fort Hardy, after the royal governor of the province. It was by far the largest and most elaborate of the forts built here, covering about fifteen acres. It could not have served any practical purpose at that time further than a shelter for troops and a depot for supplies, because it was commanded by hills on two sides within easy cannon shot.

Concerning this fort as with old forts Saratoga and Clinton, there has been much diversity of opinion. One historian argues from its bad strategical position, and the silence of all Revolutionary writers (as he claimed) regarding it, that there was no such fort here. Others affirm that it was built by the French under Baron Dieskau, in 1755. As to Baron Dieskau the fact is he never got further south with his valiant Frenchmen than the vicinity of Fort Edward. He himself, however, was brought down after the battle of Lake George in a boat, wounded and a prisoner of war.

This dispute over Fort Hardy furnishes a good test case on the value of silence, on the part of contemporary writers, as tending to prove the existence or non-existence of an object, custom, or alleged fact. Here it is shown to be untrustworthy. The writer rummaging in the State Library at Albany came across the official journal of the engineer who laid out and superintended the building of the fort.[5] He was Colonel James Montressor, chief of the Royal Engineers, in America, who was commissioned to build forts the same year at Albany, Schenectady, Halfmoon, Stillwater, Fort Edward and Fort George on Lake George. Fort George, like Fort Hardy, was of no value for defense, and for a long time it was known as Montressor's Folly. He began work on Fort Hardy August 19th, 1757. For some time he had considerable trouble to get help, but on the 7th of September he had at work about a hundred men and six teams. There had been a sawmill on the north side of the creek, about where the gristmills are

---
[5]Collections of the N. Y. Historical Society. Vol. XIV.

now located, but the provincial soldiers had torn it to pieces for firewood, so this work had to be done with whip-saws run by hand power. The stone was drawn from the hills, presumably from the ridge west of the old north burying ground, as old residents say loose stone was most plentiful there. The brick was brought down from Fort Edward in bateaux, or scow boats. Thus early Fort Edward had its brick yards. The timber was procured up the river on both the mainland and islands, floated down and dragged out with ox teams. The first buildings finished were three storehouses, which were placed on posts three feet high to preserve the stores from water in case of inundation. The capacity of the three was 2,596 bbls. of flour. The barracks for the soldiers were 220 feet long; the officers' rooms were 14x16 feet in size. One day the mechanics all struck work because the commissary tried to put them off with a gill of rum instead of their regular ration. The trouble was that "the jug was out."

This journal discloses another particularly interesting fact, that there was already standing in that same angle, north of the creek, a blockhouse, or stockaded fort. Its size and location, as also that of the afore-mentioned sawmill, appear in the adjoining pen-sketch map reproduced from the journal. It took several days to tear it down. When and by whom this fort was built is a mystery. The silence of the writers, however, does not establish its non-existence.

From old maps we learn that a road was constructed on the west side of the Hudson from Saratoga to Fort Edward in 1757. After 1758 the road approached the river opposite the Fort and island, and there was also a pontoon and ford below the island.

MONTRESSOR'S SKETCH MAP OF FISH CREEK
AND OLD BLOCK HOUSE

Campaign of 1758. The army mobilized for the campaign of 1758 was the most formidable and imposing that had yet appeared on the American Continent. This also was put under the command of one of those chicken-hearted but titled incompetents whom royalty persisted in selecting for positions of grave responsibility. This time it was General James Abercrombie. He led an army of 16,000 men up the old war path through Saratoga. It must have been a thrilling spectacle to see those gaily caparisoned warriors swinging along with measured tread to the skirl of the bagpipe or the more stirring music of fife and drum. The trains of supply wagons, ambulances, and the batteries of artillery must have seemed well nigh endless to the onlooker. One French scout counted 600 oxen in one drove that were being driven north to feed this army of British beef eaters.

Among the potent influences which served to estrange the hearts of Americans from their allegiance to the English government was the snobbery and tactless behavior generally of British officials toward colonials. For example we are told that Gen's. Loudoun and Abercrombie, like Braddock, despised all suggestions from men born on colonial soil. They would astonish the natives by their scientific European methods of conducting war; stupidly assuming that social and natural conditions here were the same as in the long settled countries of the old world.

Among other things Abercrombie proposed to remove the native officers from their regiments and substitute Englishmen thus reducing all Provincials, of whatever grade, to the common level of privates. But of course the Americans resented this and resolutely refused to serve under any officers but those of their own choosing.[6]

Perhaps Lake George never served as a setting to so

---

[6] Tarbox's Life of Putnam, p. 57. New York's Part in History, p. 84.

magnificent a pageant, as when, embarked in over 1,000 boats, with flags and pennants flying, this embattled column swept majestically over its crystal waters toward Ticonderoga.

But how great the change wrought upon this supposed invincible host in a single day of battle with the doughty Montcalm! Through bad generalship, or rather through the lack of all generalship, we see this splendid army defeated, shattered, and panic stricken, scuttling back to Fort William Henry with its boats laden with the dead and dying. In one of these was borne the body of the brave young Lord Howe, the very soul, and the acknowledged idol, of the whole army. On reaching the head of the lake, Philip Schuyler, now a major, whose deep affection he had won, begged and received permission to convey the body of his hero to Albany, where he was buried in St. Peter's church. Of those who died from their wounds many were buried at Fort Edward, and some were buried here at Old Saratoga (Schuylerville), but all in nameless graves.

Campaign of 1759. For the first time in her hundred years of occupancy, England selected as leaders for this year men who bore the semblance of generals — Amherst and Wolfe. Satisfactory results were soon apparent. With an army of twelve thousand, Amherst followed Abercrombie's line of advance, and within a week's time from landing at the foot of Lake George both Ticonderoga and Crown Point, for so long the dread and envy of the English, were in their possession. It is but fair, however, to state that owing to Wolfe's menace of Quebec, the garrisons at these forts had been greatly weakened. That same year the brave Wolfe captured Quebec, Canada's Gibraltar, and so all Canada became an English possession by the right of conquest.

"Old Put's" Thrilling Adventure at Fort Miller. Sometime during the summer of 1758 Major Israel Putnam chanced to lie with 5 men and a batteau on the left bank of the Hudson near the steep rapids at Fort Miller. Some of his men on the opposite bank signaled to him that a large body of savages were in his rear, and would be upon him in a few moments. To stay and be sacrificed, to attempt crossing against the swift current, or to go down the falls with the chances, ten to one, of being drowned, were the only alternatives for escape that offered themselves. Instantaneously he adopted the latter course. And this he did knowing that one of his men had just rambled a little way back in the woods, and must be left a victim to savage barbarity.

The Indians reached the shore soon enough to fire many bullets at them before they could get out of range. But no sooner were they beyond musket shot than death in another form, and but little less terrible, stared them in the face. Rocks, and eddies, swirling currents and steep descents, for a quarter of a mile afforded barely a single chance to escape. But Putnam trusting himself to a good Providence whose kindness he had often before experienced, coolly took the helm issuing his orders to the men at the oars with marvellous skill and well nigh superhuman strength guided the bulky boat between the savage rocks, yawning whirlpools, and over seemingly impossible falls till at last the boat glided forth into the more quiet waters below.

At sight of this it is asserted that the Indians, those rude children of nature, were affected with the same kind of veneration which Europeans in the Dark Ages entertained for some of their most valorous champions. They concluded the man bore a charmed life. He had shown himself proof to their bullets, and here he had floated in safety down a rapids and over falls which they had ever deemed impassable. They therefore concluded it would be an affront to the Great Spirit to make any further attempt to kill this favored mortal, even though they could get at him.[7]

Some of the journals kept by the soldiers during these campaigns against Canada are very interesting not only for the facts and incidents related but as primitive efforts at what we are striving for in these days, phonetic spelling; and also they serve as lurid examples of the picturesque in orthography.

Here are some specimens from Luke Gridley's diary:

"The 5 D[ay] [May 1757] they [the regiment] trained But I was garding & fiching we Being straitened for Proviccon: & hungery; Johnnathan Beamman Eate 3 Raw fich: inwards & al for 4 quarts of wine.

"Day 23 [May] wich was monday we marcht 10 mils & Picht our tents at Suratoke thare we went Into the River and Chast [cacht or caught] aboute 3000 Alewifes [herrings] for Super."

"Day 13th [Sept.] one Yorker whipt 300 lashes for gitting Drunk, a Regular [British] for ye same offense got 100."

Note that this is a sample of the Briton's estimate at that period of the comparative worthfulness of a subject born on English soil and one born in an American colony.

[Oct.] "Day 12th one Asbel moses a Simsbury man Died with ye lung fever, [pneumonia] Being ye 10th man that has died with Distempers out of our Company."

That is, at least 10 per cent of their number had died within six months, not in battle or of wounds, but of unsanitary conditions, infectious diseases, ignorance of the ordinary laws of health, etc. These journals are filled with tales of sickness and mortality which prove that

---

[7] Humphrey's Putnam, p. 54.

Camp life in those days, for Provincials, was far more deadly than pitched battles.

" Day 30th wich was ye Sabbath fifteen of our Rigment set out for home and marcht to Surrotoge.

" Day 30th we set sail two oclock & went to Capt. Lamsons."

At Saratoga they took scows, or batteaus down the Hudson to Stillwater. To this point (Saratoga) much of the provision for the army was brought by water transportation, from thence north to Lake George it was carted.

In Samuel Lyons Diary for 1758 we find this incident:

" June 25, We got 2 Battoes to carry our packs [from Stillwater] up to Salatogue, and we went afoot & 8 of our men were drawn out to stay at Salatogue. Capt. Lewis shot at an Indian and kild him & [as he?] sot in the Battoe."[8]

Archelaus Fuller a soldier in the same campaign of 1758 writes down some of his experiences as follows:

"Monday ye 19 day [May] we marched, went over there to Albany side whear we Reseavd Eleven mor arms, then marched with the hol Battalion threw Miscoycung [Niskayuna] to Senacade [Schenectady] wheare we taried al knight. it was about 20 miles, it was a fine place, very good land, it lais upon the Mohock River, so caled."

" Wednesday ye 19 [July] thair cam in a man that was lost the forst day we had our fit [at Ticonderoga July 6th] he levd the hol of the time on gren leves & nuts, he saw no bereys. 3 days before he cam in he saw 3 Ingons which gave him chas he run & fell down under a log and got clear. he came in bear feet & bear leg, he loke like a corps."

Just one more sample and then we pass on.

---
[8] Soldiers Journals, p. 16.

"Monday 3ᵈ [July 1758] Yesterday Mager [Israel] putmons Company cam up and and this morning the Connetticuts rigiment were Inbodied for to lorn how to form your front to Right & Left for Jineral Abba Cromba and his A de Camp to vieu."

"Sat. Aug. 12 Colonel Phich [Fitch] had a leter from Mager [Israel] putmon at tiantiroge, he is taken prisoner.

"Tues. 15. I was upon picit [picket] gard, & wet and stormy it was, 1 of the reglars whipt for sleeping upon gard."[9]

[9]Military Journals of two private soldiers, pp. 20, 30.

CHAPTER IX

The Revolution — The Causes of the War

THE scope and purpose of this work will admit of nothing more than a glance at the reasons which led the colonies to declare themselves independent of the sovereignty of Great Britain.

There were but few people in England that knew much or cared much about America, and still fewer who understood the Americans. The fact that they were colonists seemed of itself to reduce them to a lower plane racially than themselves. The English ruling classes behaved as though they thought the colonies were of use only to be exploited for the imperial glory and commercial profit of Great Britain. Their asserted right to self-government in matters local was a thing rarely known in England, and of course, it could not be tolerated by her in the colonies. The royal governors had all fumed and fretted themselves into hysterics over the wilfulness and perversity of colonial assemblies. But so long as France was powerful here, England dared not attempt to thwart the will of her colonists too much; for she needed their assistance to maintain herself against the assumptions of her great rival. But when France was well out of the way, and England had a free hand on this continent, she at once began to assert her sovereign authority over her refractory subjects.

The Seven Years War had left her deeply in debt; she would make the colonies help her pay that debt through her Stamp Acts. She forgot that they had already borne the brunt of the conflict and largely the expense of that war in so far as it was waged in this country. Next she set about depriving the colonial assemblies of their

THE STORY OF OLD SARATOGA 81

inherent legislative rights. She began to interfere in matters of "internal police," and was rapidly moving toward placing the administration of all law and government in the hands of men responsible to no one but the Crown. All this without consulting the colonists, or asking their consent. Her repeated acts of tyranny finally aroused the provincials to realize that they were in imminent danger of losing even the commonest liberties of an Englishman, but they did not resort to the arbitrament of arms till they had exhausted all other means of redress.

Events of 1775 and 1776. The final break came and open hostilities began in 1775. This was a year big with success and inspiration to the patriots. It was the year of Lexington, and Concord, and Bunker Hill; the important capture of Ticonderoga, and Crown Point; the invasion of Canada, with the capture of St. Johns, of Chambly, and of Montreal by Montgomery under Schuyler, a campaign which, if it had received a decent and patriotic support from the citizenship and soldiery of the north, and something more substantial than resolutions from Congress, would have gained Canada for the Union, but which ended in defeat on the last day of December, and the irreparable loss of the noble Montgomery, who breathed out his heroic life with the expiring year under the granite walls of Quebec. The end of this year also witnessed the siege of Boston under Washington, with good auguries of success.

The year 1776 brought some more good cheer at its beginning, with the expulsion of the British from Boston, the successful defense of Fort Moultrie in South Carolina, and the Declaration of Independence. This in turn was followed by disaster, in the ejection of the Americans from Canada, the defeat of Arnold on Lake

Champlain, and also of Washington at the battle of Long Island, the loss of Forts Washington and Lee, and finally the chase of Washington by the British across New Jersey into Pennsylvania. But as a breath of life to one well nigh asphyxiated, came the unlooked-for smashing of the Hessians at Trenton; the outgeneralling of Cornwallis and whipping of the British at Princeton, and the virtual expulsion of the enemy from the Jerseys in the end of that year. And all this by that same Washington after Howe and Cornwallis had solemnly and unanimously agreed that he had just received his quietus at their hands.

Campaign of 1777. After the evacuation of Boston by the British, General Burgoyne, who was present during its investment, went to Canada and served under Carleton during 1776, but becoming dissatisfied with his position he returned to England. There, closeted with King George and his favorite ministers, they planned a campaign which was certain, as they thought, to put an end to the war and reduce the colonies to submission.

The scheme was to get possession of the Hudson valley, sever the colonies, paralyze their union, and so, holding the key to the situation, conquer them in detail.

To this end an ample force under St. Leger was to move up the St. Lawrence to Oswego, strike into New York from that point, capture Fort Schuyler, (formerly Fort Stanwix, where Rome, N. Y., now stands) and sweep down through the Mohawk valley to Albany. Another army under Howe was to move up the Hudson from New York toward Albany; and the third under General John Burgoyne was to take the old route from Canada south through Champlain and down the Hudson, when they would all concentrate at Albany to congratulate one another, and divide the honors and the spoils. This admirable plan was adopted and its execution was placed in the hands of Burgoyne, under the title of Lieutenant-General.

As to the British plan of campaign doubts concerning it in the minds of the American leaders quite paralyzed all intelligent preparations. The retreat of Gen. Carleton from Lake Champlain, the preceding autumn, even after Crown Point, and practically the entire lake were in his possession, suggested a doubt whether a serious invasion was meditated from that quarter. On the contrary the impression was general after news about it had reached them, that the expedition of Burgoyne was destined for Boston, and that Sir. Wm. Howe, whose movements in New Jersey were enigmatical in the extreme, was to cooperate in an effort to resubjugate New England. The British government itself, as it is believed, contributed to the distractions of Congress and the American commander by causing reports to be circulated that Boston was to be the next point of attack. As a result Massachusetts, feeling that all her strength would be required for her own defence, set about raising troops for home protection, and was reluctant to allow any to go beyond her borders.

Before the close of June, however, the designs of the enemy became quite clear. Among other events a man, arrested as a spy, and brought to Gen. Schuyler, revealed very explicitly the plans of the enemy.

First Period of the Campaign. Early in June Burgoyne started from Canada, animated with the highest hopes and brightest anticipations. Should he succeed, as no doubt he would, he expected to find a title of nobility among other good things in his Christmas stocking.[1] Certainly all things looked favorable for his success.

His was not the largest, but it was the best appointed army that had yet appeared on these shores.[2] It was made up of British, 4,135; Germans, 3,116; Canadians, 148; Indians, 503; total, 7,902. Later the 22d regiment joined him. Burgoyne expected 2,000 Canadians, but they declined the service mainly because they had learned that the British were uniformly arrogant in their treatment of Provincials.[3]

Some of those regiments, both British and German, were ancient and honorable organizations and were veterans of a hundred battles. Europe could furnish no better soldiers.

On the 1st of July, Burgoyne was before Ticonderoga, which he at once invested. Through lack of sufficient force, General St. Clair, the commandant, felt obliged to abandon his line of communication with Lake George, likewise "the old French lines" just west of the fort. He had not over 3,500 men all told, while the works were so extensive that it would require ten thousand to man them properly. Of course, the British seized the points of vantage at once and made the most of them. Still with his meagre force and contracted lines, St. Clair felt confident that he could keep the enemy at bay for a respectable while, and time was valuable just then to Schuyler, who was laboring to collect an army and get up reinforcements to him.

The British were no sooner on the ground than the

---

[1] George III, empowered Lord George Germaine to promise Burgoyne a Knight Commandership of the Bath with other good things to follow should he succeed.—Trevelyan's Am. Revolution, Pt. III, pp. 108-9.

[2] "The brass train that was sent out on this expedition was perhaps the finest, and probably the most excellently supplied as to officers and men, that had ever been allotted to second the operations of an army."—*Lieutenant Digby's Journal, p.* 226.

[3] Belcher's First American Civil War

practiced eye of that veteran artillerist, General Phillips, noticed a mountain across a stretch of water to the south which appeared to be unoccupied, and which looked to be within range of the fort. He had it inspected and the officer reported it to be within easy cannon shot, and though difficult of ascent, still accessible. One night's labor built a road and put several cannon on the summit of the mountain, which the British then christened Mount Defiance; an appropriate name under the circumstances, and the one it still bears. When daylight came, on the 5th of July, the garrison was paralyzed with amazement to see the crest of that mountain blossoming with red-coats, and frowning with a brazen battery. A council of war was called immediately which decided that the works were now untenable, and that nothing was left but evacuation. That night, as soon as it was dark, the sick and the non-combatants, together with as much of the stores as they could load on the bateaux, were sent to Skenesborough (Whitehall) with an escort of six hundred men under Colonel Long. Having spiked the guns, the army quietly withdrew at 2 a. m. on the 6th over the floating bridge that connected Ticonderoga with Fort Independence, and started for Castleton, Vt. But the accidental, (some say intentional) burning of a house on the Fort Independence side betrayed their movements to the British, who straightway prepared for the chase. As he withdrew from Ticonderoga St. Clair partially broke up the bridge and left four men on the Fort Independence side to discharge a well shotted battery when the British should be crossing in great numbers. But disobeying orders they attacked a rum cask instead and hence were found lying dead drunk with their matches still lighted by the cannon. Apparently they had also been ordered to blow up the magazine because the powder barrels were found with their heads off and the powder scattered about.[4] On the second day of the pursuit the British caught up and the unfortunate battle of Hubbardton, Vt., was fought.

In the morning after the evacuation the British fleet, having broken through the barriers placed in the lake between Ticonderoga and Independence, gave chase, caught up with and captured several of the flying galleys and bateaux. The Americans, having set fire to everything valuable at Skenesborough, hastened toward Fort Ann. Colonels Long and Van Rensselaer were stationed at this little stockaded fort with 500 men, many of whom were convalescents just arrived from Ticonderoga. On the evening of the 7th Gen. Schuyler, fearing an attack, visited the post and urged the officers and men to withstand the British troops at all hazards, for one day, to enable him to remove the garrison, artillery, and stores from Fort George. The men and officers pledged themselves with cheers to do it. A detachment of British regulars under Colonel Hill pursued the fugitives the next day far toward the fort. The morning of the 8th, having heard of their approach, Colonels Long and Van Rensselaer sallied forth and gave battle to Hill, in a narrow pass a little to the north-east, and would have annihilated him had it not been for the, to him, timely arrival of a body of Indians, and the failure of the American ammunition.[5] Fort Ann was immediately evacuated and burned; but the British retired to Skenesborough (Whitehall). The Americans returned and occupied the post till the 16th.

---

[4] Anburey's Travels, I. p. 287.

[5] In the action at Fort Anne the Americans lost their colors, "a flag of the United States, very handsome, thirteen stripes alternate red and white, [with thirteen stars] in a blue field, representing a new constellation."— *Digby's Journal, p. 234.*

This fact found in a British journal is especially interesting as connected with the early history of Old Glory.

Was Schuyler to Blame for the Loss of Ticonderoga? Consternation and dread filled the hearts of the patriots over this unlooked-for disaster. They had fondly nursed the delusion that Ticonderoga was a veritable Gibraltar, impregnable; and this apart from the question as to whether it was properly manned or no. As soon as the direful news spread through the country, a storm of indignation and obloquy broke over the heads of Generals Schuyler and St. Clair. "They were cowards," "they were traitors," "they had sold their country for naught," "they had been bribed by silver bullets shot into the fort by Burgoyne." John Adams, in Congress, said: "We shall never gain a victory till we shoot a General." This disaster gave occasion to the enemies of Schuyler to resurrect their old prejudices formed against him before the war in connection with the boundary disputes between Massachusetts and New York, and the quarrels about the New Hampshire Grants.

As this boundary dispute obtrudes itself so frequently in the history of this region, before and during the Revolution, it is well that the reader should have some knowledge of its nature.

These disputes originated in the hazy indefiniteness of the early Royal Charters. The western boundaries of Massachusetts and Connecticut were declared by them to be the South Seas, or Pacific ocean. After the Conquest of New Netherland by the English, Charles II granted this province to his brother, the Duke of York. Since the only settlements in the province at that time were along the Hudson River, Massachusetts' and Connecticut's pathway to the west was clearly blocked by this grant. Hence a conflict of claims was inevitable which nothing but compromise could adjust. The partition line was finally located 20 miles east of the Hudson.

Soon thereafter New Hampshire came forward and

asked that an extension of this said line to the north be fixed as the boundary between it and New York. New York objected to this and claimed that the Connecticut river should be the line. Before this difference was adjudicated Gov. Benning Wentworth of New Hampshire made many grants to would be settlers in territory west of the Connecticut. Bennington, Vt., named after the Governor, stands within the bounds of this first grant. An appeal was finally made by New York to the King and his council who decided in favor of New York.

Then New York declared that all the grants made by Wentworth were null and void, and also, by proclamation, gave the settlers the choice between repurchasing their lands or eviction. Naturally the settlers on the Grants, as they came to be called, protested stoutly against this proposition and stood ready to defend their claims by force and arms. Thus originated the quarrel known in history as the Hampshire Grants controversy.

In their behavior toward these bona fide settlers the authorities of New York acted unwisely and ungenerously. Had they allowed those who had titles to their holdings from New Hampshire to remain unmolested, but warned all others that, after a certain date, only a title from New York would be recognized as valid there would have been no further trouble. But this equitable course our influential officials and land speculators refused to follow, hence the animosity of those people of the Grants against New Yorkers. And this bitter feeling never quite subsided till after New York's claims were extinguished by the erection of the State of Vermont.

It seems that Philip Schuyler had been chosen as one of the commissioners to represent New York in these disputes, and, as such, had shown himself somewhat of a leader; hence their dislike of him. In consequence the delegates from the Grants and from New England generally, set to work to poison the minds of the delegates to the Continental Congress against him, and magnify the virtues of General Gates, who had improved every opportunity to declare openly that New York had been wholly in the wrong in those disputes.

It is worth our while to tarry a bit and glance at the principal facts that we may the better know how much blame belongs to the aforementioned officers. First, as to Gen. St. Clair. We discover that a later and soberer judgment not only cleared him of all blame for evacuating Ticonderoga but commended him for having done the sanest and bravest thing possible under the circumstances. For example Col. Trumbull, a member of Gates staff, said: "Gen. St. Clair became the object of furious denunciation whereas he merited thanks for having saved a part of the devoted garrison who subsequently formed the nucleus of the force which ultimately baffled Burgoyne, and compelled his surrender at Saratoga." Someone else has sententiously said of him: "A post was abandoned, but a State was saved."

But how about Gen. Schuyler, St. Clair's superior, can he be vindicated so easily? Well, let us see. To that end we will consider:

First, his failure to occupy Mount Defiance that, no doubt, was a fatal error of judgment; but that astute Frenchman, Montcalm, and Generals Wayne and St. Clair, and Gates himself, had all been in command there, and yet none of them had thought Sugar-loaf, as they called it, any cause for serious apprehension, though their attention had been called to it more than once. It was in the summer of 1776 that Gates was stationed at Ticonderoga. Col. John Trumbull, quoted above, serving as engineer on Gates' staff, conceived the notion that that fortress was within cannon range of Mt. Defiance, and proved it by actual demonstration. He also, after a careful survey, found that cannon could be dragged to the top of it; then, too, he computed that it would take 10,000 men to properly garrison the works in and about the old fort, while 500 men could make Mt. Defiance impregnable. But Gates refused to act upon the suggestion.[6]

Abercrombie's failure to see it in 1758 cost him 2,000 men and defeat. A case exactly analogous occurred at Boston the year before. The British General Howe neglected to fortify Dorchester Heights, Washington seized it, planted his batteries, and the British forthwith evacuated Boston before he fired a shot at them from that point.

Again: Why the insufficient garrison at Ticonderoga and the general lack of preparation in his department? Because, after he had labored all the previous winter, heartily seconded by Washington, to put his department in a proper posture of defense, General Schuyler found, when spring opened, that he had accomplished but a fraction of what he had resolutely set out to do. And all this first, because of the apathy of the populace, and of most of the authorities to whom they unremittingly appealed. Again; because of the desertion and chronic insubordination of most of the militia organizations; because of jealousies among his subordinates, and rascality and sluggishness among contractors and commissaries.

Once again; we discover a sufficient cause for this state of unpreparedness in the fact that General Gates had spent most of the winter of 1776-7 hovering in the purlieus of Congress. There much of his time was devoted to quitely fomenting dissatisfaction with Gen. Schuyler, and his conduct of the war in the north. Schuyler, hearing repeatedly through his friends, in the Congress, of this criticism, but not knowing its source,

---
[6] Col. J. Trumbull's Reminiscences of his own Times, p. 31.

felt so outraged that he offered his resignation; but demanded of the Congress, as a necessary preliminary to its acceptance, an inquiry into the conduct of his department. Gates, of course, knew all about this, and quietly awaited the outcome.

Schuyler started for Philadelphia on the 25th of March. The same day Gates was appointed to relieve him. On his arrival in Albany Mrs. Schuyler invited Gates to take up his quarters in the General's mansion, but he declined the proffer with thanks, and remained in the city. But mark, we find that Gates failed to visit a single outlying post while in command of this Northern Department.

As a result of the investigation the Congress fully exonerated Schuyler of all charges, and restored him to his command with added powers. At the same time it defined the relative positions of Gates and Schuyler. Gates was to remain subordinate to Schuyler and serve as commandant at Ticonderoga. Gates insisted that by this action he had been degraded, refused to serve under Schuyler, asked permission to leave the department, and started for Philadelphia, to lay his grievances before his partizans in Congress, and continue his intrigues.

On his arrival in Albany, June 3d, about a month before the disaster at Ticonderoga, Schuyler found that Gates had done literally nothing to further preparations for the coming campaign, preparations just then absolutely imperative, such as had taxed all his time and energies up to the day of his departure in March.[7] On a visit of inspection to Ticonderoga, from June 20th to the 23d, he found the garrison in a woeful condition. Of the 3,000 men there stationed, 500 were sick or ineffective. Many of them were barefooted and nearly all of them ragged, and to crown all he discovered that their

---
[7] Letter from Peter Schuyler to Jay, Tuckerman's Schuyler, p. 187.

food and lodgings were deplorably unsanitary. Gates evidently knew nothing of all this, conditions about which, a General, alive to his calling and responsibilities, would have informed himself.

After the aforesaid inspection we can appreciate this quotation from a letter to his friend, Richard Varick, and can believe that Schuyler was not greatly surprised when the news of the fall of Ticonderoga reached him, though he was doubtless surprised that the event happened so soon.

"Albany, July 1, 1777.

Dr Sir,

Your favor of the 21st Inst. I received on the 29th with the enclosures.

The Insufficiency of the Garrison at Ticonderoga, the Imperfect state of the Fortifications, and the want of Discipline in the Troops, give me great cause to apprehend that we shall lose that Fortress, but as a Reinforcement is coming up from Peeks Kill, with which I shall move up, I am in hopes that the Enemy will be prevented from making any further progress.

Ph Schuyler

Colo. Varick."[8]

On his return Schuyler at once threw himself into the work with renewed energy because rumors were now rife of the advance of Burgoyne from the north, and of St. Leger from the west, but he was met on every hand with the same old indifference and languor, though he warned the authorities of possible disaster unless they should awake to the gravity of the situation.

Schuyler was in Albany in a fever of expectancy and impatience, waiting for the four Massachusetts regiments

[8] Mss. letter in N. Y. State Library.

which Washington had ordered up to his support from Peekskill, and as each day failed to bring them he finally fixed on the 6th of July as the last day of his wait; for he must be away to the north, if only with the few hundreds of militia at hand. But the Continentals failed to appear. So instead of the 10,000 he had called for, he had not more than 5,500 poorly-equipped, half-clad men and boys with which to meet Burgoyne's splendid army of veterans.

Just at daybreak on Monday, the 7th of July, he answered a loud knock at his door, when a messenger thrust into his hand a despatch announcing the evacuation of Ticonderoga. Of course, he was stunned by the news, not being able to account for the suddenness of the move, but he was not utterly cast down, as were those around him, even though he knew that a storm of public fury awaited him. Immediately he mounted his fleetest horse and started for the north. At Stillwater and Saratoga he despatched messengers everywhere announcing the dreadful tidings coupled with urgent pleas for help.

Schuyler Blocks up Burgoyne's Pathway. Schuyler reached Fort Edward the morning of the 8th, where he immediately issued orders for obstructing Burgoyne's advance from Skenesborough, for driving off all cattle, horses, etc., and the removal of all wagons out of the reach of the enemy. Brigades of axemen were sent to fell trees across the roads and into Wood creek, a navigable stream, to break up bridges, and destroy the corduroy roads that led through that savage, swampy, wilderness that stretched from beyond Fort Ann to Fort Edward. So effectually was this work done that on some days Burgoyne could not advance over a mile. British eye witnesses declare that they had to construct no less than forty bridges, and over one morass there was a corduroy road of nearly two miles.[9]

In all this Schuyler showed himself a master of what in military parlance is called practical strategy, which often proves more effective than pitched battles in vanquishing an enemy.

Recognized military experts were agreed that before reaching the Hudson, the wilderness, under Schuyler's quick witted leadership, had dealt Burgoyne the deadly blow of irremediable delay. A little later when Burgoyne was encamped on the Hudson, at Fort Miller and the Batten Kill, a German officer has this to say of Schuyler's success in delaying the invader: "I have called it a desert country not only with reference to its natural sterility, and Heaven knows it was sterile enough, but because of the pains which were taken, and unfortunately with too great success, to sweep its few cultivated spots of all articles likely to benefit the invaders. In doing this the enemy showed no decency either to friend or foe. All the fields of standing corn were laid waste, the cattle were driven away, and every particle of grain, as well as morsel of grass, carefully removed; so that we could depend for subsistence, both for men and horses, only on the magazines which we might ourselves establish.[10]

As a result of this work it took Burgoyne twenty days to get his army from Whitehall to the Hudson. Had he returned immediately to Ticonderoga, and advanced through Lake George, in all probability he would have captured Fort George, at the head of the lake, with its valuable stores of horses, wagons and provisions. Then, had he left his heavy cannon behind, and pushed forward with the light field pieces, he could have reached Albany

---
[9] Anburey's Travels. Lamb's Journal.
[10] Glich's Journal, in Vermont Hist. Soc. Vol. I, p. 12.

THE STORY OF OLD SARATOGA

as quickly as he did Fort Edward from Skenesborough. Schuyler's meagre forces depressed by defeat, and the citizenry obsessed by panic, could not at that juncture, have offered any effective opposition. This was the recorded judgment of some of Burgoyne's officers, and also of General Gates.

But as it turned out the time thus gained by Schuyler proved of priceless worth to the patriots, for in the interim they, in large measure,, recovered their morale and had begun to exhibit much of their old confidence. By great effort they succeeded in removing their munitions of war from Fort George and transporting them down the river. Among other things Schuyler saved 40 unmounted cannon. These were left at Saratoga (Schuylerville), where he ordered carriages to be made for them; for after Ticonderoga was evacuated he had not one piece of mounted cannon left, and not an artillery man on whom he could lay his hand.[11] For material with which to mount these cannon his mills located here were kept running night and day sawing up the stock of oak logs which had been collected for the building of bateaux for transport. Some of these cannon afterward defended the American camp at Bemis Heights, and were later used in the investment of Burgoyne at Saratoga.

Stampede of the Inhabitants. The patriotic inhabitants on the upper Hudson and near the lakes, seized with panic at the fall of Ticonderoga and the sudden appearance of Burgoyne's Indians, hastily gathered together their most valuable effects, loaded them on carts or wagons, or the backs of horses, and in some cases leaving everything behind, started pell-mell for Albany, or Manchester, Vt., whichever was the more convenient. In their panic, and dread of the

---
[11] N. Y. Historical Soc. Collns., Vol. XII, p. 138.

Indians, whom they fancied were right at their heels, they often forgot the ordinary claims of humanity. Those on horseback or in wagons paid no heed to the pleas of tired mothers, trudging along afoot, trying to escape with their children. "Everyone for himself, and the devil take the hindmost" was the code that too often ruled in those fugitive crowds.

CHAPTER X

Second Period of the Campaign

When Burgoyne reached Skenesborough on the 7th of July he found himself in a most happy frame of mind. Thus far it had seemed as if all that was necessary for him to do was to pass along, jar the trees, and the ripened plums of success would fall of their own weight into his lap. So elated was he that on the 10th of July he ordered a Thanksgiving service to be read "at the head of the line, and at the head of the advanced Corps, and at sunset on the same day, a *feu de joie* to be fired with cannon and small arms at Ticonderoga, Crown Point, Skenesborough and Castleton." That was indeed a bright day in Burgoyne's career, but alas! for him, he never again saw as bright a one. Here ended the first period of the campaign, as he calls it in his " State of the Expedition."

A contemporary historian relates that the "joy and exultation were extreme" among all the friends of King George who insisted upon the unqualified subjugation and unconditional submission of the colonies. Loyalist refugees in England had been full of hope ever since the plan of the Burgoyne campaign became known. One of these Tories writing from London in April said: "We believe the American game of independency is nearly up." And when the news of the fall of Ticonderoga came a score of such engaged births on a packet to New York; while twelve or fifteen others chartered an armed vessel to convey themselves and a large consignment of merchandise, to New York so as to be on the spot when the Royal authority was reestablished, and the American

Colonies were once more thrown open to English goods.[1]

He retained his headquarters at the house of Colonel Skene, after whom the place was named, till his men had cut their way, under a broiling July sun, through a tangled mass of tree-trunks and tree-tops, harassed night and day by exhaustless and persistent hordes of punkies and mosquitoes. When the road was cleared Burgoyne advanced with his host to Fort Ann on the 25th, and on the 28th caught his first sight of the Hudson. Then he congratulated himself and his men that their troubles were over; but they had hardly begun. The first unpleasant discovery which he made was that Schuyler had so effectually stripped the country of food and forage that sufficient supplies could not be secured for love nor money; he was therefore obliged to halt there till stores and provisions could be brought from Canada by the way of Fort George and Skenesborough, over wretched roads made worse by incessant rains.

The Jane McCrea Tragedy. While Burgoyne was encamped between Fort Ann and Sandy Hill there occurred an event, which he perhaps thought trifling, but, which wrought as powerfully for his defeat as any other one thing in the campaign. That was the murder of Jane McCrea, between Fort Edward and Sandy Hill, on the 27th of July. She was a beautiful young woman visiting a Tory family at Fort Edward, and was engaged to a young Lieutenant of Provincials in Burgoyne's army, named David Jones. She and Mrs. McNeil, with whom she was staying, were seized and carried from the house (still standing in Fort Edward) by some Indians, part of a band who were in pursuit of an American scouting party which had fled to their camp, near the old fort. On their

---

[1] Trevelyan's Am. Revolution, Part III, pp. 108-9.

way up the hill toward Gen. Fraser's camp located north of Sandy Hill (Hudson Falls) the Indians got quarrelling over their prisoners when one of them shot Miss McCrea and scalped her.

Her beautiful tresses were soon seen up at the camp dangling from the belt of the Wyandotte Panther. It was generally believed at the time that her murder was wholly the work of Burgoyne's Indians. The news of this shocking tragedy drove her lover frantic, while her story, with many embellishments, flew everywhere and aroused the people to a sense of their personal danger as nothing else had been able to do. Every man felt that his daughter, wife, mother, or affianced might be the next victim of the murderous savage.

Thus the employment by the English of Indians, as allies against their kith and kin, proved to be a veritable boomerang, for this occurrence, followed by many others, quite as revolting, wrought mightily in arousing hatred against the invaders, and in unifying the sentiment for independence.

The result was that scores and hundreds who had been wavering before, seized their muskets, hastened to the nearest recruiting station and volunteered for service against Burgoyne and his savages. It was soon discovered that the Indians in their forays made no distinction between loyalists and rebels, e. g. about the time of the murder of Jane McCrea a British officer sent his servant to a spring out in the woods for water. In a short time an Indian came from that direction brandishing the man's smoking scalp, and claimed his £2 or $10. prize money.[2]

Schuyler's Movements. While Burgoyne was eager to get himself and his army out of Skenesborough and

---

[2] Heath's Memoirs, p. 124.

over to the Hudson, Schuyler, seated at Fort Edward, was just as eager to block his way and prepare a desert waste there for his reception, and this he executed with such a measure of success as we have already seen. On the 12th of July General St. Clair joined him at Fort Edward with about two thousand men, the remnant of the army which he brought away from Ticonderoga. The same day Nixon brought up his brigade from Peekskill, but instead of the four regiments ordered by Washington, he had only 575 effectives, many of whom were mere boys.

Schuyler now found himself at the head of some four thousand five hundred troops, about fifteen hundred of whom were raw militia. Here the calumnies so industriously circulated against Schuyler and St. Clair began to produce their effect on the army, and this, together with anxiety about ripening harvests, and the total lack of shelter for the troops, engendered so much discontent and insubordination, that the militia deserted faster than he could supply their places. [See note.] In this desperate

---

NOTE.—Evidently some born trouble makers among the New England troops launched the slander, and diligently circulated it, that Gen. Schuyler was secretly, at heart, a Tory. Naturally this undermined his influence with them, and with their friends, back home, to whom they wrote, and sadly interfered with his plans for checking the enemies' advance. A letter published in B. Tuckerman's Life of Schuyler is very illuminating on this point. It was written by a Rev. C. M. Smith of Sharon, Conn., to his wife:

"You wish to know if the rumors about General Schuyler are true, if he is secretly a Tory? saying that you are requested to ask me. My dear wife they are *not* true. Say this, to any who ask you, on my authority, for I speak whereof I do *know*. Gen. Schuyler is as earnest a patriot as any in our land, and he has few superiors in any respect. I do grieve that so many of our New England men should fail to do him justice, yet they

situation Schuyler appealed afresh to the Committees of Safety and other authorities in New York, and the Eastern States, to Congress, and to Washington for more men with whom to stem the tide of invasion, but little help came to him. At such a time as this those very New Englanders who, as politicians, had been foremost in promoting the war against tyranny, ran from, or refused to go to, the one place on earth where they could show their faith by their works. Congress was notably apathetic, and for more than a month hardly so much as lifted a finger for his aid and encouragement. Washington alone appreciated the situation. He wrote urgent letters to the militia generals in Massachusetts, Connecticut, and New Hampshire, pointing out the danger to their homes and country should Burgoyne be left unopposed.

Because of the wholesale desertion of the New England troops General Schuyler had written to Washington asking that he send him an energetic General or two who

---

are not quite without excuse, not for their suspicions but for their dislike. The General is somewhat haughty and overbearing. He has never been accustomed to seeing men that are reasonably well taught, and able to give a clear opinion, and to state their grounds for it, who were not also persons of some wealth and rank; and when our blacksmith C——, came up to the General, without any preliminaries, to offer him some information and advice, but withal not disrespectfully, the General, albeit the information was of importance, and should have speedy attention — spake sharply to the poor man and bade him begone. He could have easily seen that the man meant no harm, and was far more intelligent than the most of his 'stupid Dutchmen' (as I grieve to say our N. E. men are too apt to call 'em) even when they are officers; but it was not till I had explained to him that the man was well descended and only a blacksmith by reason that his grandfather's English estates had been forfeited to the Crown, that the General could be prevailed upon to listen to him. This is our commander's one weakness,

would be acceptable to the eastern people. He responded by sending him Lincoln and Arnold. General Arnold reported to Schuyler at Fort Edward July 22d, Gen. Lincoln at Fort Miller on the 29th. The latter was at once dispatched to Manchester to assume command of the militia assembling there from the Grants. A little later Washington sent north Gen. Glover with a part of his Brigade, but he could do nothing further, as his own heart and hands were full with Howe and his erratic movements in the vicinity of New York. And yet in this hour of deepest gloom Schuyler writes to the Committee of Safety of New York: "I thank God I have fortitude enough not to sink under the load of calumny that is heaped upon me, and despite it all I am supported by a presentiment that we shall still have a merry Christmas."[3] He surely proved himself to be a prophet that time.

Fort Edward possessed no fort during the Revolution, only a camp, and this being badly situated for defense, Schuyler withdrew the main body of his army on the 22d of July, four miles south to Moses' Creek, where Kos-

---

and I would not have you repeat it to anyone. On the other hand our men are much too free with their strictures. Full one third of my time is taken up in trying to make them see that we have no warrant for suspicions of him, and every reason for the greatest confidence. I am in a position to form a good judgment, and I consider the General to be an honorable gentleman, a man of unusual probity, an excellent commanding officer, and *most devoted to our cause.* Tell all who talk to you about him just what I here do say, and bid 'em to pay no heed to aught the perverse faultfinders, like E. N. and N. W., may choose to say."

Gen. Schuyler having received his military training in the British army had naturally grown to be somewhat strict in matters of military etiquette. In this he was not unlike Washington who had in him much of the martinet. Then, too, people

[3] Collections of the N. Y. Historical Society. Vol. XII.

ciusko, the noted Polish engineer, had laid out an intrenched camp. Here he prepared to dispute Burgoyne's passage; but the army became so dispirited and so depleted by desertion, that he, with the approval of his officers, ordered a retreat further down the river, and nearer the source of supplies. The movement began on the 30th. His right wing under St. Clair took the west side of the river, and his left, under Arnold, kept down the east side. The movement was accomplished by easy stages, the army destroying the roads and bridges behind them. They reached Fort Miller on the first day's march, thence to Saratoga on the 31st of July. Here the army lay for two days.

Burgoyne's Indians, ever in advance, hung like a pestilence on the American flanks, alert for stragglers, or detached parties. For example, Aug. 1st, they killed three men, on the east side of the river, and scalped two of them. This was right in sight of the American camp then at Saratoga. August 3d, about two miles west of

---

untraveled, and of limited experience, are usually suspicious of, and often regard as stupid, those who speak their language with a dialect, or brogue, and whose habits of life are quite different from their own.

In this connection would it not be wholesome for us to take a look at the reverse side of the medal. Associated with the above, Mr. Tuckerman quotes the following as an illustration of how New Yorkers in those days regarded New Englanders. It is from Lewis Morris' will, dated 1762: "It is my desire that my son, Gouverneur Morris, may have the best education that is to be had in Europe or America, but my express will and directions are, that he be never sent for that purpose to the Colony of Connecticut, lest he should imbibe in his youth that low craft and cunning so incident to the people of that country, which is so interwoven in their constitutions, that all their art cannot disguise it from the world, though many of them under the sanctified garb of religion, have endeavored to impose themselves on the world for honest men."

Saratoga, they ambushed a scouting party, killed and wounded 20 or 30, among whom was Capt. Gray of the 10th Mass.

Schuyler's mills, and other buildings, located here, were full of public stores; these had to be removed. They were mainly floated down the river to Stillwater on rafts. General Schuyler and his staff spent all the first of August in the saddle looking for a suitable place hereabouts to entrench and make a stand against the enemy, but failing in their quest, he ordered the retreat to be sounded on the 2d, and on the 3d the army reached Stillwater. Here he selected a place and began to entrench, and while here made the house of Dirck Swart (still standing), his headquarters. [See Note.]

NOTE.—Believing that it would add the human touch and give vividness to this narrative if we could know how the actual experience of camp life and marching affected the average soldier of that day we here subjoin portions of a letter written, during this retreat from the north, by William Weeks a young paymaster in Col. Scammell's regiment.

"Still Water Aug. 6th, 1777.

Brother: Having so convenient an Opportunity, though Time be ever so precious, I will take a Minute to give you some Idea of my present Situation & of this Part of the Globe. I suppose you have heard some Information of our Retreating from Place to Place by the Letter I wrote to my Father when at Moses Creek. Since then we left that Place & march'd to Saratoga & from thence to Still Water.

. . . .

The Army are somewhat unhealthy, their Disease being chiefly the Fever Ague & Dysentery, scarcely any but have had some Complaint. . . . It is not at all to be wondered at if we have a few sick when lodging on the bare Ground covered with Dew wet Blankets, having a few Boards for Cover. But now they begin to be more healthy as they get hardened to this Method of living. I find there is a great deal

---

⁴ Journal of Col. Jeduthan Baldwin. Diary of Capt. Benjamin Warren.

THE STORY OF OLD SARATOGA

Gen. Schuyler was at Stillwater when he received news on Aug. 8th of the battle of Oriskany. Col. St. Leger in the execution of his part of the Burgoyne campaign was on his way from Oswego to Fort Schuyler (Rome), by the last of July. That post was commanded by Col. Peter Gansevoort with a garrison of 750 men. Brig. Gen. Herkimer, commander of the Tryon County militia, learning of the approach of the enemy had mobilized something over 800 men and was on his way to the relief of Col. Gansevoort. He reached the site of the present village of Oriskany on the 3d of August. That same day St. Leger had begun the investment of Fort Schuyler. While at Oriskany awaiting further reinforcements some of Herkimer's officers became impatient

---

in Use. When at "Ti" I thought I had very poor lodging when laying on my Mattress, what can I say now—this I can, that I sleep as well upon the Ground as ever I did upon a Bed. . . . . . .

Cloaths are amazing dear here as well as everything else, R[ed] Shirts are sold for 20 to 25 Dollars a piece [Continental money]. . . . I hope to get some Cloathing here to rub along for the present. . . . . . I saved none of my cloaths except what I had on when we left "Ti." . . . . Allmost all the Officers & Soldiers shared the same Fate which makes Cloathing so excessive dear.

A Soldiers' Life is such that no one can have a true Idea of it without the Trial. It is such that I am convinced it will suit no Man except he have a Constitution like Iron. . .

There is a very good Crop in these parts but soon comes a Desolation. Wherever we march we keep our Horses in the Fields among the Corn & Oats, So that the enemy if he gain the Ground may have poor fare for them and their Horses. Tories are very Troublesome here [Col. Dearborn confirms this in his Journal]. Many of these take up Arms against us & lurk in the Woods with the Indians waiting for a Sculp. It is believed many of the Tories have sculped many of their Countrymen as there is a Premium from Burgoyne for Sculps. They [Tories] are daily taken and brought in

of delay and urged him to advance immediately, but he refused to take unnecessary risks. These malcontents gradually waxed insolent in their behavior and charged Herkimer with being a Tory and a coward. Finally under great provocation he took council of his resentment rather than of his judgment and ordered the advance. St. Leger having heard of his approach prepared an ambuscade in a ravine about 4 miles east of Fort Schuyler. Into this Herkimer's men were entrapped and, being furiously assailed, there ensued what is generally reckoned, considering the numbers engaged, the fiercest and bloodiest battle of the Revolution.

It was, however, a drawn battle as neither party at-

---

by our Scouts & I believe some of them will swing [be hung] very soon. The Indians treat both Sexes with the same Barbarity, have kilt and Sculped whole Familys together, Men Women & Children. At one place as our Men were passing they saw a Man his Wife & Children sculped (by those savages) gaping and expiring & the Hogs rooting their Bodys.

A few days ago I rode a little Distance from Camp where we had a few men stationed to guard the Sick. I had just past the Place where a Party of Indians happened to lay & stopped at the first House talking with an Officer. As I set upon my Horse out rush'd those Indians and fired at some swimming in the Water & chas'd Some as they were passing. I seeing this scream'd to the Guard to pursue them, and rode towards them, they discharged their Pieces toward us. Immediately upon our pursuing them they ran into the Woods and got off. We were in such haste they had not time to get a Sculp. They kil'd two, one shot in the Water who got out & ran a considerable Distance before he fell. Since then they have cut off more of our Men. One Hundred Indians in the Woods do us more harm than 1000 British Troops. They have been the Death of many brave Fellows.

Give my best Respects to my Relations & Acquaintance, particularly to my Father & Mother.

I remain with due Respect Your L. Brother

Wm. Weeks."[5]

---

[5] From Five Straws. Letters of Wm. Weeks.

tempted pursuit after the fight, but Fort Schuyler was not relieved. Col. Gansevoort sent a trusty messenger to report the battle and his situation to Schuyler.

Gen. Schuyler at Stillwater felt that Gansevoort should be succored at all hazards. When urging the case before a council of officers he learned that some of them were echoing one of the charges of Herkimer's officers, that he was at heart a Tory because he was willing to weaken the army in the presence of the enemy. Overhearing this he resolutely assumed all responsibility and called for a General to lead the expedition. Gen. Arnold at once volunteered. Learned's Brigade was selected. This was composed of Jackson's, Bailey's, and Van Schaack's regiments. The latter was a New York regiment, as was also Col. James Livingston's which was sent on a little later. Learned and his men started on Aug. 12th, Arnold followed the next day.

St. Leger was relentlessly pushing the siege when Arnold from Fort Dayton (Herkimer), by a clever stratagem, succeeded in creating such a panic among his men, and especially the Indians, that they suddenly abandoned their camp and scurried as for life northward. And thus Burgoyne was hopelessly crippled in the right arm of his strength, while patriot hearts thrilled with new hope in consequence, and Schuyler's little army was gladdened by the assurance of a speedy accession to its strength.

It should ever be remembered that this resolute and timely action on the part of Schuyler had as much to do with shattering that important adjunct of Burgoyne's plan of campaign, viz: the conquest of the Mohawk valley, as did any other one human cause, and that St. Leger's defeat, equally with Baum's at Bennington, were the two events that made possible the great victory at Saratoga.

Schuyler having concluded that Stillwater was untenable with his present force, he withdrew to the "sprouts of the Mohawk," a place at that time admirably adapted for defense. General Winfield Scott on visiting this spot eighty years later, pronounced it the best strategic position to be found for the defense of Albany and the lower Hudson against the north, at that time.

Movements of Burgoyne. Returning to the north we find that Burgoyne remained in the vicinity of Sandy Hill and Fort Edward till the 14th of August, when he moved down with his center to Fort Miller. Brigadier General Fraser, commanding his right wing, had already been sent forward, and on the 13th we find him camped at the Battenkill. Following him came Colonel Baume, at the head of his 521 dragoons, his Indians, and Tories, equipped for the expedition against Bennington, Vermont. Its purpose was to provide Burgoyne with a lot of much needed horses for cavalry, artillery, etc., besides other supplies, all of which were sorely needed by him, and which had been stored there for the use of the American army.

Another grand purpose of this expedition was to encourage and arm the Loyalists, or Tories, who, Burgoyne had been assured, were very numerous on the Grants and in Massachusetts.

The Battle of Bennington. On the morning of the 13th Lieut. Colonel Baume forded the Battenkill near its mouth.[6] After reaching the old road from Schuylerville to Greenwich he turned to the eastward.

His was a heterogeneous force, made up of two hundred dragoons (cavalrymen) of Riedesel's regiment,

---
[6] Letters of Col. Philip Skene to Lord Dartmouth, N. Y. State Hist'ol Asso'n. Vol. V, —, 73.

Capt. Fraser's marksmen, Peters' Provincials, Canadian volunteers, and something over a hundred Indians. Think of it, three races and at least four languages represented in that small body of troopers. A motley collection, that, for a task requiring unity of thought, action, and control.

They made 16 miles the first day over a rugged road, mainly through a wilderness, arriving at Cambridge about 4 p. m. From Cambridge Col. Baume sent an express to Burgoyne reporting a skirmish with 40 or 50 rebels who were guarding cattle. On the 14th, at 9 a. m., he reported from Sancoik (Van Schaick's mills) another sharp skirmish with the rebels, the capture of the mills, with flour, grain, salt, etc., also that "people [Tories] are flocking in hourly and want to be armed." Some prisoners taken reported to him a force of fifteen or eighteen hundred, assembled at Bennington, who would probably withdraw on his approach. He also stated that "the savages would destroy or drive off all horses unless he paid for them at once in cash, and that no one seemed able to control them."

That day he advanced within four miles of Bennington. The Americans appearing in large numbers, and beginning to harass his flanks, he retired some distance and occupied a commanding hill at a bend of the Walloomscoick, which was quite well wooded, and there began to intrench.

It appears that after the battle of Trenton, General John Stark had returned to New Hampshire on a recruiting expedition, but soon thereafter hearing that the Congress had promoted junior officers over his head he resigned in disgust and retired to private life. But when the menace of Burgoyne's army appeared above the horizon his patriotism got the better of his resentment and he accepted the command of a Brigade strongly urged upon him by the General Assembly of his State.

But he would accept only on two conditions; 1st, that he should not be expected to join the main army, and 2d, that he should be subordinate to no one save the body that commissioned him.

He had been at Bennington since the 9th assembling forces intending to march to Schuyler's relief, but was being held back by the Vermont Council of Safety when, on the night of the 13th, word came that a body of Burgoyne's Indians had reached Cambridge. Col. Gregg was at once sent with 200 men to oppose their advance. The next day toward night, he received information that a large column of the enemy, with a train of artillery, was in full march for Bennington. Stark at once rallied all his forces, sent an urgent call for the militia in the vicinity, and also an express to Manchester ordering Col. Warner's Regiment to march immediately to his support. The order was promptly obeyed, and they arrived just before dawn of the 16th thoroughly drenched with rain. Col. Symonds also came with a detachment of Berkshire militia.

The 15th was a very rainy day, which rendered flint lock muskets practically useless; but Gen. Stark and Col. Baume, however, utilized the time in preparation for the conflict. Baume spent the day intrenching and disposing his force to the best advantage. But very unwisely he allowed a gap of nearly a mile, and the Walloomscoick river, to intervene between him and Peters' corps of Provincials, and Canadians.

Burgoyne having concluded from Baume's dispatches that he would need reinforcements sent Col. Breyman on the morning of the 15th with 500 men and two brass cannon. On account of the badness of the road, made worse by the rain, the excessive heat, and through getting lost in the woods, Breyman made but slow progress, arriving too late to be of service. Gen. Stark, having thoroughly reconnoitred the enemy's position, carefully planned his course of action.

The 16th being a fair day Stark issued his orders for the attack. About 3 o'clock in the afternoon Baume found himself being assailed on all sides. Col. Hubbard quickly dislodged Peters' corps, which fled in disorder to the Hessian camp. Col. Nichols attacked the Hessian left, in its rear, and Col. Herrick their right. The Indians, whose camp was in Baume's rear, beat a hasty retreat and took to the woods. Gen. Stark, with the main body, assailed the camp in front, and, clambering up the steep hillside, furiously charged the trenches defended by cannon. Two hours of fiercest fighting, much of it hand to hand, put an end to the fray. Most of the enemy were captured, though a few found their way through and escaped. Col. Baume, their brave leader, among others, was wounded to death.

After the fight Stark's soldiers broke ranks and started pell mell to loot the enemies' camp. This nearly proved fatal to them, for at that moment, Col. Breyman arrived with his reinforcements for Baume. And had it not been for the opportune coming of Col. Warner's regiment, it is doubtful whether Stark could have reassembled his men, and reformed his ranks, to withstand this unexpected assailant. As it was the battle was renewed by Warner, and continued till sunset at which time Breyman's ammunition being exhausted, the meagre remnants of his force broke and fled.

The trophies of the fight included four brass cannon,[7] 259 dragoon swords, 12 brass drums, and nearly 1,000 stand of arms. The British casualties are variously re-

---

[7] The history of these four brass cannon is very interesting They were of French manufacture, were taken by Wolfe at Quebec in 1759, captured by Stark at Bennington in 1777, surrendered by Hull to the British at Detroit in 1812, and retaken at Niagara in 1813. Fonblanque's Burgoyne, p. 273

8

ported. About 200 were killed, and something like 800 were taken prisoners. After Bennington Congress voted to make Stark a Brig. General in the U. S. army, the position which he had previously claimed of right, and which had been denied.

So this venture, from which so much was expected, brought far more foreboding than forage to the royal army waiting by the Hudson. Burgoyne was now badly crippled in the left arm of his strength. Lieutenant Digby, in his Journal (page 286) says, the British officers all carried sober faces after Bennington.

La Corne St. Luc, the leader of the attack on Fort Clinton at Saratoga in 1747, had command of most of the Indians with Burgoyne's army. He, with many of his Indians, was with Colonel Baume when attacked, but the battle had hardly opened when they ran. Nor did they stop running when they reached the camp of Fraser at the Battenkill, but hastily collecting their effects they all, with the exception of about eighty, started at night for Canada.[8] When Burgoyne arrived at Ticonderoga he had five hundred of them. Digby in his Journal says of St. Luc: "He was as cruel and treacherous as his followers, for as soon as the British were in a critical situation he deserted them." A little later quite a number of the Indians who had been with St. Leger in the west, joined Burgoyne's army.

In his "State of the Expedition" Burgoyne sharply criticises the Provincials for their reluctance to enter the service and for insubordination. He had expected about two thousand, but apparently not over eight hundred ever appeared. Peters in his defense against these charges says: "Burgoyne encouraged the Provincials (native Canadians and Refugees from the States) to

---

[8] Hadden's Journal, p. 134. Digby's Journal, p. 253.

enlist and be under their own officers, to whom he promised to issue commissions. He failed to do this, and at Fort Edward, told the Provincial officers that since they knew not the art of war, his sergeants and officers would take command of their men. Whereat the Americans mutinied and were about to go off with the Indians. Burgoyne, seeing this, recalled his orders and allowed them to proceed as before, but issued no commissions.

Peters, and other Provincial officers, advised against making the Bennington expedition with so few men, but Burgoyne treated the advice with supercilious contempt, as did Gen. Braddock before him, and had to pay a like penalty for his conceit and arrogance. Peters and the other Provincial officers, having no commissions, were in the end defrauded by the British government of pay for seven years hard service.[9]

The two battles of Oriskany and Bennington caused the hitherto depressed Americans to believe that what they had done with Burgoyne's lieutenants they could no doubt do with General Burgoyne himself, so they began flocking to the standard of Schuyler at the mouths of the Mohawk, and that of General Lincoln at Manchester, Vt.

And thus Washington's prediction was literally fulfilled which he made in a letter to Schuyler about the 1st of August: " As I suggested before, the successes Gen. Burgoyne has met with may precipitate his ruin. From your account he is pursuing that line of conduct which of all others is most favorable to us, I mean acting in detachments. This conduct will certainly give room for enterprise on our part, and expose his partys to great hazard. Could we be so happy as to cut one of them off, though it should not exceed four, five, or six hundred men, it would inspirit our people."

[9] Jones, N. Y. in the Revolution, Vol. I. p. 683.

Schuyler Relieved by Gates. Some days before these happy events at Bennington, and Fort Schuyler occurred, General Schuyler had been called to Albany on business. On the morning of the 10th of August, as he was about to mount his horse and return to the army, an officer approached and handed him a dispatch. After the General had broken the seal and read it an observant onlooker would have noticed an involuntary compression of the lips, a flush of passion crimson his face, and a gleam of righteous anger shoot from his darkling eyes. The dispatch was a resolution of Congress relieving him of his command. Oh, the injustice of it! Was this his reward for all the unselfish toil, wasting anxiety, and limitless sacrifices he had been making for his country? Well, so it seemed.

Smothering his resentment he dismissed the messenger courteously, and started for Stillwater. At such a moment could he help but remember that when he assumed command there was no northern army in existence; it must be created, officered, and equipped. There were no military supplies; he provided them. No money was given him; he procured all that was obtainable. And now everything being ready for the crucial test just at hand, he finds himself dismissed.

In this connection we will quote a criticism made by an English historian on the short sighted, childish, behavior of the Congress toward its best Generals during these years:

"Congress ousted Schuyler, insulted Greene and Knox, repremanded Stark, snubbed Benedict Arnold, courtmartialed Sullivan, Wayne and St. Clair, and promoted a cabal against Washington himself. At the same time it held Charles Lee and Horatio Gates in high repute." [10]

---

[10] H. Belcher's First American Civil War. Vol. II-322.

The best and wisest men of the Congress of 1776 withdrew from that body, preferring positions of trust in their State governments. After that the majority of the delegates to Congress were second rate, narrow minded men.

Schuyler's first impulse was to abandon the army immediately, but an imperious sense of duty together

SCHUYLER RESIGNING HIS COMMAND TO GATES

with the urgent appeals of his officers, prominent among whom were the New England generals, decided him to remain and serve till the coming of his successor, whose name was then unknown. We may judge, however, that he was not much surprised when General Horatio Gates, the appointee of Congress, arrived in camp on the evening of the 19th of August to relieve him. He was received by Schuyler with every mark of distinction, who immediately turned over to him all useful papers, and offered to render him every assistance in his power. But so far was Gates from responding to Schuyler's magnanimity and profiting by the counsel of the one man who, more than any other, was acquainted with the Department, that he did not even ask him to be present at his first council of war, although he did invite up from Albany Brig. Gen. Tenbroeck of the militia, and others.

Gates arrived just at the turning of the tide in Schuyler's ill fortune; in time to reap what he had been sowing; to profit by all the delays and harassments he had inflicted upon Burgoyne, by the successes at Fort Schuyler and Bennington, which had set free thousands of troops flushed with victory. E. g. In the second week of August Gen. Lincoln wrote Schuyler that he was on the way with 2,000 men from the Hampshire Grants; Stark wrote that he was coming with the victors of Bennington. And while Gates was on his way from Philadelphia, Arnold was returning with augmented forces from up the Mohawk. Schuyler now saw himself backed by 10,000 men and the skies clearing. Then too, just at this juncture, the northern army received a veritable windfall, which had also been mediated by Schuyler. In his correspondence with Washington, he had asked for help, and had pictured the terror caused by the murderous raids of Burgoyne's Indians. Washington bethought himself that he had a sure antidote for them in Col. Daniel Morgan and his incomparable Rangers. With great reluctance he resolved to part with them for awhile, and so ordered them north. They arrived a few days after Gates assumed command. And Burgoyne heard from those crack woodsmen and marksmen, as we shall see later on.

In addition to the command Congress had freely voted to Gates every aid and authority which had been asked by Schuyler but studiously withheld. Schuyler finding himself totally ignored withdrew to his home at Albany, resolved however, still to serve his country in some way during this crisis. And this he did zealously and efficiently. Thus he put his own nobility of character and largeness of heart in startling contrast with the littleness and coarseness of Gates.

Estimates of Schuyler's Character. The appearance of such exalted characters from time to time serves to hold us to our faith in the perfectability of human nature, and should stimulate all who contemplate them to cultivate the grace of unselfishness. Gen. Wilkinson, Gates' Adjutant, during the Burgoyne campaign, has this to say of Gen. Schuyler in his Memoirs: "The zeal, patriotism, perseverance, and salutary arrangements of General Schuyler, had aroused the spirit of the country, and vanquished the predjudices excited against him by artifice, intrigue, and detraction."

Daniel Webster once said to General Schuyler's grandson, Geo. L. Schuyler: "When a life of your grandfather is to be published I should like to write the preface. I was brought up with New England prejudices against him, but I consider him as only second to Washington in the services he rendered to the country in the war of the Revolution." Said Gov. Horatio Seymour in his Centennial speech: "We could not well lose from our history his example of patriotism and of personal honor and chivalry. We could not spare the proof which his case furnishes, that virtue triumphs in the end. We would not change, if we could, the history of his trials. For we feel that they gave luster to his character, and we are forced to say of General Schuyler that, while he had been greatly wronged, he had never been injured."[11] And Fiske, one of the sanest and most fair of our American historians, says of him: "No more upright and disinterested man could be found in America, and for bravery and generosity he was like the paladin of some mediæval romance."

Question! Why had Gen. Schuyler to wait so long for his justification before the world? And why is he still overtopped in popular esteem, at least in certain quarters, by Revolutionary Brig. Generals immeasurably below him in calibre and efficiency? Trevelyan, a recent English historian, in his American Revolution, Part III., has answered it. He says: "Schuyler had the supreme misfortune of being disliked in Boston; and a statesman, or a General of the Revolution, who was out of favor with the Bostonians, had as small a chance of making a good figure in history as an Anglo Saxon, or a Plantagenet Monarch, who had offended the clergy and monastic chroniclers," who were the only historians of that day.

But here is something conceived in quite a different vein, yet interesting. A letter from Schuyler to John Jay, dated Jan. 18th, 1779, contains the following passage: "I have long since justified Congress for depriving me of the command in 1777, convinced that it was their duty to sacrifice the feelings of an individual to the safety of the States, when those people, who only could defend the country, refused to serve under him."[12] This, as an example of magnanimity, is quite ideal; but in no way does it exonerate Gates from his intrigues. An American born General, as Greene, or Knox, or perhaps Arnold, should have been chosen.

---

[11] Memoir of the Centennial Celebration of Burgoyne's Surrender, p. 60. W. L. Stone.
[12] Magazine of Am. Hist. Vol. III, p. 760.

Question. Why has the city of Albany never reared a monument to perhaps the greatest man she has ever produced?

Burgoyne's Advance Delayed by Bennington. It had been Burgoyne's purpose to move right on toward Albany as soon as Baume should return with the spoils of Bennington, and he had already given orders to that effect. Indeed General Fraser had actually crossed the river on a bridge of rafts and boats, August 14th, and spent a day or two with his men at Saratoga.[13] but the disaster to Baume and Breyman obliged a change of plan. That defeat suddenly convinced Burgoyne of the impossibility of securing supplies from the country. He saw also that he had been deceived as to the sentiment of the citizenship, and was forced into the realization of an unwelcome conclusion that he was in the midst of a hardy people, skilled with the musket, and at home in the woods, which hemmed him in on every side. In a letter to Lord George Germaine, dated Aug. 20th, he says: " Had I latitude in my orders I should deem it my duty to wait in this position [i. e. Hudson Falls to the Battenkill] where my communication with Lake George would be perfectly secure, till some event happened to assist my forward movement." Evidently the shadows were beginning to fall upon his spirits.

In the meantime, the bridge over the river had been swept away by a freshet. Fraser with his corps got back to their entrenchments north of the Battenkill the best way they could on small boats and rafts, while the whole army was detained an entire month, till supplies could be hauled down from Lake George. This, through lack of sufficient draught animals, was a herculean task, men being forced to do the work of mules and oxen. About

---
[13] Hadden's Journal, p. 137. Digby's Journal, p. 249.

500 horses arrived from Canada on the 18th of Aug. which greatly relieved the strain.

This respite gained for us by the battle of Bennington was most opportune, because it afforded the needed time for recruiting and thoroughly organizing the American army, which was now progressing quite rapidly at the "sprouts of the Mohawk."

Fraser threw his first bridge across the Hudson, somewhere above the present State Dam at Northumberland, but finding a narrower and better place below the rapids constructed the next one there. The latter was a pontoon bridge, or bridge of boats, about 425 feet long, and its exact location is still marked by the cut through the bank on the west side, and the road excavated by the British down the east bank. The road is clearly visible from the new iron bridge, in the rear of the house of Ex. Gov. John A. Dix. Mr. Dix has very considerately left this historic road intact, and also much of the breastworks constructed by Burgoyne, behind which he posted a battery to defend the crossing. Amid so much spoliation and vandalism which has been exhibited hereabouts it is refreshing to feel that there are some among us possessed of a proper reverence for such monuments of the heroic past.

For a month after Bennington the British lay strung along the river from Hudson Falls to the Battenkill. Fraser was at the Battenkill, Burgoyne and Phillips with the center at Fort Miller or "Duer's House," and Riedesel, with the left, at Fort Edward and Sandy Hill.

Burgoyne Begins His Final Advance. On Saturday, the 13th of September, the crossing began under the lead of Fraser. Colonel Breyman followed immediately to cover his left wing. Next, on the 14th, came Burgoyne and Phillips with the train of artillery. To expedite the crossing the 20th regiment forded the river instead of crowding the bridge. Burgoyne took up his quarters in the Schuyler mansion that night.

The Marshall house and one other, standing where the old parsonage of the Reformed church now is, were then the only dwellings north of the creek. The military barracks built by the Americans in the northwest angle formed by Broadway and Spring street, were also standing. Fort Hardy was then a ruin. The heights above Broadway were nearly all densely wooded at that time; hence it was extremely hazardous for the advance guard to separate itself from the main body, cross the river, and camp in a position difficult of defense.

That the British fully appreciated this we are assured from the fact that after Burgoyne was over, and while his center was crossing, he and his generals inspected the heights and decided where each division should be posted in the event of an attack. In fact the advance or right wing camped for two nights on the heights in three columns, in order of battle.[14]

On the 15th Riedesel with the left wing crossed, when, at once, Burgoyne severed his communications with Canada by breaking up the bridge. The advance was sounded and the invading host forded the Fishkill and started forth to find the enemy posted somewhere in the woods to the south. Singularly enough Burgoyne had not provided himself with scouts, or if he had them, did not use them; hence we have here the unique spectacle of an invading army groping its way through an unmapped wilderness for an enemy, native to the soil, without sending out feelers or using its eyes to ascertain their exact whereabouts.

The British advanced in three parallel columns, one

---

[14] Digby's Journal, p. 267.

by the river along the flats, the artillery and baggage by the main road, and the right wing a half mile or more to the west through the woods. Sometimes it was difficult for the columns to keep up communication with each other. In addition to this a fleet of 200 bateaux, floated down the river carrying the baggage, the ordnance stores, and a month's supply of provisions. "The money value of that cargo amounted to a king's ransom, for (according to an elaborate calculation which found its way into London newspapers) every pound of salt meat on board that flotilla had already cost the taxpayers the sum of 30 shillings," i. e. $7.50 per lb. in our currency.[15] That day the army advanced only as far as Dovegat[16] (Coveville) and encamped.

While stationed here, Burgoyne occupied the house shown in the picture, and which was but recently torn down.[17]

The army remained at Dovegat all of the 16th, while several regiments personally conducted by Burgoyne, and accompanied by some two hundred workmen, started forth to repair bridges, and learn the whereabouts of the enemy. So rapid were their movements that they covered nearly three miles that day; they saw no enemy, but heard the sound of drums off in the woods to the south calling the men to arms. On the 17th the army advanced and

---

[15] Trevelyan's American Rev., p. 161.

[16] Dovegat is a word whose etymology has been much in dispute. That it is of Dutch origin is not doubted. The writer consulted Mr. Arnold J. F. van Laer, State Archivist at Albany, a cultured linguist, and a native of Holland. He concludes that it is a corruption of the Dutch *duevenkot*, equivalent to the English dove-cote. It must have been a favorite haunt or nesting place of wild pigeons. Burgoyne, and Hadden, and Digby, all wrote it Dovegot.

[17] When this photo was taken the house stood on the north side of the canal, but when the canal was straightened in 1888 it was left on the south side. Its exact location was just west of the south abutment of Mr. Charles Sarle's canal bridge. The large elm tree, still standing, was perhaps two rods from the south-east corner of the house. The barn in the photo stood on the north side of the present canal.

THE DOVEGAT HOUSE

took up its position at Sword's house. (This should be written Swart's house.)[18]

While the British army was lying at Swart's house, a party of soldiers and women strolled out in front of the encampment a few hundred yards to dig some potatoes in a field. While thus engaged a party of Americans swooped down upon them, killed and wounded quite a number, and led away about twenty of them as prisoners.[19]

Movements of the American Army. As we have seen, Gates assumed command the 19th of Aug., on Van Schaick's island at the mouths of the Mohawk. On the 30th Col. Morgan with his 500 riflemen reported. These men had been carefully picked from the different regiments of the main army. On the 31st Gen. Arnold came in from his Fort Schuyler expedition with five regiments. Morgan on his arrival received from Gates a most cordial welcome, and every mark of deference. Moreover, as a special token of regard, his corps was designated as "the advance of the army," and he was directed to receive orders only from the General-in-Chief. Also under Morgan was placed an additional battalion of about 300 men, selected from the Northern Army in the same way his own had been from the Southern. This battalion was led by Major

---

[18] The site of Sword's house is on the south side of a spring brook, about fifty yards west of the canal. To find it, take the private road running westward, just north of Searles' ferry, cross the canal bridge, and on a knoll a little to the left you will find a slight depression, at the foot of a higher hill. That is where Sword's or Swarts house once stood. Mr. Robert Searles told the writer that his father tore it down, and that the hall was so large that he could turn a yoke of oxen around in it. "Sword's house," is doubtless a mistake of Burgoyne's secretary, who misunderstood his informant. It should have been Swart's house. There were no Swords living in this region at that time nor since, but plenty of Swarts, one of whom is known to have owned a farm in that neighborhood.

[19] Hadden's Journal, p. 160.

Dearborn, a New Hampshire man, who had been a comrade of Morgan in the 1775 attempt against Quebec.

Gates now felt himself strong enough to start northward to contest the advance of the enemy. This movement began the 8th of Sept. On the 9th Army headquarters were established at Stillwater. That day a white flag came in from Gen. Burgoyne with a Doctor and necessaries for the sick and wounded of Bennington. A most thoughtful and fitting act.

Gates at first settled on Stillwater as the place where he would make his stand, and forthwith began intrenching himself. But the wide area of comparatively level ground at that point made it difficult to defend his left and center. Gen. Arnold and Kosciusko, the Polish engineer, having spent a day inspecting the country a little to the north, reported to Gates a site at Bemis Heights admirably fitted by nature for holding an enemy at bay. Gates approving of their judgment ordered the abandonment of Stillwater so, on the 13th, the army moved up to that position and began there the construction of defensive works. The Hudson, at the little hamlet of Bemis Heights, approaches within 30 rods of the river hills or bluffs.

Gates' right rested on the river, his left on the high ground to the west. The whole camp was fortified by strong batteries and breastworks as well as by the natural defenses of ravines and thick woods. A deep intrenchment ran from the foot of the hills to the river at Bemis' tavern, and was defended at the river end by a battery. From here a floating bridge was thrown across the river, defended on the east side by a *tete du pont*. A similar work was thrown up farther north at Mill creek. Several redoubts connected by trenches crowned the bluffs facing the river. A strong earthwork was constructed on the high knoll at the northwest angle of the camp, a mile or more west of the river. This was thrown up around a log barn, which was strengthened by a double coating of logs and named, after the patriotic owner of the property, Fort Neilson. In addition to breastworks the left and front on the high ground were made difficult of approach by an abatis formed of trees felled with their tops outward. The defenses on the high ground were not completed till after the first battle. A flank intrenchment was also begun on a knoll a little west of Fort Neilson.

Midway between Wilbur's Basin and Bemis Heights Mill Creek empties into the canal. Following up this creek you will enter first a wide and deep ravine which soon turns northward. This again separates into three principal ravines which lead toward the west. A little to the south of the first one you meet, Gates threw up his northern line of breastworks. The one called the Middle Ravine was recognized as the dividing line between the hostile camps after the first battle. This figures largely in all descriptions of the movements and incidents connected with the battles. These ravines being thickly wooded, filled with fallen timber and tangled brushwood, and with sides very steep, were practically impassable for large bodies of men equipped for battle, and of course were easily defended.

Arnold had command of the left wing till after the first battle. Under him were Morgan and Poor, with their headquarters in the Neilson house, still standing. Gates reserved to himself the command of the right, with his headquarters at Bemis' tavern. When he gave command of the right to General Lincoln he moved up on the hill into a house owned by Ephraim Woodworth, whose site is now marked by a granite tablet. A fairly correct idea of the lay of the land, the plan of the camps, and relative positions of the hostile armies, may be had by reference to the map.

Morgan and Dearborn, with their Rangers, had for some days kept themselves about two miles in advance of the main army. The same day that Bemis Heights was occupied they went scouting as far north as Saratoga and brought back a few prisoners. From that time bodies of troops were kept in the woods to the north on the lookout for the enemy. On the 18th Arnold with about 3,000 men, and Morgan with his corps started out with the hope of striking the British on their flank but found it impracticable to assail them advantageously. However it was a party of Morgan's men who swooped down on the potato diggers, previously mentioned, and stopped the fun of foraging. That day they bagged 36 prisoners. A German officer said of these annoyances: "We had to do the enemy the honor of sending out whole regiments to protect our workmen while repairing roads and bridges."

Gen. Stark came in on the 16th with his brigade of militia, the heroes of Bennington. But unfortunately the time of their enlistment was about expired. Both Gates and Stark used every argument to induce them to stay a few days longer as a battle with Burgoyne himself was now imminent, but all their pleadings were of no avail.

The men asserted it had been expressly stipulated that they were to obey no commander but Gen. Stark, and now their time being out they were going home, even though their General himself desired to stay. They left on the 18th, the day before the battle. Soon, however, Stark was enabled to take the field with a new brigade.

CHAPTER XI

BATTLE OF THE 19TH OF SEPTEMBER

EARLY on the 19th of September, Lieutenant-Colonel Colburn of the New Hampshire line and a small scouting party posted themselves in the trees across the river from Swart's house to observe the British camp. From there they counted no less than eight hundred tents, but observed also something of far more consequence, namely, a movement among those tents that strongly indicated an advance. This being immediately reported to Gates, he put his men on the alert. He at the same time issued orders for the army to strike their tents and have the teams and baggage ready for retreat. This order was repeated on five subsequent days according to the diary of Sergeant Frank Squier.[1]

Gen. Gates' army, at this time, was made up as follows: Gen. Poor's Brigade, consisting of the New Hampshire regiments of Cilley, Scammel, and Hale: Van Cortland's and Henry Livingston's New York regiments; Cook's and Latimer's Connecticut militia; Morgan's rifle corps, and Dearborn's rangers. These composed the left wing under Arnold, resting on the heights a mile and more west of the river. General Learned's brigade, Bailey's, Wesson's and Jackson's Mass. regiments, and James Livingston's New York regiment were posted on the plateau to the east of the Neilson barn. The main body under the immediate command of Gen. Gates, was composed chiefly of Nixon's, Patterson's, and Glover's brigades. These formed the right wing on the bluff, and extended across the low ground to the river.

---
[1] Mag. of American Hist. Vol. II p. 692.

The surmise of the scout proved to be correct. Burgoyne, as the result of a brief reconnaissance,, and after consultation with certain Americans in his army who knew the ground, decided that the only vulnerable point of the American lines was the left flank. He resolved, therefore, to advance, ascertain the position and strength of his enemy, and outflank him if possible. The movement was made in three columns. The right under General Fraser, composed of the 24th regiment, the English and German grenadiers, a body of Provincials and Canadians, and a light German battalion with eight six pounders under Colonel Breyman took the road west from Swart's house to a point where the present Quaker Springs road runs, and there turned south. The center column, led by Burgoyne, composed of the 9th, 20th, 21st, and 62d regiments, with a body of Indians and Canadians, took the same road for half a mile west, when he turned southeast till he struck the Wilbur's Basin ravine, crossed it and then turned west. Burgoyne's advance was very slow and laborious, as many obstructions had to be removed and several bridges thrown across ravines for the passage of his artillery. The intention was to form a junction with Fraser near the head of the Middle ravine and from there attempt to turn the American left. Phillips and Riedesel, with the balance of the army, were to follow the river road to within a half mile of the American works and there to await the report of three minute guns as notice that the aforesaid junction had been made, when they were to threaten the American right until Burgoyne had executed his flanking movement. Then the advance was to be general.

Gates, although apprised of these movements by his scouts, had planned to await the enemy behind his defenses. But Arnold, divining the intention of Burgoyne, urged Gates to permit him to go out with his men and attack the enemy before he could reach the camp, urging as arguments that if beaten in the attack they would still have the woods and their intrenchments to fall back on, and that if Burgoyne should get near enough to the camp to use his artillery, it would be impossible to hold their position. This brings to mind Napoleon's dictum, "It is a maxim of the military art that the army which remains in its intrenchments is beaten." If that be correct then Arnold here proved himself to be the better general.

Finally Gates yielded so far as to permit Morgan, and soon thereafter Dearborn, with their rangers and riflemen, to go out to observe and harass the enemy. About 12:30 p. m. they met Burgoyne's Indians and Canadians under Major Forbes scouting a little west of the Freeman cottage. These were driven back, with considerable loss, every officer in the party being either killed or wounded. Morgan's men eagerly pursued and unexpectedly struck the main body in the edge of the woods, northeast of the cottage where, after a stubborn contest, they were routed and badly scattered in the woods. Morgan, though greatly disconcerted by this accident, was soon able by the vigorous use of his "turkey call" whistle to rally his men about him. Having been strengthened on his left by the arrival of Cilley's and Scammel's regiments, they renewed the attack about one o'clock, but with indifferent results.

Burgoyne formed his line of battle in the woods on the north side of a clearing owned by one Isaac Freeman. It contained 12 or 15 acres and extended east and west about sixty rods. This clearing, called Freeman's farm, was the principal scene of the action of the 19th. Fraser with the right wing had reached the line of low hills just west of Freeman's farm when the action began. After the termination of the first skirmish, and when the contest had been vigorously renewed, Fraser wheeled to the left for the purpose of flanking Morgan and the other regiments when, to his surprise, he encountered, in the woods near the head of the Middle ravine, Arnold with several additional New York and New Hampshire regiments intent on separating Fraser from Burgoyne. It is needless to say that the dogs of war were unleashed at once, and a furious struggle ensued. The two most fiery leaders in either army were here personally opposed to each other. Arnold and Fraser both seemed ubiquitous, rushing hither and yon in the thick of the fray, giving orders and encouraging their men. The battle here raged for more than an hour, and Fraser seemed in imminent danger of being cut off from the main body when Colonel Breyman with his German grenadiers and a few pieces of artillery appeared on the field and assailing Arnold on his right forced him back. But he retired only to catch breath and regain his strength, for soon being reinforced by two regiments of Connecticut militia he returned to the field, and then the battle raged all along the line. Fraser having formed his junction with Burgoyne, the chief struggle was now on Freeman's clearing and in the open woods just to the west. The Americans attacked the British furiously and drove them into the woods on the north side, where they were rallied, and charging with bayonets drove the Americans back across the same field into the cover of the woods to the south, where they in turn recovered themselves and hurled the redcoats back with great slaughter. Morgan's sharpshooters, posted in trees, did terrible execution among the British officers as well as the rank and file. Both sides exhibited the most desperate valor, and bloody hand to hand contests were frequent, especially about the British field battery, which was taken and retaken at every charge, but the Americans, having no horses nor matches could neither get them off the field nor fire them. Gates, having been persuaded to reinforce the tired patriots, about five o'clock sent out Learned's brigade, which renewed the fight with such spirit that Burgoyne, finding himself on the perilous edge of defeat, sent to his left for reinforcements. Riedesel responded promptly and reaching the field about dusk, struck the American right, folded it back, and posted Pausch's battery on the hill south of Freeman's cottage, which was served with such efficiency that the patriots were obliged to give way and retire. Though nearly dark Riedesel and Fraser were on the point of following up their success when Burgoyne, neither energetic nor wise enough to improve his advantage, called a halt, to the infinite disgust of both generals and common soldiers. Thus twice during that eventful day the Germans saved the British army from rout, and yet Burgoyne scarcely mentioned them in his dispatches home.

Victory that day was evidently for the General who could most promptly bring up the largest reserves; but the reinforcements that Gates so sparingly doled out to Arnold were all he was allowed to receive. He had a number of brigades in reserve most of whom were, no doubt, eager for a chance at the enemy. Some of these men had already had their baptism of fire at Bunker Hill, Quebec, and Oriskany. At least Gates, if he were a really live general, could and should have made a diversion in Arnold's favor at the British left, down on the river flats. That would have kept Generals Phillips and Riedesel at their posts instead of leaving them free to go to Burgoyne's rescue as they did.

Of course Burgoyne claimed a victory, but like Pyrrhus' victory over the Romans, another such would prove his ruin.[2] Indeed it had been an unusually fierce and sanguinary struggle. On the British side the 62d regiment was nearly cut to pieces. It had three or four ensigns or color bearers killed; only sixty of the three or four hundred men who entered, with five or six officers, reported for duty, and thirty-six out of forty-eight men in Captain Jones' artillery company were either killed or wounded, the Captain himself being among the victims.

Lieut. Hadden, who worked two guns on the British left says, he lost in killed or wounded nineteen out of twenty artillerymen, and that while he was applying to Gen. Phillips for aid his cap was shot through. Lieut. Anbury, in his " Travels," says: " The officers who have been killed and wounded in the late action are much greater, in proportion, than that of the soldiers, which must be attributed to the great execution of the riflemen, who directed their fire against them in particular." Again he says: " The courage and obstinacy with which the Americans fought, were the astonishment of everyone, and we now became fully convinced they are not that contemptible enemy we had hitherto imagined them."

It is fitting to recall right here that Morgan's corps was the first on the field and the last to leave it. Where it was engaged the strife was more deadly and less interrupted than in any other position. Its loss was greater than that of any American regiment engaged, while the number who fell by its hands was nearly half of those admitted by Burgoyne to have fallen in battle. Moreover after this battle, in which Morgan's men had been specially pitted against the Indians, in the British army, and as a result of their costly experience, most of the

---

[2] It was a dear bought victory, if I can give it that name, as we lost many brave men . . . . and no very great advantage, honor excepted, was gained by the day.—*Digby's Journal, p.* 273.

OLD BATTLE WELL

savages discovered that some very pressing business called them homeward, and they went.

The Americans lost in killed and wounded three hundred and nineteen, or ten per cent of those engaged; the British lost six hundred or twenty per cent of those actually engaged. And as to the question of victory: Since it was Burgoyne's purpose to advance and not simply to hold his ground, while Gates' purpose was to hold his ground and check the advance of Burgoyne, the reader can judge for himself to whom the palm should be given. However it is fair to call it a drawn battle. Moreover, the Americans learned that they were a match for the dreaded British regulars, which discovery was in itself worth a victory to them.

Burgoyne issued orders for a renewal of the conflict in the morning. Accordingly, ammunition and rations were served early to the men, but a dense fog hindered any movement at the appointed hour. While waiting for it to clear up, Fraser observed to Burgoyne that since his grenadiers were greatly fatigued after yesterday's fighting, it might be well to wait till the morrow, when they would be in far better spirits. Acting on this suggestion, Burgoyne countermanded the order and the men returned to their quarters. The Americans, apprised of this proposed movement by a deserter, manned their works and awaited the attack in dread suspense. Had Burgoyne attacked that morning, as he had planned, in all probability he would have carried Gates' works; for the American stock of ammunition was practically exhausted, and several days elapsed before the magazine was replenished.[3]

---

[3] It was due to General Schuyler's diligence in collecting powder and lead that this deficiency was supplied. For the purpose he had the leading stripped from the windows and roofs in Albany, and sent up to the army.

The following night a dispatch from Sir Henry Clinton reached Burgoyne to the effect that he was about to move up the Hudson from New York to his aid. This decided Burgoyne to remain where he was until the expected diversion should cause either the withdrawal or diminution of Gates' army.

Why Howe Failed to Co-operate with Burgoyne. For many years after the event, students of the Revolutionary war, in both England and America, cogitated much over Howe's failure to execute his share of the carefully planned campaign. The question was, Why did he not advance up the Hudson simultaneously with Burgoyne's descent from the north? Clinton's attempted diversion in Burgoyne's behalf was afterward learned to be wholly on his own motion. This served rather to complicate than to clear up the problem. But a memorandum left by Lord Shelburne, and quite recently brought to light by Lord Edmund FitzMaurice, has solved the mystery. A number of orders, dispatches, etc., duly prepared, awaited the signature of Lord George Germaine, the colonial secretary. Among these were the orders to Howe giving explicit directions for co-operating with Burgoyne. Lord George called in the office on his way to attend some social function or fox hunt down in Kent. He hastily signed the several papers, but when he came to this particular one, on glancing it over, he refused to sign it on the ground that it was not " fair copied." Always impatient of anything that interfered with his plans, the fairer " copy " must await his signature until he returned from his holiday. But when he came back the matter had wholly slipped his mind. And thus the document on which hung the fate of an army, and the retention of a vast empire, got pigeon-holed, where it was discovered, unsigned, long after Saratoga had tipped the balances in favor of American liberty and independence. Thus

Howe being left to his own devices, planned a campaign to the south, placed Clinton in charge at New York, and left Burgoyne to shift for himself.

Those of us who believe that the Almighty Ruler takes a hand in the affairs of men and nations, reckon this to be a conspicuous proof that he favored this people in their mighty struggle for a freer and nobler life. Indeed this whole campaign is full of astonishing Providences for those who have an eye to see them.

Gen. J. Watts De Peyster, an acknowledged authority in military science, in a letter to the writer, says: " The American success of 1777 was due to 'the strategy of Providence' and not of men, as Kingsley puts it: certainly not to Gates, who was another of those English military Phantasms, as he demonstrated in South Carolina in 1780."

The Interim Between the Battles. The morning after the battle the field presented a most distressing spectacle. The dead lay everywhere like autumn leaves in the forest. Some were still clutching their weapons, or the grass and twigs they had grasped in their death agonies, and some were mangled beyond all recognition. Shallow trenches were hastily dug on the field, into which the bodies were flung (each one of them no doubt was most precious and sacred to loved ones far away) and thinly covered with earth. Here note one of the horrors of war; a violent death, far from friends; and burial like a beast in a nameless grave. The writer has heard old residents on these battle-fields tell of seeing human bones turned up by the plow and skulls of grenadiers adorning stumps in the field.

As soon as Burgoyne had resolved to await Clinton's coming, he moved the major part of his army up on the heights, occupied a portion of the late battle-field and began the construction of a fortified camp. The right embraced the Freeman farm, and also took in a hill about sixty rods to the northwest of the Freeman cottage, since called Breyman's hill.[4] On this a strong redoubt was erected; another was placed about fifteen rods north of the cottage, and the spot is now marked by a granite tablet; another called the Great Redoubt, was located on the knoll a few rods southwest of the old battle well. This defended the southwest angle of the camp. Others were located at proper intervals from this point east across the plain to the crest of the bluffs near the river. These redoubts were connected by strong intrenchments. The interval between Breyman's hill and the next redoubt to the south was defended by a breastwork, of two parallel tiers of rails laid up between perpendicular posts and the space between filled with earth. At Wilbur's Basin, a pontoon bridge was thrown across the river, its eastern end was defended by a redoubt. This bridge was intended for the use of foraging parties chiefly. On each of the three hills just north of Wilbur's Basin a redoubt was erected. The middle one was called the Great Redoubt. In addition to these defenses, breastworks of logs were thrown up at intervals along the brink of the Middle ravine as cover to the advanced pickets. Thousands of trees were cut to give clear play to the artillery. Burgoyne had his hospitals and magazine on the river flats below the hills. These were defended on the north by a line of breastworks. His headquarters were with the center on the high ground.

Burgoyne's army was disposed as follows: Fraser's brigade held the right wing; Breyman, with his Brunswickers and artillery, defended the hill with its redoubt at the extreme right; next to him were the few Indians left, and Canadians, behind the rail breastworks; next

---

[4] The residents in the vicinity now call it Burgoyne's hill; a misnomer.

to the left was Earl Balcarras, with the light infantry, and the English grenadiers. These manned the other redoubts on the right. Fraser's left rested on a ravine running north and south across the camp ground, and east of the Freeman cottage. Hamilton's brigade occupied the center at Fraser's left, while Riedesel, with his Germans, held the left wing on the plateau overlooking the river; a part of the 47th regiment and a few German companies defended the hospitals, magazines, etc., on the river flats. It is interesting to note, by the way, that the 47th took part in the battle of Bunker Hill.

Thus the hostile camps, each the counterpart of the other, were separated by the distance of a cannon shot only. Indeed so close together were they that the British officers in their journals say they could often hear talking and shouting in the American camp, while the sound of chopping and the rattle of chains were daily reminders that the Americans were strengthening their defenses. But the thick woods effectually screened each camp from the other.

Soon after the battle ended, and the hush of night was fallen, Gen. Gates sent out a picket of a hundred selected men to watch the movements of the enemy. They reported that all night long they heard the cries and groans of the wounded boys. They were anxious to offer them help, but the enemies' guard would not allow it. The day following as soon as Gates concluded that Burgoyne would not renew the attack, he gave orders to hasten the completion of the defensive works, already laid out by Kosciusko. The work on these was pushed till the camp became well nigh unapproachable to a force like Burgoyne's, should it attempt to storm it. Also, by the 30th, Col. Jeduthan Baldwin, of the Engineers, had a floating bridge completed across the Hudson.

Just before the battle of the 19th Gates had sent for

Gen. Lincoln that he might post himself immediately on Burgoyne's left. He at once started from Manchester for Bemis Heights and arrived on the 22d with 2,000 troops. He had been detailed by Gen. Schuyler on July 30th to take command at Manchester. His appearance put new heart into the inhabitants of that region, who were abandoning their homes through fear of Burgoyne's Indians. Early in Sept. he advanced northward to Pawlet, near Skenesboro, whence, on the 12th, he sent Col. Brown against Fort George, and Col. Johnson against forts Ticonderoga and Independence. On the 17th Brown captured Fort George; a party of rangers under Capt. Allen got possession of Mt. Defiance; while another detachment from Johnson surprised and captured a company of the 47th British regiment, at the old French lines within pistol shot of Fort "Ti." Capt. Brown immediately started southward, and appeared at Bemis Heights, Oct. 1st, with 315 British prisoners, and 118 Americans whom they had released from captivity. They had done the enemy much damage, and brought off plunder valued at £10,000.

In the Journals of American officers we note that many deserters from the British camp, mainly Hessians, came in daily. These poor fellows persisted in deserting despite the dreadful punishment inflicted by Burgoyne on those recaptured. On the 20th about 120 Oneida, Onondaga, and Tuscarora Indians came in, and made themselves useful for a time capturing stray Britons. One day a party of them came in with two prisoners and a scalp. Gen. Gates gave them $20 each for the prisoners, but would allow them nothing for the scalp. Whether such treatment disgruntled them doth not appear, but most of them, however, went off on the 27th to the great relief of all concerned.

Though well able to defend himself against attack, yet

Burgoyne and his men were allowed precious little peace or rest. He was subjected to constant harassments at the hands of the vigilant Americans. His advanced pickets were frequently gathered in by venturesome parties, his scouts and messengers were waylaid and captured, and no foraging party dare move abroad without a strong guard; for example 40 or 50 of the seamen who had charge of the flotilla of bateaux were captured while searching for food among the deserted farms on the east side of the river. The early morning of Sept. 23d Burgoyne sent Capt. Gerlach of the Brunswickers, across the Hudson, with a strong detachment of Provincials, to ascertain the position of the " rebels." He reported that he had been down the river several miles but failed to discover anything definite. Another party attempted to cross the ravines for the same purpose, but a chaos and tangle of brush and fallen timber defeated that venture. Packs of wolves attracted by the thinly covered bodies of the slain hovered about the camp and rendered the nights hideous with their dismal howls. At first it was thought the uncanny noises were made by camp dogs, and they were ordered to be confined. But the following night the hullaballoo was still more frightful. A scout sent to learn what it meant reported the real cause.

No soldier slept without his clothes. No night passed that the officers were not up and abroad, repeatedly, to assure themselves against surprise, while everybody was invariably up and equipped for action an hour before day. Thus two weary weeks had passed and yet no further tidings came from Clinton. Says one of the Hessian officers: "At no time did the Jews await the coming of their Messiah with greater eagerness than we awaited the coming of Gen. Clinton." Meanwhile the stock of provisions was running perilously low.

Gates though urged to attack, wisely declined, feeling

that time was fighting for him more efficiently and cheaply than could bristling battalions and belching batteries, because his own army was augmenting, while Burgoyne's was decreasing, and furthermore, a thing of far weightier import was the fact that gaunt famine could not be far away from his belligerent neighbor across the ravine to the north.

On the other hand the American camp was not altogether a heavenly place. For some time Gates had been treating Arnold with growing coolness, for reasons that were not apparent to the ordinary observer. Colonel Brockholst Livingston, writing from the camp at Bemis Heights, says it was because Arnold was an avowed friend of General Schuyler. But after the battle of the 19th this coolness rapidly developed into an open rupture. Another reason for Gates' attitude was this: He discovered that the soldiery were giving to Arnold and Morgan the principal credit for whatever was achieved in the late battle. A temperamental weakness of that General here came to the surface, viz: impatience with those above or below him whom the public delighted to honor. It reminds one of King Saul after he heard the women singing: " Saul hath slain his thousands, and David his ten thousands." I. Sam. 18:5-9. Thereafter Saul had no more use for David. In general orders for Sept. 26 Gates gives belated praise to the army. In his thanks he mentions Generals Poor and Learned, Col. Marshall and his 10th Mass. regiment, which was altogether proper, but says nothing about Arnold and Morgan. Again in his report of the battle, to Congress, Gates did not mention the name of Arnold nor did he speak of Morgan approvingly, though it was notorious that the checking of Burgoyne's advance was mainly due to Arnold's judgment and skill, ably seconded by Morgan. And when Arnold called his attention to this slight,

Gates, assuming lofty airs, treated him as an impertinent meddler. Arnold, not being specially gifted with docility and sweetness of spirit, resented this, when high words ensued, which resulted in Gates depriving him of his command. General Schuyler, replying to a letter from Colonel Richard Varick, then in the camp, says: "I wonder at Gates' policy. He will probably be indebted to him for the glory he may acquire by a victory; but perhaps he is so very sure of success that he does not wish the other [Arnold] to come in for a share of it." This conjecture of Schuyler's soon developed into a fulfilled prophecy. "Lossing truly says: 'But for Arnold on that eventful day, Burgoyne would have marched into Albany at the autumnal equinox, a victor,' and yet Gates behaved toward Arnold as if he had done him an injury instead of a favor." At the earnest entreaties of the officers of his division, Arnold pocketed his insults and determined to remain with the army till after the next battle, which then seemed imminent.

After the rupture between Gates and Arnold, Gen. Lincoln was given the command of the right wing, and Gates moved his quarters from Bemis' tavern up on the heights and occupied Capt. Ephriam Woodworth's house, at the junction of the Saratoga and Quaker Springs roads. A few days before the second battle Gates received a request from Washington, that Morgan and his corps be returned if he could possibly be spared. From his reply to Washington one can easily draw Gates' real estimate of Morgan's worth to him. After describing the two armies as still facing each other, waiting to renew the struggle, Gates says: "In this situation your Excellency would not wish me to part with *the corps that the army of Gen. Burgoyne are most afraid of.*" Italics our own.

CHAPTER XII

Battle of the 7th of October

Burgoyne, not having heard anything from Clinton, and his commissariat running low, called a council of his principal officers on the evening of the 5th of October, laid the situation before them, and asked their advice. Riedesel advised a hasty retreat to Fort Edward; Fraser conceded the wisdom of this, but was willing to fight; Phillips declined to give an opinion. Burgoyne, strongly averse to a retreat, decided to ascertain first, the position and strength of his enemy, by a reconnaissance in force; and secondly, to learn if the high ground to the west commanded Gates' camp; then if he should think it unwise to attack, he would retreat. With a body of fifteen hundred picked men, and two twelve pounders, six six-pounders, and two howitzers, he set out from the camp between ten and eleven o'clock on the morning of the 7th. Generals Phillips, Riedesel and Fraser accompanied Burgoyne to assist in the reconnaissance. They moved toward the southwest about two-thirds of a mile and deployed in an open clearing and sat down while a detail of drivers and batmen from Fraser's brigade foraged in a wheat field. The place is the southern slope of the rise of ground just north of the Middle ravine. The highway running from Quaker Springs to Bemis Heights passes through the left of the center of the British position. The light infantry, under the Earl of Balcarras, were stationed on the right, Riedesel, with his Germans and a battery of two six pounders under Captain Pausch, held the center; Majors Ackland and Williams, with the grenadiers and most of the artillery, were posted on the left. General Fraser with five hundred grenadiers had occupied some high ground in the advance to the right with the intention of stealing around to the left of the American works and holding their attention while the main body could gain the high ground to the west of the American camp.

Gates having been apprised of the movement, sent out his adjutant, Wilkinson, to ascertain if possible its purpose. Having posted himself on the high knoll at the turn of the road, about fifty rods south of the Middle ravine bridge he saw the enemy arrayed in the fields over against him, and several officers posted on the roof of a log house, with glasses, trying to get a glimpse of the American works. He reported that Burgoyne apparently offered battle. Gates said, "what would you suggest?" Wilkinson replied, "I would indulge him." Then, said Gates, "order out Morgan to begin the game." After a little consultation it was decided that Morgan should make a circuit to the west and strike the enemy in flank. General Poor, with his brigade, was to assail their left flank, while Learned's brigade and Dearborn's light infantry were to engage the center and left. Sufficient time was to be given Morgan to reach his position before the attack should begin. General Poor having formed his line of battle ordered his men not to fire till after the first volley from the enemy.

At about 2:30 p. m. the advance began, and Poor's men descended into the ravine with perfect coolness and ascended the opposite bank with the steadiness of veterans. They were well up and were nearing the enemy before a shot was fired, when suddenly a tremendous volley of musketry and cannon thundered forth, but the pieces being elevated too much, the missiles of death harmed only the tree tops in their rear. At once they rushed forward in open order and forming again on their flanks, they literally mowed down the grenadiers with their accurately aimed volleys. Then charging, they closed with the enemy, and a desperate hand to hand conflict ensued; the combatants surging back and forth as each for the moment gained an advantage. The most furious contest, however, raged around Williams' battery. One of the twelve pounders was taken and retaken no less than six times, till finally Major Williams was taken prisoner, and Major Ackland, of the grenadiers, was seriously wounded, when the men, seized with panic through the loss of their leaders, abandoned the contest and fled. Colonel Cilley at this moment leaped upon the much disputed gun and having "sworn it true to the cause of America," turned it upon its late defenders.

About the time the action began on the right, Morgan having discovered Fraser in his advanced position, managed to gain the ridge to the west and then rushing down upon him like an avalanche, compelled him to retire to the main body; then by a quick movement to his left he soon placed himself where he could flank the British right, and then struck with such tremendous force as to fold them back and compel Balcarras to change front. Almost simultaneously with Morgan's flank attack Dearborn with his men leaped the fence and charged their front with such effect as to force them to give way, but Earl Balcarras, their skillful and intrepid leader, rallied and formed them again behind a second fence, where they held their ground for a little time; but being overborne by numbers, and skill in the use of the deadly rifle, they soon broke into disorderly retreat.

But where is Arnold all this while? Arnold of the quick eye and lightning action; Arnold the thunderbolt? Why, he is being held in leash by the will of the jealous Gates. There deprived of all command he is pacing the ramparts of Fort Neilson like a caged lion. He hears the roar of battle; his ear catches the shouts of the combatants, but half a mile away, and the trumpet tones of command. A passing breeze brings to him a whiff of the battle's smoke. That, sir, is his native element; it kindles a raging fire in his veins; his soul is in his face; his eyes are ablaze; all the instincts of his nature urge him thither. He has asked Gates to allow him to serve as a volunteer in the ranks, but has been refused. The stress is too great for his unruly spirit. Breaking through all restraint he mounts his splendid bay, rushes through the sally port and is off for the scene of action in a trice. Suspecting his intention, Gates dashes off a dispatch ordering his instant return, and giving it to Major Armstrong, bade him deliver it to him at once " lest he should do some rash thing."

Once on the field Arnold took in the situation at a glance, and putting himself at the head of a detachment of Learned's brigade, he directed them in a furious charge against the Germans at the center; but being stoutly repelled by them again and again, he finally in a charge, which he personally led, forced himself through their lines closely followed by his men. Their lines thus broken, they retreated in confusion. Meanwhile Major Armstrong had been trying to fulfil his commission, but Arnold, divining his errand, managed to keep out of his way, till finally his course becoming so erratic and perilous, Armstrong decided to await a less hazardous occasion.

But let us glance at the struggle from the British standpoint. Burgoyne was evidently disconcerted by the suddenness and vigor of the American attack. Fraser having been forced back from his advanced position, put in where he could be of the most service. Nor was there any lack of opportunity. Under the withering fire and tremendous pressure of the American attack, the lines were being constantly broken. Fraser on his splendid iron gray charger rushed fearlessly here and there rallying and animating the men and directing their movements. When the right wing was broken and in danger of being cut off, Burgoyne ordered Fraser to form a second line to cover and reinforce them. This movement was executed with such energy that Morgan's men were effectually held in check. The falling back of both wings uncovered the center, but the Germans stubbornly held their ground. It was at this juncture that Arnold's desperate charge forced them into disorderly retreat. Fraser noticing their peril, hastened to their relief with the 24th regiment, which soon brought order out of chaos. Indeed wherever Fraser appeared everything seemed to prosper for King George, for the men believed in him and would follow him anywhere. Morgan, who was directly opposed to his brigade, noticing that the contest seemed to be wavering in the balances, called for a few of his best sharpshooters and directing their attention toward the enemy, said: "That gallant officer on the gray horse is General Fraser; I admire and respect him, but it is necessary for our cause that he should be put out of action—take your station in that clump of trees and do your duty." But a few minutes had elapsed when the gallant Fraser fell mortally wounded, and was tenderly borne from the field by a detail of his brave grenadiers.

After the fall of Fraser, General Burgoyne assumed the personal direction and bravely exposing himself, tried to rally his men and stem the tide, but in vain; for at this juncture General Tenbroeck, at the head of his brigade of New York militia appeared on the field, and the British overwhelmed and beaten at every point, were forced to abandon the field and seek refuge in their intrenched camp, leaving nearly all their artillery in the hands of the Americans.

To avoid confusion on the part of the reader it will be well to note that the rout of the two wings and the center of the British force was nearly simultaneous, and that from the opening of this part of the contest to the retreat of the British only fifty-two minutes elapsed.

The British in retreating to their defenses were hotly pursued through the woods by the Americans, who assailed the front and entire right flank of Fraser's camp. The war demon raging in Arnold's bosom, not yet sated with blood and carnage, prompted him to lead portions of Glover's and Patterson's brigades in a dare-devil assault upon the Great Redoubt, which defended the southwest angle of the British camp. He drove the enemy through and beyond the abatis at the point of the bayonet, and then made desperate attempts to scale the works, but was finally beaten off with loss. This place proved to be a veritable "bloody angle" to the Americans, because in assaulting the redoubt they found themselves exposed to the fire of a strong battery shotted with grape and canister, and with little shelter to themselves save stumps and brush. Suffice it to say, they got out of that. Arnold seeing little chance for success here, recalled the men and then darted off alone northward toward the extreme British right in search of a more favorable opening. On his way he insanely urged his horse between the firing lines, but escaped unscathed. Meanwhile the redoubt on Breyman's hill, with its flanking breastworks, the strong defense of the British extreme right, had been thoroughly invested, but no assault had as yet been attempted. General Learned having just appeared on that part of the field with his brigade, asked Wilkinson, Gates' aide, who had surveyed the situation, where he could "put in to the best advantage." He replied that he had noticed a slack fire from behind the rail breastworks in the interval between Breyman's redoubt and Balcarras' camp, and suggested an assault there. On his way to the place Arnold appeared on the scene, and putting himself at the head of the brigade (Arnold was of right Learned's superior officer) led the assault. It chanced that there were but few men to defend those works at the moment, as the Provincials and Indians stationed there had been withdrawn for scouting and other service before the battle, and had on the retreat taken refuge behind Fraser's breastworks instead of their own; hence the slack fire from that point. The few that were there, finding themselves overmatched by the assaulting party, soon abandoned the position and fled. This left the flank of the Brunswickers in the redoubt exposed. Arnold following up his advantage, razed a section of the breastworks, rushed with his men through the opening, struck them in the rear, and quickly possessed himself of that important work without serious opposition. The Germans who defended it fled precipitately, but left their brave commander, Colonel Breyman, behind in the works shot to death. Arnold had his horse shot under him by the parting volley and himself was wounded in the same leg that was hurt at Quebec. There in the moment of victory he was overtaken by Major Armstrong with the order for his return to camp "lest he should do some rash thing." He was now ready to go, but had to be carried. And he had done a very "rash thing," he had gone to the field without any official authority to fight, much less *to command,* and had contributed greatly to the winning of one of the most important battles in all history. A blessed thing were it for his memory had that bullet gone through his heart instead of his leg.

As Arnold fell an American soldier rushed forward to bayonet the German soldier who had shot him, the German himself having been wounded. Arnold shouted:

"Don't hurt him, he did but his duty; he is a fine fellow!" Thus with an expression of truest chivalry he saved the life of the one who had just attempted his life.[1] One bright spot, that, in Arnold's career.

Lieutenant Colonel Speht, then in Balcarras' camp, hearing of Breyman's disaster to the right, undertook to recover the position, but having trusted himself to the guidance of a supposed royalist, he with his four officers and fifty men, were delivered into the hands of an American detachment and found themselves prisoners.

The Americans thus possessed of this right flank defense, found it to be an open gateway to the whole British camp. The British recognizing the significance of its capture, knew that the game was up for them. But night put an end to this struggle, as it did to the battle of the 19th of September. Both conflicts also ended on practically the same ground. The loss to the British in this battle in killed and wounded and missing was about seven hundred. The loss of General Fraser alone was equal to that of a small army; there, too, were Sir Francis Clerke and Colonel Breyman wounded to death, and Majors Ackland and Williams, and Lieutenant Colonel Speht prisoners in the hands of the Americans; the loss of these men was well nigh irreparable. The American loss was inconsiderable, there being only one hundred and fifty killed and wounded. Arnold was the only commissioned officer wounded. This wide diversity in casualties was chiefly due, no doubt, to the superior skill in marksmanship on the part of the patriots.

Colonel Wilkinson having occasion to pass over the field just after the British had retreated from their first position, records the following among other things which he saw: " The ground which had been occupied by the British grenadiers [where the battle was begun by Poor's

---

[1] Stone's Burgoyne's Campaign, p. 66.

brigade] presented a scene of complicated horror and exultation. In the square space of twelve or fifteen yards lay eighteen grenadiers in the agonies of death, and three officers propped up against stumps of trees, two of them mortally wounded, bleeding, and almost speechless. With the troops I pursued the flying enemy, passing over killed and wounded until I heard one exclaim, 'protect me, sir, against this boy.' Turning my eyes, it was my fortune to arrest the purpose of a lad in the act of taking aim at a wounded officer who lay in the angle of a worm fence. Inquiring his rank, he answered, 'I had the honor to command the grenadiers;' of course I knew him to be Major Ackland, who had been brought from the field to this place by one of his men. I dismounted, took him by the hand and expressed hopes that he was not badly wounded. 'Not badly,' replied the gallant officer, but very inconveniently, I am shot through both legs; will you, sir, have the goodness to have me conveyed to your camp?' I directed my servant to alight and we lifted Ackland to his seat, and ordered him to be conducted to headquarters."

It was fitting also, at this point, to give an instance of the courage and hardihood of the private soldier; for he represents the average man. Thomas Haines, a private in the 1st N. H. Regt., was one of those who fought for Maj. Williams' 12 pounders in the second battle, Oct. 7th. In the desperate hand to hand conflict he killed three British soldiers, then was himself struck by a musket ball which, passing through the mouth, tore out 11 of his teeth, a portion of his tongue, and came out near the left ear. He fell as one dead, and was left on the field two nights and a day. When a detail went out to bury the dead Haines was picked up, carried and deposited on the ground for burial. An officer present, who had known him well, noticed that his body was not stiff like the rest, and refused to allow him to be buried. His breast was then bared and he was found to exhibit symptoms of life. He was at once tenderly carried to the hospital where, to the surprise of all, he soon recovered sufficiently to be taken to Albany. After months of convalescence he fully recovered his strength and reenlisted, and served out his full term of three years. He finally returned home and lived to the remarkable age of ninety, dying at Loudon, N. H., the place of his nativity.[2]

Two things this man possessed in a remarkable degree, animal vitality, and persistency of purpose.

Note the difference in spirit exhibited by the generals in chief in these two battles. Whatever the failings of General Burgoyne, he certainly was not lacking in the grace of personal courage; for he exposed himself right in the thick of the fight in both battles, a target for sharpshooters, who succeeded in putting a ball through his hat, and tearing his clothes but failed to touch his person. Gates, on the other hand, never ventured within a mile of either field, nor even got a whiff of the smoke of battle, unless, perchance, there was a stiff wind from the north that day. Besides being a coward, Gates again showed himself to be the small minded, jealous ingrate, that we have already noticed, in that he barely mentioned Arnold or Morgan[3] in his report of the battle, and meanly

---

[2] Kidder's 1st. New Hampshire Regt.

[3] Col. Daniel Morgan was living on a farm in Virginia, when the news of the battle of Lexington reached him. He mustered a picked company of riflemen and marched with them to Cambridge, Mass., a distance of 600 miles, in twenty-one days, an average of 28½ miles per day. It was in the dusk of the evening when Morgan met General Washington, who was riding out to inspect the camp. As they met, Morgan touched his broad-brimmed hat, and said. " General—from the right bank of the Potomac." Hastily dismounting, Washington " took the captain's hand in both of his, and pressed it silently. Then passing down the line, he pressed, in turn, the hand of every soldier, large tears streaming down the noble cheeks as he did so. Without a word, he then remounted his horse, saluted, and returned to headquarters."

Graham in his biography of Morgan relates how, upon his return to head

ignored the commander-in-chief, General Washington, in failing to report to him at all, which, to say the least, was a gross breach of official courtesy.

On one of his returns from the battle field with reports Wilkinson found that Sir Francis Clerke had been brought from the field badly wounded and was laid upon Gates' bed, and that while the conflict was still raging, and the outcome was yet trembling in the balance, Gates was engaged in a heated argument with Sir Francis over the merits of the questions at issue between England and America, apparently more anxious to win in that wordy contest than in the awful life and death struggle raging just outside his camp. Gates not being able to make his wounded prisoner yield to the force of his arguments turned away in unconcealed disgust and said to Wilkinson: "Did you ever see such an impudent son of a b—h!" The whole scene discloses the real fibre of the man's character.[4]

Wilkinson in his Memoirs, written in later life, says:

---

quarters the night of the 7th of Oct., to report, he was met by Gates who warmly embraced him, saying: "Morgan you have done wonders to day. You have immortalized yourself, and honored your country; if you are not promoted immediately I will not serve another day." But wait a bit and we shall see how genuine was this boisterous enthusiasm.

Later in life Morgan saw fit to relate the following incident. Soon after the surrender at Saratoga he visited Gates on business, when he was taken aside by the General and confidentially told that the main army was extremely dissatisfied with the conduct of the war by the present leader, and that several of the best officers threatened to resign unless there was a change. Morgan quickly caught Gates' drift, then sternly replied: "I have one favor to ask of you General: Never mention that subject to me again; for under no other man than Washington, as Commander-in-Chief, would I consent to serve."

About that time it was noted that Morgan was treated by Gates with growing coolness and neglect, and it afterwards became known that in a covert way he hindered his promotion by Congress. To us New Yorkers it is interesting to note that on his return to Virginia, in 1778, Morgan rechristened his home SARATOGA as a constant reminder of his most important battle.

[4] Sir Francis Clerke was taken the next morning to the house of Dirck Swart at Stillwater and there he died some days later.—Clinton Paps. II, 430.

"The same force which enabled Gates to subdue the British army would have produced a similar effect under the orders of Gen. Schuyler, since the operations of the campaign did not involve a single instance of professional skill, and the triumph of the American arms was accomplished by the physical force and valor of the troops under the direction and protection of the God of battles." All of which means, so complete were the preparations, and so favorable the conditions on the 19th of August, when Gates assumed command, that thereafter the rôle of commander was largely perfunctory.

CHAPTER XIII.

Third Period of the Campaign — The Retreat

BURGOYNE now finding his position on the heights untenable, withdrew his army during the night of the 7th to the low ground near the river, retaining, however, so much of the high ground as lies immediately north of the Wilbur's Basin ravine. His leading generals urged him to abandon his heavy artillery and unnecessary camp equipage and push with all speed for Canada. But No! life on the way would not have been worth the living without that precious park of artillery, his generous stock of liquors, and his packs of showy millinery; so all must be risked that they might be kept.[1]

If Burgoyne could have brought himself to abandon everything except necessities, as did St. Clair when he evacuated Ticonderoga, or as did Morgan and his men in 1775 who, in their light equipment, made 600 miles in twenty-one days from Winchester, W. Va., to Boston, he could have crossed to the east side of the Hudson on his floating bridge, and, made Ticonderoga without a question, and saved his army; for Gates at that time had not a sufficient force at the north to materially obstruct him.

The ancients had a saying, "Whom the gods propose to destroy they first make mad." While a commission of lunacy would hardly have voted General Burgoyne *non compos mentis,* yet for the next few days his behavior was so lacking in sound sense and vigorous action that had he been really mad he could not have compassed the

---

[1] It took thirty carts to transport Burgoyne's personal baggage. No other officers in the army was allowed a single cart for his private use after they left Fort Edward.—*See Hadden's Journal, p.* 314.

ruin of his army with greater certainty or celerity than he did.

General Fraser died the next morning after the battle. Before his death he requested that he might be buried at 6 p. m. within the Great Redoubt on the second hill north of Wilbur's Basin. This hill had been with him a favorite spot on account of the beauty of the view. Such a request proves that General Fraser was not himself, or that he did not realize the situation when he made it. It was no time for Burgoyne to take counsel of sentiment, yet he resolved to fulfil the dying soldier's request to the letter; so he spent that, to him, precious day in preparing leisurely for retreat and in sharp skirmishes with the advanced lines of the Americans who had occupied his old camp ground.

On this day General Lincoln, who had command of the American right, while personally leading a body of militia to take post near the enemy on the river flats, fell in with an advanced party of Germans in a thick wood. Mistaking them for Americans, because of their blue uniforms, he approached within a short distance of them before he discovered his error. At once he wheeled his horse and, as he did so, they fired a volley, and a shot fractured his leg. He escaped and was carried back to his quarters.[2]

Wilkinson writes that the same day (the 8th): " The enemy refused a flag with which I attempted, at every point of his line, to convey a letter to Lady Harriet Ackland from her husband, a prisoner in our hands."

Death of Fraser. General Fraser was evidently the idol of the army, for among other eulogists, Lieut. Anbury in his Travels, has this to say of him: " Gen. Fraser was brought back to camp on his horse, a grenadier on

---

[2] Sparks' Am. Biography, Vol. 13, p. 260.

each side supporting him. The officers all anxious and eagerly inquiring as to his wound—the downcast look and melancholy that was visible to every one as to his situation, and all the answer he could make to the many inquiries was a shaking of the head, expressive that it was all over with him. So much was he beloved that not only officers and soldiers, but all the women, flocked around solicitous for his fate."

General Fraser died in a small farm house which at the time was occupied by the Baroness Riedesel, wife of the General of the German contingent. The house was located near the foot of the hill whereon he was buried. When the road was changed it was moved and stood on the present highway near the river till 1873, when it was torn down. The Baroness in her Memoirs gives a touching account of the death of the General.

On the morning of the 7th, before the reconnaissance and battle, Generals Burgoyne, Phillips, and Fraser had promised to dine with herself and husband, and she was still waiting for them when General Fraser was brought in on a litter mortally wounded. Afterward, when told that his hurt was fatal and that he had but a few hours to live, she heard him exclaim repeatedly and sadly: "Oh fatal ambition! Poor General Burgoyne! My poor wife!" Then he frequently begged the Baroness' pardon for causing her so much trouble, because he was laid in her apartment, and she was so assiduous in her efforts to add to his comfort. His brave spirit took its departure at eight o'clock a. m. of the 8th. The corpse having been washed and wrapped in a sheet, was laid on the bed and she, with her three children, was obliged to remain in the room most of the day.

Precisely at 6 p. m. he was carried by his beloved grenadiers to the spot he had selected for his sepulture, accompanied by the chaplain Brudenell, the generals and

BURGOYNE'S CAMP AT WILBUR'S BASIN. FROM ANBUREY'S TRAVELS, PUBLISHED IN 1790. THE LINE OF MEN REPRESENTS GEN. FRASER'S FUNERAL PROCESSION. TAKEN FROM EAST SIDE OF THE HUDSON.

all other officers whose duties would permit them to be present. The Americans noticing the procession, and imagining that some hostile movement was on foot, opened a battery upon them. The balls flew thick and fast, some of them tearing up the ground and scattering the dirt over the participants during the ceremony; but fortunately their aim was high and all the shots went wild.[3]

Burgoyne Describes Fraser's Burial. Burgoyne's eloquent description of the burial of Fraser is well worthy of a place here. He says: "The incessant cannonading during the solemnity, the steady attitude and unaltered voice with which the chaplain officiated, though frequently covered with dust, which the shot threw up on all sides of him, the mute but expressive mixture of sensibility and indignation upon the mind of every man who was present, the growing duskiness added to the scenery, and the whole marked a juncture of such character that would make one of the finest subjects for the pencil of a master that the field ever exhibited. To the canvas and to the pen of a more important historian, gallant friend, I consign thy memory. There may thy talents, thy manly virtues, their progress and their period find due distinction, and long may they survive, after the frail record of my pen shall be forgotten."

Retreat and Delay at Coveville. After the burial service was fittingly closed, Burgoyne issued orders for the retreat, an order sadly at variance with his grandiloquent announcement of three months agone that "this army must not retreat." He felt obliged to leave behind him his hospital, with some four hundred sick and wounded, whom he commended to the tender

---

[3] The old story about the Americans substituting the solemn peal of the minute gun for their savage cannonade, after they learned the nature of the gathering on the hill top, we have found to be entirely **mythical.**

mercies of General Gates and his insurrectionists. His confidence in their humanity was not misplaced, for as soon as he learned of it Gates sent forward a body of light horse to protect the sick and wounded from insult and plunder.

It was nine o'clock before the army got under way. During the night a pouring rain set in, which, together with the inky darkness and the narrow road, and the inability of the poor horses, weakened by starvation, to pull the loads, permitted only a snail's pace movement. Burgoyne reached Dovegat (Coveville) about 4 a. m., the same hour that his rear guard left Wilbur's Basin, or two hours before day, when he ordered a halt. It was generally supposed that this was for the better concentration of the army, and that they would move on again shortly; but, to the unspeakable chagrin and disgust of the whole army, the delay was protracted till 4 p. m. before the retreat was resumed. This was a criminal blunder under the circumstances, for not only was much precious time lost but the continued rain rendered the roads so soft that further movement with his artillery and baggage train was well nigh impossible. As a result he was obliged to abandon most of his tents and camp equipage, which, by the way proved a most acceptable contribution to the comfort of the Americans, who promptly appropriated such as were not too badly damaged by the fire set by Burgoyne's orders.

During this interval of twelve hours the British army was strung along from within a mile of Saratoga to below Coveville, General Riedesel in charge of the advance and General Phillips bringing up the rear.

Digby in his Journal says: "During our march [retreat] it surprised us their not placing troops on the heights we were obliged to pass under, [i. e. the bluffs which for a long way overlook the river flats] as by so

THE STORY OF OLD SARATOGA 159

doing we must have suffered much." Others likewise have wondered much about the same thing. On the 8th a Brigade marched through the woods nearly to Saratoga, and returned. Why were there not other Brigades sent forward to harass the enemy on the 9th? We have not been able to discover any sufficient reason, except rain, and Gates' lack of initiative, for such failure to improve an opportunity.

Woes of the Bateaumen. Burgoyne's bateaumen on their retreat up river were greatly annoyed by the American militiamen, who posted themselves along the bank to waylay them. An interesting writer who, as a boy, native to this locality, followed up Gates' army after the battles " to see what was going on," relates the following incident in this connection: "A few bateaux and scows were passing along as I arrived — they were loaded with military stores, the baggage of the officers, and the women who followed their ' soger laddies.' A few well directed shots brought them to the bank. A rush took place for the prey. Everything was hauled out and carried back into a low swampy place in the rear, and a guard placed over it. When the plunder was divided among the captors, the poor females, trembling with fear, were released and permitted to go off in a boat to the British army, a short distance above. Such a collection of tanned and leathern visages was never before seen. Poorly clad, their garments ragged, and their persons war-worn and weary, those women [4] were objects of my sincere pity."[4]

Lady Ackland's Adventure. While Burgoyne was delaying at Dovegat, there occurred one of

---
[4] There were over 300 women connected with Burgoyne's army.—*Hadden's Journal, p.* 81.
[4a] The Sexagenary.

those incidents which display in the most engaging light the heroic fortitude of womankind under the most trying conditions, particularly in cases where her affections are involved. The heroine on this occasion was the Lady Harriet Ackland, before mentioned, wife of Major John Dyke Ackland, of the grenadiers. She had already nursed him back to health in a miserable hut at Chambly, in Canada, and afterward when she heard that he was wounded at the battle of Hubbardton, Vt., she, contrary to his injunctions, came up the lake to Skenesborough (Whitehall) with the determination not to leave him again. From there she shared his tent through all the vicissitudes of the campaign. Judge then of her state of mind when word was brought from the field that her husband was mortally wounded and a prisoner in the hands of the Americans. After spending two nights and a day in an agony of suspense, she resolved to ask General Burgoyne for permission to go over to the enemy's camp to seek out and care for her husband. She was urged to this step also by the Baroness Riedesel. Burgoyne was astounded by such a request from a woman of her quality at such a time, and especially as she was then in a most delicate condition. Finally he yielded to her importunities, furnished her with a boat and crew, and allowed the chaplain Brudenell [5]—he of the steady nerves — and her husband's valet who still carried a ball

---

[5] The Rev. Edward Brudenell, chaplain to the artillery, was nearly lost in a man-of-war's barge while coming over Lake George, July 27th, in one of those sudden squalls so common on that sheet of water.— *Hadden's Journal, p.* 106.

Major Ackland was a gallant officer and a generous foe. While in New York, on parole, he did all in his power to mitigate the treatment of distinguished American prisoners. After his return to England he sacrificed his life in defence of American honor. At a dinner of military men, the courage of Americans generally was questioned. He repelled the imputation with great energy. High words ensued, in the course of which the lie was passed between him and a subordinate officer named Lloyd. A duel was the consequence, in which the Major was killed. As a result Lady Harriet lost her senses, and continued deranged for two years.

in his shoulder received in the late action, to accompany her, and then armed with a letter of commendation from Burgoyne to Gates, she set out in the edge of evening, during a storm of wind and rain, on her venturesome trip. She reached the American advanced pickets about ten o'clock, and being hailed, went ashore, where she was courteously received and hospitably lodged for the night by Major Dearborn, who was able to relieve her mind with the assurance that her husband was in a most comfortable and hopeful condition. In the morning she passed on down the river to Bemis Heights, where she was met and most graciously received by General Gates, whence she was taken to her husband, who was lodged in the roomy tent of one Joseph Bird. General Burgoyne's letter to Gates in her behalf, though written in haste and on a piece of dirty wet paper, has ever been regarded as a model of gracefulness and point in epistolary literature. Here it is:

"SIR:

Lady Harriet Ackland, a Lady of the first distinction by family, rank, and by personal virtues, is under such concern on account of Major Ackland, her husband, wounded and a prisoner in your hands, that I cannot refuse her request to commit her to your protection.

Whatever general impropriety there may be in persons acting in your situation and mine to solicit favors, I cannot see the uncommon perseverance in every female grace, and exaltation of character of this Lady, and her very hard fortune, without testifying that your attentions to her will lay me under obligation.

I am, Sir,

Your obedient servant,

October 9, 1777.   J. BURGOYNE.
MAJOR GENERAL GATES."

Fellows Anticipates Burgoyne's Retreat to Saratoga. General Gates, in anticipation of an early retreat on the part of Burgoyne had sent forward General Fellows, before the battle of the 7th, with thirteen hundred men to occupy the heights of Saratoga, north of Fish creek (whereon Schuylerville stands) to waylay stragglers and dispute the passage of the creek with any advanced parties of the enemy that might be sent forward. The day after the battle the Americans discovering signs that the British were preparing to decamp, Gates sent two messengers, one on each side of the river, to apprise Fellows of the probable movement and order him to recross the Hudson and defend the ford. This ford was located at the upper end of the island over which the Schuylerville and Greenwich highway bridge now passes. Before this notice reached him General Fellows had a narrow escape from surprise and possible capture.

On the night of the 8th, and some hours before his army started, Burgoyne had sent forward Lieutenant Colonel Sutherland with a scout to make observations. He discovered Fellows' situation, and guided by the fires, he completely encircled his camp without once being challenged. He hastened back and begged Burgoyne to allow him to go on with his regiment and attack him, assuring him that since they lay there unguarded he could capture the whole body. Burgoyne refused peremptorily; but had he permitted it, in all probability, Sutherland would have succeeded. The reasons for the refusal were probably, first, because he had no men to lose, and secondly, he had neither place nor provender for so large a body had they been captured.

At four o'clock p. m. on the 9th, the British army was again set in motion, and wading the now swollen Fish creek, bivouacked wet, shivering and hungry, without tents or covering, on the cold wet ground. They were over just in time to see the rear of General Fellows' detachment ascend the eastern bank of the Hudson and place himself in a position to bar their passage that way and to take possession of their old camp north of the Battenkill. Previously to his withdrawal across the Hudson, Fellows destroyed the bridge over Fish creek.[6]

Burgoyne did not forget to make himself very comfortable that night, though his men were most miserable. He remained on the south side of the creek and occupied the Schuyler mansion, retaining Hamilton's brigade as a body guard. The officers with their men slept on the cold, wet ground, with nothing to protect them but oilcloth. Nor did the wives of the officers fare any better.

Discomforts of the Ladies. Supposing that Burgoyne's advance to Albany would be little else than a triumphal march, with but feeble opposition to overcome, these fine ladies, with adventurous spirit, had come along to enjoy a novel excursion and picnic, and, incidentally, to select for themselves a fine mansion from the estates sure to be confiscated from the rebels. Among these were Lady Ackland, as we have seen, and the Baroness Riedesel, wife of the General (pronounced Re-dáy-zel; the British soldiers called him Red-hazel), a woman of rare culture, intellectual force, and vivacity of spirit, and withal possessed of unusual literary ability. Colonel Wilkinson, Gates' adjutant general, speaks of her as "the amiable, the accomplished and dignified baroness." She was accompanied by her children, three little girls. The oldest was Augusta, 4 years and 7 months; the 2d Frederika, 2 years; and 3d Caroline, 10 weeks old when they started.[7]

---

[6] Digby's Journal, p. 297.

[7] Describing her experience in getting started from home Frau von Riedesel writes: "Not only did the people tell me of the dangers of the sea, but they also said that we must take care not to be eaten by the

Of her experiences on this particular night she writes: "Toward evening, we at last came to Saratoga, which was only half an hour's march from the place where we had spent the whole day. I was wet through and through by the frequent rains, and was obliged to remain in this condition the entire night, as I had no place whatever where I could change my linen. I, therefore, seated myself before a good fire, and undressed my children; after which, we laid ourselves down together upon some straw. I asked General Phillips, who came up to where we were, why we did not continue our retreat while there was yet time, as my husband had pledged himself to cover it, and bring the army through? 'Poor woman,' answered he, 'I am amazed at you! completely wet through, have you still the courage to wish to go further in this weather? Would that you were only our commanding general! He halts because he is tired, and intends to spend the night here, and give us a supper.' In this latter achievement, especially, General Burgoyne was very fond of indulging. He spent half the nights in singing and drinking, and amusing himself with the wife of a commissary, who was his mistress, and who as well as he loved champagne."

The Marshall House Cannonaded. Early in the morning of October 8th, General Gates, expecting that Burgoyne would retreat, had ordered General Bailey, with 900 New Hampshire troops, to cross the Hudson and hasten to the aid of General Fellows, opposite Saratoga. Captain Furnival was ordered to fol-

---

savages; and that the people of America lived on horseflesh and cats. But all this frightened me less than the thought of going to a land where I did not understand the language. However, I made up my mind to everything, and the idea of following my husband and doing my duty, held me up through the whole course of my journey." In these days that would be equal to a wife following her husband on a military expedition into the heart of Africa. The Baroness became the mother of 9 children.

low with his battery. The same evening they were reinforced by a Massachusetts regiment under Colonel Mosley. On the evening of the 9th Captain Furnival was ordered to cross the Battenkill and erect some earthworks. This battery was placed on the hills north of Clark's Mills, and was erected during the night of the 9th of October.[8] General Matoon, then a lieutenant of this company, relates that on the morning of the 10th, "seeing a number of officers on the steps of a house [The Marshall house] opposite, on a hill a little north of the mouth of the Battenkill surveying our works, we opened fire on them. I leveled our guns and with such effect as to disperse them. We took the house to be their headquarters. We continued our fire till a nine or twelve pounder was brought to bear on us, and rendered our works untenable."

This battery, in company with a Massachusetts regiment, was then ordered to Fort Edward to defend the fording place there, which they did effectually till recalled on the 14th, after the armistice was declared.[9] There was no more cannonading from this hill during the siege of Burgoyne.

On the 10th the force of General Fellows on the east side of the Hudson was augmented to three thousand, made up of New Hampshire and Massachusetts troops, chiefly militia.

---

[8] Mr. Hiram Clark of Clark's Mills, told the writer that he could remember the remnants of that work. It consisted of two lengths of heavy timbers, locked together at one end, placed at an obtuse angle, and filled in with dirt behind.

[9] Burgoyne's Campaign, by W. L. Stone, p. 376.

CHAPTER XIV

The Siege

Burgoyne waded Fish creek the morning of the 10th, dragged across his heavy artillery, and seeing that it was now too late to cross the river at the Battenkill, took up the positions he had determined upon on the 14th of September, in case of an attack at that time. He erected a fortified camp on Prospect Hill, or the heights of Saratoga, as it was then called. This camp began north of the house of Counsellor William S. Ostrander, and embraced Prospect Hill Cemetery, also the land between the cemetery and the terrace east of George M. Watson's orchard and extended south into the Victory woods. Part of the 20th, and six companies of the 47th regiment, with the German grenadiers and Berner's battalion, had their camp on the flat where Green and Pearl streets now run and north of Burgoyne street. The German Yägers (riflemen) and Canadians camped each side of the Saratoga road on the flat or terrace above the Boston & Maine R. R. station. The balance of the 20th British regiment, and the Germans under Riedesel, occupied the ground north of Spring street, bounded on the east by Broadway and on the west by a line running north from Dr. Webster's house and reaching toward the Marshall house. The artillery was parked on the spur of high ground east of Broadway and on the continuation of Spring street, now called Seeleyville.

The same day (the 10th) Burgoyne sent forward a working party made up chiefly of loyalists, under Capt. Mackey, to repair roads and bridges, also a detachment of the 47th Regt., all under Lieut. Col. Sutherland. They were also to learn if the enemy had occupied Ft. Edward and, if feasible, to build a bridge and take possession of the fort. Sutherland sent back word that he had met none of the enemy, and that the bridge was already building. His express had not reached Saratoga before the Colonel received orders to return to camp with his force. He at once started with the regulars, but left Mackey with his company to continue work on the bridge. Soon a large party of Americans appeared on the Ft. Edward side and put an end to their bridge building. About then Capt. Mackey and his Provincials, and the few Indians with him, discovered that Canada was a far more attractive place than Saratoga, so they struck for the north. Sutherland was recalled because Burgoyne had been apprised of an attack by the Americans.

Gates Tardy Pursuit. Through some mismanagement in the commissary department, Gates could not immediately follow up the advantage which the victory of the 7th gave him. In consequence of this, his main body was not ready for the pursuit till about noon of the 10th. The road and fields on the way northward were found to be strewed with abandoned wagons and carts, carcasses of horses starved or driven to death, ammunnition, tents and every sort of baggage, all of which had been purposely damaged. Besides this the bridges had been destroyed, and many of the buildings along the way had been burned. Among these were the fine dwelling and all outbuildings of Col. Cornelius Van Veghten at Coveville.

Colonel Wilkinson in his "Memoirs" says: "It rained and the army did not march until the afternoon; our front reached Saratoga about four o'clock, where we discovered the British army encamped on the heights beyond the Fish creek, General Fellows' corps on the opposite bank of the river, and the bateaux of the enemy at the mouth of the creek, with a fatigue party busily employed unloading and conveying their contents across the plain to the heights. The commanding officer of artillery, Major Stevens, ready to improve every advantage, ran a couple of light pieces down on the plain near the river, and opened a battery upon the bateaux and working party at the landing, which soon dispersed it; but he drew the fire of the enemy's whole park upon him from the heights, which obliged him to retire after the loss of a tumbrel, [ammunition cart], which was blown up by a shot from the enemy, and caused a shout from the whole British army."

"The army took a position in the wood on the heights in several lines, their right resting on the brow of the hill, about a mile in the rear of the Fish creek, Colonel Morgan being in front and near the church."[1]

The same authority says that Gates appropriated a small hovel about ten feet square with a dirt floor for his headquarters. It was located at the foot of a hill, along the road something over a mile south of Fish creek. It was probably the older portion of what is now the Edward Dwyer house. [See Note.]

NOTE.—Benson J. Lossing, in his Field Book of the Revolution, asserts that what is now (1900) the Edward Dwyer house was Gates' headquarters. He gives a cut of the house and then adds this: "It is of wood and has been enlarged since the Revolution. It was used by General Gates for his quarters from the 10th of October until after the surrender of Burgoyne,. on the 17th. It belonged to a Widow Kershaw, and General Gates amply compensated her for all he had, on leaving it."

Lossing got his information from Walter Van Veghten, in 1848. Walter was a son of Col. Van Veghten, of Revolutionary fame, and succeeded to the old homestead at Coveville. Despite Wilkinson's statement, several facts make Van Veghten's asser-

---

[1] Wilkinson's Memoirs. Vol. I.

After Gates had posted his army south of the creek, Burgoyne ordered the Schuyler mansion with the mills and other outbuildings, to be set on fire. These with their contents were valued at $50,000.

Gates' Abortive Attack. That same evening (the 10th) word came to Gates that Burgoyne had gone on toward Fort Edward, and that only a guard was left behind with the baggage. His informant had mistaken the two regiments sent ahead for the whole army. Gates at once issued orders for the entire force to cross the creek in the morning and assault the British camp under cover of the fog, which usually rises from the river and remains till after sunrise at that season of the year.

Burgoyne in some way received notice of this proposed assault and posted his men to the best advantage to receive it.

Agreeably to orders, Morgan crossed the creek at Victory Mills, below the old dam at the stone bridge, and advancing through the fog soon fell in with a British picket, which fired and cut down a lieutenant and two privates. This led him to think that there must be some

---

tion altogether probable. It is the uniform testimony of other writers that at the time of the surrender, Gates had his quarters much nearer the front. This would indicate that he must have moved up after negotiations had opened to avoid loss of time in transmission of dispatches. Since Wilkinson does not mention this removal, which must have occurred, it is quite probable that he in writing his Memoirs some years later, got the two places mixed in his mind, and in his story transferred the "hovel" down to where the house stands, which, according to Lossing, was but a small affair at the time. Walter Van Veghten was in a position to know the facts, and being an intelligent and also a prominent citizen, was not liable to be in error as to such a matter.

mistake about the retreat of the British, which misgiving he reported to Colonel Wilkinson, who came up at this moment. As a result Generals Learned and Patterson were sent to his support with their brigades.

Wilkinson then hastening down to the right, learned from a deserter, and from a squad of thirty-five of the enemy just captured, that Burgoyne had not retreated, but was posted and awaiting the American attack. At once he dispatched an aide to Gates with the message: "Tell the General, that his own fame and the interests of the cause are at hazard; that his presence is necessary with the troops." But in obedience to orders, Nixon's and part of Glover's brigades had forded the creek and were deploying for action; Captain Nathan Goodale,[2] of Putnam's regiment, swung to the right and captured a party of sixty men at the mouth of the creek and also the bateaux they were guarding. Suddenly the fog lifted and disclosed to their astonished gaze the whole British army drawn up and ready to give them a fiery greeting. They at once opened with musketry and cannon upon the Americans who, realizing their ugly situation at a glance, broke for the south side of the creek, without much regard as to the order of their going.

Wilkinson fearing that the left might be badly entrapped, hastened up and found Morgan and Learned within two hundred yards of Burgoyne's strongest position on Prospect Hill, and just entering ground which had been cleared by the enemy in front of their works. He found Learned near the center and begged him to

---

[2] This Capt. Nathan Goodale was one of the most efficient of Gates' scouts. He gave Gates the first reliable information concerning the situation of Burgoyne's army during its advance as it lay along the river opposite and above Saratoga. Before the surrender of the British army, no less than 121 prisoners fell into his hand. In 1899 a descendant of Captain Goodale erected a tablet to his memory on Prospect Hill, near the monument. He was killed by the Indians, in Ohio, in 1790.

halt, which he did. Wilkinson said to him (quoting from his Memoirs), "'You must retreat,' Learned asked me, 'have you orders?' I answered, 'I have not, as the exigency of the case did not allow me time to see General Gates.' He observed, 'Our brethren are engaged on the right, and the standing order is *to attack*.' I informed him 'our troops on the right have retired, and the fire you hear is from the enemy;' and, I added, 'although I have no orders for your retreat, I pledge my life for the General's approbation.'" Several field officers coming up and approving the proposition, the order for the retreat was given. They were hardly turned when the British, who had been quietly awaiting the assault, fired a volley and killed several men, among whom was an officer.

Thus Gates got out of a tight place, and escaped dire disaster, by a very narrow margin. Had he been the great general that his friends pictured him, he would not have ordered such an attack without knowing for a certainty whether the main body of his enemy had decamped or not. He would also have been near the front, when the attack began that he might be able quickly to recall or give new orders as the exigency might demand. For this escape, as for his victories, Gates could thank his subordinates. He never allowed his sacred person to be seen along danger lines if he could avoid it. Only once during the Revolution was he under fire, at Camden, S. C., and then he beat the record in getting away, for he made two hundred miles on horseback in three days.

Burgoyne had hoped great things from this move on the part of Gates, feeling sure that he could annihilate the assaulting force, but was sorely disappointed at the outcome. He described it as "one of the most adverse strokes of fortune during the campaign."

Gates Decides Upon a Regulation Siege. Gates now decided to starve Burgoyne into a surrender by siege, rather than compel him by force of arms as some of his officers urged, thus avoiding much bloodshed. He at once took steps to make sure of his prey by completing his lines of circumvallation. Morgan and his Virginians, Learned's brigade, and a Pennsylvania force occupied the high ground to the west of Burgoyne. Their lines stretched from the creek, up back of the Victory school house, through the French burying ground, in the rear of the house now owned and occupied by Mr. David H. Craw, and along the elevated ridge to the north. The east side of the river was held by New Hampshire, Massachusetts and Connecticut troops, while New York, New England and New Jersey held the south. New Hampshire and Vermont, under the redoubtable Stark, a day or two later filled the gap to the north, and so practically corked the bottle. Thus New England, the Middle and Southern States were all represented at that crucial moment in our national history, and all very appropriately had a share in the decisive stroke that determined the severance of these colonies from the mother country, and assured their independence.

But as late as the 12th there was still a chance for Burgoyne to escape. There was an opening northward on the west side of the river, as it had not yet been occupied by our people. He called a council of his generals, laid the situation before them, and asked their advice. Riedesel strongly urged that they should leave artillery and baggage behind, and, thus lightened, attempt to escape by avoiding Fort Edward, now held by the Americans, cross four miles above, and strike for Ticonderoga through the woods on the west of Lake George. Orders were at once issued to move out that night if the provisions could be distributed by ten or eleven o'clock. Pre-

COLONEL DANIEL MORGAN

cisely at ten o'oclock Riedesel notified Burgoyne that the provisions had been distributed, and everything was ready, when he and all the rest were astonished to receive orders to stay where they were, as it was now too late. What decided him that it was "too late" is not known. But when the morning broke, sure enough, it was too late; for during the night Stark and his men had crossed the river just above the mouth of the Battenkill on rafts, occupied the gap and erected a battery on a hill, (probably the bare one back of Mr. D. A. Bullard's farm buildings). This was the springing of " the trap," about which General Riedesel had talked, the corking of the bottle which sealed the fate of the British army.

They were now completely surrounded. Gates had thrown a floating bridge across the Hudson below Fish creek. The approach to this bridge was just below the mouth of the deep ditch that runs east from Chubb's bridge. This gave easy communication with Fellows to the east; and on this with the raft just built above, Gates could pass in safety all around his foe, if he dared.

The Americans now made it very warm for the Britons. Fellows' batteries on the bluffs, east of the river, were echoed by Gates' from the heights south of Victory, and then the new battery on the hill to the north bellowed Amen! we are with you! while Morgan's sharpshooters to the west, and the Yankee marksmen everywhere else popped at any hostile head that dared show itself from behind a tree, or above the breastworks. All this, with the answering thunder of Burgoyne's heavy artillery, must have made terrific music, such as these Saratoga hills never heard before nor since.

Woes of the Besieged. The experiences of those shut within this fiery and thunderous arena whereon Schuylerville now stands, must have been appalling beyond description. There were but few places of safety except behind trees, in a few hollows, or immediately behind breastworks. Hundreds of dead horses and oxen lay everywhere, which had been killed by cannon or musket shots, or which had died from starvation. Without hospital tents or any hospital conveniences, the sick and wounded soldiers would drag themselves to some sheltered spot and there breathe out their lives in agony on the cold, damp ground. There were but few places where the surgeons could dress the wounds without being interrupted by cannon shot dropping or crashing through the trees. Fellows' battery on the bluffs opposite Schuylerville was especially annoying to the British, and they were unable to silence it. It was from thence that the Marshall house was chiefly cannonaded;[3] from there the shot was fired that carried off the ham from Burgoyne's table, and so broke up one of his dinner parties,[4] and thence the cannon ball came that lodged in an oak tree by the side of which General Burgoyne was standing.[5] No soldier dare lay aside his arms even to sleep. There was constant firing on the picket lines, and a man on duty there hardly dared show himself from behind a tree, or his head above a rifle pit, lest a whistling bullet should perforate him. And though there were rivers of water all about, yet for those beleaguered Britons there was hardly a drop to drink. A few springs and the rivulets running down the hills could not supply the needs of six thousand men with their horses and cattle. Any man who attempted to reach the creek or river became a mark for a dozen rifles. Some of the wives of the common soldiers risked a trip to the river with their buckets for water, and found the

---

[3] See Baroness Riedesel's account, which immediately follows.
[4] Burgoyne's State of the Expedition. Edition of 1780, p. 55.
[5] Digby's Journal, p. 304.

Americans too chivalrous to harm a woman. And, by the way, there were no braver hearts in that army than beat in the breasts of those women. Baroness de Riedesel tells of one who supplied the occupants of the Marshall house, and how they rewarded her.

Baroness Riedesel Relates Her Experiences. The account given by that most estimable lady of her experiences in the Marshall house are of so interesting and thrilling a character that we should wrong our readers not to allow her to tell them her own story. She proved herself to be a veritable angel of mercy to those poor officers and men, yes a forerunner of Florence Nightingale, Clara Barton and the Red Cross. She writes:

"About two o'clock in the afternoon [of the 10th], the firing of cannon and small arms was again heard, and all was alarm and confusion. My husband sent me a message telling me to betake myself forthwith into a house not far from there. I seated myself in the calash with my children, and had scarcely driven up to the house when I saw on the opposite side of the Hudson river five or six men with guns, which were aimed at us. Almost involuntarily I threw the children on the bottom of the calash and myself over them. At the same instant the churls fired, and shattered the arm of a poor English soldier behind us, who was already wounded and was also retreating into the house. Immediately after our arrival a frightful cannonade began, principally directed against the house in which we had sought shelter, probably because the enemy believed, from seeing so many people flocking around it, that all the generals made it their headquarters.[6] Alas! it harbored none but wounded soldiers, or women! We were finally obliged to take

---
[6] This was from Furnival's battery, north of the Battenkill.

THE BARONESS RIEDESEL

refuge in a cellar, in which I laid myself down in a corner not far from the door. My children lay down on the earth with their heads upon my lap, and in this manner we passed the entire night. A horrible stench, the cries of the children, and yet more than all this, my own anguish, prevented me from closing my eyes. On the following morning [the 11th], the cannonade again began, but on a different side.[7] I advised all to go out of the cellar for a little while, during which time I would have it cleaned, as otherwise we would all be sick. They followed my suggestion, and I at once set many hands to work, which was in the highest degree necessary; for the women and children being afraid to venture forth, had soiled the whole cellar. After they had all gone out and left me alone, I for the first time surveyed our place of refuge. It consisted of three beautiful cellars, splendidly arched. I proposed that the most dangerously wounded of the officers should be brought into one of them; that the women should remain in another; and that all the rest should stay in the third, which was nearest the entrance. I had just given the cellars a good sweeping, and had fumigated them by sprinkling vinegar on burning coals, and each one had found his place prepared for him—when a fresh and terrible cannonade threw us all once more into alarm. Many persons, who had no right to come in, threw themselves against the door. My children were already under the cellar steps, and we would all have been crushed, if God had not given me strength to place myself before the door, and with extended arms prevent all from coming in; otherwise every one of us would have been severely injured. Eleven cannon balls went through the house, and we could plainly hear them rolling over our heads. One poor sol-

---

[7] This was from Fellow's battery, opposite Schuylerville and south of the Battenkill. Furnival's battery had been ordered to Fort Edward.

ORIGINAL MARSHALL HOUSE
REFUGE OF BARONESS RIEDESEL AND THE WOUNDED OFFICERS

CELLAR IN MARSHALL HOUSE

dier [a British surgeon by the name of Jones], whose leg they were about to amputate, having been laid upon a table for this purpose, had the other leg taken off by another cannon ball, in the midst of the operation. His comrades all ran off, and when they again came back they found him in one corner of the room, where he had rolled in his anguish, scarcely breathing. I was more dead than alive, though not so much on account of our own danger, as for that which enveloped my husband, who, however, frequently sent to see how I was getting along, and to tell me that he was still safe.

" The wife of Major Harnage, a Madam Reynels, the wife of the good lieutenant who the day previous had so kindly shared his broth with me, the wife of a commissary, and myself, were the only ladies who were with the army.[8] We sat together bewailing our fate, when one came in, upon which they all began whispering, looking at the same time exceedingly sad. I noticed this, and also that they cast silent glances toward me. This awakened in my mind the dreadful thought that my husband had been killed. I shrieked aloud, but they assured me that this was not so, at the same time intimating to me by signs, that it was the lieutenant—the husband of our companion—who had met with misfortune. A moment after she was called out. Her husband was not yet dead, but a cannon ball had taken off his arm close to the shoulder. During the whole night we heard his moans, which resounded fearfully through the vaulted cellars. The poor man died toward morning. We spent the remainder of this night as the former ones. In the meantime my husband came to visit me, which lightened my anxiety and gave me fresh courage. On the following morning [the 12th], however, we got things better regulated. Major Harnage, his wife, and Mrs. Reynels

[8] Seventy soldiers brought their wives with them also.

made a little room in a corner, by hanging curtains from the ceiling. They wished to fix up for me another corner in the same manner, but I preferred to remain near the door, so that in case of fire I could rush out from the room. I had some straw brought in and laid my bed upon it, where I slept with my children—my maids sleeping not far from us. Directly opposite us three English officers were quartered—wounded it is true, but, nevertheless resolved not to be left behind in case of a retreat. One of these was Captain Green, aide-de-camp of General Phillips, a very valuable and agreeable man. All three assured me, upon their oaths, that in case of a hasty retreat, they would not leave me, but would each take one of my children upon his horse. For myself one of my husband's horses constantly stood saddled and in readiness. Often my husband wished to withdraw me from danger, by sending me to the Americans; but I remonstrated with him on the ground that to be with people whom I would be obliged to treat with courtesy, while perhaps, my husband was being killed by them, would be even yet more painful than all I was now suffering. He promised me, therefore, that I should henceforward follow the army. Nevertheless, I was often in the night filled with anxiety lest he should march away. At such times I have crept out of my cellar to reassure myself, and if I saw the troops lying around the fires, (for the nights were already cold), I would return and sleep quietly. On the third day, I found an opportunity for the first time to change my linen, as my companions had the courtesy to give up to me a little corner; the three wounded officers meanwhile standing guard not far off.

"Our cook saw to our meals, but we were in want of water; and in order to quench our thirst, I was often obliged to drink wine, and give it also to the children. The continued danger in which my husband was encompassed, was a constant source of anxiety to me. I was the only one of all the women whose husband had not been killed or wounded, and I often said to myself—'shall I be the only fortunate one?'

"As the great scarcity of water continued, we at last found a soldier's wife who had the courage to bring water from the river, for no one else would undertake it, as the enemy shot at every man who approached the river. This woman, however, they never molested; and they told us afterward that they spared her on account of her sex.

"I endeavored to divert my mind from my troubles, by constantly busying myself with the wounded. I made them tea and coffee, and received in return a thousand benedictions. Often, also, I shared my noon day meal with them. One day a Canadian officer came into our cellar who could scarcely stand up. We at last got it out of him that he was almost dead with hunger. I considered myself very fortunate to have it in my power to offer him my mess. This gave him renewed strength, and gained for me his friendship. One of our greatest annoyances was the stench of the wounds when they began to suppurate.

"One day I undertook the care of Major Bloomfield, adjutant to General Phillips, through both of whose cheeks a small musket ball had passed, shattering his teeth and grazing his tongue. He could hold nothing whatever in his mouth. The matter from the wound almost choked him, and he was unable to take any other nourishment except a little broth, or something liquid. We had Rhine wine. I gave him a bottle of it, in hopes that the acidity of the wine would cleanse his wound. He kept some continually in his mouth; and that alone acted so beneficially that he became cured, and I again acquired one more friend.

"In this horrible situation we remained six days. Finally, they spoke of capitulating, as by temporizing for so long a time, our retreat had been cut off. A cessation of hostilities took place, and my husband, who was thoroughly worn out, was able for the first time in a long while to lie down upon a bed.

"On the 17th of October the capitulation was consummated. Now the good woman who had brought us water at the risk of her life, received the reward of her services. Everyone threw a handful of money into her apron, and she received altogether over twenty guineas. At such a moment the heart seems to be specially susceptible of gratitude."

CHAPTER XV

THE CAPITULATION.—BURGOYNE SUMMONS COUNCIL OF WAR

BURGOYNE knowing himself to be surrounded by overwhelming numbers; for the American militia had been pouring in from everywhere since the battles; called a council of war on the 13th, laid the situation before it, and inquired if in its opinion a proposition to surrender would be warranted by precedent, and would it be honorable. The council agreed that surrender was the wisest course. They were doubtless urged to this conclusion by a forceful argument in the shape of a cannon ball that swept across the table about which they were sitting.

Accordingly General Burgoyne sent a flag of truce asking if Gates would receive a "field officer from him, on a matter of high moment to both armies." Gates replied that he would receive such an officer at 10 o'clock the next morning, the 14th. Major Robert Kingston, of Burgoyne's staff, was selected to bear the message to Gates. The next morning at the appointed hour Kingston descended the hill, and, crossing the creek on some sleepers of the bridge that had been left, was met there by Colonel Wilkinson, who represented Gates, and who, after blindfolding him, conducted him on foot down to headquarters, over a mile away.

Burgoyne Sues for an Armistice. Through him Burgoyne asked for a cessation of hostilities while terms might be arranged for an honorable surrender. General Gates sent back the terms on which he would accept the surrender of the British army, and granted a cessation of hostilities during the negotiations. Gates' terms seemed to offend the pride of Burgoyne and his generals, who thereupon refused point blank to treat upon such conditions. The offensive articles were, first: that the British should surrender as prisoners of war; and, second: that they should lay down their arms within their intrenchments at the command of their adjutant general.

At sunset Burgoyne returned Gates' propositions with the answer that he and his army would die to a man rather than submit to conditions involving such humiliation. Along with this answer he presented the terms on which he would consent to a surrender. Gates, evidently frightened by the news just received that Sir Henry Clinton had broken through the obstructions and had passed the forts in the Highlands; that he had destroyed Kingston, and was advancing upon Albany, tamely accepted Burgoyne's proposals, and thus allowed the British general to dictate his own terms.

Terms of Surrender Agreed Upon. But before any treaty could be signed, there were several subordinate questions and items which must be settled; for this purpose two men from each side were selected, at Burgoyne's suggestion, who were to meet at some convenient place, to be selected, to arrange the final terms. A tent was pitched upon the bluff, just south of the Horicon mill, where the representatives met and, after due discussion, signed and exchanged the articles of capitulation, and moreover agreed when they separated, at 8 p. m. of the 15th, that their respective chiefs should sign and exchange in the morning. Burgoyne expressed himself as well pleased with everything, but objected to calling the instrument a "treaty of capitulation;" he would term it a TREATY OF CONVENTION. To this also Gates agreed.

During the night of the 15th, a spy managed to get through to the British camp with the news that Clinton was on the way with relief, and was now nearing Albany. Burgoyne saw here a ray of hope, and the next morning called another general council of his officers, told them what he had heard, and asked whether in their opinion he would be justified, under the circumstances, in repudiating his agreement with the American General. The majority decided that the public faith had been pledged, and therefore voted that it would be dishonorable to abrogate the treaty. However, instead of signing the Convention, as he had agreed, he sent Gates an evasive letter, in which he charged him with having reduced his army since negotiations were opened, and asked that two of his officers might be permitted to inspect his army, that he might know if it was as large as reported. Gates was evidently nettled by the rudeness and impudence of the request, but sent Wilkinson to allay Burgoyne's apprehensions. This parley was spun out to such a length that finally Gates, who had just heard of the burning of Kingston by the British, got impatient, drew up his army, and sent Burgoyne word that he must either sign or fight. Burgoyne, urged by his generals, came down from his perch, on Prospect Hill, signed the Convention and sent it over to Gates in proper form.

And let us never, never, forget that this was wholly an American victory; foreign elements had little or nothing to do with it. With the exception of Gates, a mere figurehead, native born soldiers, led by native born officers, fought all the battles that culminated at Saratoga. For the first time in her history proud old England here surrendered an army, and that to a host of embattled farmers, the sort of men her ruling classes, then and for long, regarded with lordly contempt. A French fleet and a French army helped round up Cornwallis at Yorktown.

Articles of Convention

The instrument as finally agreed to and executed is herewith subjoined.

Articles of Convention between Lieutenant-General Burgoyne and Major-General Gates.

I.

"The troops under Lieutenant-General Burgoyne, to march out of their camp with the honors of war, and the artillery of the intrenchments, to the verge of the river where the old fort stood, where the arms and artillery are to be left; the arms are to be piled by word of command from their own officers."

II.

"A free passage to be granted to the army under Lieutenant-General Burgoyne to Great Britain, on condition of not serving again in North America during the present contest; and the port of Boston is assigned for the entry of transports to receive the troops whenever General Howe shall so order."

III.

"Should any cartel take place, by which the army under General Burgoyne, or any part of it, may be exchanged, the foregoing article to be void as far as such exchange shall be made."

IV.

"The army under Lieutenant-General Burgoyne, to march to Massachusetts Bay, by the easiest, most expeditious and convenient route; and to be quartered in, near, or as convenient as possible to Boston, that the march of the troops may not be delayed when transports arrive to receive them."

V.

"The troops to be supplied on their march, and during their being in quarters, with provisions by General Gates' orders at the same rate of rations as the troops of his own army; and if possible, the officers' horses and cattle are to be supplied with forage at the usual rates."

ELM TREE UNDER WHICH BURGOYNE SIGNED THE CONVENTION

VI.

"All officers to retain their carriages, batt-horses and other cattle, and no baggage to be molested or searched; Lieutenant-General Burgoyne giving his honor that there are no public stores secreted therein. Major-General Gates will, of course, take the necessary measures for the due performance of this article. Should any carriages be wanted during the march for the transportation of officers' baggage, they are, if possible, to be supplied by the country at the usual rates."

VII.

"Upon the march, and during the time the army shall remain in quarters in Massachusetts Bay, the officers are not, as far as circumstances will admit, to be separated from their men. The officers are to be quartered according to rank, and are not to be hindered from assembling their men for roll call, and other necessary purposes of regularity."

VIII.

"All corps whatever, of General Burgoyne's army, whether composed of sailors, bateaumen, artificers, drivers, independent companies, and followers of the army, of whatever country, shall be included in the fullest sense and utmost extent of the above articles, and comprehended in every respect as British subjects."

IX.

"All Canadians and persons belonging to the Canadian establishment, consisting of sailors, bateaumen, artificers, drivers, independent companies, and many other followers of the army, who come under no particular description, are to be permitted to return there; they are to be conducted immediately by the shortest route to the first British post on Lake George, are to be supplied with provisions in the same manner as the other troops, and are to be bound by the same condition of not serving during the present contest in North America."

X.

"Passports to be immediately granted for three officers, not exceeding the rank of captain, who shall be appointed by Lieutenant-General Burgoyne, to carry dispatches to Sir William Howe, Sir Guy Carleton, and to Great Britain, by the way of New York; and Major-General Gates engages the public faith, that these despatches shall not be opened. These officers are to set out immediately after receiving their despatches, and are to travel the shortest and in the most expeditious manner."

XI.

"During the stay of the troops in Massachusetts Bay the officers are to be admitted on parole, and are to be allowed to wear their side arms."

XII.

"Should the army under Lieutenant-General Burgoyne find it necessary to send for their clothing and other baggage to Canada, they are to be permitted to do it in the most convenient manner, and the necessary passports granted for that purpose."

XIII.

"These articles are to be mutually signed and exchanged to-morrow morning at nine o'clock, and the troops under Lieutenant-General Burgoyne are to march out of their intrenchments at three o'clock in the afternoon."

    (Signed) "HORATIO GATES, Major-General.
    (Signed) " J. BURGOYNE, Lieutenant-General.
" Saratoga, Oct. 16th, 1777."

THE SURRENDER

" All was decided here, and at this hour
 Our sun leaped up, though clouds still veiled its power.
 From Saratoga's hills we date the birth,—
 Our Nation's birth among the powers of earth.
 Not back to '76, New Yorkers' date:
 The mighty impulse launched our ' Ship of State '
 'Twas given here—where shines our rising sun
 Excelsior! These hills saw victory won.
 This vale the cradle where the colonies
 Grew into States—despite all enemies,
 Yes, on this spot—Thanks to our gracious God
 Where last in conscious arrogance it trod,
 Defil'd as captives Burgoyne's conquered horde;
 Below their general yielded up his sword,
 There to our flag bowed England's, battle-torn.
 Where now we stand th' United States was born."
         —*J. Watts De Peyster.*[1]

As the echoes of the sunrise gun reverberated through the valley, on that eventful morning of the 17th of October, it awoke within the breasts of the thirty thousand warriors encamped within and about the arena whereon Schuylerville now stands, emotions as diverse as the antipodes. On the one hand was the sense of utter defeat and humiliation, on the other was felt the very ecstasy of lofty achievement and success.

This was a high day in liberty's history, a red-letter date in the annals of human progress, and, that there should be no lack of artistic setting worthy of the occa-

---

[1] From ODE read at the laying of the corner-stone of the Saratoga monument, October 17, 1877.

sion, dame Nature had decked herself in her most gorgeous apparel. It was one of the rarest of those rare Autumnal days when all the elements seem to conspire to give a witching charm to the calm landscapes of October. The progress of the month had been like the stately march of an Orient army, with all the splendor of blazing banners, and the wealth and pageantry of olden story. The forest primeval, then regnant here, looked as though the glories of the sunset had been distilled into it. Here and there were clusters of trees, decked with the glowing hues of crimson and scarlet and gold, that lighted up those ancient woods like pillars of fire. The scarlet uniform of the Briton and the blue and white of the Teuton, fitted admirably into this picture of beauty; but neither showy uniforms nor their proud wearers had availed against the embattled farmers, innocent of all uniform save the uniformity of homespun, and zeal for liberty.

But, alas! to the vanquished this autumnal glory was only the glory of fading leaves, the hectic flush that presages a speedy dissolution, the approach of a barren and cheerless winter. And as the haughty Briton looked out upon the scene, from the heights of Saratoga, he could exclaim with the still more haughty Roman of old: "Sic transit gloria mundi." As fades these leaves, so fade the glory and prestige of British arms amid this people; as fall the leaves, so this day must witness the fall of these puissant weapons from our grasp, and here comes on apace "The winter of our discontent."

To the American, on the contrary, the scene was suggestive of far brighter things; for recalling that every falling leaf leaves behind it a fully-developed bud which the coming spring will awaken to a larger life, so the fall of British power and pride here gave room and occasion for the rise of a nobler and broader civic life,

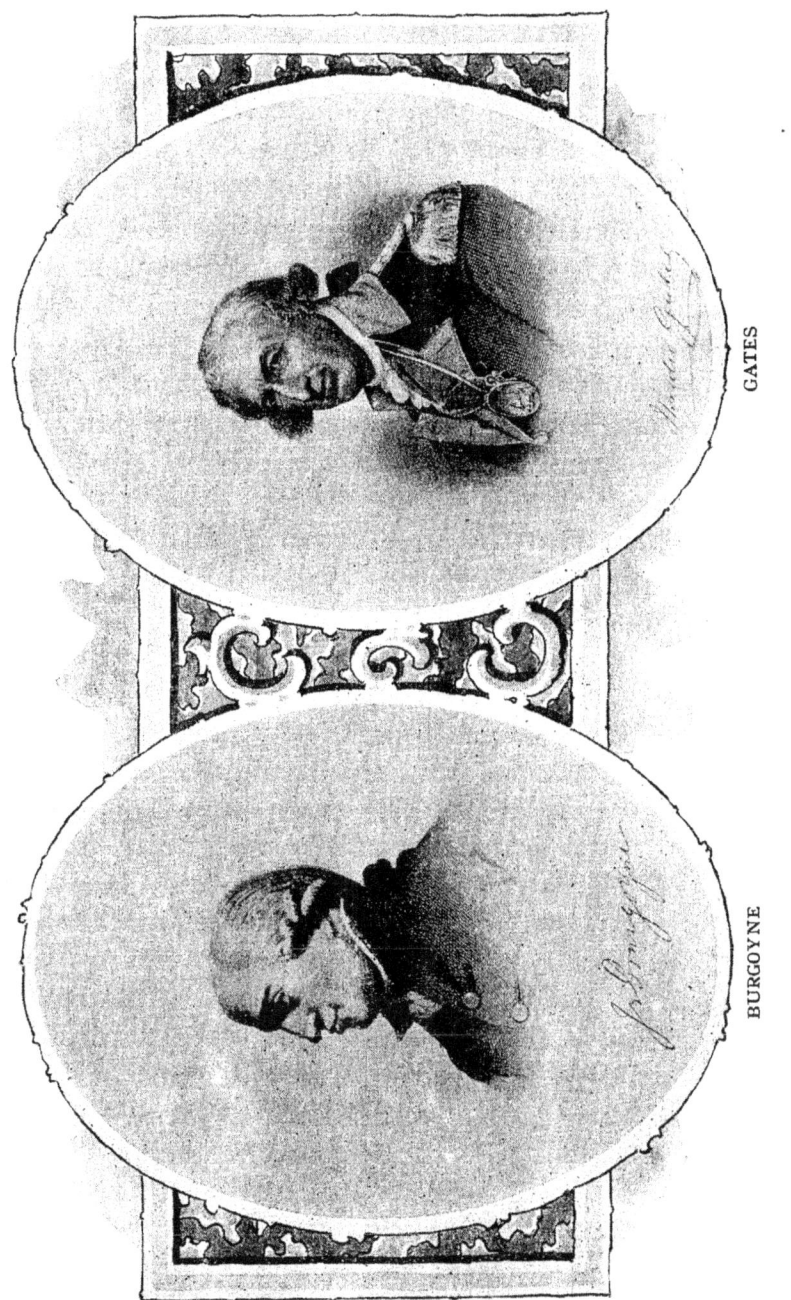

GATES

BURGOYNE

which the rising sun of freedom would surely quicken and nourish into a grandeur as yet undreamed.

The Formal Surrender. In the early hours of that day Colonel Wilkinson had been dispatched by General Gates to the British camp, to wait upon General Burgoyne and serve him in any way that courtesy might suggest. Burgoyne having arrayed himself in his most showy regimentals, mounted his horse and, together with Wilkinson, visited and inspected the ground where his army was to lay down their arms. From there they rode out to the bank of the river, which he surveyed attentively for a few moments, and then inquired if it was not fordable there. "Certainly, sir!" was the reply, "but do you observe the people on the opposite bank?" "Yes," replied he, "I have observed them too long."

He then suggested that he be introduced to General Gates. At once they wheeled, retraced their steps and crossed the Fish creek at the ford, General Burgoyne in the lead with his staff, followed by General Phillips and the Baron de Riedesel, with the other General officers and their respective suites according to rank. Says Wilkinson: "General Gates, advised of Burgoyne's approach, met him at the head of his camp, Burgoyne in a rich royal uniform, and Gates in a plain blue frock. When they had approached nearly within sword's length they reined up and halted; I then named the gentlemen and General Burgoyne, raising his hat most gracefully, said: 'The fortune of war, General Gates, has made me your prisoner,' to which the conqueror replied, 'I shall always be ready to bear testimony that it has not been through any fault of your excellency.' Major-General Phillips then advanced and he and General Gates saluted and shook hands. Next the Baron Riedesel and the other officers were introduced in their turn, and as soon as the ceremony was concluded I left the army and returned to the British camp." Gates' leading officers were now in their turn introduced. With them also appeared General Schuyler, in citizen's dress, who had come up from Albany to congratulate Gates on his success, and share in the delights, if not the honors, of the occasion. When Col. Morgan was presented Burgoyne took his hand and said: "Sir, you command the finest regiment in the world." As to that matter Burgoyne was just about then fully competent to judge.

In the meantime General Riedesel had sent for his wife, who came over to the enemy's camp with much fear and trembling, but met with a reception which soon allayed her apprehensions and quite won her heart. Let her tell her own story, for she takes occasion to eulogize and exalt one whose memory Schuylerville especially delights to honor. Says she: "In our passage through the American camp, I observed with great satisfaction that no one cast at us scornful glances. On the contrary, they all greeted me, even showing compassion on their countenances at seeing a mother with her little children in such a plight. I confess I feared to come into the enemy's camp, as the thing was so entirely new to me. When I approached the tents a noble-looking man came toward me and took the children out of the wagon, embraced and kissed them, and then, with tears in his eyes, helped me also to alight. He then led me to the tent of General Gates, with whom I found Generals Burgoyne and Phillips. Presently, the man who had received me so kindly, came up and said to me: 'It may be embarrassing to you to dine with all these gentlemen; come now with your children into my tent where I will give you, it is true, a frugal meal, but one that will be accompanied with the best of wishes.' 'You are certainly,' answered I, 'a husband and a father, for you show me so much kindness.' I then learned that he was the American General Schuyler."

At eleven a. m. the British army left its camp, marched down the hill to the flat and piled their arms just to the east of the Champlain canal. General Matoon, who afterward inspected them, said that the piles reached from near the creek to the vicinity of the Marshall house. The only Americans present to witness this part of the program were Colonels Wilkinson and Morgan Lewis, who had been appointed by Gates for this purpose.

It was with dread reluctance that those brave men parted with their weapons. Some, with tears in their eyes, kissed them as they gave them up; some gnashed their teeth and slammed them down with vengeful oaths; while others ruined their muskets or stamped in their drum heads.

Lieutenant Digby, in his Journal of the Expedition (p. 320), describes the grief of heart exhibited by the officers on the eve of the surrender. In the last council of war Burgoyne could with difficulty control himself sufficiently to speak. "As to my own feelings," says he, "I cannot express them. Tears (though unmanly) forced their way. I could have burst to give myself vent."

After leaving "the field of the grounded arms," the captured army forded the creek, and at once passed between the lines of the American army, which had been drawn up on either side of the road. But no shout of exultation greeted them, neither taunting word nor scornful look wounded their feelings, at which they were greatly astonished, and for which they afterward confessed themselves as profoundly grateful. This was by the order of General Gates; a most considerate and humane act, by which he greatly honored himself and his army. They were, however, met by an escort of soldiers and a drum corps, which could not refrain from administering a small dose of poetic justice to these captive Britons in the form of that good old martial tune, "Yankee Doodle." The words, and perhaps the tune, had been composed by a British humorist during the French and Indian war in mockery of the variegated and ludicrous costumes of the provincial troops and citizenship. It was sure to be played whenever a colonial regiment marched by on parade. It had been British property exclusively till Saratoga, and now the waggish drum-major thought it a good time to put "Yankee Doodle" on the other foot. It took so well with our people that it was immediately adopted as an American martial air. [See note.]

In the volume, "Letters of Hessian Officers," we learn how their conquerors looked to them: "We passed the enemies' encampment in front of all their regiments. Not a man of them was regularly equipped. Each one had on the clothes he was accustomed to wear in the field, to the tavern, and in every day life. Few of the officers in Gen. Gates' army wore uniform, and those that were worn were evidently homemade, and of all

---

NOTE.—During the Albany Bi-Centennial celebration "The Argus" gave a brief sketch of the "Crailo," the old Van Rensselaer homestead in Greenbush. In that sketch the writer says: "It was in the rear of this mansion that Yankee Doodle was composed. While Abercombie's army was encamped there [in 1758] by the old sweep well at the rear of the house, waiting for reinforcements, the country people came straggling in, in all manner of costumes and dress. Their ludicrous appearance so excited the humor of a British surgeon [Dr. R. Shuckburg] that he, while sitting by the bed, composed the original version of 'Yankee Doodle,' words and music both." It is worth noting in this connection that the above Dr. Shuckburg, in 1754, was a surgeon in Capt. (General) Horatio Gates' Independent Co. of New York. He was afterward nominated by Sir Wm. Johnson as Secretary of Indian Affairs for Northern New York.

colors. For example, brown coats with sea green facings, white linings, and silver dragons, and gray coats with yellow buttons and straw facings, were to be seen in plenty. All the men who stood in array before us were so slender, fine looking, and sinewy, that it was a pleasure to look at them."

It is also worthy of special note, that at the same time and place our American flag, Old Glory, was unfurled for the first time at army headquarters and also to grace a victory. It had been adopted by the Continental Congress, June 14th, of that year. [See note.]

After the meeting of the Generals, and their mutual introduction, dinner was served in the marquee, or tent, of General Gates, which he had had pitched nearer the advanced lines during the negotiations. It was not a full course dinner, but, no doubt, those half-starved captives never afterward enjoyed anything more toothsome. Burgoyne magnanimously drank the health of Washington, whereat Gates, not to be outdone, drank to King George.

Dinner being over, they stepped outside, and for a

NOTE.—Regarding this flag the following facts were communicated to the writer by Mr. E. R. Mann, of Ballston, N. Y., an enthusiastic student of American history. They were related to him by Mr. George Strover, in 1877, who got the story from his father, who was a resident in the neighborhood, at the time, and was present at the surrender of Burgoyne. "When it became apparent that Burgoyne must surrender, the ladies of the settlement and the wives of some of the American officers took their flannel petticoats, etc., of the required colors, and made them into a United States flag, having heard of the adoption of the Stars and Stripes, in the preceding June, by the Continental Congress. They presented it to General Gates, and when, on October 17th, Burgoyne approached Gates' marquee to make the formal surrender, that flag was hoisted to the top of the staff and the fifes and drums saluted it with 'Yankee Doodle.'"

time watched the royal army as it passed by toward Stillwater. Then at a pre-arranged signal, the two generals faced each other, when General Burgoyne drew his sword and presented it to General Gates, in view of the two armies. Gates received it with due courtesy, and in a few minutes returned it to Burgoyne. General Schuyler witnessed this ceremony, and no doubt felt that in all justice that sword should have been placed in his hands.

On this occasion Schuyler showed his rare exaltation of character and magnanimity, when General Burgoyne expressed to him his regret at the great loss he had inflicted upon him in the destruction of his property, valued at $50,000. To which he replied: "Think no more of it, General, the occasion justified it according to the rules of war." And after all this, he opened his fine home in Albany to Burgoyne and a suite of twenty persons, and made him a welcome guest so long as he stayed in that city.

The number of prisoners surrendered amounted to five thousand seven hundred and ninety-one. Four of the eleven on General Burgoyne's staff were members of Parliament. Besides these our people already had eighteen hundred and fifty-six prisoners, including the sick and wounded, which had been abandoned to the Americans. The American force which, as we have already seen, had been rapidly augmenting during the last few weeks, at the time of the surrender was composed of nine thousand and ninety-three Continentals, or regular soldiers, and some sixteen thousand militia, in all about twenty-five thousand men. Hence there were assembled here in the wilderness, on that day of grace, over thirty thousand soldiers, besides the camp followers and civilian visitors, who had flocked hither to witness the last act in that heroic drama. It is also worthy of note

SURRENDER OF BURGOYNE

that the largest American army mustered during the Revolutionary war was assembled here at that time. [See note.]

Saratoga a Decisive Battle—Why? Historians by common consent regard the battle of Saratoga as one of the few decisive battles in history. The average reader will naturally inquire: What is meant by a decisive battle, and what did Saratoga decide? Hallam, a great English historian, in his " Middle Ages " defines decisive battles as "those battles of which a contrary event would have essentially varied the drama of the world in all its subsequent scenes." Mr. E. S. Creasy, late professor of history in the University College of London, acting on this suggestion found only fifteen among the thousands of battles that have been fought that answer to Hallam's standard; the first was Marathon, fought 490 B. C., the last was Waterloo, fought in 1815. The one preceding this in his list is Saratoga. Of it he says: " Nor can any military event be said to have exercised more important influence on the

---

NOTE.—After the battle of Saratoga, Captain John VanPatten, of Col. Wemple's regiment, was publicly commended for his bravery, and as a further tribute to his worth was, on Oct. 17th, honored with the charge of conveying the official dispatches to Albany, announcing the surrender of Burgoyne. He died in 1809, and is buried in the town of Charlton, Saratoga Co., on the farm that was the home of his family at the time of the battle. It is veritable family history that here, huddled at their mother's knees, the children of Capt. VanPatten listened in fear to the booming of cannon to the eastward, telling with clamorous tongues of the battle in progress, in which their father and three uncles were taking an active part.

The sword carried by Capt. VanPatten is now in the possession of a great-great-grandson, Percy VanEpps, a prominent citizen of Glenville, Schenectady Co., N. Y., who gave the author the facts.

future fortunes of mankind than the complete defeat of Burgoyne's expedition in 1777." Take notice: that is the judgment of an Englishman! Momentous indeed were the results that followed upon Saratoga in which all the world is interested.

But the skeptical might naturally ask: How could such a little, beggarly, affray as that, fought in the woods, and by so few men, ever be classed as a battle of such great moment to the world? Well, sure enough, in point of mere size or bulk, a matter of 3,000 men in each of the fighting lines, and a battle front of only half a mile, seems but a Liliputian compared with some of our modern battles, with their millions of men arrayed, and their hundreds of miles of battle front. But over against this we note the fact, that it is not always the event biggest in bulk and pageantry that fills the largest angle in history. Palestine, ancient Greece, and Latium, all insignificant in area, fill a vastly larger place in the thought of to-day than do those ancient world empires of Assyria, Egypt, and Babylonia, because their contributions to the forces that make for civilization were far more numerous and valuable than all those of the latter put together. At Marathon the Greeks had arrayed only 10,000 men against the barbarous hordes of Asia, and only 192 Greeks were killed, but the outcome of that battle has remained as a benediction to the world in all the subsequent story of humane progress.

First. It preserved to the cause of liberty in America the precious Hudson valley by which New England and the Southern colonies were linked together, and which was absolutely necessary to their unity and coöperation.

Second. It taught the Americans that they could meet, and overthrow, in a fair contest, what they had been taught to believe were invincible troops; hence their hopes of success were amazingly strengthened, and from that day the leaders believed that our independence was assured.

Third. The outcome of Saratoga convinced European nations that the Americans could organize, fight and win battles, and that their union possessed elements of stability; hence France immediately thereafter acknowledged our independence and entered into an alliance with us. This naturally caused war between England and France, in which Spain was soon involved. As a consequence much of England's fighting strength was diverted from us to the defence of her own coasts. France sent us fleets, and armies, and much money, by whose aid we were able to give the finishing stroke to English power, over these colonies, at Yorktown.

"Saratoga was the wand that 'smote the rock of the national resources.' It was the magic that revived the 'dead corpse of public credit.'"[2]

Holland, after Saratoga, also gave most substantial aid, in supplying us with the sinews of war, in the shape of seven million guilders.[3]

Fourth. Having once seen that Saratoga not only made possible but probable our independence, anyone can see how after independence came naturally the establishment of this glorious republic which has proved herself a fount of all material, civil, and religious blessings, not only to her own citizens, but to the whole world. This is a much better world, and the average of human comfort and happiness has been vastly raised, because of the birth, the development, and example of this republic.

"*17th. A day famous in the annals of American history.*"

Lieut. Digby, of Burgoyne's army, uses the above as the opening words of his journal for October 17, 1777.

---

[2] Hon. S. S. Cox, in the U. S. Senate, 1884.
[3] Bolle's Financial History of the U. S. Vol. I., p. 258.

He packed far more of truth in that sentence than he dreamed.

In the Fifteenth Century humanity cried for more room, and Christopher Columbus, by the grace of God, discovered a continent. In the Eighteenth Century humanity cried for greater civil liberty and the citizen soldiery of America, under the smile of the Almighty, won it at Saratoga. All hail thou morning of the 17th of October, 1777! Light from the four corners of heaven streams upon thee, making thee the brightest that had yet dawned upon this virgin continent. Farewell, ages of tyranny; farewell, sceptred brutes and crowned despots! The triumphant day here dawned which ultimately assured to every man the privilege of becoming equal to any other man, and which should see every man anointed a king and every woman a queen in her own right, and ushered in the era that should witness the realization of that dream of the poet: "The parliament of man, the federation of the world."

> "The nation that forgets its Marathon
> Has lost the choicest glory it has won.
> Then let yon granite shaft of grace
> Forever be a rallying place
> For liberty and honor, till the day
> The stone is dust, the river dried away."
> —*C. H. Crandall.*

The reader will remember that this crushing defeat, inflicted on England, by no means ended the war, which dragged its slow length along through five more weary years, but the stroke at Saratoga tipped the scales in freedom's favor, it turned the tide which thenceforward set unfalteringly for victory and independence.

The Fate of the Armies. The captured army marched south and stayed the first night on their old camp ground at Wilbur's Basin, whence they

SURRENDER OF BURGOYNE (From an Old Print)

THE STORY OF OLD SARATOGA

had been driven ten days before. The next day our people separated the Germans from the British. The British crossed the river on the floating bridge which had been thrown across by Gates at Bemis Heights, and took the old Hoosac road through Northampton, Mass., for Boston. The Germans crossed in boats near Mechanicville, and stayed the next night at Schaghticoke; thence marched south through Troy and Kinderhook to Claverack; thence east through the Berkshires by the way of Springfield to Boston. [See note.]

Congress did not keep the contract made by Gates to send the surrendered army back to England immediately. The reason for this was that several of the regiments, in defiance of the capitulation, failed to surrender their colors; " Riedesel by his wife's help, saved the flags of his regiments and returned them safely to Brunswick."[4] And besides this the military chest was effectually concealed in various ways by the officers. And furthermore, rumors reached Congress, and it was led to believe, that the British soldiers meant to break their parole, join Howe's army and renew the fight against us. There was evidently some grounds for this belief, for in a letter to his friend, Col. Phillipson, dated Albany, Oct. 20th, 1777, Burgoyne says: "Under all these circumstances of distress, among all these causes of despair, I dictated terms of convention *which save the army to the State for the next campaign."* Italics our own. So they marched them from Boston down to Virginia, whence they were moved hither and yon till after peace was declared.

NOTE.—Rosengarten in his German Soldier in the Wars of the U. S., says: "Of 30,000 Germans who were in the Revolution hardly half returned." Gen. George A. Custer, of the Civil War, was a great grandson of a Hessian officer who served under Burgoyne. Küster was the original German spelling.

[4] German Allies in the Revolution, p. 142.

Washington himself advised Congress to this course. Burgoyne was permitted to return to England, where he received but a cold reception at the hands of the king and people. Afterwards, however, he largely regained his popularity. He died in 1792, and was honored with burial in Westminster Abbey.

Several days before the surrender word had reached General Gates of the burning of Esopus, or Kingston, by Gen. Vaughan. Immediately after the surrender he ordered several Brigades of regulars to start very early on the 18th and hasten southward to check the advance of the enemy; for Albany was just then practically defenceless. Several regiments made the entire distance to that city in one day; i. e. 30 to 36 miles, depending on their position the previous night.

Three days after the surrender Gates' host of militia started for their various homes and so vanished from the scene like the mists of the morning.[5] Morgan, with his illustrious corps, and several brigades, were reluctantly and tardily returned by Gates to the grand army under Washington. Washington was being hard pressed by Howe at the south about this time. The Delaware forts were attacked on the 10th of November. He had already sent north for reinforcements, but they failed to arrive when expected. He writes: "I am anxiously waiting the arrival of troops from the northward, who ought, from the time they have had my orders, to have been here before this. Col. Hamilton, one of my aides, is up the North River, doing all he can to push them forward, but he writes me word that he finds many unaccountable delays thrown in the way. The want of these troops has embarassed all my measures exceedingly." Nov. 2d Hamilton found Morgan with his riflemen a little below Newburg moving slowly south. Morgan promised to

---
[5] The Sexagenary, p. 124.

quicken his pace. He found on reaching Albany that preparations were making for most of the northern army to go into winter quarters in that vicinity. On urging Washington's need, Gates gave all sorts of pretexts for keeping the troops at the north. Finally the Brigades of Poor and Patterson were detached to the aid of the commander-in-chief. "I doubt," writes Hamilton to Washington a little later, "whether you would have had a man from the northern army, if the whole could have been kept at Albany with any decency." Washington afterward said if he could have had those troops ten days earlier the Delaware forts would have been saved, and Howe made unsafe in Philadelphia.

The regulars lingered here at Saratoga for some time, restored the barracks destroyed by Burgoyne, and helped General Schuyler to resurrect from the ashes the home which the same enemy had wantonly cremated. So much of the army as did not finally go to reinforce Washington wintered at Saratoga and Albany.

CHAPTER XVI

A Word More About Gates After Saratoga

On November 5th, 1777, General Gates was ordered by Congress to regain possession of the Highlands, which had been captured by the British under Gen. Sir Henry Clinton, in October. That expedition ended in the burning of Kingston. The defeat and surrender of Burgoyne seem to have filled Sir Henry Clinton, and General Vaughan with dismay. For, at the news of it, they quickly faced about and headed for the south; and furthermore, to the surprise of all Americans, at least, abandoned the valuable prize they had won for Britain, viz: the Highlands and their forts. On the news of this Congress requested Gates to proceed there immediately and superintend the construction of stronger defensive works in more eligible positions than were the last.

For some time the enemies of Washington had been developing that faction which came to be known in history as the Conway Cabal. Gen. Thomas Conway was another of those ambitious trouble makers of foreign birth, and training, who, like Lee and Gates, were more at home in the lobbies of Congress than in the field. The evident purpose of these intriguers was to oust Washington and substitute Gates as commander-in-chief. The connection of Gates with this cabal has been much in dispute, but it seems clear that he at least " bent a pliant ear " to its suggestions, and willingly but guardedly, played into its hands. At all events he was made president of the new Board of War in which Generals Mifflin and Conway, known to be bitterly hostile to Washington, were ruling spirits. When apprised of his election Gates immediately gave notice that he was due in York,

Pa., where Congress was at that time holding its sessions. Gov. Clinton begged Gates, who was still at Albany, to defer his departure from the State, if only for a few days, that he might look through the Highlands, fix upon locations for the new forts, etc., and at least begin the organization of the men detailed to do the work. The Governor again requested him to stop a little while at Pokeepsie, then the State capital, on his way down, that he might confer with him on this important matter. But Gates, in his eagerness to reach the congenial atmosphere of the Congress, would not give so much as a day to this most urgent public service.[1] Gates was ambitious, and it was evidently the idea of the cabal, then in full swing, that Gates was henceforth to be the master spirit of the war. With Gates in York making himself altogether comfortable for the winter, one cannot help but think of the woeful contrast to this situation which at that time existed over at Valley Forge, where Washington and his soldiers were shivering and starving rather than desert the work given them to do.

About this time an extract of a letter from Gen. Conway to Gates was brought to the notice of Washington which aroused his suspicions that Gates was in sympathy with his detractors. This disclosure of his correspondence, coming to the notice of Gates, threw him into spasms of apprehension. His state of agitation was such that he wrote an hysterical letter to Washington concerning it. The correspondence which followed served only to assure Washington that Gates was at least in the confidence of the plotters. In one of his letters Gates solemnly affirmed that Conway's letter to him contained nothing derogatory to Washington; but he failed to produce the letter in evidence which, if its character was as innocent as he claimed, would have cleared his skirts

---

[1] See Clinton Papers, Vol. II.

without further words. It emerged in this correspondence that Col. James Wilkinson, late Adjutant General to Gates, had, at a wine supper, indiscreetly betrayed his superior, all of which involved Gates in two duels with Wilkinson from which he escaped with neither wounds nor added lustre.

Another Attempt at Canada. During the winter of 1777-78 the new Board of War planned a notable winter campaign against Canada. The scheme was laid before Congress and promptly approved by that body. Lafayette, then a mere boy of twenty, was to be the commander with General Conway as second in command. This was evidently designed to separate Lafayette from Washington, to whom he seemed greatly attached. Washington, though he had not been consulted as to the proposed expedition, advised Lafayette, when he asked his opinion of it, to accept the appointment, which he did. The Board was profuse in its blandishments, its promises of succor to Lafayette, and in its assurances of success. Gates told him that he would find at Albany a well equipped army of 3,000 veterans, and that Gen. Stark, with his Green Mountain Boys, would join him and heartily second his leadership. Lafayette, though young, was acute enough to catch the drift and meaning of all this unctuousness. He knew of Conway, and had little admiration for him. He therefore said to the Board that he would accept the appointment provided Baron DeKalb could also be appointed to go with him. To this they readily agreed; but at the time they did not know that Baron DeKalb's commission made him Conway's superior. On his arrival at Albany Lafayette found to his deep chagrin barely half the troops promised, and those nearly naked and, of course, wholly unprepared for a winter campaign; nor indeed had there been any serious attempt at preparation made.

And instead of seeing the redoubtable Stark, impatiently waiting and eager for the fray, he found a letter from him, dated somewhere in New Hampshire, asking for information about the proposed expedition, and what might be expected of him.

So complete was the fiasco and so loud was the condemnation of the public, when the details of the plan came to its notice, that it served to awaken Congress from its infatuation. The orders for the expedition were recalled, Gates and Mifflin were dismissed from the Board of War, and the former was ordered to resume his place in the northern department, and look after the defenses of the Highlands which he had neglected; and he was particularly cautioned, at the same time, to report statedly to the Commander-in-Chief.

Gates chafed in this, to him, cramped and subordinate position for a while, then in some way got himself transferred to a command in Rhode Island. But ere many days he withdrew from the army, and retired to his plantation in Virginia. In 1780 he was offered the command of the southern department which he accepted with avidity. But soon came the overthrow and rout of his army at Camden, South Carolina, which served to end his career.

Conditions at Saratoga in 1778. It is uncertain how many or what particular body of troops remained at Saratoga during the winter following the surrender of Burgoyne. But it is known that a detachment of Col. Van Schaick's Continental regiment was there during March, 1778, because the records say that he with all the regular troops here, and up the Mohawk valley, were ordered to the Highlands for the defense of that important post.

Col. Seth Warner's regiment of militia, from the

Grants, was ordered to Saratoga to take Col. Van Schaick's place, but it was the 22d of April before he reported himself and men, and then, not at Saratoga but at Albany. The delay was claimed to be due to lack of arms. But it was shown that his regiment was fully armed and equipped when disbanded the previous Oct. It was quite evident that many of the men had appropriated the guns, which were public property, had sold them and pocketed the money.

The notorious Gen. Thomas Conway had been left in command of this department by Lafayette when he and Baron DeKalb were ordered back, by Washington, to the main army. While in command here he made a tour of inspection as far north as Saratoga and Fort Edward.

The departure of the troops early in April, created quite a panic among the inhabitants both to the north and west of Albany. It appears that after the surrender of Burgoyne many refugees of this region had ventured back to their homes, and were making preparations to cultivate their farms the coming season. All this was done on the assumption that a sufficient body of the soldiery were to be kept at Saratoga to protect them. On the strength of such expectations Gen. Schuyler had, by the 1st of April, moved his family up from Albany. He had just been chosen by the State Legislature as a delegate to Congress, and Gov. Clinton wrote him an urgent letter pleading with him to speed his going, as the State needed stronger representation in that body. But he replied that he was obliged to remain at home to protect his family. He argued against the wisdom of leaving this region defenseless, as such a course would serve as an invitation to marauding parties of the enemy from the north to swoop down upon them. The people generally realized this and numbers of them were already beginning to leave, and he too would have to follow their example unless speedy relief were afforded. Moreover he urged that these people should be protected because not only would the crops they could raise be needed for their own support, but for the maintenance of the army. Petitions were sent to the Governor from the Saratoga district, and Cambridge, asking for protection. Early in May Col. Warner, with his regiment, was sent to Fort Edward, which, in a measure, allayed apprehension.

Gen. Stark Takes Command. About the 20th of May Gen. Conway was relieved by Gen. John Stark who made his headquarters in Albany, and remained in command of the department through the summer and early fall. So far as we can learn he visited none of the exposed places on the frontiers, nor did he apparently give himself much concern about the proper distribution of the troops. Indeed Gov. Clinton and other public officials repeatedly expressed dissatisfaction with the conduct of his department.

That the fears of the people were by no means groundless was amply, yes sadly, proven by the wanton destruction of Cobleskill, on May 30th, by a band of Indians and Tories; and not long thereafter Andrestown, and Springfield, a few miles south of Little Falls, on the Mohawk, shared the same fate.

Gen. Edward Hand Relieves Stark. Gen. Hand succeeded Stark on October 22d. He, unlike his predecessor, at once set out to visit the frontier settlement on a tour of inspection. He was up the Mohawk valley when Cherry Valley was attacked by Brant and Butler and utterly destroyed, many of the inhabitants were massacred, and others carried into captivity. German Flatts would have shared a like fate but for a seasonable warning, which gave the inhabitants time to take refuge in Forts Herkimer and Dayton. But as it was, vast stores of grain were destroyed, a great number of cattle, horses, &c., were either killed or driven off, and scores of buildings were consigned to the flames. And, think of it, all this on the verge of winter!

The Situation in 1779. Colonel Seth Warner's regiment spent the year for which it had enlisted, at Fort Edward, and left there about the 1st of May, 1779. Detachments of Gen. Jas. Clinton's Brigade had been stationed at Saratoga, and Fort George, but about the same date they were withdrawn to join their command, which was to form part of the proposed Sullivan expedition against the Six Nations. Capt. Levi Stockwell was placed in command of 100 men, 25 of whom were to be posted at Fort Edward, and the rest at Skenesborough. They were ordered to be constantly on the lookout for enemies from the north, and report their discoveries to Gen. Ten Broeck at Albany. Apparently there was no garrison detailed for Saratoga during the greater part of '79.

It will no doubt be of interest to relate that in September of this year the inhabitants of Saratoga district sent a petition to Gov. Clinton praying for a permit to trade some of their wheat with the New England people for salt. It seems that an embargo had been placed on the exportation of wheat, &c., from this State, because it was needed for home consumption, and for the main army. A salt famine would seem unthinkable to us in these days but they suffered much from that cause in this State during the Revolution. At that time New York had no available source of supply, it had to import its salt. The salt springs at Syracuse, then recently discovered, could not be worked, as that country was at the time a wilderness, in the hands of the Indians.

CHAPTER XVII

BEGINNING OF DARK DAYS OF THE REVOLUTION

THE question of the ability of the States to continue the war reached an acute stage in 1780. To maintain an army's efficiency it must be well fed, clothed, and comfortably housed, especially in the winter. But as a rule our Revolutionary armies were poorly fed, scantily clothed, and insufficiently sheltered. One frequently wonders, as he reads the story of their sufferings, how the soldiery ever submitted to such hardship and neglect.

The heart of the difficulty lay in the lack of the wherewithal to purchase the necessities. There always seemed to be a sufficiency of food and clothing in the country, but neither the Congress nor the State governments had money with which to buy them. By the beginning of 1780 their credit with the producers was practically gone. We must remember that there was at that time no such thing as a general government, recognized as paramount by the States. The Congress was mainly an advisory body; it had no power to enforce its decrees. The only place where it exercised real control was over the so-called Continental army. In the early days of the war it issued several millions of paper money, and for a time this was received at its face value, but by 1780 it had so depreciated that a continental dollar would pass for only $2\frac{1}{2}$ cents. Someone said, it would take four months pay of a private soldier to buy a bushel of wheat, and an officer's pay would do little more than keep his horse in oats.

At last it became necessary for the States to levy taxes in kind for such articles as were needed for the maintenance of the troops, i. e. taxes were paid in cattle, sheep, grain, forage, &c. But despite this, sometimes the soldiers were reduced to the necessity of going out to forage for themselves among the nearby farmers, or starve. The lack of provisions for the army at this time was partly due to the shortage of crops in 1779. But such measures, as the above, very naturally, served only to make a bad matter worse.

The Tories Become Troublesome. Then too, certain Loyalists, or Tories, who had felt themselves crushed, and for a time silenced, by the overthrow of Burgoyne, were assuming a bolder front. In many quarters and in various ways they were doing what they could to aid the enemy. Possessed, as they were, of such an intimate knowledge of the people, and the country, they were able to keep the British authorities posted on the exact state of affairs in both civil and military quarters. Their homes were much used as places of refuge for bands of the enemy, or by spies, while others volunteered to act as guides to marauding parties of Indians and Loyalists, and many of them, who had enlisted in the British service, proved a menace and scourge to their old time neighbors, often aiding in the capture of prominent citizens, and dragging them off to Canada.

Many Frontier Settlements Destroyed. This year the frontier settlements reaped to the full the harvest of savage vengeance whose seed had been sown the previous season in the Sullivan expedition. That crusade had destroyed much more of Indian property than it had Indians, hence, according to their savage code, they must get even with the whites, and they had no trouble to find plenty of Tories to help them.

Before the snow was off the ground in the Spring the campaign of destruction and butchery was under way.

On the 15th of March Remensnyder's Bush, near Little Falls, was destroyed; on the 24th Brant and a party of his Indians fell upon Harpersfield, killed three men and took away twelve, leaving their families destitute and far from the nearest white settlement. In March there were only 13 men left at Skenesborough, and 5 at Ft. Edward of the 100 sent there in the fall previous. On the 22d, about sixty Indians led by a renegade Tory, the noted Joe Bettys of Ballston, attacked the little garrison at Skenesborough. A man and his wife were killed and scalped, and only 3 of the 13 men escaped, Col. John McCrea, brother of the ill fated Jeanie, having visited Fort Edward reported that the military stores there were guarded only by Capt. Chipman with three men, and that he had ordered up reinforcements. These quickly arrived.

Early in May well founded rumors of an invasion from Canada were spread abroad. These created throughout this region the greatest possible alarm. Because of such rumors, Col. Van Schaick, writing from Albany on the 17th of May, informed the Governor that he was receiving daily applications from the north and west for aid; that the remote settlements were rapidly breaking up, and moving down the country, and that unless something was speedily done, the whole region north and west of Albany would be abandoned. Under this spur four regiments of militia were ordered to assemble at Saratoga.

That this was not a mere scare-crow rumor is proved by the fact that near the middle of May Sir John Johnson with 400 whites and 200 Indians came up Lake Champlain, landed near Crown Point, then struck through the woods west of Lake George, and came out on the upper Hudson at its junction with the Sacandaga. They followed up this river to the Fish House, Sir Wm. Johnson's famous summer camp, thence turning southward they appeared at the Johnson manor house, where they rested a bit. Thence they issued on the 21st of May, attacked and laid waste the settlements on the Mohawk from Tribes Hill to Anthonys Nose, murdering many people and taking captives. Then they retired by the way they came.

Meanwhile there was no little stir and anxiety throughout the Saratoga district, as may be judged from the following appeal sent by the officers of militia regiments recently arrived at Saratoga. In it one cannot fail to note how it sets forth the forlorn condition of these would be defenders, who are rendered helpless by the want of everything essential to the accomplishment of the task assigned them:

"Sir:

The Regiments assembled at this Time at this Place, in consequence of an Alarm occasioned by the sudden and unexpected Descent made upon the Mohawk River.

It is true when we have assembled, we find ourselves entirely unable to do anything to defeat the Present Operations of our Enemies, occasioned by the entire want of the necessary supplys, and provisions, for the support of the Militia when they are ordered out on duty, and does happen very frequently this Spring.

We find upon trial that it is not in the power of the Officers to order out any detachments to Counteract the doings of the Enemy. The Reason assigned is the lack of Provisions. It is not in the power of the Militia to furnish their own Provisions on account of past distresses, Being greatly distressed for the present necessary support of their own Families.

We must also mention that Ammunition is not to be had. Our situation is truly very deplorable, our Country under every Apprehension of being Depopulated by the immediate incursions of the savages, and others connected with Them, as little acquainted as they with the tender feelings of Humanity.

These are Things we have considered our duty, as Repre sentatives of the Different Regiments, to suggest to your Excellency, hoping you will take these Things in consideration, and Point out such Relief as shall most effectually answer our Present distressed Situation.

We are Sir with Esteem Your Excellencies' Humbel Sevts.

      Peter Yates, Colonel.
      John McCrea, Colonel.
      Lewis VanWoert, Colonel
      Nicholas VanSchoonhoven, Colonel.
      Cornelius VanVeghten, Lieut. Colonel.
      John M. Groesbeck, Major.
      Daniel Dickenson, Major.
      Samuel Ashton, Major.
"His Excellency, Governor Clinton."

"P. S. The Inhabitants of Saratoga are all on the move downward, and the greatest reason to expect all the country north of Albany will drive in."[1]

In response to this Gov. Clinton himself came north to lead the troops, Gen. TenBroeck having been crippled by an accident. Clinton's purpose and hope was to head off and destroy Johnson's force on its retreat before he could reach Lake Champlain. But so much precious time was wasted in procuring the necessary ammunition, and a few days rations for the troops, that when he reached Crown Point he found that Johnson had just preceded him, was already paddling for the north, and so had slipped through his fingers.

Again on the 2d of Aug. Brant with some 400 Indians and Tories attacked Canajoharie, and did a vast amount of damage in that vicinity on the south side of the Mohawk. Besides burning many buildings they massacred fourteen of the inhabitants and carried into captivity fifty of them. Unfortunately the militia were just then on duty further up the valley, and so Brant and his miscreants again escaped. Tory spies doubtless kept

---
[1] Legislative Papers.

Brant informed as to the whereabouts of American troops.

Destruction of Schoharie. The rumor of another foray from the north by Johnson caused Gov. Clinton on Aug. 26th to order Brig. Gen. TenBroeck with a part of his Brigade, to assemble at Saratoga. But that proved to be a false alarm, and doubtless had been caused to be spread abroad by Johnson as a blind to his real purpose. It afterward became known that he with his red and white savages were heading toward Niagara as a rallying point having another objective in view.

About the 1st of Oct. the people up the Mohawk were startled by a word from the west that Johnson, Brant, and Butler, were again on the war path, but of course no one knew where the blow would fall. It might, however, be expected where the defenders were fewest. At all events they suddenly appeared, on the 17th among the settlements of Schoharie, and utterly laid waste that most beautiful and fertile valley. Thence hastening northward, following the Schoharie Kill, they swooped down upon the Mohawk, at Fort Hunter, and destroyed much of what was left of their previous raids.

Ballston also Suffers. Coincident with Johnson's incursion from Niagara another force was reported advancing by way of Champlain. This comprised about 1,000 men under Major Christopher Carleton, nephew of Gen. Sir Guy Carleton. They landed at South Bay and suddenly appeared before Ft. Ann, on the 10th of Oct. and demanded its surrender. The garrison consisted of 75 men, under Capt. Sherwood. Knowing that he had but a scanty supply of ammunition, and sure that his little stockaded fort could not defend itself against cannon, the Capt. after consulting with his subordinates, decided to surrender. On the next day Fort George, at the head of Lake George, shared the like fate. These forts were destroyed, and the buildings of nearby settlements were reduced to ashes.

A detachment from the above force, under Capt. Munro, a Tory, came down the old Kayadrosseras Trail, surprised and destroyed Ballston. On good grounds it is believed that this foray was planned by the miscreant Joe Bettys. The first assault was made under the immediate guidance of one McDonald, (a Tory who lived in the neighborhood,) upon the house of Mr. James Gordon, an influential citizen, whose zeal for the cause of Independence had made him obnoxious to the Tories. Soon after midnight he was awakened by the crash of his windows, and in a brief space he found himself a prisoner, and his house pillaged. His wife and child were permitted to escape. In this raid they killed one man, who tried to save Mr. Gordon, wounded another, took 29 prisoners, including some negroes, and returned with them to Canada by the way they came. Mr. Gordon was held in captivity for nearly two years. One of his negro slaves, taken with him, afterwards escaped, returned to Ballston, and delivered himself to his old master. Note the coincidence that the sacking of Schoharie and Ballston occurred on the same day, the 17th of October, the anniversary of Burgoyne's surrender.

Apropos of the above event, and to show the lack of readiness of our people at this juncture to meet the enemy, due to the condition of the commissary, we quote from a letter of Gen. Schuyler to Gov. Clinton:

Saratoga, Oct. 20th, 1780.

When your letter arrived we had about 150 men at Ft. Edward, and as many more had arrived here, about ten in the morning. Those at Ft. Edward were without any beef, and those here with none but what I could furnish them. All my cattle fit for the knife are already killed, and I have sent to try and collect some more, but I fear a supply will arrive too late to push a party in pursuit of the enemy who were at Ballstown.

I am Sir your most Humble Servt.
Ph. Schuyler.[2]

Soon after the above letter was written a body of troops of ample strength, and sufficiently equipped to take the field, was collected at Saratoga. Having learned this fact through the medium of Loyalist friends, Major Carleton prudently decided not to attempt to penetrate the country further. Therefore, he, with his force, retired to Canada about Nov. 10th.

Tory Women Stranded at Saratoga. During the month of September, of this year, there was gradually assembled at Saratoga a body of five hundred women and children, whose husbands and fathers, loyal to King George, had gone to Canada. They were waiting for some favorable opportunity to be exchanged for prisoners, or in some way to be taken to Canada. On September 18th these unfortunates were reported as being in the direst need of food and clothing. In a letter dated Saratoga, Oct. 20th, Gen. Schuyler says to Gov. Clinton: "The women and children, whose husbands have gone to Canada, still remain here. They will become an intolerable burden to the country if they remain in it all winter."

About the first week in November Gen. James Clinton sent a messenger to Major Carleton to arrange with him, if possible, for their transportation to the north. In a letter dated Albany, Nov. 12th, he says to the Governor that his man reported that " all the shipping of the enemy had

---

[2] Hough's Northern Invasion, p. 609.

gone down the lake except one schooner. That Major Carleton consented to send five boats, which were half the number required, as far as Skenesborough, where they were to wait till the 14th inst. and receive such of the families as were included in an enclosed list. In consequence of which, upwards of two hundred of them were sent off yesterday in waggons as far as Fort Ann; but as the road from that to Skenesborough is impassable with waggons, many of them unable to walk, and the season so intensely cold, I have every reason to fear, many of them must unavoidably perish on the way. Capt. Humphreys with upwards of sixty Levies, and Mr. Vanvechten, D. W. M. Genl. were sent to assist them on." How this all turned out we have not been able to discover.

An Appraisement of 1780. Because of the many depressing events, above recounted, we are constrained to write down 1780 as a year of defeat and disaster to the forefathers, struggling for a larger liberty. Little or nothing happened during its twelve months to cheer the hearts of the patriots. Besides the destruction of many populous frontier settlements in New York, which brought thousands of well-to-do people to the verge of starvation, and cut off many valuable lives, the tide of warfare seemed everywhere to set against us. It was the year of Gen. Lincoln's surrender of Charleston, S. C., with his army of two thousand, and Gen. Gates' humiliating defeat at Camden, in the same State. But the battle of Kings Mountain, also in South Carolina, won by a body of unorganized mountaineers against trained men, and superior numbers, came as a breath of life to one nearly smothered.

And then, as if something were lacking to add blackness to the gloom that seemed to be shutting out the light of life, there came, the last of September, the heart sickening news of the cold blooded treachery of Benedict Arnold. He was just on the point of betraying the strongholds of the Highlands into the hands of the enemy when the plot was Providentially discovered. After such a shocking disclosure what wonder that, for a time, our people were in perplexity and asked anxiously: "Whom now can we trust?"

> "So disasters come not singly;
> But as if they watched and waited,
> Scanning one another's motions,
> When the first descends, the others
> Follow, follow, gathering flockwise
> Round their victim, sick and wounded,
> First a shadow, then a sorrow,
> Till the air is dark with anguish."

But still there is more of the like to follow ere the day breaks and the shadows flee away.

CHAPTER XVIII

1781 AT SARATOGA

THE year 1781 opened and closed most auspiciously, though the intervening experiences were quite of a pattern with those of 1780. The first event to which we refer was the battle of The Cowpens, which was fought Jan. 17th on the border line between North and South Carolina. A special interest attaches to this because the leader in that fight was Col. Daniel Morgan, of Saratoga battle fame, but who had recently become a Brigadier General. Morgan was pitted against Gen. Tarleton, Lord Cornwallis' ablest and most energetic chieftain. The result of that collision was that Tarleton's force was practically annihilated. That affair, in its plan, execution, and outcome, was then, and still is, considered the most brilliant battle of the Revolution.

At the north, in New York State, the small garrison which had been posted at Fort Edward had to be withdrawn because of the lack of provisions. They were marched down and quartered at Saratoga, but here the men were quite determined not to stay for the same reason. For the rest of the year Saratoga was the northernmost military post in the State.

Gen. Schuyler, writing from Saratoga May 4th, says: "The garrison here has now been ten days without any meat, except what they procure by marauding. Every eatable animal in this part of the country is already expended. Not a single scout can be kept out, and I fear that a great many of the troops here will go off to the enemy unless provision is instantly procured for them. Flour, equal to about a hundred barrels, I have procured on my own account, and have prevailed on the Schaktikoke people to furnish in advance their quota of the flour to be raised under the late act [of the State Legislature]. This will probably amount to forty or fifty barrels more."

Again writing to the Governor on the 19th of May he says: "As only 39 Levies are as yet come up, and that we have not above 150 Continental troops here, and none of either that I can learn of expected, I cannot in justice to myself and family any longer risk them here, and intend to move to morrow, unless I receive letters this day announcing the coming of more troops. It is a mortifying reflection that so fine a country must be abandoned for want of men and provisions." However because the people in the neighborhood were all of them ready to fly, he decided to stay a few days longer lest all would follow his example.

These facts are given to show that Gen. Schuyler, though he would not again take a command, still continued to exert every energy, and make every sacrifice to keep up the people's courage, and supply the means for continuing the fight against tyranny and also as an answer to certain New England writers who, to this day, try to minimize his patriotism and traduce his character. And we might add, right here, that for a long period the General at his own expense, employed private scouts and spies to visit Canada, and the haunts of the Tories, through whom he was able to give the first reliable warnings of the enemies movements.[1]

Gen. John Stark Ordered to Saratoga. Major John McKinstry of Col. Robert Van Rensselaer's militia regiment, was commandant here during the spring and early summer of this year. But on the 25th of June Gen. Stark was ordered by Washington to take

---
Lossing's Schuyler, Vol. II —, 405.

command at Albany and to the north. In his orders Washington says: " I am induced to appoint you to this command on account of your knowledge and influence among the inhabitants of that country." [He means the people to the east whence most of the soldiery were drawn to man this post.]

" You will be pleased, therefore, to repair to Saratoga and establish your headquarters at that place, retaining with you four hundred of the troops from Mass. and sending the other two hundred to Col. Willet who will remain in command of the Mohawk river.

" You will advise with Gen. Schuyler with respect to the disposition of the troops destined for the defense of that quarter."[2]

Stark arrived at Saratoga early in July. Gen. Schuyler having abandoned his home and removed to Albany, Gen. Stark made Schuyler's house here the garrison headquarters. In a letter to Washington, Aug. 9th, Stark says this: " General Schuyler is polite enough to show me every assistance in his power, either in advice, or knowledge of the country, and property, if need be."

In the early autumn of this year Mrs. Schuyler and some of her daughters returned to Saratoga to preserve fruits, and prepare various stores against the winter. In a letter of acknowledgment from Schuyler to Stark, we learn that the General, and his son, Major Caleb Stark, were assiduous in their attentions, and detailed a sergeant and body of men to attend and guard them. From all this and more, we gather that the personal touch of a strong and kindly man had wrought a radical change in the attitude of the doughty Stark toward this New York Dutchman.

Early in September rumors came that another expedition from Canada was afoot quite similar in plan to that

---

[2] Watson's Men and Times of the Revolution.

of Burgoyne's. The succeeding days ripened these rumors into veritable fact. It developed that a Major Ross was to play the part that St. Leger did in the campaign of 1777, while St. Leger himself was to impersonate Burgoyne, though the numbers engaged were by no means as formidable as in the former expedition.

When the authorities became assured that St. Leger's force was really under way, and the fact became generally known, panic seized the people on the upper Hudson because of their nearly unprotected condition.

At this time Washington had Sir Henry Clinton corralled in New York City, and seemed to need the bulk of the army in that vicinity, and in the Highlands, to maintain his advantage. Gen. Stark from Saratoga made the most urgent pleas to Washington, to Gen. Heath, and to Gov. Clinton for reinforcements. They responded as they felt they safely could, and troops began to move in this direction. Finally Major Gen. Lord Sterling was given command of the Northern Dept., i. e. Albany and the region to the east, north and west of it. He took command the 15th of Oct., with headquarters at Albany. This of course did not mean the removal of Stark, but Lord Sterling was his superior officer, and was sent to take charge of the entire department. Gansevoort's and VanRensselaer's Brigades of militia were ordered to take the field immediately, and troops from the east and south were reported to be on the way. Col. Weisenfel's N. Y. regiment was already at Saratoga.

Major Ross' incursion was evidently conducted with great secrecy. With a body of six hundred British regulars, Tories, and Indians, he ascended the St. Lawrence to Oswego; thence he followed the line of previous forays, struck through the woods, west of Fort Schuyler, to the head of Otsego lake, passed through Cherry Valley, made a raid in the Schoharie valley; thence northward to the Mohawk, where they managed to destroy much property to the east of Fort Hunter; thence they veered northwest to the vicinity of Johnstown, where, Oct. 25th, they were attacked and defeated by Col. Willet, who pursued them westward with great loss to the marauders. That infamous Tory, Walter Butler, who led in the butchery at Cherry Valley, and other murderous raids, was shot and scalped by an Oneida Indian during this retreat. And thus the last battle of the Revolution was fought in New York State.

St. Leger came up Lake Champlain with about 3,000 troops, and pushed southward through Lake George. Quite an army was assembled at Saratoga to dispute his advance. On the 30th of Oct. Lord Sterling, accompanied by Gen. Schuyler, came up from Albany to assume personal direction of the army's movements. There he perfected his plans to give St. Leger a warm reception, should he venture as far south as Ft. Edward or Saratoga. He drew up a plan of battle whose lines extended from Fish creek, at Saratoga, to the Snook Kill, about three miles below Ft. Edward, which for a body of 4,000 men, would seem somewhat attenuated. His purpose was to dispute St. Leger's crossing the Hudson, but not knowing where such attempt might be made, he so arranged it that the extremities of his army could concentrate within an hour and a half.

St. Leger, doubtless apprised of the formidable force which had been collected to oppose him, concluded that discretion was the better part of valor, and decided not to try conclusions with my Lord Sterling. This, with the extreme lateness of the season, urged him to seek the more hospitable shores of Canada. At all events it was discovered that the retreat was in progress on the 2d of Nov.

On the 29th of Oct. up from the south came news that

sent thrills of joy surging through every loyal frame that heard it. It was nothing less than that Lord Cornwallis had surrendered to General Washington, at Yorktown, Va., on the 19th of October. On the 1st of Nov. at the command of Lord Sterling, thirteen cannon, loaded to the muzzle, announced at noon, that day, the glorious event, and one extra one was fired in compliment to Vermont, then eagerly seeking admission to the Union, and which had given material aid in this year's campaign.

The 3d of Nov., after councelling with his officers, Lord Stirling dismissed the militia with warmest thanks, then, after suggesting to Stark that he build a couple of block houses on adjacent hills, indicated by him, for the better defense of the barracks, he with his suite departed for Albany.[3]

Gen. Stark remained in command at Saratoga during the following winter. That the present generation may be impressed with a proper sense of what it cost in the way of deprivation and suffering to win our liberties, and establish in the earth a government of the people, by the people, and for the people, and that they may know that Valley Forge was not the only encampment where the soldiers of the Revolution suffered, the writer here inserts some letters taken from "Stark's Memoirs:"

"To Major General Heath.

Saratoga, 29th November, 1781.

My Dear Sir — Your two letters of the 14th and the 21st inst. came to hand. I have discharged Col. Reynolds' regiment. The militia and levies at this post were dismissed previous to the arrival of your letters. The two block-houses mentioned in my last are nearly completed. The barracks are repairing by the soldiers, as well as they can be without materials, but I cannot hope that the

---
[3] Life of Lord Stirling, p. 237.

soldiers can be rendered very comfortable without considerable alterations in clothing, fuel, &c. With respect to the latter you observe [in your letter] that I have it 'at command.' In that suggestion you are certainly mistaken, for it cannot be got without going a mile and a half for it. In your observation on the clothing, you mention that the materials are to be sent, and the clothes to be made by the regimental tailors. I must observe that there is but one tailor in the New Hampshire Line, and he a drunken rascal, that could be hardly compelled to make three coats in a winter.

You observe that a few horses should be kept with the troops, and that the remainder should be sent to places where forage can be obtained. This argument I think very reasonable; but I cannot find a man in this district who knows where that place is.

I cannot sufficiently admire the magnanimous conduct of our soldiers. They certainly put knight errantry out of countenance; and all those whimsical tales, which are generally supposed to have existed nowhere but in the brains of chimerical authors, seem realized in them right here. But I fear that this virtue will not last forever; and indeed it is my opinion that nothing but their too wretched situation prevents an insurrection. However I have not heard a syllable of the kind yet, and shall take every imaginable precaution to hinder it; and I hope that their firmness and my endeavors will prove efficatious."

"To Major General Heath.

Saratoga 12th Dec. 1781.

Dear Sir.— I am sorry to hear that any troops suffer more than in this quarter, (our enemy excepted); but since some are more wretched, we must submit to our fate like good soldiers. [Gen. Heath, at this time, was in command of the Northern Dept., and had his headquarters in the Highlands.] I am sure it is not practicable for the troops that are here to go to the Mohawk River until they are clothed. Indeed I am obliged to detain the six months men to do the necessary camp duty, on account of the nakedness of the Continental troops. In the last duty report only 36 'three years,' and 'during the war' men were fit for duty in the two Regiments. The remainder are so naked that they cannot procure fuel for their own use."

In a letter addressed to the President of Congress, Sept. 1st, 1781, Gen. Stark appeals for at least part pay for his services. In said letter these words appear:

"I must inform you that it is going on the third year since I have received any cash from the public as pay, (except $2,000 at Providence in 1779) which you must know is very incompetent to the expenses of a General officer since that time. However, I have tamely awaited the liberality of Congress without asking for my due, until my means, as well as my credit, is exhausted.

Yr most obedient and humble servant

John Stark."

A Garrison at Saratoga, 1782. The surrender of Cornwallis practically put an end to the war. Minor engagements and desultory fighting occurred, here and there, but no great collision of armies. In May 1782 Sir Guy Carleton returned from England with preliminary overtures from his Majesty King George for peace. But Washington and the other leaders thought it not wise to disband till the treaty of peace was definitely signed. So the bulk of the Continental troops were retained in their several encampments.

General Stark continued in command at Saratoga till

the beginning of summer. He was succeeded by Colonel Dearborn, who had been coupled up with Morgan in 1777, and had proved himself so efficient in the Burgoyne campaign. He had under him mainly a body of New Hampshire troops. Dearborn's Journal contains several passages recounting his experiences here, which are of interest to a modern Saratogan. He had been on duty with the main army at Newburg, but after being ordered north says: "On the 9th of July I set out to join my regiment at Saratogea. On the 27th I began to erect fortifications at this Garrison for its better security."

Col. Dearborn's Opinion of the Springs. " Oct. 5th. Having heard much said of several springs, of an uncommon kind that are situate about 12 miles west of the Garrison, I was induced to pay them a visit this day in company with several other Gentlemen. I was much disappointed [surprised?] in finding the quality or taste of the water, as well as the very extraordinary situation of it, infinitly more curious than I expected. The water is clear, the taste is hard to describe; to me it appeared at first tasting to partake much of alkoline qualities, but on drinking freely it appeared to be between good porter and cyder, and was not ungrateful to my taste. Many are excessive fond of it."

"Oct. 17th. This being the anniversary of the Capture of General Burgoyne and his Army, we had an entertainment, at which were all the Officers of the Garrison, & some other Gentlemen. We spent the day and evening in festivity and mirth. The soldiers had a gill of Spirits over their allowance served out to them, to enable them to keep the day with the spirit, as well as with the understanding." [4]

---

[4] The chief source of the facts presented in the last three chapters is the nine volume edition of The Clinton Papers. Other authorities have been given either in the text or foot notes.

On Nov. 7th, Dearborn left with his regiment to join the main army, still at Newburg, and was relieved by the Rhode Island Regiment.

It is of interest to observe that General Washington made two visits to Saratoga, once in this year of 1782, and again the following year. The details of these visits will be given, later, in the Civil History section.

CHAPTER XIX

ANECDOTES OF THE REVOLUTIONARY PERIOD

Introductory — The Sexagenary — Who was He? Among the very few early residents of the upper Hudson valley who left behind them a written record of incidents connected with Colonial and Revolutionary days was one who signed himself the Sexagenary, (that is, the man in his sixties). Indeed, he gives us about the most entertaining and realistic pictures we have of the hardships and sufferings, the toils and sacrifices, which the common folk of those days had to undergo, especially the dwellers in those communities into whose precincts the common enemy chanced to intrude himself. His real name was never divulged, so far as we can learn, hence his identity has ever remained a profound mystery, but at the same time a prolific cause of wonderment and conjecture on the part of students of New York history.

On the first reading of the Sexagenary's book, the writer was inclined to regard it as largely fictitious; but after a more critical study of it he discovered the author to be thoroughly accurate in all cases where it has been possible to verify him. His constant reference to sites, and localities and personages, in and about Old Saratoga, showed a familiarity with the lay of the country and its people which was possible to one only after a protracted residence. All this served to arouse the curiosity of the writer to the point of getting on his track and running down this coy and evasive author. The clues were furnished us chiefly by the book itself, showing that the author did not cover his tracks as thoroughly as he fancied.

Having collated the evidence and reached a conclusion as to the authorship of the book, we laid the results before several gentlemen, in whose judgment we had confidence, among whom was Hon. Charles R. Ingalls, Justice of the Supreme Court, and all agreed with us that the name of the man who furnished the facts for the Sexagenary was John P. Becker. This evidence was published in detail in the first edition of this work. We thought it not worth while to encumber this 2d edition with its repetition, especially since no one has appeared to question those conclusions. On the contrary confirmation of our findings have since come to us. E. g. one link was lacking in the pedigree of Mr. Becker. This was furnished by Mr. Leroy Becker who was a result of his ancestral researches confirmed our inference that Peter Becker was indeed the father of John P. Becker. Again in Dr. Asa Fitch's Survey of Washington Co. we found this paragraph: " Rich in historical material as is this district, it is surprising that there has not been to this day a Campbell, a Simms, or a Stone, to gather up the various details of its local history and present them to the world, with the exception of the incidents furnished from his memory by one of our citizens to an Albany editor, some twenty years ago, and by him written out and published in a small duodecimo entitled The Sexagenary." Dr. Fitch was a fellow citizen with Mr. Becker of Greenwich, and Fitch's work was published in 1849.

John P. Becker was born at Middleburg, Schoharie Co. in 1764. In 1768 his father, Peter, with Johannes, a brother, came this way, bought an 820 acre tract of land of Phillip Schuyler, on the east side of the river, built a substantial house, established himself, and became one of the prominent citizens in this locality. Everybody familiar with the road down the east side of the river has noticed the stately mansion adorning the bluff up to your left, and overlooking the river, about two miles south of the bridge.. The place now comprising 226 acres is owned by Thomas Gleason, but for many years was known as the Slade place.

This was the early home of the Sexagenary, though the original house was removed to make room for the present brick structure. Just to the north of the house is a hollow, and a ravine running into the high bluffs, or river hills. From underneath the bank up in the ravine gushes a spring. This ravine was frequently used by the Beckers as a place of refuge from the periodic raids of Indians and Tories.

Some years after the Revolution J. P. Becker moved up on the Battenkill and became one of the founders of the village of Greenwich, and was the owner of the fine property now the home of Henry Gray, M. D. In later life, through too implicitly trusting men, supposed to be friends, he lost his property. The condition in which this left him was the occasion for the book with the source of its facts left nameless. From the original publication preserved in the State Library, since destroyed by fire, I quote the following: "Induced by the cares of poverty, which now press upon me with a weight, unfelt in happier years, I have, at the instance of a gentleman, who has befriended me in adversity, consented to entrust to his hands the incidents of my life for publication." The gentleman to whom he refers was S. Dewitt Bloodgood, a prominent citizen of Albany at that time, and a regular contributor to the press. The reminiscences were first published as contributed papers in the *Albany Gazette,* in 1831-'3. The Sexagenary is a book that deserves to be more widely read, as it is written in a very entertaining style, and is thoroughly trustworthy in everything where the author was in a position to know the facts from experience, or could consult the witnesses, and he attempts to meddle with very little else. The book being out of print and quite rare, we have taken the liberty to quote it very freely in these pages.

Stampede of the People—Its Cause. During the entire period of the Revolution the farmers up and down the valley, who happened to possess teams of horses, were frequently pressed into service as wagoners; compelled to leave their own homes and business to serve the public. Mr. Becker (the Sexagenary) tells how his father, like his neighbors, was frequently made a victim of this presumably necessary policy. Once, while a boy of only eleven, he was forced to drive one of his father's teams all the way to Montreal, in the dead of winter, with supplies for General Montgomery's army. They used the ice on Lakes George and Champlain as a highway.

The following incident related by Mr. Becker, occurred after the fall of Ticonderoga, and just after the vanguard of Burgoyne's army had reached the Hudson at Fort Edward:

"For some days no information was received from our troops, who were supposed to be intrenched at Moses creek for the purpose of making a stand. We were wrapped in fond security until our danger was suddenly brought home to us by one of the startling incidents attendant on an enemy's approach. It was in August, and we had just risen from dinner, when one of my uncle's negroes came running to the house with eyes dilated with terror. After waiting for a few moments for the return of his natural functions, we learned from him that an Indian had been seen in the orchard near the house, evidently intending to shoot a person belonging to the family, who was at work in the garden; the blacks, however, had given the alarm, and the man escaped into the house, while at the same time six other savages rose from their place of concealment and ran into the woods. This was on our [the east] side of the river. The savages that remained with Burgoyne were continually, for miles in advance of him, on his flanks, reconnoitering our movements, and beating up the settlements. My father, on learning the fact of their approach, went immediately over to his brother's house, which was about one-fourth of a mile off, to ascertain what was to be done for the safety of their families. He found him making every exertion to move away. During my father's absence, my mother, who was a resolute woman, one fitted for the times in which she lived, was industriously placing the most valuable of her clothing in a cask; and at her instance, I went out with some of our servants to catch a pair of fleet horses, and harness them as fast as possible to the wagon." Several loads were hastily taken down to the river placed in a light bateau, some of the farming utensils were buried in the road; a half dozen porkers were turned loose into the woods; the father and family, with a couple of teams, ferried[1] themselves across the river to Schuyler's Flats, while the son, who tells us the story, with a black, paddled down the river. They reached H. Vandenburg's [now Ephraim Ford's place], between Wilbur's Basin and Bemis Heights, that night. "We found, on landing there, a number of people who, like ourselves, had been driven from their homes. I scarcely ever witnessed a greater scene of hurry and confusion than was now presented to our view. I had been amused by the novelty, and pleased with the variety of incidents which attended our own flight, but the distress of the groups around us changed

---

[1] The cut in the bank, excavated by the Beckers as an approach to their private ferry, and mentioned by the Sexagenary in connection with the above story, is still used for a crossing place in the winter, and for drawing ice from the river by the neighboring farmers.

the current of my feelings and excited my deepest sympathy. Some of them obtained accommodations that night within doors; some were happy to be under the cover of the cattle sheds, while others stretched themselves in their wagons, and endeavored to snatch a few moments of repose. The next morning my father, with a few congenial spirits, went back home to try to save some of their stock, which they succeeded in doing safely. At the same time the whole body of people at Vandenburg's moved off toward Stillwater; a general panic now prevailing among them, which seemed every hour to increase. Our procession of flying inhabitants wore a strange and melancholy appearance. A long cavalcade of wagons, filled with all kinds of furniture not often selected by the owners with reference to their use or value on occasions of alarm, stretched along the road, while others on horseback, and here and there two mounted at once upon a steed panting under a double load, were followed by a crowd of pedestrians. These found great difficulty in keeping up with the rapid flight of their mounted friends. Here and there would be seen some humane person assisting the more unfortunate, by relieving them of their packs and bundles with which they were encumbered, but generally a principle of selfishness prevented an interchange of friendly offices." After many vicissitudes, young Becker, with his father and family, reached Bethlehem, about ten miles below Albany, where they found refuge among relatives.

Some Tories at Stillwater. It is well known that the sentiment in this vicinity, as elsewhere, was divided concerning the propriety of severing our connection with England. We think it, therefore, worth while to give the following incident as an example of the measures some vould take to maintain and exhibit their loyalty to the crown: It occurred during Schuyler's retreat to the Mouths of the Mohawk.

"Aug. 16th 1777. This morning I was ordered up to Stillwater [from below Mechanicville] with 280 men to burn the boards left cut, and burn the bridges and break up the roads. About one o-clock we discovered two men carrying packs, crossing the river, from the upper to the lower island. A sergeant and six men went over to learn who they were. One of the men returned and said there was a considerable number encamped on the island. I immediately sent 50 men, well armed, [under Capt. Benj. Warren] to take the party and bring them off. In about an hour some of my party returned with four men and several women and children in a canoe they had picked up, for they waded the rapids. The whole party, men, women, and children, numbered 28. They were Tories, inhabitants of Stillwater, and people of wealth. They had secreted their household stuff, clothing and movables, in the woods, then went to the island that was thickly wooded, where they proposed to remain till our army was gone down, and Burgoyne had come; then they would place themselves under his protection.

> They were John Jeffers, his wife and three children.
> Benjamin Burrows, wife and four children.
> John Vise [Weis?] wife and four children.
> Thomas Jeffers, Jr., wife and four children.
> Mrs. Mageer, and one child.
> One negro woman, and two Jeffers children."[2]

Experience of the Marshall Family. Mrs. Thomas Jordan, a daughter of Abram Marshall, who settled upon the farm now owned by W. H. Marshall, south of Victory, in 1763, related to Benson J. Lossing,

---

[2] Journal of Col. Jeduthan Baldwin, p. 116. Diary of Capt. Benj. Warren.

the historian, in 1848, her experience of the Burgoyne campaign. She was a young lady of twenty when independence was declared, and was living with her parents on the farm when Burgoyne came down the valley. She was then betrothed, but her lover had shouldered his musket, and was in Schuyler's camp. When the people were hastily fleeing toward Albany, on the approach of Burgoyne, she and her parents were among the fugitives. So fearful were they of the Indian scouts sent forward, and of the resident Tories, who were emboldened by the proximity of the invaders, that for several nights previous to their flight they slept in a swamp, apprehensive that their dwelling would be burned over their heads, and themselves murdered. When they returned home, after the surrender of Burgoyne, all was desolation. "It was a sad return, for we had but little to come to," she said. "Our crops and our cattle, our sheep, hogs and horses, were all gone, yet we knelt down in our desolate home and thanked God sincerely that our house and barns were not destroyed." She wedded her soldier lover soon after his discharge. He had been in the bateau service. She was personally acquainted with General Schuyler, and used to speak feelingly of the noble-heartedness of himself and lady in all the relations of life. Thomas Jordan cleared and owned the farm now occupied by Mr. Frank Marshall, who is a grand-nephew of Mrs. Jordan.

Experience of the Rogers Family. Among the interesting incidents of Revolutionary times connected with citizens who have been prominent in the history of Schuylerville, one of the most thrilling relates to the ancestry of Rev. Thomas L. Rogers, for a number of years pastor of the Baptist church here.

His grandfather, James Rogers, son of Rev. James

Rogers, was living, in 1777, with his family, on a farm at the junction of the Battenkill with the Hudson river, at the place now known as Clark's Mills. When the army of Burgoyne was approaching that point, he thought it wise to seek shelter under the protection of General Stark, at Bennington, about thirty miles to the eastward. Hastily packing a wagon with such of his goods as he could carry, he started, with his wife and two young children, for Bennington, on August 13th, 1777. He reached Walloomsac on the eve of the 15th, and camped for the night. The next morning he saw coming down the creek some American soldiers, and soon after saw, coming up the valley, some British troops; in fact, he was right between the lines, and a battle was imminent, for Stark had come out to prevent Burgoyne's men, under Colonel Baume, getting to Bennington. The mother and children were hastily secured in the cellar of a hut by the creek, and the father and the oxen were impressed into the service of Stark. Baume planted his cannon to stop the Yankee advance, but they were soon taken by a charge (the first charge upon a battery in the open field made by Americans in the Revolutionary war). Soon thereafter those guns were hauled to the rear by James Rogers' oxen. One of them was exhibited and fired in the salute at the dedication of the Bennington battle monument, August 16, 1891.

Mr. Rogers and his family remained in the vicinity of Bennington for two weeks, during which time the younger child died. He returned as soon as it was safe to his farm, where he died in September, 1793. He left three sons and four daughters, all of whom married and settled in Greenwich. James Rogers was only 49 when he died, but his wife lived to the age of 88 years, dying in 1837. She is well remembered by her grandchildren, one of whom, Samuel Rogers, of Bald Mountain, is still living [A. D. 1900] at the age of ninety-three.

The farm of James Rogers has been held continuously in the Rogers family since 1770, being now occupied by A. Yates Rogers, Esq.

The maiden name of Mrs. James Rogers was Mercy Tefft. Her family emigrated to Greenwich from Rhode Island and was among the earliest and most substantial settlers of that town.[3]

Joseph Welch's Narrow Escape. Joseph Welch was one of the ante-Revolutionary settlers in Old Saratoga, and perhaps was the only representative from this locality who fought in the battle of Bunker Hill. Sometime after this, he had the misfortune to be captured by some Indians and taken to Canada. They evidently intended to adopt him into their tribe if they could tame him. They kept him pretty snug for a time, but he managed in various ways to win their esteem and confidence. One day the chief asked him if he had a squaw and any papooses back home, and he said no, which was not true, for he had a young wife and a child or two. The chief then said: " Before many moons, we will give the white man a squaw."

After a while they allowed him to go out hunting with them, but he was too politic to allow himself to shoot more game than the Indians, lest he should arouse their jealousy. But all this time Welch was only "playing possum." By no means had he forgotten his old home and loved ones, nor had his determination to see them again abated; for after he had been with the Indians, perhaps a year or more, and noticed that they had relaxed their vigilance, he began to lay his plans for escape.

---

[3] The above facts were kindly given the writer by Mr. Thomas L. Rogers, of Boston, Mass., son of the Rev. Thomas L. Rogers.

He secreted some provision, secured a hatchet, and finally one summer night, when all were sound asleep, he arose wrapped his blanket around him, stole out of the wigwam, and was off for liberty, intending to make the nearest English settlement or military station.

Of course, the next morning he was missed, and at once the Indians gave chase. Ere long he discovered that they were on his track, and despite every effort to elude them, found that they were gaining on him. Finally he espied a hollow log, and in sheer desperation, crawled into it. His pursuers were soon up with him, and losing the trail, hunted around for it in the vicinity of the log the balance of the day, and in fact camped near him for the night. The next morning they gave up the search and went off.

He crawled out of his cramped hiding place, congratulated himself on his escape, took his bearings, and made a new start. He had not covered many miles ere the tire of the previous day's race, together with the sleepless watchfulness of the last night, compelled him to stop and rest, so he lay down alongside a big log, threw his blanket over him,—head and all,—to keep off the mosquitoes, and went to sleep. He had not lain there long before he was awakened by a loud stamping and a whistling snort. He seized his hatchet, thumped it over a stone, and a clatter of heels told him that the herd of deer, which had disturbed his slumbers, were off. He knew what they were as soon as he heard the peculiar snort.

After his rest he renewed his journey, and on reaching a large stream was startled by seeing a man coming up the opposite bank. At first he thought him an Indian, but on a closer view saw that he was a white man. Then he disclosed himself, related his experience and asked the way to the nearest settlement. The man guided him to an English military post, where he was received and treated as a prisoner of war, but soon thereafter was exchanged. Shortly after his return he enlisted as a Continental, and became a member of the "4th N. Y. Regiment of the Line" (Regulars) and served till honorably discharged.

It was apparently before the Revolutionary war that he had the following adventure. While roaming the woods, and evidently far from home, he espied a party of Indians coming down the banks of a stream, near which he chanced to be. On their closer approach he noticed that one of them was carrying a white baby, which they had, no doubt, stolen away from its mother. He revealed himself, and soon saw them trying to still the infant's cries, and satisfy its hunger by feeding it some water, into which they had steeped or soaked some crushed hickory-nut meats. He succeeded in buying the baby of them, perhaps for a little powder and tobacco, and then he took it into the first white man's cabin he came across and gave it into the hands of a motherly woman, who cared for it, but who, on ultimately finding its parents, gave them back their lost baby.

Joseph Welch emigrated from Ireland, and came to Saratoga (Schuylerville) about 1770. For some time he worked for General Schuyler. He was a shoe-maker by trade. After the Revolution he leased a farm of the General, made a clearing, built a log house, and settled down for life. His farm was the one now owned by J. E. McEckron, in the angle formed by the road to Grangerville and the back road to Bacon hill. He married a Miss Bowen; they had a large family, and are the ancestors of the numerous Schuylerville Welches. The old patriot and his wife are buried in the Finch burying ground up near the monument.

We obtained these facts from Mrs. Isaac Bemis, of

Bacon Hill, a grandaughter of Joseph Welch, and who heard them from the lips of the old man while sitting on his knee as a little child, and also from John B. Welch, a great-grandson.

Loyal to the Limit. As a specimen of firmness for the right as he had been led to see the right, we insert the following. This happened a few days before the murder of Jane McCrea.

"Some Ottawa Indians fell in with an American scouting party near Ft. Edward. The Americans fled to their boats and crossed the river. The Indians fired but failed to hit. Whereupon greatly exasperated, finding a hog trough they placed their guns in it, stripped and swam across the river pushing the hog trough before them. The Indians gained the shore lower down than the Americans, surprised and took them, and brought them back in the bateaus over the river and delivered them to General Fraser. The Captain of the party was taken also, badly wounded. Fraser quizzed him but he would give no answers, and behaved in the most undaunted manner. The General thinking that by showing him some attention he might gain the desired information, ordered him some refreshments. After examining his wound the surgeon said his leg must be amputated, which being performed, he was advised to keep himself quiet else lockjaw would set in. To this he replied with great firmness: 'Then I shall have the pleasure of dying in a good cause, that of gaining the independence of the American Colonies.' I mention this circumstance to show how cheerfully some of them will sacrifice their lives in pursuit of their favorite idol." The Captain died the next morning.[4]

Indian Children Amphibious. "The Mohawks, driven from their homes by the Americans, joined

---
[4] Anburey's Travels, p. 324.

the British army at Saratoga, and encamped at the creek from whence this place takes it name. They came with their squaws, children, cattle and horses. When the army crosses the river the squaws and children are to go to Canada, and the men remain. Upon their arrival I visited them at their encampment, and had an opportunity of observing the mode they adopt in training up their children. They are in a manner amphibious. There were several of the men bathing in the creek, and a number of little children, the eldest could not have been more than six years old, and these little creatures had got into the creek upon planks, which they paddled along, sometimes sitting, then standing on them, and if they overbalance the plank and slip off, with a dexterity almost incredible, they get on it again. As to diving they will keep a considerable time under water, nearly two or three minutes."[5]

Neilson's Encounter with the Big Indian. The two following anecdotes are selected from "Burgoyne's Campaign," by Charles Neilson. His father, John Neilson, owned the property and buildings at the northwest angle of the American works at Bemis Heights, and from whom it was named Fort Neilson. The property is still in the Neilson family.

This first event must have been nearly coincident with the preceding ones. The writer says: "About this time, small parties of Indians were seen prowling about the vicinity, of whom my father and a few resolute fellows had been in pursuit. On their return, he had occasion, while the others passed on, to call at a Mr. Ezekiel Ensign's, who afterwards, and for a number of years, kept a public house a little north of Wilbur's Basin. While sitting there, about nine o'clock in the evening, in

---
[5] Anburey's Travels, p. 351.

THE STORY OF OLD SARATOGA

conversation with Mr. Ensign, a ferocious-looking giant-like Indian, armed and accoutred in the usual costume of an aboriginal warrior, ushered himself into the room, and after eying them sharply for a moment, he, with one hand drew from his belt a huge tomahawk, which he flourished about his head in true Indian style, and with the other a long scalping-knife, with which he exhibited, in pantomime, his dexterous manner of taking scalps. At the same time, with eyes flashing fire, and turning alternately from one to the other, as they sat in opposite directions, he accompanied his daring acts in broken English with threats of instant death if they attempted to move or speak. Ensign being crippled in one arm, having at some former time accidentally received a charge of shot through his shoulder, and feeling his own weakness, should resistance become necessary, and being in momentary expectation of receiving the fatal blow, became fixed and immovable in his chair with a countenance of ashy paleness. On the other hand, my father being a man of great muscular strength, and of uncommon agility, and having had many encounters with the Indians, for which they owed him a grudge, prepared himself with much presence of mind for a desperate encounter. To this end, while the Indian would momentarily direct his attention to Ensign, he would imperceptibly and by degrees turn himself in the chair, and in this manner would, from time to time, keep silently moving, by little and little, until he succeeded in placing himself in a position in which he could grasp, with both hands, the back of his chair. Thus situated, and knowing the lives of both of them depended altogether on his own exertions, he watched his opportunity, and the moment the Indian turned his eye from him he grasped the chair and, with almost the rapidity of lightning, sprang upon his feet, whirled the chair over his head, and aimed at him a desperate blow; but the chair raking the ceiling above, and the Indian at the same time dodging the blow, he missed him. The Indian, having recovered his position, immediately sprang with a hideous yell, and with his tomahawk uplifted, ready to strike the fatal blow. But before he could effect his direful purpose, the chair was brought around the second time, and with redoubled force, athwart his head and shoulders, which brought him to the floor.

"No sooner had he fallen than his assailant, dropping the chair, sprang upon him and wrenched from his firm grasp the dreadful weapons of death; and would have disabled him on the spot, had not Ensign begged of him not to kill him in the house. He then, holding him in his firm grasp, called for a rope, and then, with the assistance of Ensign, he succeeded, though not without a dreadful struggle, in binding the savage monster. By this time two neighbors, who had been alarmed by some female of the family, came in, when he was shut up in an outhouse, and left under their guard." But while they slept he managed to escape, to the extreme disgust of his captor.[6]

---

[a] This farm is still owned by a descendant of Ezekiel Ensign.

CHAPTER XX.

ANECDOTES — Continued

Capture of the British Picket by Young Farmers. Between the first and second battles, and " while the two armies were thus encamped near each other, about twenty of the most resolute inhabitants in the vicinity collected together for the purpose of having a frolic, as they termed it, of some kind or other. After their arrival at the place of rendezvous, and a number of propositions had been discussed, they finally concluded, with more courage than prudence, that by a *coup de main* they would go and bring in one of the British advanced pickets, which was posted on the north bank of the Middle ravine. Having with much formality selected their several officers, and furnished themselves with suitable arms and other equipments, they marched off in *ir*-regular military style. Thus they ventured forth about ten o'clock at night, fully determined to conquer or die in the glorious cause of their beloved country.

"As they approached within musket-shot distance of their unsuspecting enemy, they formed themselves in order of battle, and advanced in three *grand* divisions; one by a circuitous route, to gain their rear, while the other two posted themselves on their flanks. After giving time for each party to gain their several positions, the resolute captain, who was prepared for the purpose, gave the preconcerted signal by a deafening blast on an old horse trumpet, when all with fearless step, ' rushed bravely' on with clattering arms, through rustling leaves and crackling brush, with the usual parade of a hundred men. As they closed in, the leader of each division, in a bold and commanding voice, and before the guard could say: 'Who comes there?' called, or rather bawled out, 'Ground your arms, or you are all dead men!' Supposing they were surrounded by a much superior force, and deeming resistance of no avail, the officer of the guard gave the orders, when their arms were immediately grounded, and the thirty British soldiers surrendered themselves 'prisoners of war' to only two-thirds of their number, and those undisciplined American farmers."

The following is related by Wilkinson in his Memoirs:

"Prior to the action of the 19th [Sept.] Lieutenant Hardin had been detached with a light party to the rear of the British army to take a prisoner and pick up intelligence. On his return, near Saratoga, on the 22d, he met an Indian courier in a path on the summit of a sharp ridge [south of Victory Mills]. They were within a few rods when they caught sight of each other, presented and fired at the same instant; the Indian fell, and Hardin escaped with a scratch of his antagonist's ball on his left side. Letters of Burgoyne to Powell, and several others, were found in the shot pouch of the dead Indian, and delivered by the Lieutenant to Gates at headquarters."

About Two of Burgoyne's Plucky Messengers. The office of messenger between Burgoyne and Sir Henry Clinton, in New York, was a risky business; not alone because of watchful guards, but our people along the route were very suspicious of a strange face, just at that time. And yet there were those who had the hardihood to undertake it. As we have seen two of them got through, one at Bemis Heights, and one at Saratoga. Fonblanque, in his Life of Burgoyne, has the following to say about two others:

" Burgoyne, after having received the cypher dispatch from Gen. Clinton on Sept. 20th, sent back the Messenger the same night with an urgent appeal for help. His dispatch was placed in a hollow silver bullet which the bearer was ordered to deliver into Clinton's hands. The man succeeded in making his way to Fort Montgomery, in the Highlands, where he supposed Gen. Clinton must be by this time. On inquiry he learned that a Gen. Clinton was there, and on request he was led into his presence. There, to his surprise, he discovered it was not Gen. Henry Clinton of the British army, but the American Gen. James Clinton. On discovering his mistake the unfortunate man swallowed the bullet; but this being observed, he was at once forced to take an emetic when up came the silver pill with its tell tale message. Result, the unhappy man was hung as a spy."

But Burgoyne took the precaution to send other messengers, one of these was a Capt. Scott of the 53d Regt. whose Journal furnishes a vivid picture of the difficulties he had to encounter.

Captain Scott's Journal. "The 27th of September, in the evening, I left Gen. Burgoyne's camp, at Freeman's Farm, with dispatches for Sir Henry Clinton, at which time I passed the Hudson to the east side on a bridge that was upon the left of our camp; but could not get further into the woods than a mile and a half, owing to the darkness of the night, and a swamp which we got into. Set out the 28th in the morning keeping the woods until we got to the banks of the Husick creek which we found was guarded at all the fords by the enemy, to prevent the friends of Government [Tories] from getting into Gen. Burgoyne's camp, which obliged us to remain quiet all that day.

Passed several of their guards that night and by the assistance of a thick fog passed the creek early in the morning of the 29th, and got 4 miles beyond Pittstown

[Renss'l Co], at which place my guide from Burgoyne's camp left me, and recommended me to a German, where I stayed part of the night.

The 30th, got a guide who brought me through the woods to another friend of Government where I got horses. It being night I kept the road until I arrived at Kinderhook, where I stayed the remainder of the night. Oct. 1st, passed the Hudson river in a canoe to the west side, and stopped a few hours at Cusocky, [Coxsackie] at a friends house who furnished me with horses that carried me 8 miles where was obliged to stop that night. 2d. Prevailed on a German, for a sum of money, to carry me down the Hudson River, concealed in a canoe as far as the other side of Esopus creek, which he did that night. Being landed half mile below Esopus [Kingston], I continued marching the rest of the night and some part of the next day, it being the 3d, but was obliged to stop, not being able to procure a guide. The 4th proceeded to the back of New Windsor, where I stayed until the evening of the 5th at a friend's house, at which time I set out having prevailed on a guide to try to conduct me to New York, as I could get no intelligence at that time relative to Sir Henry Clinton. Coming up the North River were a good many parties of rebel militia, making toward New Windsor and the Forts. Got the same evening as far as Smith's Clove, at which place I had great reason to suppose my guide betrayed me, having brought me close to the rebel guard, who challenged us, and ordered us to come in, which the guide did. Upon seeing which I immediately fell back, was fired at by two sentinels, at a distance of three or four yards from me. I made my escape into a wood about 300 yards distance from the guard, along with a man who came with me from Gen. Burgoyne's army, where we remained all the rest of the night. Heard one of the rebels at daybreak, being the 6th, in search of us, and was obliged to remain hid all day. Set out in the night and got past their guards. The 7th we made for the Jerseys, steering by a compass having no guide. The 8th met an inhabitant who informed us of Fort Montgomery being taken. He seemed much dejected, and thought their cause at that time in a bad way. Altered our course for Fort Montgomery, lay that night in a house by itself in the Highlands which was the only one we ventured into since the 5th, during which time our provision did not consist of a pound of bread and cheese. Still steering by a compass got into Fort Montgomery by ten o-clock that day; went immediately and waited upon Sir Henry Clinton, aboard the Commodore Hotham. Set out the next day, being the 10th, on my return to Gen. Burgoyne, on board the fleet of armed vessels going up the Hudson River, under the command of Sir James Wallace. Sailed the 11th, but as the fleet at that time did not proceed higher up the river than 20 miles below Esopus, we were obliged to land in the night, when we lay hid in the woods until morning. The 12th we marched all day, and crossed Esopus creek in the night. The 13th marched all day, and was conducted in the night by a guide to a friend's house where I got a wagon that carried me the same night to Cusocky, where I was obliged to remain hid until the 15th, not being able to secure a guide that would undertake to carry me through to Gen. Burgoyne's army, declaring he was entirely surrounded, and had capitulated. Likewise finding those that were well inclined to Government, would upon no account Venture either for to harbor me, or give me the least assistance. I was obliged for to try to make my way back to our fleet in the North River; set out in the night and by the assistance of a canoe got 12 miles. The 16th was obliged to lie hid all day up a small creek, set out in the evening in the canoe and got on board the fleet that night opposite Livingston's Manor, whereof I continued until they arrived in New York."

The Saving of the Old Dutch Church. The following incidents are taken from the Sexagenary:

"It was the 8th of October, if I am not mistaken, [the 9th], that Burgoyne's retreat was first discovered. The news created an intoxication of joy in the American camp. My father being well mounted and anxious to see everything that could be seen, and also having a thorough knowledge of the country roads, proposed to two friends, Mr. (Dirck?) Swart, and Mr. Schuyler, [not the General], to go forward for the purpose of obtaining intelligence. They started, taking a private road which came out at Saratoga opposite the church, [which then stood in the fork of the river and Victory roads, south of the creek], and there, at a short distance from them, actually saw the British troops passing by. In consequence of their excessive fatigue and a tremendous rain, they were all day getting there. My father always claimed the credit with his companions for having saved the old church from being burned. A soldier was seen approaching it with fire when they shouted to the man with all their might. He dropped the brand and ran off. They in the same instant turned their horses into the woods, and made off at full speed. My father, although he arrived late that afternoon in the camp, obtained a fresh horse, and reached Albany at 11 o'clock that night, bringing the joyful news of Burgoyne's retreat."

Return to Saratoga. "The intelligence brought by my father [Peter Becker] was indeed joyful to us. He ordered the black to get three horses ready, early in the morning, to take us back to Saratoga. Early as the day dawned, all were on the move, but my mother, who remained behind. We met on the road great numbers of wounded men, belonging to both armies. A great many were carried on litters, which were blankets fastened to a frame of four poles. I never saw the effects of war until now. In camp there was something of 'pomp and circumstance,' which rather animated than depressed the spirits. But the sight of these wretched people, pale and lifeless, with countenances of an expression peculiar to gun-shot wounds, as the surgeons have truly informed us, and the sound of groaning voices, as each motion of the litter renewed the anguish of their wounds, filled me with horror and sickness of heart. And is public happiness then bought at the price of individual wretchedness? Must blood and tears and sorrow be the result of even the most just and righteous controversies? The human heart, 'a tangled yarn,' brings a curse on its own plans.

"We reached the American camp, and drove through it to the bank of the river, opposite my uncle's farm. We got out and walked along the bank to see if there was any chance to get across. My father luckily recognized a Captain Knute, of the bateaumen, who kindly offered us the use of a scow, and indeed saw us safely over the river. We drove that night to our own home. But, oh, how much changed! It looked like a military post, to which use it was actually converted. A thousand eastern militia were quartered around the premises. We began to think we had not gained much by coming on at this juncture." They secured lodgings in their house that night, however. "The next day brought its variety; we discovered that our fellow lodgers were troops from Sheffield, Mass., and, if I remember right, were some of those militiamen who refused to stay with the army until Burgoyne should be compelled to surrender."

The Cannonade of the Old Dutch Church. Young Becker, with a companion, made numerous excursions over to the American camp "to see what was going on." On one of these trips the following occurred: "Every moment the scene was growing more interesting. As we came near the main body of the enemy, which we approached within three-fourths of a mile, and while we were looking round to observe the movements of the different detachments about us, which we could do very distinctly, we observed a flash from a cannon, and almost instantly saw a ball come out of the Saratoga church, apparently deadened by the resistance it had met. It passed over our heads, with a slight whizzing, and struck in the bank behind us, at the distance of three hundred yards. In a few moments another, its fellow, passed through the church in the same manner, and struck in the bank behind us.[1] I judged that the range of these shots was about a mile. The church long exhibited the marks of the balls; but it was pulled down some years ago, [1822] and another of more modern appearance is now devoted, in its place, to religious worship. We did not remain in our position longer. We concluded that we had seen enough for the present."

The Capture of Burgoyne's Horses. "An anecdote recurs to my recollection, which shows the daring of our soldiers. It is well known that the east side of the river was lined with militia. One of them discovered a number of the enemy's horses feeding in the meadow of General Schuyler's, opposite; he asked permission of his captain to go over and get one of them. It was given, and the man instantly stripped, and swam

---

[1] These shots must have been fired from the battery stationed on the bluff at what is now called "Seeleyville." From statements made by various writers of the time, we conclude that the banks of the river and creek were then practically free from trees.

across the river. He ascended the bank, and selecting a bay horse for his victim, approached the animal, seized him, and mounted him instantly. This last was the work of a moment. He forced the horse into a gallop, plunged down the bank, and brought him safely over to the American camp, although a volley of musketry was fired at him from a party posted at a distance beyond. His success was hailed with enthusiasm, and it had a corresponding effect on his own adventurous spirit. After he had rested himself, he went to his officer and remarked, that it was hardly fitting that a private should ride a-horseback while his commander went on foot. 'So, sir, if you have no objections, I will go and catch another for you, and next winter when we are home, we will have our fun driving a pair of Burgine's horses.' The captain seemed to agree with him, and gave a ready consent. The fellow actually went across a second time, and with equal success brought over a horse that matched exceedingly well with the other. The men all enjoyed this prank very much, and it was an incident familiar to almost every one in the army at that time."

Romance of the Maguires. During the time of the cessation of arms, while the articles of capitulation were preparing, the soldiers of the two armies often saluted, and talked with each other from opposite banks of the river. Among the British was a soldier of the 9th regiment [which had its camp just south of the monument] named Maguire, who came down to the river side with a number of his companions, and engaged in conversation with a party of Americans on the further shore. In a short time something was observed to strike the mind of the Hibernian very forcibly. He suddenly jumped up and darted like a flash down the bank and into the river. At the same moment one of the American soldiers seized with a like impulse, resolutely dashed into the water. The wondering soldiers beheld them eagerly swim toward the middle of the river, where they met. Fortunately it was shallow enough for them to stand on the bottom. They embraced, and hung on each other's necks and wept; and the loud cries of 'me brother! me dear brother!!' soon cleared up the mystery to the astonished onlookers. Indeed they were brothers; one had emigrated to America, while the other had entered the British army, and unbeknown to themselves had been engaged in mortal combat against each other".[2]

Reminiscences of the Surrender. On the day of the surrender the "Sexagenary," being only a boy, was allowed by some good-natured officers to get very near to the tent, or marquee, of General Gates, where he had an opportunity to witness what there occurred. He, boy like, watched his chance to peep into the tent while the generals were at dinner. He relates the following, among other things he saw: "At the moment they [the British troops] **stepped foot** within our lines, our drums and music struck up, 'Yankee Doodle.' At this moment the two generals came out together. The American commander faced the road, and Burgoyne did the same, standing on his left. Not a word was said by either, and for some minutes, to the best of my recollection, they stood silently gazing on the scene before them. The one, no doubt, in all the pride of honest success; the other, the victim of regret and sensibility. Burgoyne was a large and stoutly formed man, his countenance was rough and hard, and somewhat marked with scars, if I am not mistaken, but he had a handsome figure and a noble air. Gates was a smaller

---

[2] Stone's Campaign of Burgoyne.

THE STORY OF OLD SARATOGA

man with much less of manner, and destitute of that air which distinguished Burgoyne."[3] His description of the delivery of the sword tallies with that already given. He next describes the captured troops as they passed. He says: "I saw the whole body pass before me. The light infantry, in advance, were extraordinary men. Finer and better looking troops I never saw. They were not seen to much advantage, however, for their small clothes and gaiters having been wet in the creek, the dust[4] adhered to them in consequence. Some of the officers were very elegant men.

"The Hessians came lumbering in the rear. I looked at these men with commiseration. It was well known that their services had been sold by their own petty princes, that they were collected together, if not caught at their churches, and if we may credit the account given us, they were actually torn from their homes and handed over to the British government at so much a head, to be transported across the ocean and wage war against a people of whose history, and even of whose existence, they were ignorant. Many of them deserted to our army before and after the convention of Saratoga. Fifty have been known to come over in one party before the surrender.

"A very remarkable disease prevailed among them, if the accounts of some respectable officers attached to Burgoyne's army may be credited. While on their way down from Canada a presentiment would take possession of twenty or thirty of them at a time that they were going to die, and that they would never again see their fatherland. The impression could not be effaced from their minds, notwithstanding every exertion of their officers

---

[3] Anburey's Travels, p. 324.
[4] The "dust" proves that they had clear weather at the time of the surrender.

and the administering of medicines. A homesickness of the most fatal kind oppressed their spirits and destroyed their health; and a large number actually died of this disorder of the heart.

"The Hessians were extremely dirty in their persons, and had a collection of wild animals in their train—the only thing American they had captured. Here you saw an artilleryman leading a black bear, who every now and then would rear upon his hind legs as if he were tired of going upon all fours, or occasionally growl his disapprobation at being pulled along by a chain. In the same manner a tamed deer would be seen tripping lightly after a grenadier. Young foxes were also observed looking sagaciously at the spectators from the top of a baggage wagon, or a young raccoon securely clutched under the arm of a sharpshooter.

"On the evening of the surrender a number of Indians and squaws, the relics of Burgoyne's aboriginal force, were brought over for safe keeping to my uncle's farm, and quartered under a strong guard in the kitchen. Without this precaution their lives would not have been safe from the exasperated militia. The murder of Miss M'Crea was but one of a number of their atrocities which hardened every heart against them, and prevented the plea of mercy from being interposed in their behalf. Among those savages were three that were between six and seven feet in height, perfect giants in form, and possessing the most ferocious countenances I ever saw. [Neilson claims that the big Indian with whom his father had his life and death struggle at Ensign's was one of these.]

"It was three days after the surrender that our camp began to be broken up. The militia were assiduous in exploring the fields for plunder and the concealed treasure of the vanquished. Immense quantities of camp

THE STORY OF OLD SARATOGA

furniture and fragments of every description were strewed about, 'and they spoiled the Egyptians.' Opposite our own house my father found a large number of hides and a considerable quantity of tallow. This, however, neither graced his store nor greased his boots. Our friends, the *irregulars,* spared him the trouble of carrying them home. In this way closed the eventful history of Saratoga. Blood and carnage were succeeded by success and plunder. My father once more commenced the labors of a husbandman, and after preparing the ground in a great hurry, and sowing his winter wheat, went off to Albany to bring home his wife."

Elbow Room for Burgoyne. " I'll make the rebels give me plenty of elbow room when I get in Albany!" was one of the many boasts uttered by Burgoyne on his way down from Ticonderoga, and which happened to be overheard by some one, who besides being a rebel, was likewise guilty of eaves-dropping.

By some means the above expression became known in Albany before his arrival. Generals Burgoyne and Riedesel were riding side by side, attended by some American generals. Many people had assembled from the surrounding country to witness the grand *entree.*

As the cavalcade struck the pavement in North Market street (Broadway), there appeared suddenly, a little in advance of the generals, a witty, waggish son of the Emerald Isle, accompanied by a few kindred spirits. At once he began elbowing his comrades right and left and shouting with stentorian lungs: "Now, shure and ye'll shtand back an' giv' Gineral Bergine plenthy av ilbow room right here in Albany; I say, ye darthy ribels, fall back and giv' th' great Gineral room to come along here in Albany! Och, fer hiven's sake, ye cowardly shpalpeens, do ye shtand aside to th' right and lift and make more ilbow room for Gineral Bergine or, by Saint Patrick, I'll murther iv'ry mother's son av ye!!" The proud General was not a little disconcerted and annoyed by these hard rubs of this Irish *quidnunc,* but apparently not so much as the German General.[5]

Burgoyne was greatly astonished when, after halting and dismounting before a palatial residence, he was ushered into the presence of Mrs. Philip Schuyler, wife of the General, and found that the man whom he had so greatly injured was to be his host. He afterward paid a glowing tribute to Schuyler's generosity in a fine speech delivered in the British Parliament.

After the surrender, General Schuyler remained at Saratoga to look after his private affairs. He sent on Colonel Varrick to Mrs. Schuyler, in Albany, to announce the speedy coming of some guests from the vanquished army. He sent thither the Baroness Riedesel and her children in his own carriage, while Generals Burgoyne and Riedesel, and officers of their staffs, were escorted on horseback, the latter in company with General Glover. Mrs. Schuyler received these guests with her accustomed cordiality, and all of them, with the Baroness and her little daughters, were treated as friends and not as enemies.

Not long after their arrival one of Madame Riedesel's little girls, after frolicking about the spacious and well-furnished mansion, ran up to her mother and, with all the simplicity of youthful innocence, inquired in German: "Mother, is this the palace father was to have when he came to America?" The blushing Baroness speedily silenced her child, for some of the family who were present could understand German.

Saratoga After the Departure of the British. It is certain that a good-sized force wintered here at

---

[5] Simm's Frontiersmen of New York. Vol. II, p. 132.

Old Saratoga after the surrender, but it was withdrawn in the early spring and sent southward. This left the inhabitants hereabouts utterly defenseless, whereat General Schuyler and many others protested vigorously.[6] This was remedied soon afterwards.

The Sexagenary has bequeathed us several interesting facts connected with that period. He says:

"During the winter, [of 1777-'78] notwithstanding the utter annihilation of anything like a regular and effective force by the capture of Burgoyne, yet the country was considered liable to the incursions of small parties of the enemy. Among other things, the church at Saratoga was occupied as a public depot, and the commissary in addition had it partitioned off inside and lived in it. Many a time have I seen barrels of pork and beef rolled in at the sacred porch, which so often had been proclaimed the gate of Heaven. One of the evils of war is the perversion of the most sacred things to the necessities of the moment. In Boston the famous Old South church was converted into a riding school by the British officers. A church in New York was made a prison for our sick and captured countrymen. The conversion of the church at Saratoga into a commissary's store was the only instance within my knowledge of a similar voluntary abuse by the Americans. [This was no doubt because the church was the only building of size left in the vicinity.] During the same winter, General Schuyler had twenty-four men constantly in attendance at his residence as a life guard, and, if I am right in my recollection, during the remainder of the war."

The Search for Cannon, etc. During the season of 1778 a part of the 1st N. Y., Van Schaick's regiment, was stationed here. The troops were under

---
[6] Public Papers of George Clinton. Vol. III, p. 177.

the immediate command of Lieutenant-Colonel Van
Dyke. That summer, Colonel Quackenboss of the
quartermaster's department came up to Saratoga with
boats and all proper equipment to look for cannon
which Burgoyne was supposed to have sunk in the river
between the rapids and the mouth of Fishcreek. They
hunted diligently and the only thing found was a barrel
of British smoked hams of royal quality. That same
summer a militia captain from Schenectady, by the name
of Clute, while swimming in the river where Quackenboss had dragged, discovered a small brass howitzer.
Calling on some of the neighboring farmers for help, he
succeeded in landing it. He sold it to the government
for a good round sum. It was then dragged up to the
barracks.[7]

Raids of Tories and Indians. The following year,
1780, the inhabitants north of Albany and Schenectady
were kept in continual alarm by the frequent raids of
Indians and Tories from the north. It was the year
when Ballston was pounced upon by Colonel Munro with
two hundred followers, who captured and carried into
Canada Colonel Gordon and a number of his neighbors.
The Sexagenary writes of this time:

" In Saratoga we continued constantly exposed to the
harassing incursions of the Tories and Indians. Almost
the whole country was alarmed by them, and, with the
subtilty peculiar to the savage intellect, they seemed to
escape every attempt at capture. Often we have seen
them running across the fields upon the opposite [west]
side of the river, now stooping behind fences which
afforded them a partial cover, and now boldly running
across the open ground, where the fences were down, to

---

[7] These facts are taken from the Sexagenary.

some other enclosed field, along which they skulked as before. During these alarms our neighbors used to come and live with us for weeks together, until the danger was over. The principal men of the country had guards stationed at their dwellings."

Colonel Van Veghten's Narrow Escape. "One of our neighbors, a Colonel Van Veghten, who lived about three miles below the barracks [at Coveville], had a narrow escape about the same time. He was in the habit of riding from his own house up to General Schuyler's and to the barracks in order to receive and communicate intelligence.

"Those acquainted with the road will remember the ravine and creek just before you reach the [Dutch Reformed] church. [It is just south of what is now called Chubb's canal bridge.] In this ravine, concealed behind the trees, a Tory placed himself to shoot Van Veghten as he passed, who had rendered himself obnoxious to the partisans of the English by his constant assiduity in the service of his country. As he approached, mounted on his favorite gray, the assassin raised his gun to fire. His finger was on the trigger, when, as he afterwards confessed, the bold and manly air which Van Veghten possessed, joined to his unsuspecting manner, unnerved his arm. The weapon of death dropped from its position, and Colonel Van Veghten rode by unharmed. It so happened, however, that an alarm, which was given while he was at Saratoga, about a body of Indians and Tories having been seen, induced him to take the river road on his way home, and to give it the preference ever afterwards."[8]

[8] This indicates that there was a road at the time of and before the Revolution, near the river bank, as there still is north of Wilbur's Basin, and used to be between Wilbur's Basin and Bemis Heights.

The Dog Gagged by a Garter. The following incident was related to the writer by Mrs. E. M. McCoy, daughter of the late George Strover:

Her grandfather, John Strover, lived on his farm, over near Bryant's bridge, during those precarious times. The refuge selected for his family in case of danger was a sort of cave under the bank of the creek, and not far from the house. This could be entered only at low water during the summer. One day, being warned of the approach of Tories and Indians, she, with her children and a little dog, ran to the cave. For fear lest the dog, a noisy little cur, should bark and betray their hiding place, she took off her knitted garter and wrapped it tightly around his muzzle. It proved to be a most effective gag, and they escaped without being discovered.

Dunham's Daring Capture of Lovelass, the Spy. It was during this or the previous season that the following incident occurred. Thomas Lovelass, a bold, resolute, and powerful man, was a noted leader among the Tories. He had succeeded in the capture of a number of his neighbors and in the destruction of much property among the patriots, and was considered a most dangerous partisan.

A goodly number of the people hereabouts were attending some entertainment or social function. While there, a boy was seen to emerge from the woods on horseback, and then riding up to the house asked if he could buy some rum there. On being answered, No, he went on down the river road. Among those present who observed him were Colonel Van Veghten and Captain Hezekiah Dunham. Dunham was a captain of militia, and a man of large influence among his neighbors. There was something in the behavior of the boy which aroused their suspicions, so he decided to watch the outcome. In a little while the boy was seen to ride back up the road at full speed, re-enter the woods and vanish. Dunham turned to Colonel Van Veghten and said: "The enemy is near us, the Tories are in the neighborhood, and not far off." They separated with a determination to act immediately. Dunham, when he reached home, went to see a person by the name of Green, who was a kindred spirit and a great leader among his neighbors. On relating the circumstance to him, they went and got three other men, and with these started out on the search. Every suspected place was carefully examined. They continued the search until near daylight without avail, when they separated; Green and one man going in one direction, and Dunham, with two, taking another course. The latter, as a last resort, returned to the house of one Odeurman, who he believed would be in communication with an enemy, if near him. Near the house they discovered a path leading through a meadow toward a thicket about three acres in size. At once they suspected that this led to the object of their search. Following it they passed nearly around the thicket, when it entered the bush. Toward the center a big log blocked the way; on peeping over it cautiously there, sure enough, was the remains of a camp-fire and a group of five fierce-looking men. They were in the act of putting on their shoes and stockings. And one thing more which Dunham particularly observed was a musket by the side of every man, ready for instant service. He drew back, reported to his companions and in a whisper asked, "Shall we take 'em?" A nod of assent was the answer; then moving forward to the log, they all mounted at the same instant, and Dunham shouted, "Surrender, or you are all dead men! All of them but their leader seemed petrified by the suddenness of the apparition. He was not disposed to yield without an effort at defense. Twice he was reaching for his gun when he found Dunham's rifle ominously near his head, at which he prudently desisted. They were then ordered out, one by one, when they were securely bound. Immediately they were marched off to the barracks at Saratoga.

They were tried and condemned at a court martial, of which the celebrated General Stark was the president. Lovelass alone was adjudged worthy of death, as he was considered too dangerous a man to be allowed to escape. In defense, he protested that he had been taken with arms in his hand, and ought therefore to be accounted a prisoner of war. But the court was inexorable.[9]

He was hung on the top of the gravel hill, just south of the Horicon mill, which then extended beyond the present highway to the east. The traditional spot is just east of the angle made by the picket and board fences and across the road from the brick house. He was buried in an upright position. John Strover was present and marked the spot. He told his son, George, about it, and when the bank was excavated for the Whitehall turnpike he was on hand and identified the skeleton. The skull of the Tory is preserved by Mrs. J. H. Lowber in the Schuyler mansion.

About the Number Thirteen. That there were not wanting in the British armies those who could extract a bit of fun from what they saw in America, among the rebels, the following extract from the Diary of the Rev. Frank Moore will prove. Evidently he was a chaplain in some one of their regiments stationed in New York city.

Abridged from the Sexagenary's account.

"Thirteen is a number peculiarly belonging to the rebels. A party of naval prisoners, lately returned from Jersey, say that the rations among the rebels are thirteen dried clams per diem; that the titular Lord Sterling takes thirteen glasses of grog each morning, has thirteen enormous rum bunches on his nose, and that (when duly impregnated) he always makes thirteen attempts before he can walk; that Mr. Washington has thirteen toes on his feet, (the extra ones having grown since the Declaration of Independence) and the same number of teeth in each jaw; that the Sachem Schuyler has a top knot of thirteen stiff hairs which erect themselves on the crown of his head whenever he gets mad; that it takes thirteen congress paper dollars to equal one penny Sterling; that Polly Wayne was just thirteen hours subduing Stony Point, and just thirteen seconds in leaving it; that a well organized rebel household has thirteen children, all of whom expect to be Generals, or members of the High and Mighty Congress of the Thirteen States, when they attain thirteen years; that Mrs. Washington has a mottled tom cat (which she calls in a complimentary way 'Hamilton') with thirteen yellow rings around his tail, and that his flaunting it suggested to the Congress the adoption of the same number of stripes for the rebel flag." And we moderns might add that there were just thirteen articles in the document known as the Convention of Saratoga, by the signing of which Gen. Burgoyne agreed to surrender himself and army to these same contemptible thirteen States, and that he marched through thirteen towns and cities on his way to Boston, following the lead of that rebel flag with its thirteen stars and stripes. Sure, thirteen proved an unlucky number for Britons in this country.

CHAPTER XXI

War of 1812 and the Civil War

The war of 1812, our second war for independence with old England, naturally aroused a great deal of interest in this quarter, and awakened not a little apprehension among the dwellers in this valley. For they knew not but they might be called upon to undergo a repetition of the sacrifices and sufferings of the fathers in Revolutionary days. But fortunately for them, the scenes of actual warfare, in this department, were confined to the northern end of Lake Champlain. The glorious naval victory of Macdonough in Cumberland bay, and of General McComb at Plattsburgh, on September 11, 1814, put an effectual end to British attempts at entering the country through this ancient gateway. It is interesting to note in passing that Macdonough's flagship was named the Saratoga; and right worthily did she behave herself that day, under her heroic commander, brightening the halo of glory which already surrounded the name. This locality sent its full quota of soldiery at that time to aid in the general defense. No armies of size passed up through this way during that war, as was expected, and even feared.

The Civil War. Fourscore years after our Revolutionary fathers had " brought forth on this continent a new nation, conceived in liberty and dedicated to the " realization of the proposition that all men's inalienable rights should be acknowledged and defended by the government under which they live, we found ourselves engaged in a great civil war, " testing whether that nation, or any nation, so conceived, and so dedicated, could long endure."

Splendid Exhibition of Patriotism. Many at the time believed that the spirit of patriotism was practically dead in our land, and when brought to the test, few would be found ready to venture "their lives, their fortunes, or their sacred honor," in the "deadly breach" for the preservation of the nation's life. But when the crisis arrived, it was found that love of country, so far from being dead in the hearts of the people, exhibited a more vigorous life than had ever yet been seen; that when the people found themselves face to face with the awful question of union or dis-union and our ultimate disintegration as a nation, their patriotism arose to such a pitch of enthusiasm that they counted no sacrifice too great, if only by such sacrifice the nation's life could be preserved.

The way in which the people of the North arose to the occasion when the news spread that the flag had been fired on, and blood had been spilt by traitorous hands, affords one of the grandest and most thrilling spectacles in the history of the nations.

New York State stood second to none of her eighteen sisters, at the North, in the ardor with which she devoted her sons and poured forth her treasure to insure a sufficiency of force with which to repel the invader, and crush out the rebellion. No county in the State excelled Saratoga in the alacrity with which she responded to every call made upon her to take up and bear her share of the burdens, and no township in the county was represented by a larger proportion of her sons on the perilous edge of battle than was Old Saratoga.

"Bull Run" Dispels an Illusion. The first troops that hastened to the defense of the Nation's capital, when menaced by the insurgents, were the militia regiments, which were already old organizations. Soon President Lincoln felt constrained to issue a call for 64,000 men for the army and 18,000 for the navy, in the belief that the insurrection could be quelled in a hundred days. Quite a number from this township responded to that call. But the disastrous battle of Bull Run effectually dispelled the illusion that the rebellion could be easily, or speedily, put down, and wrought mightily in awakening the country to the gravity of the situation. Soon the President issued a proclamation calling for 300,000 men to serve for three years, or during the war.

Judge McKean's Call to Arms. The Hon. James B. McKean, of Saratoga Springs, the representative in Congress from this district at that time, issued the following stirring circular to his constituents:

"FELLOW CITIZENS OF THE FIFTEENTH CONGRESSIONAL DISTRICT:—Traitors in arms seek to overthrow our constitution and to seize our capital. Let us go and help to defend them. Who will despond because we lost the battle of Bull Run? Our fathers lost the battle of Bunker Hill, but it taught them how to gain the victory at Bemis Heights.

" Let us learn wisdom from disaster, and send overwhelming numbers into the field. Let farmers, mechanics, merchants, and all classes—for the liberties of all are at stake—aid in organizing companies. I will cheerfully assist in procuring the necessary papers. Do not misunderstand me. I am not asking for an office at your hands. If you who have most at stake will go, I will willingly go with you as a private soldier.

"Let us organize a Bemis Heights Battalion, and vie with each other in serving our country, thus showing that we are inspired by the holy memories of the Revolutionary battle fields upon and near which we are living.

"JAMES B. McKEAN.

"Saratoga Springs, August 21, 1861."

Judge McKean followed this up by a campaign of patriotic speeches throughout his district. At once the young men began to enlist by scores and hundreds, and military companies were organized here and there and began to drill. Soon Saratoga Springs was appointed as a recruiting station and rendezvous. The fair-ground was appropriated for the camp, and was christened Camp Schuyler. Thither the recruits were sent, and by the middle of November, 1861, had been drilled into some semblance of a regiment.

Judge McKean was fittingly selected as colonel of the regiment, and he proved to be a most excellent selection. At first this body called itself the Bemis Heights Battalion, but in the numbering of the regiments of the State, the number 77 fell to it, which considering the fact that it was chiefly raised and recruited in Saratoga county, and that the great battle of Bemis Heights, or Saratoga, was fought in 1777, that number seemed eminently appropriate.

On Thanksgiving Day, November 28, 1861, the regiment marched out of camp, 864 strong, and started for Washington, where it arrived December 1st. On the 15th of February following, it joined the 3rd Brigade, of the 2nd Division, of the 6th Army Corps, which connection it retained throughout the whole period of its service. Immediately on coming into close proximity with the enemy, the usual sifting process began. The poltroons and cowards got out on one pretext or another, leaving only the true hearts and brave to face the music. But fortunately the latter were in the vast majority.

Hardships Decimate the Regiment. The regiment received its first baptism of fire at Lee's Mills, Va., on the 4th of April 1862. But that proved to be only the preliminary skirmish of many a hard-fought battle. The Penninsular Campaign, which immediately followed, with its hardships of mud marches, and battles, and camp fevers, sadly decimated the regiment. Because of this, some of the most efficient officers were sent back to recruit the depleted ranks. Colonel McKean among others, lost his health and was forced to retire.

Schuylerville Raises a Company. At that time Schuylerville greatly distinguished herself by raising an entire company of men, which became known as Company K of the 77th. The first ten men received a bounty of ten dollars apiece. Those who enlisted afterward received all the way from fifty to three hundred dollars, bounty money. The company chose for its captain, John R. Rockwell, then editor of the Saratoga *American, (the local paper).* First lieutenant, William H. Fursman; second lieutenant, Cyrus F. Rich. This company by no means represented all that went from this township; for no less than 340 marched from this historic town to the defense of the Union. Three-fourths of them, however, were members of the 77th, and shared in the glory of her achievements. Colonel W. B. French became commander of the regiment after the retirement of Colonel McKean. Quite a number of the men from this township served in other distinguished regiments, as the 30th and the 44th, also in other arms of the service.

List of Battles in Which the 77th Participated. The history of the achievements and experiences of each of these regiments, especially the 77th, and the famous Sixth Corps, of which it formed a part, is well worthy of the volumes that have been written upon them. Dr. George T. Stevens' history of the 77th is especially worthy of perusal. To that and other works we refer the interested reader for details. We must give space, however, to the following important facts: The 77th served under Generals McClellan, Burnside, Hooker, Meade and Grant, each of whom for a time had command of the Army of the Potomac. It went through the Peninsular Campaign in 1862, the Campaign of 1863, which took it again into Virginia and afterward into Maryland and Pennsylvania. In 1864 it served for a time in the Wilderness Campaign under Grant; but after Spottsylvania it was withdrawn with the Sixth Corps for the defense of Washington; thence it was sent into the Shenandoah Valley, where it served through that remarkable campaign under Sheridan, participating in the battles of Winchester and especially of Cedar Creek, where a reinforcement of one man (Sheridan) turned ignominious defeat into a glorious victory.

The 77th was in the following battles:
Lee's Mills, April 4, 1862.
Williamsburg, May 5, 1862.
Mechanicsville, May 24, 1862.
Golding's Farm, June 5, 1862.
Garnett's Hill, June 28, 1862.
Savage Station, June 29, 1862.
White Oak Swamp, June 30, 1862.
Malvern Hill, July 1, 1862.
Crampton Gap, September 14, 1862.
Antietam, September 17, 1862.
Fredericksburgh, December 13, 1862.
St. Marye's Heights, May 3, 1863.
Franklin's Crossing, June 5, 1863.
Gettysburg, July 2 and 3, 1863.

Spottsylvania, May 10, 1864.
Defense of Washington, July 13, 1864.
Winchester, September 19, 1864.
Cedar Creek, October 19, 1864.

It was at Cedar Creek that the stand made by the 6th Corps, of which the 77th formed a part, saved the day, and was holding the Confederates in check when Sheridan arrived on the scene—"From Winchester, twenty miles away."

Mustered Out. Says Colonel French, in his sketch of the 77th, " With this grand and wonderful battle, the fighting experience of the 77th regiment closed, and its term of service having expired, it was ordered to Saratoga Springs to be mustered out, where it arrived on the 23rd of November, 1864, just three years after the day of its mustering in. The regiment of 105 men and 14 officers, all that returned of the 1,369 that had served with it, was received with all the love and honor a patriotic people could bestow. They were received by a series of speeches in the public hall, and were then treated to a splendid banquet tendered by the citizens of Saratoga Springs, at the American hotel." [So much of Company K as returned at this time to Schuylerville, after having marched through the streets, were given a collation by the ladies of the Reformed church.]

" This is the history in brief of Saratoga county's pet regiment, the 77th, a record of noble deeds without a single blot. It never, by any act on the field or in the camp, on the march or in the fight, disgraced the county from which it was sent. It never flinched or wavered from any duty, however perilous, which was assigned to it, nor until properly ordered, did it ever turn its back upon the foe. From the beginning to the end of its service the regiment bore its colors untouched by the hand of the enemy. They were often shattered and torn by shot and shell, often leveled to the dust by the death or a wound of their bearers, but they were always kept sacred, and on the muster out of the regiment, were deposited in the Bureau of Military Statistics at Albany."

What Colonel French has said of the 77th could be said with equal truth, we are assured of the other regiments which were partially recruited from the town of Saratoga.

Suffering and Sacrifices of the Wives and Mothers.
Thus we see that many of the boys who marched forth returned no more forever; those who came back were greatly changed. The health of many was shattered. Some were maimed and crippled in body, most of them returned with new habits and altered ambitions. There were empty places in almost every household in those days. Everywhere was to be seen the badge of mourning worn by women; old and young were in black gowns, or, if there was no crape on their persons, it was quite sure to be upon their hearts. For the men at home as well as at the front, there was excitement in the description of a charge, the fierce struggle and victory. But precious little excitement or consolation was there in this for the wife, the mother or the betrothed, left behind at home; no glory in it for her, only silent suffering and abiding anxiety. No adequate history could ever be written of the women of the Civil War; but it is strange indeed, that no great sculptor, or architect, has been commissioned to erect some mighty monument to commemorate in enduring marble and bronze her heroism, her sacrifices and her achievements.

19

Most fittingly has the poet said:

"The maid who binds her warrior's sash,
   With a smile that well her grief dissembles,
The while beneath her drooping lash
   One starry teardrop hangs and trembles,
Tho' heaven alone record the tear,
   And fame shall never know her story,
Her heart doth shed a drop as dear
   As ever dewed the field of glory.

"The wife who girds her husband's sword
   'Mid little ones who weep and wonder,
And bravely speaks the cheering word
   What though her heart be rent asunder,
Doomed nightly in her dreams to hear
   The bolts of war around him rattle,
Hath shed as sacred blood as e'er
   Was poured upon a field of battle.

"The mother who conceals her grief
   When to her heart her son she presses,
Then breathes a few brave words and brief,
   Kissing the patriot brow she blesses,
With no one but her secret God
   To know the pain that weighs upon her,
Sheds holy blood as e'er the sod
   Received on Freedom's field of honor."

BOOK II

CIVIL HISTORY

CHAPTER I

SCHUYLERVILLE is fittingly named, and yet the student of the history of this locality cannot repress a sentimental wish that the ancient name (Saratoga) had been retained. Indeed, the older inhabitants hereabouts speak of the district between here and Coveville as Old Saratoga. We have not been able to ascertain when the name Schuylerville was given to the place, but can trace it back to 1820.

Saratoga—Significance of the Name. The name Saratoga passed through many vicissitudes at the hands of public officials before the spelling became settled. Note the variety of spelling as it appears in the Documentary History of New York: Cheragtoge, Sarachtitoge, Sarachtoga, Saractoga, Saraghtoga, Saragtoga, Saratoge, Saraktoga, Sarastague, Sarastaugue, Schorachtoge, Sarasteau, Saraston, Saratogo, Sarrantau, Serachtague, Seraghtoga, Soraghtoga, *Saratoga*. Thus the modern spelling of this name affords a good example of the survival of the fittest in orthography.

Saratoga is an Indian word. The red men applied it to one of their favorite hunting and fishing grounds located on the west side of the Hudson river, extending from three to ten miles back from the stream, and an indefinite distance both north and south of Fishcreek, which empties into the river at Schuylerville. The colonists adopted this name and applied it to a district covering both sides of the Hudson and extending from the mouth of the Mohawk, north to the vicinity of Fort Miller. Afterward it began at Mechanicville instead of Cohoes.

Quite naturally when they established the first settlement within this district, that at the junction of Fishcreek with the Hudson, they named it Saratoga.

As to the significance of the name several traditions are extant. One is that it means "the hillside country of the great river;" another says it means "place of the swift water," in allusion to the rapids just above Schuylerville. Two men, Horatio Hale, M. A., of Clinton, Ontario, and Dr. D. G. Brinton of Philadelphia, Pa., who made a special study of the Iroquois and Mohican languages, agreed that Ochserantongue, as it was written in the original Saratoga Patent, means "at the beaver dam," or, "the place of beavers." One who knows the lay of the land hereabouts, and the habits of the beaver can regard this as credible.[1]

Mr. J. L. Weed of Ballston, N. Y., told the writer that an old uncle of his, Joseph Brown, an early settler, who had native Indians for neighbors on Saratoga lake, used to say the word means "place of herrings," suggested by the vast number of those fish which they used to catch in the river and creeks hereabouts. To the writer this seems very satisfactory for the reason that both the Dutch and English gave the analogous name Fishkill or Fishcreek to the outlet of Saratoga lake, because of the myriads of herrings which used to swarm up through it in the spring of the year into that lake; and secondly, because of the extensive fish weirs which the Indians constructed along the outlet of the lake for catching herring.

---

[1] See Proceedings of the N. Y. State Historical Ass'n, Vol. VI, part Second, p. 180. This Part Second is an exhaustive study of Indian place names.

THE STORY OF OLD SARATOGA 283

The Saratoga Patent. The circumstances under which the white man first settled here are as follows: In the year 1683, four Albanians, Cornelis Van Dyk, Jan Jansen Bleecker, Peter Phillipsen Schuyler and Johannes Wendel, purchased from the Mohawks their old hunting grounds called "Ochserantogue, or Sarachtogie."

On November 4, 1684, Governor Dongan granted a patent for this tract to seven persons, Cornelis Van Dyk, John J. Bleecker, Pieter Phillipse Schuyler, Johannes Wendel, Dirck Wessels Ten Broeck, David Schuyler and Robert Livingston, for which they were to pay an annual rental to the crown of twenty bushels of wheat. This was confirmed by Lord Cornbury, in June, 1708. In this confirmatory patent the name of Johannes Schuyler appears in the place of Johannes Wendel.

This patent took in both sides of the Hudson river, from the Anthony's Kill, at Mechanicville, north to opposite the mouth of the Battenkill, and from the Hoosac river north to the Battenkill (then called Dionoondahowa), on the east side. It extended six miles back from the river on both sides, and being, as was supposed, twenty-two miles long, made a tract of 264 square miles.

The next year the patentees made a division of the arable lands lying along the river. The division was made by five disinterested men, then seven numbers written on slips of paper were thrown in a hat, and the children of the patentees drew the numbers. Lot 4, which lay just south of Fish creek, fell to Johannes Wendel; Lot 5, north of the creek, fell to Robert Livingston; Lot 6, which extended south from the Battenkill to Titmousekill, fell to David Schuyler. In March, 1686, David Schuyler sold his seventh share to Robert Livingston and Peter Schuyler for 55£ 16s ($279). Livingston took the part opposite his own Lot 5, and Schuyler that part opposite Lots 2 and 3, which would take in from opposite Bemis Heights to opposite a point about a mile and one-half north of Coveville. On this section lived a Frenchman by the name of Du Bison.

Johannes Wendel seems to have taken immediate steps to improve his property. The inducements were sufficiently strong to lead several to venture up this way and settle. But at that day, and for a long while after, it proved to be a very risky undertaking.

First Settlers. We get our first hints of any settlement at Saratoga from the minutes of the Council of Albany. There we learn that several families were living in the region of Stillwater and Saratoga in the winter of 1688-9. Most of them were French refugees. Those were the days of religious persecution, now happily a thing of the past. It was then the policy of the French to permit none but Roman Catholics to settle in Canada, and to banish all others who might find their way there. The province of New York being the most accessible, the exiled Huguenots were sent this way, and several of them found a home in Albany or its vicinity. A few families were induced to settle on the Saratoga patent. After they were thus located, it was suspected, and with good reason, that the Canadian government caused some of its friends to emigrate and settle among them as refugees, and then acting as spies, to keep them acquainted with what was going on among the English colonists. During the winter of 1688-9 the Council caused several of the suspected ones to be arrested on the rumor that they were aiding soldiers to desert to Canada. The names of those arrested were Antonie Lespenard, John Van Loon, Lafleur, and Villeroy. They proved to be innocent. Antonie Lespenard afterward moved to New York, where he became the founder of a prominent family. One of the streets of America's metropolis still bears his name.

It was in the mid-summer of 1689 that the Iroquois confederacy made its famous raid into Canada, which came near wiping out that infant colony in flames and blood. On the 1st of September, that year, a report reached Albany that three people had been killed at Bartel Vrooman's, at Saratoga, by some Indians from Canada; the first blow struck on this side the big waters in King William's war, and the forerunner of Schenectady. The Council assembled and resolved to dispatch Lieutenant Jochem Staats, with ten men, to Sarachtoge to learn the situation and report at once. Robert Sanders and Egbert Teunise were also commissioned to go with some friendly Indians on a scout thither for the like purpose.

At the same session (September 5th), the Council resolved to build a fort around Vrooman's house, and "that twelve men be sent there to lie upon pay." Their stiped was 12d per day besides provisions. Schaghticoke Indians were to act for them as scouts.

This fort, together with the houses it protected, were evidently abandoned for the winter of 1689-90, else the French and Indian expedition against Schenectady, which came this way and from this point took the Saratoga trail, would have been discovered by these settlers.

Johannes Wendel died in 1691, and left his Saratoga property to his son, Abraham, who in turn sold it to Johannes Schuyler, in 1702, for 125£ ($600).

Schuyler was soon able, after he got possession, to induce some families to venture up this way again, for Lord Cornbury reports their settlement here in 1703, and adds that they should be protected by a fort or they would probably desert the locality. In 1709, the fort was built, as preliminary to an expedition against Canada, by Peter Schuyler, but it was located on the east side of the river. This was in Queen Anne's war, during which period Saratoga was made a depot of supplies for the invading armies. It is well to recall that Pieter and Johannes Schuyler, large owners in the Saratoga patent, were among the chiefest heroes of that war in this country.

A long peace of thirty-two years ensued after Queen Anne's war, which furnished both the time and the conditions necessary for colonial development.

The Schuylers, being energetic men, improved their opportunity; settlers flocked in, to whom they sold no land, but gave long leases. There being here an excellent water power, and the means of transportation good, saw and grist mills were erected, and the products of the soil and forests found a ready market down the river, whither they were floated on bateaux or large flat boats.

Location of Old Saratoga and the Mills. The old village of Saratoga and most of the mills were on the south side of the creek till after 1765. The Livingstons apparently did little to develop their holdings here, where Schuylerville now stands, so long as they owned it. There seems to have been not more than one or two houses north of Fish creek at the time of the massacre, in 1745. The village and the fort were below the creek, on the flats, and hillside.

But few records have been preserved concerning Old Saratoga, between Queen Anne's war, 1709, and King George's war, 1745. The following may prove of some interest to modern Schuylervillans.

In 1720, we find the Indian commissioners reproving some Mohawk Indians for killing cattle at Saratoga.[2] Domestic animals were unknown to the Indians before the advent of the white man, and the idea of personal

---

[2] Documents relating to Colonial Hist. of N. Y. Vol. V, p. 566.

THE STORY OF OLD SARATOGA 287

ownership in an animal so large as cattle, sheep, horses, etc., was apparently hard for them to grasp. The deer and the elk, that roamed the forests, belonged to any one who could get them.

In 1721, they began to take an interest in the improvement of highways in this part of the colony. The Legislature appointed as first commissioners for the district of Saratoga, north of Half Moon, Robert Livingston, Jr., Col. Johannes Schuyler and Major Abraham Schuyler. Livingston then owned the site of Schuylerville; Johannes Schuyler was the grandfather of Gen. Philip Schuyler.[3]

In 1723, several families of Schaghticoke Indians were living here. Through fear of the New England Indians, they emigrated to Canada.[4]

In 1726, the Legislature, in pursuance of a petition from a number of those primitive Saratogans, passed an act prohibiting swine from running at large, as they had heretofore, to the great annoyance and damage of the good people. The limits of that provision were from "Dove Gatt" northward, on both sides of the river.[5]

In 1729, the names of Philip Schuyler, Garrett Ridder and Cornelius Van Beuren appear as the highway commissioners, by appointment.[6] These names are all familiar to this locality. This Philip Schuyler, son of Johannes, was the one shot in his house in the massacre. The De Ridders settled on the east side of the river. When they came does not appear, but the fact that Garrett (De) Ridder's name appears as such commissioner, would indicate that he was already located in this vicinity, or, at least, had property interests here.

---

[3] Colonial Laws of N. Y. Vol. II, p. 69.
[4] Documents relating to Colonial Hist. of N. Y. Vol. V, p. 722.
[5] This is the first time the name Dovegat (Coveville) appears in the records.
[6] Colonial Laws of N. Y. Vol. II, p. 301. Ibid, p. 516.

The tragic story of the destruction of Old Saratoga has already been told in our military annals. Unfortunately the names of but few of those carried captive into Canada have been preserved.

Resettlement After the Massacre. Despite the hard and bitter fate of those primitive Saratogans, there were found a number of people willing to venture hither and settle again on the land that had but recently been wet with the blood and tears of so many victims of the late war. Who they were, we have not as yet been able to discover. De Ridder is the only name preserved to us from that lot of plucky pioneers who dared, immediately after King George's war, to attempt the resurrection of Old Saratoga from the ashes.

Visit of Kalm. Peter Kalm, the great Swedish naturalist and traveler, came up through here in the summer of 1749, on his way to Canada. He has left behind a very interesting record of his travels and observations in America.

On the 22d of June, 1749, he started for the north, from Albany, in a white pine dugout, or canoe, accompanied by two guides. They lodged the first night in the vicinity of the falls at Cohoes. On their way up the river, the next day, they had great trouble in getting over the rapids. The greater part of both sides of the stream was densely wooded, though here and there was to be seen a clearing, devoted to meadow and the growing of maize.

He says: "The farms are commonly built close to the river-side, sometimes on the hills. Each house has a little kitchen garden, and a still lesser orchard. Some farms, however, had large gardens. The kitchen gardens afford several kinds of gourds, [squash] watermelons and kidney beans. The orchards are full of apple trees. This year the trees had few or no apples, on account of the frosts in May, and the drought which had continued throughout the summer.[7]

He tells of seeing quantities of sturgeon toward evening, leaping high out of the water, and how he saw many white men and Indians fishing for them, at night, with pine-knot torches and spears. Many of them, which they could not secure, afterward died of their wounds, lodged on the shore, and filled the air with their stench.

"June 23d. This night we lodged with a farmer, who had returned to his farm after the war was over. [This must have been in the vicinity of Stillwater.] All his buildings, except the great barn, were burnt. It was the last in the Province of New York, toward Canada, which had been left standing and which was now inhabited. Further on we met still with inhabitants; but they had no houses, and lived in huts of boards, the houses being burnt during the war."

That night, the 24th of June, he accepted the hospitality of a settler at Saratoga and lodged in one of those huts. We have elsewhere given his version of the French attack on Fort Clinton. The morning of the 25th, he resumed his journey northward. They had a hard struggle getting up the rapids, below the State dam, at Northumberland, and were obliged to abandon the boat entirely at Fort Miller. He described the road to Fort Nicholson (Fort Edward) as so overgrown that it was reduced to a mere path; while the site of Fort Nicholson was a thicket, well-nigh impenetrable. The mosquitoes, punkies, and wood-lice, made life miserable for them on their way to the head of Champlain, at Whitehall.

The fact that there was a sawmill on the north side of Fish creek, and that a blockhouse fort had been erected here as early as 1755, would indicate that there were a

[7] Kalm's Travels in North America. Vol. II, p. 284.

goodly number of families living hereabouts at the beginning of the French and Indian war.

Its Development Under Philip Schuyler. In 1763, the heirs of Johannes Schuyler divided his property among themselves. About this time, we find Philip Schuyler in possession of that part of the ancestral estates located here at Saratoga. In 1768, we learn that he purchased some four thousand acres north of the Fish creek, from the Livingston heirs, and afterwards other large tracts hereabouts.

With characteristic energy, he at once set to work to develop his holdings. He rebuilt the saw and grist mills destroyed by the French in 1745. According to the map of Saratoga, made by Burgoyne's engineer, in 1777, and Sauthier's map of 1779, (preserved in the State Library, Albany,) these mills were all, with one exception, on the south side of Fish creek. He found a ready market in New York and the West Indies for all his surplus products.

Philip Schuyler had an eye for all improvements in agriculture and manufacture, and was in correspondence with the most progressive men in both England and America. Here at Old Saratoga he erected and successfully ran the first flax, or linen, mill in America. Soon thereafter he read a paper before the Society for the Promotion of Arts, in which he gave a detailed statement of the workings of the machinery, and exhibiting samples of its work compared the output with that of hand power. The Society was so highly pleased with his venture, and considered the enterprise of such great public importance and utility, that it decreed a medal should be struck and given him, and voted him their "thanks for executing so useful a design in the Province."[8]

---

[8] Lossing's Life of Philip Schuyler. Vol. I.

THE STORY OF OLD SARATOGA 291

The productions of his farms and mills became so great that he found it to his advantage to establish a transportation line of his own between Albany and New York, consisting of a schooner and three sloops. The freight was taken down the river from here (Schuylerville) on flat boats and rafts.

Before 1767 he had built his first country mansion here. It was located a few rods south-west of the brick one assaulted and burned by the French, as we have before mentioned. After the building of this house, he spent more than half of each year at Saratoga, that he might give his personal attention to his extensive and growing business.

All fear of further war-like incursions from the north being removed by England's late conquest of Canada, and Schuyler and other landed proprietors offering sufficiently attractive inducements, settlers began to pour in from the east and the south, and from across the sea. Soon many open spaces began to appear in the interminable woods back and away from the river, in the midst of which the sturdy pioneer erected his log hut and made ready to start life anew.

Mrs. Grant on Colonel Schuyler's Saratoga Enterprise. Mrs. Grant, of Lagan (Scotland), in her "Memoirs of an American Lady," draws a very interesting picture of Old Saratoga as it appeared about 1768, as also of the master spirit who was then the director of its fortunes.

"The Colonel, since known by the title of 'General Schuyler,' had built a house [yet standing] near Albany, in the English taste, comparatively magnificent, where his family resided, and where he carried on the business of his department. Thirty miles or more above Albany, in the direction of the Flatts, and near the far-famed

Saratoga, which was to be the scene of his future triumph, he had another establishment. It was here that the Colonel's political and economical genius had full scope. He had always the command of a great number of those workmen who were employed in public buildings, etc. They were always in constant pay, it being necessary to engage them in that manner; and were, from the change of the seasons, the shutting of the ice, and other circumstances, months unemployed. At these seasons, when public business was interrupted, the workmen were occupied in constructing squares of buildings in the nature of barracks,[9] for the purpose of lodging artisans and laborers of all kinds. Having previously obtained a large tract of very fertile lands from the Crown, on which he built a spacious and convenient house, he constructed those barracks at a distance, not only as a nursery for the arts, which he meant to encourage, but as the materials of a future colony, which he meant to plant out around him.

"He had here a number of negroes, well acquainted with felling of trees and managing of saw mills, of which he erected several; and while these were employed in carrying on a very advantageous trade of deals and lumber, which were floated down on rafts to New York, they were at the same time clearing the ground for the colony the Colonel was preparing to establish.

"This new settlement was an asylum for everyone who wanted bread and a home. From the variety of employment regularly distributed, every artisan and every laborer found here lodging and occupation; some hundreds of people, indeed, were employed at once. Those who were, in winter, engaged at the sawmills,

---

[9] These are the barracks spoken of by Burgoyne in his State of the Expedition, and by Sergeant Lamb, as having accidentally caught fire on the night of the 9th of October, 1777.

were in the summer equally busied at a large and productive fishery.[10]

"The artisans got lodging and firing for two or three years, at first, besides being well paid for everything they did. Flax was raised and dressed, and finally spun and made into linen there; and as artisans were very scarce in the country, everyone sent linen to weave, flax to dress, etc., to the Colonel's colony. He paid them liberally, and having always abundance of money in his hands, could afford to be the loser at first, to be amply repaid in the end.

"It is inconceivable what dexterity, address and deep policy were exhibited in the management of this new settlement, the growth of which was rapid beyond belief. Every mechanic ended in being a farmer—that is, a profitable tenant to the owner of the soil; and new recruits of artisans, from the north of Ireland chiefly, supplied their place, nourished with the golden dews which this sagacious projector could so easily command. The rapid increase and advantageous result of this establishment were astonishing. 'Tis impossible for my imperfect recollection to do justice to the capacity displayed in these regulations. But I have thus endeavored to trace to its original source the wealth and power which became afterwards the means of supporting an aggression so formidable."[11]

---

[10] The "fishery" here alluded to was doubtless one of shad and herring, and perhaps sturgeon. During the months of May and June, annually, immense schools of these fish used to run up the river and its tributary creeks, before the dams were erected in the Hudson. Local tradition says that farmers used to drive into Fish creek and with a dip or scoop-net literally load their wagons with shad and herring. Stephen Newberry, an aged resident of Greenwich, told the writer that he could remember helping his older brothers fish with a seine in the river below the rifts at Thomson's Mills, near the iron bridge. They salted down the shad in barrels and sold them to merchants and farmers. This is also confirmed by Mr. D. A. Bullard.

[11] Memoirs of an American Lady. Edition of 1846, p. 228.

This pleasant description of Old Saratoga and its famous proprietor, leads one to the conclusion, if the picture is correct, that in his notions about co-operation, and the proper relations which should subsist between the employer and his employees, Philip Schuyler was a hundred years and more ahead of his time. One thing, however, we cannot fail to note in passing, that, from earliest times, Old Saratoga has been a manufacturing and milling center.

CHAPTER II

THE FIRST PERMANENT SETTLERS

AMONG the earliest permanent settlers in this locality were the De Ridders. They settled on the east side of the river, just across from Schuylerville. We include them here because that was part of Old Saratoga, and because they figured largely in the early history of this place.

The first of this family, whose name appears, is that of Garett De Ridder. His name is found in connection with Philip Schuyler (uncle of the General) and Cornelius Van Beuren, as a road commissioner for the district between Saratoga and Half Moon, in 1729. Again, in 1750, Garett De Ridder, Killian De Ridder and Waldron Clute are appointed to the same office.

Tradition says that five brothers De Ridder came over from Holland. Their names were Walter, Simon, Hendrick, Killian and Evert. Though there is no direct authority for it, still it would be fair to presume that they were the sons of Garett De Ridder, who appears in history 21 years before the others. Killian was a bachelor, and appears to have been the largest land-holder among the brothers, at least in this locality. Walter De Ridder's house stood on the east bank of the Hudson, just north of the road as it turns east from the river going to Greenwich. This house was ruined by the ice in a freshet. Some of the timbers in this old house are in the one now called the Elder Rogers' house. This latter house was built by General Simon De Ridder, for his son, Walter. General Simon's house stood on the site of the house now owned by Robert and William

Funston. The original house was of brick, burned on the farm, and was twice as large as the present structure. The present kitchen is a relic of the original mansion, which was burned in 1837.

The De Ridders are now the oldest family that have lived continuously in this locality.

Abraham Marshall came from Yorkshire, England, leased a farm of Philip Schuyler about 1763, and situated perhaps a mile south of Victory village. This farm is still owned by his grandson, William H. Marshall. He and his family suffered all the hardships incident to the Revolution. Many of his descendants are still residents in this vicinity. Besides the above, we recall Mr. John Marshall, a prominent citizen on Bacon Hill; Mrs. William B. Marshall, still the owner of the house made historic by the experiences and writings of the Baroness Riedesel, and also Mr. Frank Marshall, of Victory, a great-grandson.

Thomas Jordon came here before the Revolution. He was then a young man. He served in that war as a bateauman. After the war he married a daughter of Abraham Marshall, settled upon and cleared the farm now occupied by Mr. Frank Marshall.

Conrad Cramer (Kremer), a German, came about 1763, and settled on the farm now owned by John Hicks Smith. He married Margaret Brisbin, by whom he had five children. His descendants are numerous, but are now scattered far and wide. A grandson, Hiram, and great-grandson, Charles, still cling to the old haunts.

John Woeman was living near Coveville in 1765. William Green also settled here about the same time. His sons were Samuel, John and Henry.

Thomas Smith moved from Dutchess county about 1770, and settled on the place still owned by his great-

THE STORY OF OLD SARATOGA

grandson, Stephen Smith, on the hill about four miles west of Schuylerville.

About 1770, John Strover bought the farm now owned by the Cornings. He was an active patriot during the Revolution, and did valuable service as a scout. He held the rank of orderly sergeant. His son, George, bought the old Schuyler mansion about 1838, which is still owned by two of his daughters.

Hezekiah Dunham was also one of those sturdy pioneers who was not only strong to clear the forests, but was equally efficient in clearing his country of tyrants. He was a captain of a militia company, and was one of the most prominent patriots in these parts. He was leader of the captors of the notorious Tory, Lovelass. He settled on the farm now owned and occupied by Charles Cramer.

James I Brisbin made his clearing on the farm now owned by Michael Varley, previously owned by Oliver Brisbin.

George Davis settled the farm still called the Davis farm. The stone quarry known as the Ruckatuc is on that place. The following story is told as an illustration of pioneer honesty, which measures up pretty close to the ideal: On one occasion James I. Brisbin and George Davis swapped horses. But on reaching home and looking his horse over very carefully, Brisbin concluded that he had the best of the bargain, and that he ought to pay over about five dollars to even the thing up. Strangely enough, Davis had also been going through the same judicial process with his conscience and had arrived at Brisbin's conclusion, precisely. Both concluded to go over at once and straighten the thing up while in the mood. They met each other about half way, but just how they settled it the tradition saith not. It would perhaps be hazardous to assert that Saratoga horse-fanciers have ever since invariably followed this model in similar transactions.

James Brisbin settled, before the Revolution, on the farm until recently owned by his great-grandson, James Caruth Brisbin, but now by Hiram Cramer.

Peter Lansing, of Albany, built what is now known as the Marshall house in 1773, for a farm house, but who occupied it is not known.

Sherman Patterson was the first settler on the place now bounded by Spring street and Broadway, and owned by Patrick McNamara. That was before the Revolution.

A Mr. Webster, one Daniel Guiles, and a Mr. Cross, lived here before the Revolution. Mr. Cross' place was near the present one of Mr. Orville C. Shearer. Mr. Guiles lived where Victory village now is.

Three brothers by the name of Denny came to this town as early as 1770, and built three log houses on what is now the John McBride place, near Dean's Corners.

Col. Cornelius Van Veghten was among the first settlers at Coveville. He had three boys, Herman, Cornelius and Walter, and was a very prominent Whig in the Revolution. He was a friend of General Schuyler, and was most cordially hated by the Tories. The story of his narrow escape from assassination at the hands of one of them is told elsewhere. The old Van Veghten homestead is now owned and occupied by Mr. Charles Searles.

The historic Dovegat house is supposed to have been built by Jacobus Swart; at least, according to an old field book in possession of Mrs. Charles Searles, he owned it soon after the Revolution. At the time of Burgoyne's excursion down this way, another man, by the name of Swart, lived just south of Coveville, near Searles ferry. Doubtless his was the "Sword's house" where Burgoyne camped the 18th of September, 1777. It is now owned by Robert Searles. A short distance below

Swart's, lived Ezekiel Ensign, on a place still owned by a descendant, George Ensign.

A little further south was the house of John Taylor in which General Fraser died. The first settler on Taylor's place was John McCarty, who ran away from home, in Limerick, Ireland, to avoid marrying a red-headed girl whom his parents had selected for him. In 1765 he leased from Philip Schuyler the land just north of the Wilbur's Basin Ravine, and on which are the three hills fortified by Burgoyne, and on one of which General Fraser was buried. The lease called for one-tenth of the produce as rental. The original parchment, signed by the contracting parties is now in the possession of Edwin R. Wilbur, at Wilbur's Basin, a great grandson of John McCarty. Evidently John found a wife better suited to his tastes in America. F. Patterson's little barn west of the canal stands on the site of McCarty's house. Near him Thomas and Fones Wilbur had settled before the war. Frederick Patterson now owns the homestead of Fones Wilbur. Wilbur's Basin received its name from these brothers. Below Wilbur's Basin, on the flats near the river, were two homes owned by J. Vernor and H. Van Denburg. Joseph Holmes now occupies the Vernor place, and Ephraim Ford the Van Denburg homestead. It was here that the fugitive inhabitants stopped over night in 1777, as told by the Sexagenary. The buildings were burned by the British on the 19th of September, 1777.

Next below Van Denburg's was Bemis' tavern, occupied by Gates as headquarters for a short time. Fothem Bemis was the first settler at Bemis Heights. (Bemus is the spelling in the original document in the county clerk's office, Albany.) On the heights back from the river Ephraim Woodworth purchased a farm and built a house afterward occupied by General Gates as headquarters. We are already familiar with the historic home of John Neilson, also with Isaac Freeman's cottage and farm, the site of the great battle. A number of other clearings had been made and log cottages put up in that immediate vicinity. According to Neilson one Asa Chatfield owned the one just south of the middle ravine, from the top of whose house Colonel Wilkinson reconnoitered the British as they deployed into line of battle just before the second day's fight. Simeon Barbour and George Coulter owned the clearings and cottages where the second day's battle opened, and one S. McBride had his homestead to the north of them, apparently where the farm buildings of the late Mrs. Ebenezer Leggett stand.

Gabriel Leggett and Isaac Leggett were settled near the borders of Stillwater and Saratoga when Burgoyne came down to make good Englishmen of them. They were prominent Friends, and we presume therefore that neither they nor their co-religionists shouldered a musket to stop his progress.

David Shepherd's pioneer home has also become hereditary in his family; it now being owned by his grandson, David Shepherd. John Walker also settled in the southern part of the town of Saratoga. His descendants now own part of the battlefield. It is interesting to note, in this connection, that E. R. Wilbur, a grandson of Fones Wilbur, married Phœbe Freeman, a granddaughter of Isaac Freeman, and that they now own that part of the camp ground of the British army whereon Burgoyne had his headquarters.

Besides the above there were doubtless many others settled in this town whose names have thus far escaped the searching eye of the historian.

CHAPTER III.

Revolutionary Trials

AFTER the conquest of Canada by Britain in 1760, people very naturally believed that Old Saratoga had seen the last of war and bloodshed, hence, as we have learned, they began to flock to this fertile vale. But hardly had they settled here in appreciable numbers before Mother England began to stir up strife with her Colonies. Parliament started in to vex the righteous souls of the Colonists with the most unwise and impolitic legislation. Their constitutional rights as freeborn subjects were ruthlessly circumscribed. Naturally enough this was resented, and respectful remonstrances were sent to the home government in the hope that the obnoxious acts might be reconsidered, but in vain. The Stamp Act of 1765 aroused the indignation of every thinking and self-respecting freeman. But nowhere did the flame of resentment burn more fiercely than in the province of New York. In New York City the first liberty pole was erected, and there that patriotic order of the Sons of Liberty originated which did so much to nerve the people for the struggle.

The People Take Sides. News traveled very slowly in those days, but all of it finally reached the inhabitants of this district and kindled the same fires in their breasts as it had elsewhere. But when they came to talk about armed resistance to England's encroachments, here, as in other localities, there was a diversity of opinion, and heated discussions were sure to be held wherever men congregated. But when the news came that British soldiers had wantonly spilt American blood, at Lexington and Concord, many of the wavering went over to the majority and decided to risk their all for liberty. Some, however, remained loyal to the king. In this they were no doubt conscientious, and their liberty of conscience was quite generally respected except in the cases of those violent partisans who talked too much, or who took up arms for Britain against their neighbors or gave succor or information to the enemy.

Philip Schuyler had several times been chosen to represent the County of Albany in the New York Colonial Assembly. Says Lossing in his life of Schuyler: "Schuyler espoused the cause of his countrymen from the beginning, fully understanding the merits of the controversy. His judgment, his love of order, and his social position made him cautious and conciliating till the time for decisive action arrived." But when that time came we find him standing alone in the Assembly with George Clinton and one or two others against the satellites of King George, for the rights of the people and the constitution. He was also chosen a delegate to the Provincial Convention, after the aforesaid Assembly had refused to coöperate with the other colonies in their hostility to the unlawful acts of Parliament. By that convention he was chosen a delegate to the Continental Congress on the 20th of April, 1775.

The News of Lexington. The news of the battle of Lexington reached New York on the 23d of April, just after Schuyler had started for his home. It followed him up the river, but did not overtake him till he reached Saratoga, on Saturday afternoon the 29th; *i. e.*, the news was then six days old in New York and ten days old in Boston. That same evening, writing to his friend John Cruger, he said among other things: "For my own part, much as I love peace, much as I love my domestic happiness and repose, and desire to see my countrymen enjoying the blessings of undisturbed industry, I would rather see all these scattered to the winds for a time, and the sword of desolation go over the land, than to recede one line from the just and righteous position we have taken as freeborn subjects of Great Britain." That this was not mere gush and sentiment is proved by the fact that Philip Schuyler lived right up to the level of that heroic declaration, as we have already seen. In a private letter to James Duane, dated here at Saratoga, December 19, 1778, he says: "I am £20,000 ($100,000) in specie worse off than when the war began," and that was five years before the war closed. Excepting Robert Morris, the financier of the Revolution, it would be interesting to know if the struggle for Independence cost any one man more in money and property than it did Philip Schuyler.

The next day after the receipt of the aforesaid news Schuyler, as was his custom, attended divine service at the old (Dutch) Reformed Church, then standing in the angle of the river and Victory roads. The "Sexagenary" (John P. Becker), who was present at the same service, writes of it thus: "The first intelligence which gave alarm to our neighborhood, and indicated the breaking asunder of the ties which bound the colonies to the mother country, reached us on Sunday morning. We attended at divine service that day at Schuyler's Flats. I well remember, notwithstanding my youth, the impressive manner with which, in my hearing, my father told my uncle that BLOOD *had been* SHED *at Lexington.* The startling intelligence spread like fire among the congregation. The preacher was listened to with very little attention. After the morning discourse was finished, and the people were dismissed, we gathered about Gen. Philip Schuyler for further information. He was the oracle of our neighborhod. We looked up to him with a feeling of respect and affection. His popularity was unbounded;

his views upon all subjects were considered sound, and his anticipations almost prophetic. On this occasion he confirmed the intelligence already received, and expressed his belief that an important crisis had arrived which must sever us forever from the parent country."

This news had a very warlike ring to it. Soon after this the militia began to organize hereabouts and train for service. It is to be presumed, however, that when those good people heard of Lexington that Sunday morning, they did not dream that the dogs of war were about to be let loose at their own doors, and that they would soon be called upon to pass through a very gehenna of suffering and loss, the like of which neither Lexington, nor Concord, nor Boston ever knew. Nor had these dwellers in this warworn valley long to wait before they began to experience the realities of the mighty struggle thus inaugurated. In less than two weeks after the news of Lexington had reached them the country was electrified by news of the capture of Ticonderoga and Crown Point, just to the north.

About this time Schuyler left for Philadelphia to be in attendance at the Continental Congress. On the 15th of June he was appointed as one of the four Major Generals. He was immediately placed in command of the Northern Department, which included the Province of New York, and all New England. Not long thereafter the farmers and others along the upper Hudson, who owned teams of horses, were employed to transport part of the captured military stores to safer places south and east.

Farmers Impressed Into Service. At the beginning of the winter, 1775, these farmers were again pressed into the service of Congress to transport some of the captured cannon from Lake George to Boston, where Washington needed them to help persuade the British that

THE STORY OF OLD SARATOGA 305

they should evacuate that city and leave it to its lawful owners.

Among those in this vicinity who assisted in that work was Peter Becker, the father of the "Sexagenary," who lived across the river from Schuylerville. Col. Henry Knox, who afterward became the noted General, and chief of artillery, was sent on to superintend their removal. He first caused to be constructed some fifty big wooden sleds. The cannon selected for removal were nine to twenty-four pounders, also several howitzers. They already had been transported from Ticonderoga to the head of Lake George. From four to eight horses were hitched to each sled, so that when once under way, they made an imposing cavalcade. They were brought down this way to Albany, taken across the river, thence down through Kinderhook to Claverack, thence east to Springfield, Mass. There the New Yorkers were dismissed to their homes, and New England ox teams took their places. Those cannon once in the hands of Washingon proved to be potent persuaders indeed, for when the morning of the 5th of March, 1776, dawned the British were astounded to see a whole row of them frowning down from Dorchester Heights, prepared to hurl death and destruction upon them. The British lion loosened his grip at once and got out.

During the fall of that same year, 1775, the army under Schuyler and Montgomery, destined for the conquest of Canada, passed up through here. Subsequently there followed in its wake great trains of supply wagons, or fleets of bateaux, carrying provisions for its sustenance. The following spring the people here were compelled to witness the harrowing spectacle of detachments of the wounded, the diseased and dispirited troops returning from that ill-starred expedition. The barracks located here were filled with the sick and disabled soldiers, many of whom died and were buried here in nameless graves.

The Flight. But it was the year of 1777 that was fullest of distress for those pioneer Saratogans. In our military annals we have endeavored to depict the way in which they were compelled to abandon their homes, and seek shelter among their sympathetic compatriots below. While the loss of Ticonderoga, that year, filled the hearts of the patriots everywhere with despondency, it spread consternation among the people hereabouts who lived right in the track of the invading host, and who felt that it would soon be upon them.

General Schuyler had agreed to give timely notice to the leading citizens here, should he feel compelled to retire before Burgoyne; but apparently he had not reckoned upon the peculiar tactics of Burgoyne's Indians. They slipped by him on either side and spread terror down through the valley of the Hudson by their many atrocities. It was their appearance, not Burgoyne's main army, that caused the sudden stampede of the inhabitants. Seized with panic they, in many cases, abandoned much valuable property, which might have been saved. Cattle and sheep were often turned into the woods, which might have been driven along; and many of their household treasures could have been carried away or hidden had they been a little more deliberate in their departure. But easy is it always to say what ought to have been done after the event.

After the Return, Tory Raids. After the surrender of Burgoyne many of the fugitive families ventured back to their homes; but if they fancied that the annihilation of his army had conquered an immediate and unbroken peace for this locality, they were doomed once more to disappointment. While no considerable force ever again got as far as this from Canada, yet small bands of malignant Tories, accompanied by Indians, made frequent forays, destroying property and carrying away leading citizens into Canada. These periodic raids kept the inhabitants on the rack of apprehension until the end of the war.

Gen. Edward F. Bullard, in his Fourth of July (1876) address on the History of Saratoga, relates the following incident characteristic of that time: "The raid of May, 1779, more immediately affected this locality, and the few inhabitants scattered in the interior fled from it to avoid certain destruction. After the surrender of Burgoyne, Conrad Cramer had returned to his farm (now the John Hicks Smith place) and was living there with his wife and four small children, when, on the 14th of May, they had to flee for their lives. They hastily packed their wagon with what comforts one team could carry, and started on their flight southerly. They reached the river road and proceeded as far south as the farm now owned by Jacob Lohnas, about five miles south of Schuylerville, when night overtook them. At that place there was a small house used as a tavern, but as it was already full, the Cramer family were obliged to remain in their wagon, and that same evening the mother gave birth to a child (John Cramer) who afterward became, probably, the most distinguished person ever born in this town. He weighed less than four pounds at his birth, and his parents had little hopes of rearing him. At manhood he became a very broad-chested, large-headed man, with an iron constitution and a giant intellect. The next morning the family continued its flight to what is now known as the Fitzgerald neighborhood, about three miles below Mechanicville, where they obtained a small house in which they remained until it was considered safe to return to their home in the wilderness."

The "Sexagenary" relates how their family had been threatened by the Tory Lovelass and his band one night, but that he had been frightened off by the barking of their dogs, which clamor also awoke the family and put them on their guard. He also relates how the farmers made watch towers of their straw and haystacks, leaving a sort of nest on the top, in which two watchmen would station thmselves, one remaining on guard while the other slept.

After the farmers had threshed their grain in the fall, they would take it down to Albany for safe storage; going after it from time to time as they needed it. During the Burgoyne campaign, Gates' quartermasters often compelled the farmers, along the valley, to give up their grain, etc., for the use of the army. These goods were appraised, and receipts were given. These receipts were really governmental promises to pay the price of the goods named therein on presentation of the same. But few of those receipts were ever honored; because of an empty public treasury.

It is a fact which has never been sufficiently emphasized that the inhabitants of the Mohawk and upper Hudson valleys paid, as their share of the price of our precious liberties, a sum out of all proportion to their numbers and wealth. Parts of New Jersey, however, suffered much; but not one of the states suffered as did New York in life and property, and yet she was the only one who furnished her full quota of men to fight the common battles. These facts do not appear in our ordinary histories, most of which have been written in New England.

It is well for us at least to attempt an estimate of what our liberties have cost, that we may the better realize their value, and so be the more ready to guard them.

CHAPTER IV

The Several Schuyler Mansions and Their Occupants

THE house now standing is the last of a series of three. Its predecessors met with a tragic fate, as we have already had occasion to notice. They were both offered as a burnt sacrifice to the insatiable Moloch of war. A brief résumé of their story, however, seems necessary as a fitting introduction to the history of the present mansion.

Mansion No. 1. When the first of the three was built is now known; but it was doubtless erected by Johannes Schuyler anywhere between 1720 and 1745. All we know certainly about it is, that it was of brick, two stories high, with thick walls pierced for musketry, and was designed to serve as a fort as well as a dwelling. It was burned by the French on the night of the 28th of November, 1745. Its sole defender on that awful night was Philip Schuyler, the son of Johannes, and uncle of General Ph. Schuyler. The Frenchman, Beauvais, who confesses to the slaughter of Schuyler, says that on summoning him to surrender, he replied by calling him bad names and by shooting at him. Beauvais then gave him one more chance for his life, but receiving the same defiant answer, thereupon he fired and shot him dead. Having pillaged the house, they then burned it over his bleeding body. An indefinite number of other occupants having sought refuge in the cellar, perished in the flames. Beauvais compliments Schuyler by saying that had the house been defended by a dozen men as brave and resolute as himself they would have been unmolested. Such is the Frenchman's story. The picture drawn by him, as is perfectly natural, is no doubt presented in the lightest shades possible. It makes one wish, however, that he could know Capt. Philip Schuyler's side of the story.

This house stood about twenty rods directly east of the present structure, on the bank of the canal. When the canal was widened in 1855, parts of the cellar walls were exposed, and in 1895 they were completely unearthed, when many interesting relics were found in the ruins. The terrace on which the house stood has been excavated for a long distance back by the canal authorities. Twenty-six feet was the north and south dimension of the house, or at least of the cellar; but the work of excavation proceeded so slowly, the walls being removed in the process, that the east and west dimension was never ascertained. One regrets that those walls, and the well-preserved fire place there discovered, could not have been preserved as relics, of, and monuments to, the brave but hapless victims of that frontier village.

Mansion No. 2. For perhaps eighteen years after the massacre old Saratoga remained but sparsely settled, until another Philip Schuyler appeared on the scene about 1763. Soon after his advent the mills began to whirr and the meadows to blossom again. Under his magic touch the business developed so rapidly here that he found he must spend less time in Albany and more in Saratoga, so he built a spacious summer home for himself and family here about 1766. Tradition has it that this house was considerably larger and more pretentious than the present one. The ground plan of it, given on Burgoyne's map of Saratoga, tends to confirm this tradition. We have copied this plan, as also of the other buildings, in our map of old Saratoga (which see). Lieut. Digby, a British officer, in his Journal of the Expedition, says of this home: "General Schuyler's house

SCHUYLER MANSION NUMBER TWO

THE STORY OF OLD SARATOGA 311

was the best we had seen in that part, and much superior to many gentlemen's houses in Canada. This second house was located about twelve rods southeast of the present mansion. Parts of its walls were unearthed and removed by the ruthless hand of the canal excavator. Many relics of pottery, etc., were found at that time.

This house served as the summer home of the Schuylers seven or eight months in the year, for at least ten years. During that period its illustrious owner was less occupied with public affairs than at any other period in his active life and could give more attention to the demands of the home and his private business than at any other subsequent time.

Philip Schuyler and Family. Philip Schuyler was the son of John Schuyler and Cornelia Van Cortlandt, and grandson of Johannes Schuyler, the hero of the French expedition of 1690. He was born at Albany in 1733, on the southeast corner of State and Pearl streets. Catherine Van Rensselaer, who became Angelica Livingston and John Van Rensselaer, who became his wife, was born in the Crailo, Greenbush (still standing), in 1734. Philip Schuyler, at the age of twenty-one, was commissioned Captain of an Albany company in the French and Indian war. It was after the battle of Lake George, September 8th, 1755, where Johnson defeated Dieskau, that his Colonel considerately granted him a furlough to return home and consummate his marital bargain with his "sweet Kitty V. R."

Mrs. Catherine Schuyler is described as being a very beautiful woman, rather small and delicate, but "perfect in form and feature, extremely graceful in her movements, and winning in her deportment." Her tastes seemed to lead her to prefer the quiet seclusion of domesticity to the excitement incident to society and official life. Her youngest daughter, writing of her says: "She possessed courage and prudence in a great degree, but these were exerted only in her domestic sphere. At the head of a large family of children and servants, her management was so excellent that everything went on with a regularity which appeared spontaneous." Saratoga tradition pictures her as a noble and charitable lady. Quoting her daughter again on this point, we catch a glimpse of the basis for such tradition: "Perhaps I may relate of my mother, as a judicious act of kindness, that she not unfrequently sent a milch cow to persons in poverty."

She became the mother of eleven children, eight of whom reached maturity. The names of these and the marriages they contracted are as follows:

Angelica, married John Barker Church, son of a member of Parliament.

Elizabeth, married Alexander Hamilton, the great statesman and first Secretary of the Treasury of the United States.

Margarita, married Stephen Van Rensselaer, the last of the Patroons.

John Bradstreet, married Elizabeth Van Rensselaer, sister of Stephen.

Philip Jeremiah, married (1) Sarah Rutzen, of New York; (2) Mary A. Sawyer, of Boston.

Rensselaer, married Eliza Tenbroeck.

Cornelia, married Washington Morton, son of General Morton.

Catherine Van Rensselaer, married (1) Samuel Malcolm, son of General Malcolm; (2) James Cochran, son of Dr. Cochran, surgeon-in-chief of the American army.

The old mansion with its romantic environment became the summer playground of these children, and was, no doubt, to them, as it has been to their many succes-

JOHANNES SCHUYLER AND WIFE.

sors, the dearest spot on earth. In those days when there were no public schools, all who could afford it employed tutors and French governesses for their children who, while engaged in their work, often became members of the family. The Schuyler mansion here had its particular apartment known as the school-room, since much attention was given by the Schuylers, generally, to the education of their children.

According to all accounts the busiest place within twenty-five miles around, before, and immediately after, the Revolution, was within the precincts of the old Schuyler house on the south side of Fish creek. Not only were many artisans employed here, as we have learned in a previous chapter, but teamsters, bateaumen and raftsmen were much in demand to transport the products of the mills and farms down to tide water at Albany.

Revolutionary Experiences. But the agitation connected with the troubles with England ere long began to ruffle the smoothly flowing tide of business, which had set so strongly in this direction. Colonel Schuyler began to be more and more in demand to represent the County of Albany in Provincial Assemblies, Indian Councils and Conventions, but when freed from these public duties he would hasten eagerly back to his beloved Saratoga. It was here that he heard the news of 'Lexington. From here he sent forth most of those stirring appeals that proved so influential in holding many of New York's leading families to the cause of liberty. It was from here that he went as an honored delegate to the Continental Congress at Philadelphia in 1775, which body soon appointed him to the high and responsible office of Major General. The acceptance of that office meant good-by to the quiet of home and the pursuits of a business delightfully congenial to him, and the launching out upon the treacherous sea of military life as a leader in a rebellion which might easily cost everything dear to his heart, and which did cost him a vast sum of treasure, and suffering unspeakable in both body and mind; but from which he emerged with honor untarnished, an ornament to American manhood, and a credit to the cause he had espoused. Much of the time during those eventful years of 1775 and 1776, which saw the expedition led against Canada under his supervision, and its utter defeat, through no fault of his own, he was confined at Old Saratoga by a most painful hereditary malady (the gout), brought on by overexertion.

During those years the great storehouses and barracks, which he had erected here, proved to be of incalculable service as shelter to the soldiery marching either north or south and as a depot for army supplies.

Distinguished Guests. This house, like its successor, harbored many distinguished guests, among which was the brave, the much loved, but ill-fated Montgomery. It was also especially honored by the presence of three distinguished men sent by Congress in 1776 as special Commissioners to conciliate Canada and attach its people to the cause of America. They passed through here early in April of that year and returned from their fruitless mission in time for each of them affix his signature to the Declaration of Independence on the 4th of July following.

These men were first: Samuel Chase, delegate to Congress from Maryland, a most zealous patriot, and afterward a judge of the Supreme Court of the United States.

The second was Charles Carroll, another delegate from Maryland. Of the fifty-six signers of the Declaration, Charles Carroll of Carrollton is noted as having been the wealthiest man, the only Roman Catholic, and the last

THE STORY OF OLD SARATOGA 315

survivor of the immortal band who pledged their lives, their fortunes, and their sacred honor, for the support of the cause of liberty in America. On their arrival at Albany from the south they were invited to partake of the hospitality of General Schuyler. Charles Carroll, in his journal wrote that, "He behaved to us with great civility; lives in pretty style; has two daughters (Betsy and Peggy), lively, agreeable, black-eyed gals."[1]

The third was Benjamin Franklin, one whose memory the world yet delights to honor as a statesman, as a journalist, as a diplomatist, as an inventor, and a philosopher; for in each of these spheres he achieved undoubted greatness. We should especially remember that it was through his skillful diplomacy at the court of Louis XVI, and the use he was enabled to make of the victory over Burgoyne and the capture of the British army here at Saratoga that the French alliance was consummated and through which we were enabled to carry that war to a successful issue.

Attempt on Schuyler's Life. During the Campaign of 1777, interest in house No. 2 reaches its culmination. It was no doubt while stopping here for the night on one of his frequent trips up and down the valley connected with Burgoyne's advance that General Schuyler came near figuring as the victim of a tragedy. An Indian had insinuated himself into the house, evidently for the purpose of murdering the General, on whose head a price had been set by the British. It was the hour of bedtime in the evening, and while he was preparing to retire for the night, a female servant coming in from the hall, saw a gleam of light reflected from the blade of a knife in the hand of some person, whose dark outline she discovered behind the door. The servant was a black slave who had sufficient presence of mind not to appear to

---

[1] Afterwards the wives of General Hamilton and Stephen Van Rensselaer, last of the Patroons.

have made the discovery. Passing directly through the door into the apartment where the General was yet standing near the fireplace, with an air of unconcern she pretended to arrange such articles as were disposed upon the mantelpiece, while in an undertone she informed her master of her discovery, and said aloud: "I will call the guard." The General instantly seized his arms, while the faithful servant hurried out by another door into a long hall, upon the floor of which lay a loose board which creaked beneath the tread. By the noise she made in tramping rapidly upon the board, the Indian, who was led to suppose that "the Philistines were upon him" in numbers, sprang from his concealment and fled. He was pursued, however, by the guard and a few friendly Indians attached to the person of General Schuyler, overtaken, and made a prisoner.[2]

Mrs. Schuyler Burns the Wheat Fields. Coincident with the arrival of the vanguard of Burgoyne's army at Sandy Hill (Hudson Falls), about the 26th of July, 1777, the Indians made those raids down through the valley which frightened away the inhabitants as we have before related. It must have been about the last of July of that year when the following incident occurred which not only exhibited the quality of Schuyler's patriotism, but also tried the metal of his noble wife. Apprised by her husband that there was little prospect of checking Burgoyne's advance down the Hudson, Mrs. Schuyler decided that everything valuable must be removed from the country home at Saratoga. So with her "coach and four," accompanied by a single guard on horseback, she started for the north. In the vicinity of Coveville she encountered the vanguard of what proved to be a regular procession of panic stricken inhabitants fleeing "from the wrath to come" in the shape of a horde of plumed and painted

---
[2] Gen. J. Watts De Peyster in Godchild of Washington, p. 396.

savages, allies of Britain. Many of the people recognized Mrs. Schuyler and warned her to proceed no further. They recited the fate of Jane McCrea, and the murder of the Allen family at Argyle. They assured her that by going further she took her life in her own hand and was riding straight into the jaws of death. After facing a crowd of men and women, crazed by fear, and listening to such terrifying tales of atrocities committed only yesterday, and especially since she knew that just before her was a dense wood through which she must pass for two miles, and which might easily be the lair of savages watching for prey, and that she had but one man as guard, it required an unusual amount of nerve to press on. Did she have it? Yes, and a wealth of it. To her solicitous advisers she replied: "The wife of the General must not be afraid," and bade her coachman to proceed. She reached her home in safety and succeeded in her purpose.

While employed in this work she received a letter from her husband, the General, in which he directed her to set fire to the wheat fields, which she did with her own hands, to the great astonishment of her negro servants.[3] The reason for this was to induce their tenants and others to do the same rather than suffer their crops to be reaped by the enemy for the support of his troops. Having completed her task, it occurred to her that the army might have need for more horses at this critical juncture, so she sent her own up to Fort Edward, while for herself she extemporized a conveyance of more modest mien. She ordered to the door an ox team hitched to a wooden sled, which she boarded and started for Albany. Truly a woman of such heroic mould was worthy to be mated with such a man. That was the last time she saw

---

[3] Godchild of Washington, p. 395.

the old home where she and her little ones had spent so many happy summers.

Burgoyne's Carouse. The next time the old house plays a noteworthy part in story was the night of the 9th of October following. On the 15th of September its vacant windows stared out upon the serried hosts of King George, recently from Canada, as they streamed by with airy step confident in their ability to drive the dastardly rebels before them like a flock of sheep. On the 9th of October it beheld the same host file past on the backward track, defeated, crestfallen, wet and bedraggled, and every man's breast heaving with sighs for another sight of Canada. But apparently the least anxious man in that entire army was its commander. The late battle, the preparation for retreat, the all-night march in the rain, with its attendant confusion and extra labor, had served to keep this sybarite General from indulging his accustomed carouse. So when late on the 9th the army moved up from its protracted and unwelcome rest at Dovegat, it supposed that the race for Canada was now really on; not so Burgoyne, who had other plans in mind. He had bethought himself of the home of Schuyler, with all its conveniences and comforts, which he had sampled on his way down. Such an opportunity for a good time must not be lightly thrown aside, therefore, what though his Generals were eager to make the most of the precious moments for escape; what though the poor soldiers were forced to bivouac on the cold, wet ground, without covering—all such considerations must be thrust aside as of little worth compared with the opportunity to hold wassail for one more night at this wayside hostelry.

Having summoned the several kindred spirits in the army to meet him there, not forgetting the frail wife of a commissary who served as his mistress, together with

GENERAL PHILIP SCHUYLER

MRS. PHILIP SCHUYLER

his principal Generals, some of whom we know accepted the invitation with vigorous, though silent, protest, the feast began. General Hamilton's brigade was retained on the south side of the creek to see that his Excellency's pleasures should not be rudely disturbed by inconsiderate rebels. Soon the old house is brilliant with hundreds of candles and plenty of pine knots blazing on the hearths, the fire-waters flow freely, glasses clink, rude jokes, drinking songs, and shouts of ribald laughter make the empty rooms above echo to the Bacchanalian orgies. Being both a poet and a dramatist, Burgoyne was a prince of entertainers; full of

> Quips and cranks and wanton wiles,
> Nods and becks and wreathed smiles.

But it is "no time to break jests when the heart strings are about to be broken." In the midst of their revels, when all, but the few who felt the gravity of the situation, were maudlin with drink, they were startled by an angry glare from without which quickly paled the lights within, accompanied by a cry of fire, that put a sudden and effectual stop to the untimely feast. All rushed forth to learn that the barracks in which many of the sick and wounded had found shelter for the night had caught fire accidentally[4] and were all ablaze. It was only by the most heroic exertions that the poor fellows were saved from a horrible death.

The next morning Burgoyne with the rear of his army forded to the north side of Fish creek. That was the nearest he and his army ever got to Canada, so greatly longed for, on their return trip.

Burgoyne Burns Mansion No. 2. During Gates' abortive attack on the British camp the morning of the

---
[4] See account of Sergeant Lamb, in Stone's Burgoyne's Campaign, p. 344; also p. 387.

11th, Burgoyne discovered that such of the Schuyler buildings as had escaped the fire, shielded his enemy and interfered with the play of his artillery. He thereupon ordered them to be set on fire.[5]

Since General Schuyler acknowledged to Burgoyne, as he alleged, that their burning, from the British standpoint, was a military necessity, it is clearly unfair to charge Burgoyne with wantonness, as is so often done. But General Schuyler's magnanimous behavior at the scene of the surrender when General Burgoyne attempted to apologize for the destruction of his property, his courtesy toward the Baroness Riedesel, and his hospitable treatment of them all at his home in Albany afford one of the finest exhibitions on record of the "golden rule" in practice. The like of it is seldom seen outside the lives of the saints.

On October 12th, Col. Richard Varick writing to General Schuyler, then in Albany, says: "No part of your buildings escaped their malice except a small outbuilding, and your upper sawmill,[6] which is in the same situation we left it. Hardly a vestige of the fences is left except a few rails of the garden."[7]

---

[5] Seventeen buildings are marked down on the British map; six of them evidently were very large, and were doubtless the barracks aforementioned.

[6] This sawmill was located at Victory. The dam was where the stone bridge now is, and the mill was on the right side of the stream, on the little flat a short distance below. The dam and mill stood till about 1848.

[7] N. Y. Historical Society Collections. Vol. XII. Schuyler Papers.

CHAPTER V.

Mansion No. 3

AFTER the surrender and the departure of the British army General Schuyler remained behind to survey the ruins of his property, and make plans for resurrecting his home from the ashes. Local tradition, in perfect agreement with the Schuyler family tradition, says that house number three (yet standing), was built by the soldiers of Gates' army in seventeen days. Many have doubted the credibility of this story, but the writer in his researches has found that which renders it altogether probable.

In a letter to Congress dated Saratoga, November 4, 1777, Schuyler says: "On the 2d instant two British officers on their way to Canada took shelter in a violent storm of rain in my little hut, the only remains of all my buildings in this quarter." These men got into an altercation over the respective merits of General Burgoyne and Sir Guy Carleton, and inadvertently let some state secrets out of the bag, which Schuyler thought worthy of transmission to Congress, hence this letter. Toward the close of it he says, incidentally: "In less than twenty days I shall nearly complete a comfortable house for the reception of my family." Here is another letter touching the same subject, written to John Jay, dated Saratoga, Nov. 6th: "As I shall shortly be altogether out of public life, I am earnestly engaged in building me a house at this place, that I may be as far out of the noise and bustle of the great world as possible. I am confident (provided we repel the enemy) that I shall enjoy more true felicity in my retreat than ever was experienced by any man engaged in public life. My hobby-horse has long been a country life; I dismounted with reluctance, and now saddle him again with a very considerable share of satisfaction, and hope to canter him on to the end of the journey of life." . . . Farther along he speaks of this house as the one " which I began on the first instant, and which will be under cover and will have two rooms finished by the 15th, unless the weather should prove remarkably wet. But observe that it is only a frame house, sixty feet long, twenty-one broad, and two stories high, filled in with brick."

In his reply dated Fishkill, Dec. 11, 1777, Mr. Jay says: "The rapidity with which the desolation of your seat at Saratoga is repairing does not surprise me. I remember the despatch with which the preparations for our first expedition into Canada were completed." Schuyler then had command of the Northern Department, and organized that expedition, as he did the Burgoyne campaign before Gates took command.[1]

It is fair to presume, therefore, that having quickly decided to rebuild he secured Gates' consent to use such mechanics as he could find in the army. He at once set his mill at Victory to work sawing the lumber, (there is no hewed timber in the building), set men and teams at the cellar and drawing stone from the hills; sent to Albany for windows, hardware, trimmings, etc., and then when the material was ready put as many men on the job as could work without interference, and no doubt had the building habitable in the specified time. It was such a remarkable feat in house-building that the story of it would very naturally live in any neighborhood for a long while thereafter. The like of it would create a sensation even in these days of much machinery. Schuyler evidently engineered the whole work, and by the way, it required generalship of no mean order to keep

---

[1] See Wm. Jay's Life of John Jay, Vol. II, pp. 15-16.

SCHUYLER MANSION NUMBER THREE

hundreds of men of different craft coöperating on one small job without getting in each other's way, or awaiting each other's motions.

Description of Mansion No. 3. Only the main structure, 22 by 60 feet, was built at that time; additions on the east side and also the present kitchen were put on later. The cellar extends under the whole of this part, and is deep, dry and airy. It is divided into three parts. The south end has in it a large fireplace, and for a while was used as the kitchen; the center one was the wine cellar, and the north end was used as a storeroom for provisions, but not vegetables. The vegetable cellar was separate from the house and was located about twenty-five feet from the southeast corner of the main house. The floor timbers are of oak 10 by 12 inches in size and four feet apart.

On entering the house you first pass under the spacious veranda 10½ by 60 feet. One tradition says originally there was no veranda, only a Dutch porch over the front door, with side seats. But this is disputed. At all events there have been several changes here, for we have been told by those who can remember, that the first pillars were round, coated with stucco, and that they were not so high as the present ones by several feet. Mr. George Strover, after he came into possession, raised the roof of the veranda to let more light into the upper rooms, and substituted the present square pillars for the round ones. The main door is made of two thicknesses of plain boards laid at right angles to each other. It is furnished with the conventional brass knocker, but the hinges, and especially the lock, are curiosities. The lock is iron 7 by 15 inches in size and 2 inches thick and furnished with a prodigious key, about the size of the key to the Bastile preserved at Mount Vernon.

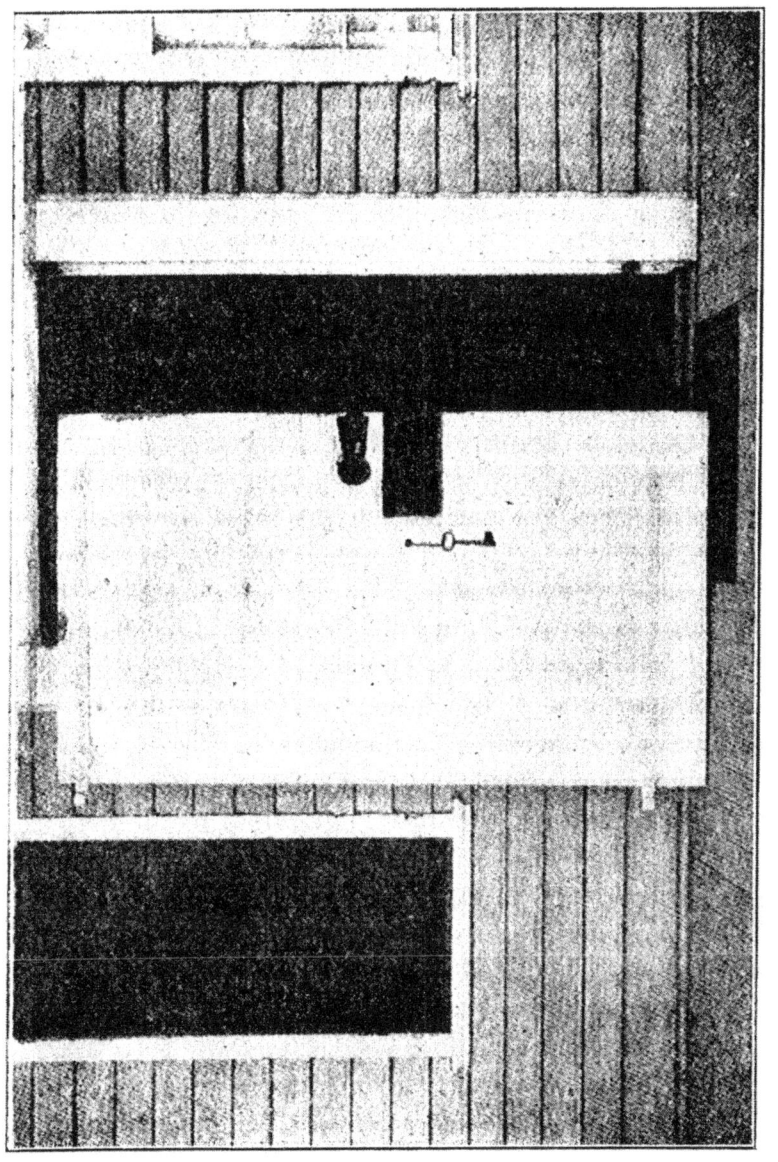

FRONT DOOR OF SCHUYLER MANSION

Entering you find yourself in a large reception hall 17 by 19 feet. The ceiling is 9 feet 3 inches high. The original stairway, with its landing and turn, was long ago replaced by the present enclosed staircase. The hall is flanked on the left and right by spacious rooms; on the left by a room 18 by 20 feet used by the Schuylers as the dining room, now the sitting room; on the right by the parlor 20 by 22 feet. This room is still adorned by paper put on by Philip Schuyler, 2d, in preparation for the marriage of his daughter Ruth to Mr. T. W. Ogden, of New York, in 1836. The paper on the room immediately above it was also renewed at the same time. All of these rooms are beautifully lighted by spacious windows which retain the original small panes of glass. The great fire-places at either end of the house are also left undisturbed; in fact the present occupants have very considerately endeavored to keep the house in its original state, that is, so far as necessary repairs would admit. Back of the parlor is a long room formerly used as a guest chamber, and which was assigned to Lafayette during his visit here to the Schuylers in 1824. This is now used as a museum and contains many interesting relics. Opening out of the reception hall to the east is a smaller room which was used by General Schuyler and all his successors as an office. Between this and the guest chamber just mentioned is a passage through a closet; a door once led from this to an addition or L which ran to the east and which contained two guest chambers on each floor. This was removed after the property changed hands. In the rear of the present sitting room, you pass into a hallway which leads on the right to a back door, and on the left to the kitchen; across this hall from the sitting room is the school room of the Schuylers, now used as the dining room. This tier of three rooms with the rear hall and kitchen were added by General Schuyler, and are all one step lower than the floor of the main edifice. Passing through this rear hall to the north you come to the great kitchen, which is by no means the least interesting part of the house. It is 23 by 25 feet interior dimensions. The opening in the fire-place is 7 feet wide by 4 feet high. The old brick oven on the left has been removed. Just to the left, as you pass out doors, the milk-room was formerly situated, surrounded with lattice work and containing sunken places in the stone floor to keep the butter cool.

Above the kitchen are four rooms. In the second story of the main house are seven bedrooms, most of them very large, and all provided with ample closet room. On the third floor is found just one's ideal of a colonial attic, stored with quaint old relics. In the north end of this attic is a very pleasant and spacious bedroom with sloping sides. All the doors were originally fitted with large brass locks, but all save two were stolen soon after the departure of the Schuylers. The house is full of fine old furniture, quite in keeping with the style and age of the structure, and which helps amazingly in one's effort to think himself back into the times of the fathers.

A few feet to the north of the present wood-house formerly stood a much larger one. In the second story of this were the slaves' quarters. The present well is the same from which General Schuyler and all his distinguished guests slaked their thirst. There were also several penstocks on the premises which poured forth their waters in perennial streams.

The spacious grounds in front were not so full of trees in the early part of the century as now. They were then arranged in clumps and considerable space was given to shrubs and lawn. At that time a lawn ran unobstructed from the rear of the house eastward to the banks of the canal. The lilac bushes at the bottom of the excavation southeast of the house are descendants of the large ones that once ornamented the garden of house No. 2, burned by Burgoyne. The children were provided with great swings hung in the trees, and permanent see saws nicely made and painted dark green.

The rebuilding of his house by General Schuyler was no doubt a necessary preliminary to the rehabilitation of his business enterprises here, that he might have a place of shelter while restoring his mills, etc., which had been destroyed. His reasons for rebuilding were no doubt, first, because he had faith in the ultimate success of the cause for which the States were struggling, and was ready to prove his faith by his works; secondly, because there was a great demand in the country at that time for such merchandise as he could produce; and thirdly, that he might encourage by his example the fugitive farmers to return to their homes.

In pursuance of this purpose the General moved his family up to Saratoga during the winter of 1777-'78, with the intention of residing here altogether.[2] But as the troops were entirely withdrawn from this section in the spring of 1778, thus leaving the upper Hudson defenseless against the ever frowning north, he, with many others, did not think it safe to remain, and so retired to Albany again. There he remained until the authorities awoke to the unwisdom of their action, which they speedily did, and reinstated the garrisons at Saratoga and other places farther to the north. After the Tories had kidnapped several prominent citizens and taken them to Canada, the authorities thought it necessary to detail twenty-four men as a constant guard to General Schuyler, and despite the guard he came near being captured

---

[2] See Schuyler's letter to Governor Clinton, in Public Papers of George Clinton Vol. III, p. 177.

at his home in Albany, as we shall have occasion to relate hereafter. You see he was a much wanted man in both Canada and the States. Why? Because he was a great leader; from the Canadian standpoint, of the rebels; from the home standpoint, of the patriots.

After resigning his post in the army he was much at Saratoga looking after his business, but his time and abilities were by no means wholly devoted to the promotion of his own private interests. His withdrawal from public life was not followed by loss of interest in the cause of liberty, for which he still labored in season and out of season. Washington was anxious that he should again take command of the Northern Department, but the bitter experiences of the past had effectually cloyed his appetite for military glory, so he chose to serve his country in less conspicuous, but none the less efficient, ways, as an adviser and counsellor, and a procurer of valuable information.

Schuyler Builds First Road to Saratoga Springs. But few details of the experiences of the Schuylers at Saratoga between the years 1777 and 1783, have come down to us. General Schuyler, like others at that time, had heard of the wonderful properties of the spring a dozen miles to the west, in the wilderness. As a result of his own and other people's investigation he became so convinced of its medicinal value that he determined to cut a road from his country home through the forests to the "High Rock," the only spring then known. This he did in the year 1783, at his own expense, and so to him belongs the honor of constructing the first highway by which the public could reach this now world famous watering place. Thus for several years thereafter the popular route to the Springs was by way of old Saratoga. But we may not suppose that the General ever dreamed that the name of his ancestral estates, "Saratoga," the name vitally connected with historic events of such vast and far reaching importance, would be successfully filched, transported over that road of his own building, and affixed to a village yet to grow up around a bubbling spring in the dense woods.

For the first season the General and his family camped near the spring in a tent, but the next year he built a cottage of two rooms with an ample fire-place in the middle, and thus he became the first of that long line of cottagers who have since spent their summers there.[3]

The Two Visits of Washington. In May, 1782, there came the gratifying intelligence that King George was ready to talk peace with the Americans. This of course meant a cessation of hostilities, for which all concerned were quite ready, and duly grateful. The Continental army, at that time, was encamped from Newburg south at various points along the Hudson. There being no campaigning on hand, Gen. Washington decided to spend a little time on a trip to the north. He reached Albany on June 27th, when the citizens, led by the Mayor and Aldermen gave him a spectacular and altogether fitting demonstration of their regard for him. The next day the minister and officers of the Reformed Dutch church presented him with an appropriate address, to which he cordially responded.

On the 29th, accompanied by Gov. Clinton, Gen. Schuyler, and many other distinguished gentlemen, he started for old Saratoga to inspect the theatre of the glorious campaign of 1777. Brig. General Gansevoort, with 40 volunteers, acted as escort. On the way up they made a careful survey of the battlefield where Burgoyne and his legions were vanquished, and then hastened north

---

[3] Sylvester's Hist. of Saratoga County, p. 149.

to the scene of the surrender. At that time Saratoga was garrisoned by New Hampshire troops under the command of General Stark. These were reviewed by Washington, after which he inspected the block houses that served as part of the defenses of that post. That night he lodged in the Schuyler mansion, and early the next morning started for Schenectady. To get there he probably took the route through Half Moon and Niskayuna, as at that time there was no road from old Saratoga to the Springs or Ballston.

The people of Schenectady gave General Washington a royal welcome, and in the most elaborate way displayed their appreciation of his person and services. The same evening, or June 30th, he with his party returned to Albany.

The year and more that elapsed before the arrival of the definitive treaty proved to be a long and tedious wait for the army. The bulk of the forces were still encamped in the vicinity of Newburg. Many of the soldiers had been allowed to go home on furloughs, but under the circumstances it would have been most unwise to disband the army. Washington found little to do at headquarters, and being incessantly teased with applications and demands which he had neither the means nor the power to satisfy, he resolved to seek a little respite by taking a more extended trip to the north and west. He would visit other scenes of the late military operations, but he especially desired to learn from personal observation more about the natural resources of the country.

Accordingly on the 18th of July, 1783, he left headquarters in company with Governor Clinton, Alexander Hamilton and a few others. Brief was his stay in Albany at this time. With his suite he hastened to the north, passed through old Saratoga, Fort Edward and on to the head of Lake George, where they embarked on light boats; traversed that beautiful sheet of water, so full of historic interest; proceeded to Ticonderoga, the scene of notable Colonial as well as Revolutionary exploits, and thence to Crown Point. Returning they came back to old Saratoga.

His curiosity having been aroused by the reports about the remarkable medicinal springs a little to the westward, he was eager to see them. So, with his party, Washington took the road only just completed by General Schuyler, and in due time reached the goal. So impressed were both Washington and Clinton with the value of the water, and by their visions of the great watering-place sure to spring up there, that they agreed to make a joint purchase of the springs, and so much of the adjoining country as possible. The consummation of the plan was left in the hands of Governor Clinton; but he discovered that the Waltons and Livingstons had already secured the land and perfected their title. Washington later expressed himself as greatly disappointed over the defeat of their project.

From the High Rock spring the party took the trail through the woods that led southward by the newly discovered spring at Ballston, afterward known as the Iron Rail Spring. On their route through the woods between the two springs they struck the path leading west by Factory Village to the Middle Line Road, but continuing too far they lost their way. Near Factory Village lived one Tom Connor, who was chopping wood at his cabin door. They inquired of him the way to the spring, and Tom cheerfully gave the requisite directions. The party then retraced their steps by the road they came, but again getting bewildered, rode back for more explicit directions. Tom now lost his temper, and petulantly cried out to the spokesman of the party—who happened to be Washington himself—"I tell you, turn back and take the first right hand path into the woods, and then *stick to it*—any d—d fool would know the way.' Afterwards, when Tom learned that he had addressed the great Washington in this unceremonious and uncivil manner, he was extremely chagrined and mortified. His neighbors never afterward allowed poor Tom to forget about his reception of General Washington.[4]

Right here we believe it will be of interest to quote a letter from Washington to the Marquis de Chastellux, in which he gives a brief outline of this entire trip. It is dated Oct. 12th, 1783. He says: " I have lately made a tour through the Lakes George and Champlain as far as Crown Point; thence returning to Schenectady I proceeded up the Mohawk River to Fort Schuyler, formerly Fort Stanwix, and crossed over to Wood Creek, which empties into Oneida Lake and affords water communication with Ontario. I thence traversed the country to the head of the eastern branch of the Susquehanna and viewed the Lake Otsego; then another portage between that Lake and the Mohawk River at Canajoharie."

In a letter of Washington to Gov. Clinton, dated Nov. 25, 1784, he says: "I am sorry that we have been disappointed in our expectation of the mineral spring at Saratoga, and of the purchase of that part of the Oriskany tract upon which Fort Schuyer stands."[5]

---

[4] Stone's Reminiscences of Saratoga, p.14.

[5] As to above letters see Magazine of American Hist., Vol. IV, pp. 156 and 159.. See also, Baker's Itinerary of Washington, pp. 302-3, and Spark's Life of Washington.

CHAPTER VI

Mansion No. 3—Continued

Its Later Occupants—John Bradstreet Schuyler. When his oldest son, John Bradstreet Schuyler became of age—the General decided to establish him in business by placing him in full charge of the Saratoga estate, assuring him that it should be his to hold and possess after the death of his father. We here insert the letter from the General to his son in which he announces his purpose concerning the property. We do this not alone because it contains matter of local interest, but mainly because its author, having achieved great success as a business man and a public servant, having been universally regarded as a model gentleman, most approachable and urbane, and one possessed of a very noble character, discloses in this letter the secret of such success, the source of his affable manners, and the basis of his exalted character.

Observe that it is dated here at his best loved home.

"Saratoga, December 3d, 1787.

"My Dear Child:

"I resign to your care, and to your sole emolument a place on which I have for a long series of years bestowed much care and attention, and I confess I should part from it with many a severe pang did I not resign it to my child.

"I feel none now because of that paternal consideration. It is natural, however, for a parent to be solicitous for the weal of a child who is now to be guided by, and in a great measure to rely on, his own judgment and prudence.

"Happiness ought to be the aim and end of the exertions of every rational creature, and spiritual happiness should take the lead, in fact temporal happiness without the former does not really exist except in name. The first can only be obtained by an improvement of those faculties of the mind which the beneficent Author of Creation has made all men susceptible of, by a conscious discharge of those sacred duties enjoined on us by God, or those whom he has authorized to promulgate His Holy Will. Let the rule of your conduct then be the precept contained in Holy Writ (to which I hope and entreat you will have frequent recourse). If you do, virtue, honor, good faith, and a punctual discharge of the social duties will be the certain result, and an internal satisfaction that no temporal calamities can ever deprive you of.

"Be indulgent, my child, to your inferiors, affable and courteous to your equals, respectful, not cringing, to your superiors, whether they are so by superior mental abilities or those necessary distinctions which society has established.

"With regard to your temporal concerns it is indispensably necessary that you should afford them a close and continual attention. That you should not commit that to others which you can execute yourself. That you should not refer the necessary business of the hour or the day to the next. Delays are not only dangerous, they are fatal. Do not consider anything too insignificant to preserve; if you do so the habit will steal on you and you will consider many things of little importance and the account will close against you. Whereas a proper economy will not only make you easy, but enable you to bestow benefits on objects who may want your assistance —and of them you will find not a few. Example is infinitely more lasting than precept, let therefore your servants never discover a disposition to negligence or waste;

if they do they will surely follow you in it, and your affairs will not slide but Gallop into Ruin.

"In every community there are wretches who watch the dispositions of young men, especially when they come to the possession of property; some of these may hang about you; they will flatter, they will cringe, and they will cajole you until they have acquired your confidence, and then they will ruin you. Beware of these, they are the curse of society, and have brought many, alas! too many to destruction.

"Be specially careful that you do not put yourself under such obligations to any man as that he may deem himself entitled to request you to become his security for money. You are Good natured, and Generous, keep a Watch upon yourself, and do not ruin yourself and family for another.

"Directly on my return to Albany I shall make you out a Deed of Gift for all the Blacks belonging to the farm except Jacob, Peter, Cuff and Bett, and for the Stock and Cattle, Horses, &c., &c., with a very few exceptions. For all the farming utensils, household furniture, &c., &c.

"The crops of the last year I must of necessity appropriate to the discharge of Debts, and they must be brought down in Winter, except what may be necessary for the subsistence of your family and to satisfy those whom you may have occasion to employ. This I shall hereafter Detail.

"The logs now in the Creek will be sawed at our joint expense and you shall have half the boards which I hope will net you something of Value. We will consult on the best and cheapest terms to have this done.

"Althou' for reasons which prudence dictates, I shall now not give you a deed for any part of my estate, yet you ought to know what of this farm I intend for you, and which I shall immediately make you by Will; it is all on the South Side of the Fishkill, and as far down as Col. Van Vechten's, and as far West as to Inclose Marshall's & Colvert's farms, Besides a just proportion of all my other Estates. But all the tenants now residing on the farm either on the South or North side of the Creek are to pay their rents to me and Preserve the right of settling people on the west side of the road and to the north of the Little Creek, which runs by Kiliaen Winne's, the blacksmith. For altho' you will have the occupancy of all the rest of the farm on both sides of the Creek, yet that on the North side of the Creek I intend for one of your Brothers.

"Should you die before me, which I most sincerely pray may not happen, your children, if God blesses you with any, will have this farm and such share of my other Estates as I intend for you; and should you die before me, and without children, your wife, who is also my child, will be provided for by me. In short, it is my intention to leave you without any excuse if you fail in proper exertions to improve the property intrusted to you; and it is with that view that I so fully detail my intentions, and Give you this written testimony of them, and that no unworthy conduct may induce me to change my intentions is my hope and my anxious wish, and I have the pleasure to assure you that I believe when once the heat of youth is a little abated, I shall enjoy the satisfaction of seeing you what I most ardently wish you to be, a Good man and an honor to your family.

"I must however not omit to inform you that the Income of all my estate except what you and your Brothers and Sisters may actually occupy at my decease will be enjoyed by your dear Mama; she merits this attention in a most eminent degree, and I shall even give her a power to change my Disposition of that part of my estate the income of which she will enjoy, should unhappily the conduct of my Children be such as to render it necessary; but I trust they are and will be so deeply impressed with a Sense of the infinite obligations they are under to her as not to give her a moment's uneasiness.

"I must once more recommend to you as a matter of indispensable importance to Love, to honor, and faithfully and without guile to serve the Eternal, incomprehensible, beneficent and Gracious Being by whose will you exist, and so insure happiness in this life and in that to come. And now my dear child, I commit you and my Daughter and all your concerns to his Gracious and Good Guidance; and sincerely intreat Him to enable you to be a comfort to your parents and a protector to your Brothers and Sisters, an honor to your family, and a good citizen. Accept of my Blessing and be assured that I am your affectionate father,

"Ph. SCHUYLER.

"To JOHN B. SCHUYLER."

The immediate occasion for making such a disposition of the Saratoga property at this time was the recent marriage of this son, John Bradstreet, which event took place in Albany, the 18th of September preceding. Parental interest evidently prompted him to thus start the young man in business that he might be the better able to support the dignity of his new position as head of a family.

John B. Schuyler takes Possession. Accepting with alacrity his father's offer, he took immediate possession, with his young wife, only daughter of the Patroon Van Rensselaer—"a most lovable woman who united in herself the good qualities of two of the most substantial families of the early Republic—the Van Rensselaers and the Livingstons." No portrait of her is extant, but tradition pictures her as a brunette, with an oval face and dark hair and eyes. Her husband was a handsome young fellow, with blue eyes and flaxen curly hair.[2]

Although brought up for most part in the city of Albany, and accustomed to the usual life of a young man of leisure, John Bradstreet Schuyler entered on the life of a country gentleman with much enthusiasm. We may suppose that he came to Saratoga with the more readiness because youthful associations combined with the romance of the wars had greatly endeared the old place to him as it also had to the rest of the family. After his coming we are told that "the intercourse with Albany was kept up regularly through the faithful family slaves" who passed back and forth like shuttles between the Saratoga and Albany homes. For example "Jim" goes down from Saratoga with an order "for a fashionable beaver hat for Betsy," as Mrs. J. B. Schuyler was called by her family; also twelve pairs of shoes, intended no doubt for the household slaves; for every person of substance in those days owned slaves.

Two sons were born to Mr. and Mrs. John Bradstreet Schuyler at Saratoga. The eldest, Philip, was named for his grandfather, the General; the second for his maternal grandfather, Stephen Van Rensselaer. Stephen died in infancy. Philip was a strong and vigorous child.

The young proprietor evidently prosecuted the business, established by his father, with energy and success; for we find that he received large orders for the products of the Saratoga mills and farms, which were transported to market mainly in the old way, on rafts and flatboats.

Death of John B. Schuyler. The career of this promising young man came to a sudden close in 1795, at the age of thirty-two. He had been spending some time up the Mohawk valley with his father, apparently assisting in the construction of a waterway from Sche-

---
[2] MSS. in possession of Miss Fanny Schuyler, of Pelham-on-Sound.

nectady to Lake Ontario. His father, the General, was president of the Inland Lock and Navigation Company, which had in charge the execution of this important work. The General had from the start been a most zealous promoter of the enterprise, which, ever since, has had so much to do with the commercial preeminence of New York. Locks had just been completed at Little Falls and Fort Herkimer to help the boats around the rapids in the Mohawk at those points, and on the 10th of August he was to meet the Indians in council at Oneida to secure the right of way for a canal between the Mohawk and Wood Creek, which empties into Oneida Lake.

His son, John Bradstreet, evidently feeling unwell, started for his home at Saratoga, where he arrived on the 7th of August. His wife, with her little son, was away at the time; family tradition says in New York. The fever which had been developing was thought to have been aggravated by showing a gentleman over the battle field under a broiling sun. This was in all probability the Duc de La Rochefoucauld-Liancourt. (See Stone's Burgoyne's Campaign, p. 381.) The record of this sad event, found in the Schuyler family Bible, reads as follows:

"August 7, 1795, John B. Schuyler arrived at his house in Saratoga from the westward. Taken sick on Wednesday, the 12th, of a Bilious Fever. Died the 19th August, 1795. Buried in the vault of Stephen Van Rensselaer, Esq., at Watervliet, 20th August, 1795."

Local tradition has it that his body was taken down the river in a canoe, which is quite probable. The absence of Mrs. Schuyler, together with the extreme heat, no doubt accounts for the speedy removal of the remains to the family vault.

That was a sad home-coming to both the young wife and the father; for when they bade him good-by, neither had dreamed that it was for aye. His sudden death proved to be especially distressing to his father, who had built on him many high hopes. That he was a young man of unusual intelligence, stability of character and influence, is proved by the fact that he had already been elected as one of the trustees of Williams College, Massachusetts; that he had been chosen the first Supervisor of his town after the new County of Saratoga had been erected; and by the fact that he was sent to the New York Assembly in 1795.

Philip Schuyler, 2d. Philip Schuyler, 2d, was seven years of age, when his father, John Bradstreet, died. His grandfather, the General, was appointed his guardian, who first placed him in a school on Staten Island, under the charge of Dr. Moore, afterwards Bishop of Virginia, and later he was sent to Columbia College. During his collegiate course he lived in New York, and for part of the time in the family of his talented uncle, Alexander Hamilton; a rare privilege, that, for a young man in the formative period of his life.

Philip Schuyler, 2d, selected for his wife Miss Grace Hunter, sister of Hon. John Hunter, of Hunter's Island, N. Y. They were married in New York, September 12th, 1811. She was a beautiful and lovable woman, and she willingly left the charms of city life for the quiet scenes and more romantic life in the old historic home at Saratoga.[3]

Being an only child, Philip inherited so much of the Saratoga estate as fell to his father, which ran for three miles along the Hudson River. He also inherited from

---
[3] Most of the above facts relating to J. Bradstreet, and Philip Schuyler, 2nd, were taken from the Schuyler MSS., in possession of Miss Fanny Schuyler, of Pelham-on-Sound.

his father and grandfather a large measure of their public spirit, which manifested itself through an active interest in anything that tended to promote the public welfare, multiply common luxuries for the people, or increase the comforts of living. He was an enthusiastic promoter of inland navigation, or the canal projects, which so stirred the public mind of this State from 1807 to 1825, at which latter date both Champlain and Erie canals had been completed.

It was through his influence that the great canal basin was built at Schuylerville and also the slip or back-set from the basin to the rear of the mills; and to guard against the evils of stagnant water he obtained a perpetual grant to tap the end of the slip and use the water for running a mill; the sawmill now operated by Mr. G. Edward Laing gets its power from this source. This is the only place where the State allows water to be drawn from the canals to furnish power for a private enterprise. This franchise was secured not only for sanitary reasons, but as part pay for the right to pass through Mr. Schuyler's estate.

He early became interested in cotton manufacture, and erected here at Schuylerville the second cotton mill in the State of New York—the old Horicon, which still stands, though somewhat enlarged, as a monument to his enterprise.

In 1822 his fellow citizens sent him to represent them as Assemblyman in the New York Legislature.

Philip Schuyler, 2d, and his charming wife maintained the ancient family reputation for hospitality. So long as a Schuyler lived here open house was kept for every one who could formulate a decent excuse for crossing their threshold. During the summer season the old house was usually thronged with guests from everywhere, among

PHILIP SCHUYLER, 2D

which were sure to be a goodly sprinkling of notables of every type.

Visit of Lafayette. Perhaps during the whole stretch of the nineteenth century the Schuyler mansion was never more highly honored than by the visit of the Marquis de Lafayette, the friend of Washington, the one Frenchman who made the greatest sacrifices for American liberty. On his last visit here, in 1824, he was voted the nation's guest, and was everywhere lionized and feted as no foreigner since has been. Though it was quite out of his way, he could not resist turning aside to visit the old Saratoga home of General Schuyler, whom he had greatly loved, and the scene of the humiliation of one proud army of France's ancient foe.

Such details of this interesting visit as have been preserved we here give verbatim from a manuscript in possession of Miss Fanny Schuyler, of Pelham-on-Sound N. Y., a daughter of Philip Schuyler, 2d[4]

"The general came in the coach-and-four which my father had sent to convey him from the town beyond. His son, who was with him, had a round face and wore gold spectacles. His secretary and another gentleman filled a second carriage. Lafayette received the villagers, who had assembled on the lawn in front of the house, with very courteous bows, and spoke some appreciative words.

"Being greatly fatigued from his journey, Lafayette was shown into the guest chamber (on the southeast corner, first floor) where, having stretched himself on the bed, he slept for several hours. After a collation was served and before his departure, he stepped to the sideboard, and while resting one arm on its polished surface, with the other poured a glass of Madeira, which he drank

---

[4] The facts which the MSS. preserve were given to her by her eldest sister, Ruth, now, 1900, 88 years of age.

MRS. PHILIP SCHUYLER, 2D

to the health of 'the four generations of Schuylers he had known'—the fourth generation was represented by his host's three little daughters (Ruth, Elizabeth and Grace). Just as he was about to depart, Lafayette lifted little Grace Schuyler up in his arms and kissed her. Afterwards, being asked how she liked General Lafayette, she said: "I don't like that man, 'his face pricked me.' "[5]

Hospitality of the Schuylers. Quite early in the century Saratoga Springs became the most popular, indeed the one fashionable watering place in America. Thither the blooded aristocracy, the merchant princes, the leaders in fashion and politics, flocked from all parts of the States. One of the most popular drives in those days for those who had the *entree* of the mansion was from the Springs to Old Saratoga (Schuylerville).

Dinner parties were frequently given here by the Schuylers at the then fashionable hour of three or four o'clock; the guests returning to the Springs in the early evening. Among such, one might mention Martin Van Buren, President of the United States, who had become a warm personal friend of Philip Schuyler, 2d, accompanied by his popular son, "Prince John," as he was then called.

Departure of the Schuylers. But changes came to the old homestead at last. Perhaps the worst financial panic in our nation's history was that of 1837. Com-

---

[5] The above-mentioned mahogany brass-mounted sideboard, together with the high-post French bedstead on which Lafayette slept, are now in possession of the family, at Pelham-on-Sound, in the house occupied by Miss Fanny Schuyler there, as are also many other interesting pieces of furniture once used by Gen. Philip Schuyler, including a mirror, which is known to have reflected the faces of most of the Revolutionary notables, among whom may be mentioned General Burgoyne and his suite; also General Schuyler's silver spurs, pocket sun-dial, gold pen and pencil case, double-cased gold-embossed watch, silver-mounted pistol—all used in his military campaigns. A high, mahogany hall clock, French white marble and gilt parlor clock, white silk vest, embroidered in gilt thread, etc., are also in possession of the family there.

merce and manufactures were prostrate; hundreds of wealthy mercantile houses in every quarter of the country suddenly found themselves bankrupt, and the crash was consummated when the banks universally suspended specie payments. Philip Schuyler, like thousands of others, was caught in this financial whirlwind and swamped. To meet his obligations, the ancestral estate was sold.

President Van Buren ere long, having need of a man of Schuyler's calibre in an important position, unsolicited, sent him as consul to the port of Liverpool, England. No better selection could have been made, according to the judgment of the English press. For example, the Liverpool *Courier* of June 1, 1842, had this to say, after it became known that Mr. Schuyler had been recalled:

"Among other removals we regret to announce that of Philip Schuyler, Esq., the late consul of this port. The United States never had, nor never can have, a more efficient officer than that gentleman to represent their great nation; for besides the official capacities which are indispensable to the fulfillment of the multifarious duties of a consulate, he possessed in an eminent degree the no less necessary and agreeable faculty of ingratiating himself into the respect and esteem of our people. Circumstances led us on several occasions to know these facts, and we feel it our duty, as it is our pleasure, to record them." He was recalled by President Tyler for purely party reasons, and that after he had been orally assured by him that he would be retained at the post.

After his return from England, Mr. Schuyler was at one time on the point of repurchasing his old home and returning to Schuylerville; but as their son John was in New York preparing for college, Mrs. Schuyler preferred to remain near him and so the project was abandoned. They finally built a new house on a fine site, including seventy acres of land, at Pelham-on-Sound, a favorite residence of New Yorkers, and within easy distance of the city.

As an indication that he retained an undying affection for the home of his fathers and the scenes of his boyhood, and that he was held in highest esteem by his neighbors, we here insert a paragraph from a letter of one of his daughters to the writer:

"One of my childish remembrances is a visit with my father to Schuylerville, on his return from England, when an ovation was tendered him in the evening, a serenade given and speeches made by the leading men of the place. And there, surrounded by his early friends, and many of his former stalwart workmen, as he stood among them once more the tears coursed down his face, as well as down many other faces about him. On another occasion, when present there, as one of the committee, with the Hon. Hamilton Fish, to select the position for the Saratoga monument, his son-in-law, Charles de Luze, Esq., of New York, who was also present, again saw him brushing away tears as he gazed over the old familiar scenes of his childhood."

The departure of the Schuylers was an irreparable loss to the commercial, social and religious interests of Schuylerville. In short, we have ever since had "Hamlet" with Hamlet left out.[6]

The Strovers. When the place was thrown upon the market by the assignee of Mr. Schuyler, it was purchased by Col. George Strover. Thus for 135 years this property had been in the hands of the Schuylers.

Col. George Strover was born near Bryant's bridge, in the town of Saratoga, in 1791. His grandfather had been

---

[6] Grace Hunter, wife of Philip Schuyler, 2nd, died at Pelham-on-Sound, December 24, 1855. Philip Schuyler died at the same place, February 12, 1865.

a soldier in the French and Indian war. His father, John Strover, became a noted scout in the Revolution; hence, with such antecedents, it was altogether natural that George Strover should be eager to serve his country in a similar way should the opportunity offer. The war of 1812 was his chance and he was among the first to enlist. It was in that war that he gained the title of Colonel through promotion.

Col. Strover became one of the leading and most public spirited of Schuylerville's citizens, and enjoyed the highest esteem of his fellow townsmen, because of his kindly spirit and integrity of character. He was largely instrumental in founding the old Academy, and in the erection of the Episcopal church. And it was at his house, the old Schuyler mansion, that the first meeting of patriotic gentlemen was called to consider what steps should be taken toward the erection of a suitable monument to commemorate the glorious events of the decisive campaign of the war for Independence.

When next this place changes hands it should go into the possession of the State, and be placed in the custody of a local historical society, which, by the way, ought to have been in existence long ere this, but which, in fact, is not yet born. In this building should be collected the many relics of colonial and Revolutionary times which are scattered about, here and there, in this vicinity, but which are being rapidly collected and carried away by the ever increasing horde of relic hunters.

The Marshall house too, like the Schuyler mansion, should ultimately belong to the public. Houses like these, so closely connected with great historic events, are very rare in our country, and hence what we have left should be guarded and preserved with the most jealous care.

CHAPTER VII

About William Duer, and Colonel James Livingston

Besides General Schuyler there were several other men, more or less native to Old Saratoga, who rendered valuable service to the country during the war for Independence, but whose names and achievements have in large measure been forgotten. This should not be permitted. We shall, therefore, in this connection, devote a little space to a pair of them, viz.: William Duer, and James Livingston.

William Duer was born in Devonshire, England, in 1747. He spent some time with the army in India under Lord Clive. He came to New York in 1768 to arrange for a supply of lumber for himself and some friends. In looking about he came in contact with Phillip Schuyler, by whose advice he bought a large tract of timberland at Fort Miller, which also included the falls, and there he erected extensive mills. In 1773 he obtained a contract to supply the royal navy with masts and spars.

Evidently expecting to make Fort Miller his permanent home he built there a spacious mansion. It was located on the bluff directly east of the modern village. This house was used at least for a month by Burgoyne, as his headquarters, during his excursion toward Albany in 1777. All his correspondence while here was dated "Duer's House." One of the Hessian officers in a letter home describes this house as follows: "Duer's house is built in very good taste, it has two stories, and the roof is in Italian style. On each side of the house is a small building serving as kitchen and storehouse. Both of these are connected with the main house by a covered passage. It is large and is the first real country seat that I have seen since my departure from Portsmouth."

DUER HOME

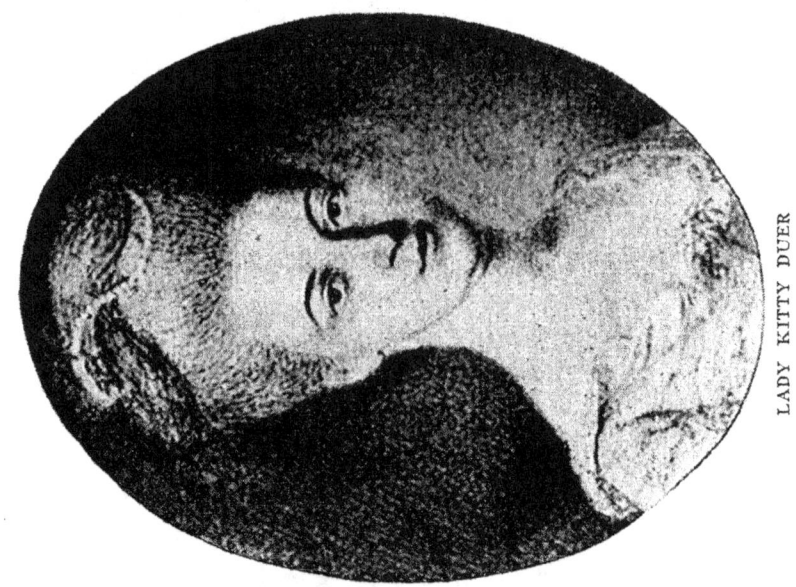

LADY KITTY DUER

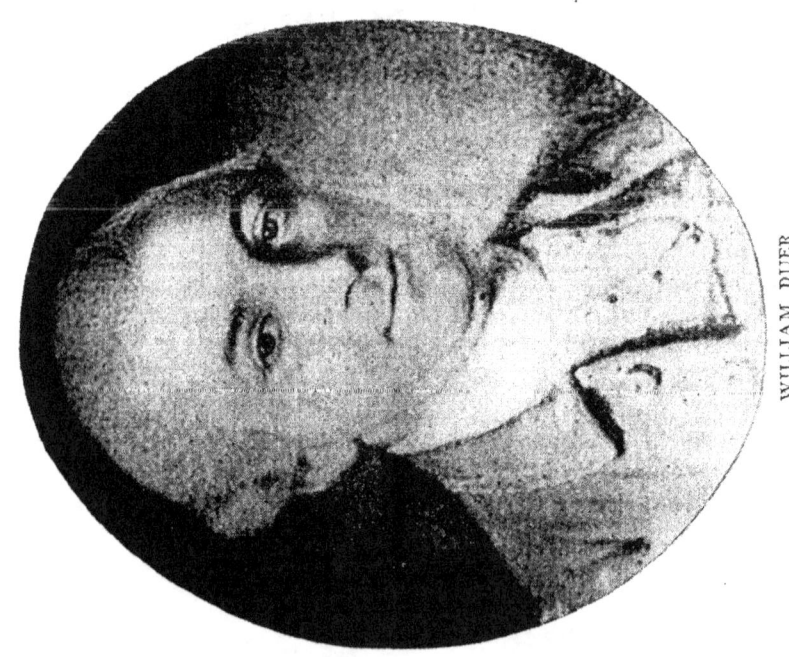

WILLIAM DUER

After the erection of Charlotte County, which included a part of what is now Washington Co. and a large slice of Vermont, William Duer was appointed its first Judge. It is related that in March, 1775, Judge Duer held Court at Fort Edward which was defended by the bayonets of Captain Mott's company of British soldiers, who had been halted by him on their way to Ticonderoga. He was enabled to find indictments against certain lawless men who had for some time been able to defy the civil authorities. These outlaws had killed Judge William French and dispersed the Cumberland Co. Court, over in what is now Vermont, but they found Judge Duer a man not to be frightened.

In the troubles with old England he believed the claims of the Colonies to be just, and when hostilities broke out he cast in his lot with the friends of liberty. He was appointed Colonel by the Continental Congress, but as he seemed better fitted for civil than military service he early consented to serve in the Provincial Congress, the successor of the Provincial Assembly. He became a member of the Committee of Safety, a very responsible position at the time. He was appointed chairman of the Committee on Conspiracies in September, 1776, and was also a member of the Committee of Correspondence. He was a member of the Committee of Thirteen which drafted the first Constitution of New York State.

After this he was sent to represent the State in the Continental Congress, and by that body was appointed Secretary of the Board of the Treasury where, for years he rendered valuable service. In a letter written by Alexander Hamilton to Governor Clinton, in Feb. 1778, wherein he severely criticises Congress, as a body, for its lack of energy, dignity, and wisdom, he makes an exception of Duane, Morris, and Duer, New York's representatives.

24

Early in 1778 he, with Gouverneur Morris, and Francis Dana of Mass., were appointed by Congress to draft instructions to General Gates as to his conduct of military affairs in the Highlands of the Hudson, and of the northern department generally. This was after the collapse of the Conway Cabal, which tried to put Gates in Washington's place. (In this connection read chapter IV of New York's share in the Revolution.) During this same year of 1778 he advanced money to the State for defraying the expense connected with the printing of the first Constitution. When Mr. Duer resigned his seat in Congress in 1779 the New York Assembly passed a resolution commending him for "his zeal in the cause of his country, and his exertions in her behalf."

In 1776 he married Catherine, youngest daughter of William Alexander (Lord Sterling), who was familiarly known as "Lady Kitty." After the war Col. Duer, with his family, returned to Fort Miller, where he resided in his mansion for a number of years, running his mills and managing his large estate. He somewhat later removed to New York where he died in 1790, survived by his wife and eight children.

James Livingston

Col. James Livingston was the son of John Livingston, who was the son of Robert, nephew and namesake of that Robert, first lord of the Manor, whose seat was at Clermont on the middle Hudson. John and his son James were living at Montreal when the Revolutionary war broke out. Then the former immediately moved back to New York, and settled near Stillwater, on a portion of the Saratoga Patent allotted to Peter Schuyler, his maternal grandfather.

James was engaged in the practise of the law at Montreal during the troublous years immediately preceding open hostilities. At that time it was the hope of the Colonies to the south that Canada might be induced to make common cause with them in the approaching struggle with the mother country. Livingston, being on the ground, was one of the few who engaged in the hazardous enterprise of trying to arouse the spirit of resistance to old England among the Canadians. His exertions soon attracted the notice of the Provincial authorities, and quickly he found himself possessed of the equivocal honor of being denounced as a traitor. The next move of the Canadian government was to confiscate his property, and set a price on his head.

He managed to escape into New York, and soon was able to organize, and was voted the command of, a corps made up of Canadian refugees, and immediately entered upon active duty.

The parts assigned to him showed that great confidence was placed in his ability and courage; nor was that confidence misplaced, for he shared largely of those sterling and heroic qualities that distinguished the leaders of our revolution. In the fall of 1775 he, with his battalion, joined the little army of the gallant Montgomery on that ill starred attempt at the conquest of Canada. On their arrival before St. Johns, he with Col. Brown were sent on the hazardous business of surprising Chambly, a post some miles in the rear of St. Johns, which contained a large quantity of military stores of which the Americans were very much in need. They were entirely successful, and this made possible the capture of the fortress of St. Johns. From there he pushed forward with Montgomery, and was present at the taking of Montreal, and later encamped with him on the far famed plains of Abraham, in the rear of Quebec. Of the hardships connected with that campaign Col. Livingston bore his full share; while his knowledge of the country acquired during his former residence in it, made him specially useful. In the desperate attack on the city, on the last day of December, 1775, in the midst of a violent snowstorm, Col. Livingston led one of the columns against the upper town. But, as is well known, the assault failed, the brave Montgomery fell, and his men, who escaped capture, beat a hasty retreat.

As a result of this defeat Livingston's battalion was permanently dispersed, but soon thereafter Congress voted to make him Colonel of one of the regiments of the New York Line. In August, 1777, his regiment formed part of the Brigade commanded by Arnold, and sent by Gen. Schuyler to the relief of Fort Schuyler, besieged by St. Leger and his savage allies. After St. Leger and his men had taken to their heels, and fled to the north, Arnold and his force hastened back eastward, and were in time to take part in the glorious battles of Saratoga, where Burgoyne was made to feel and bow to "the might of a freeman's arm." Col. James Livingston was stationed on the right of Arnold's division, which with Morgan's men, bore the brunt of both the battles that shattered the strength of Burgoyne.

He afterwards marched with his men to Rhode Island, and served with them there under the command of the illustrious LaFayette. In 1779 he with his regiment took part in the Sullivan expedition against the Indians. In 1780 Washington placed him in command of the garrisons at Stony and Verplanck's Points, just below the Highlands. While stationed there he, early one morning, noticed that a British vessel was lying at anchor not far from Tellers' Point. This proved to be the Vulture on which Major Andre had come up to bargain with Benedict Arnold for the surrender of West Point. As we know Andre had got ashore and met his man, but Livingston not liking the look of things sent post haste to

West Point for powder with which to serve a 4 pounder, the only cannon he had. Col. Lamb sent him the powder, and also a curt lecture on the folly of firing at a man-of-war with a little 4 pounder. Livingston reported that having moved the cannon to Tellers' Point he opened on her and "raked the vessel fore and aft." The result was that the Vulture was obliged to weigh anchor, get out of range, and leave poor Andre to his fate. And thus, by his prompt and timely action, Col. James Livingston proved himself an essential factor in defeating the treason of Arnold, and saving West Point and the American army. After Arnold's treachery became known Washington sent for Col. Livingston to come to headquarters, when he said to him: "It is a source of gratification to me that the post [of Verplancks, and Stony Points] was in the hands of an officer so devoted as yourself to the cause of your country,"[7]

Such among others, were the soldierly services of Col. James Livingston. The peace left him poor in purse, but rejoicing with a patriot's joy at the deliverance of his country, which he deemed cheaply purchased with the sacrifice of the valuable estate he inherited. At the close of the war he turned his attention to rural arts, and spent the greater part of the remaining years in the cultivation of a farm at Stillwater, near the scene of one of his greatest martial exploits. But his services to his country did not end here. He was, soon after his retirement from the army, elected to the legislature of New York, and the same mark of confidence was bestowed on him by his fellow citizens for eight successive years, at a period when "honesty, capability, and faithfulness to the constitution" were essential requisites in

---

[7] Lossings Field Book, 1-729. For a long while it was supposed that this officer was Col. Henry Livingston, but later researches have proved him to be Col. James, as above related. See The Livingstons of Livingston Manor.

the character of a representative of the people. His devotion to his country ceased only with his life.

He died in 1832 at the advanced age of 86, at the residence of his son, Richard M. Livingston in Schuylerville, N. Y., and his honored remains repose within the public cemetery on Prospect Hill, and under the shadow of the Battle Monument. It is believed that he is the only officer, who took part in the battle of Saratoga, that is known to be buried at Schuylerville. As an expression of our appreciation of what this man did and suffered for his country in those crucial times would it not be altogether fitting if the citizens of Schuylerville, or the Sons and Daughters of the Revolution in this vicinity, were to erect a more conspicuous monument than the one which now marks the last resting place of Col. James Livingston?

CHAPTER VIII

A Historic Church

OLD Saratoga was served by one church edifice. It was the scene of so many stirring incidents during the Revolution that we feel its share in the story should not be passed over. Its later history, as that of the other churches of Schuylerville, was told in the first edition of this work, which see.

The Reformed Church. The first religious society organized here was the Reformed Church, originally called, The Reformed Protestant Dutch Church. Since the ante-Revolutionary records of this church were destroyed, or lost, during that war, we are left to conjecture as to the date of its founding. It must have been as early as 1770, and very likely a few years before; for in 1771 it had developed enough strength to erect a house of worship.[1] Towards this most worthy object Gen. Philip Schuyler and Killaen De Ridder were the chief contributors. De Ridder gave a hundred acres of land, located to the southwest, on Lot 24, of the Saratoga Patent.

Location of Church. From the early church records we learn that the church edifice stood east and west, that it had a stoop, was adorned with a steeple, and had three aisles. The church stood on a four-acre lot given by General Schuyler, south of the creek, in the angle of the river and Victory roads. During the war the society was broken up and scattered. The cut is from a pen and ink sketch, made by the author, and submitted to Mr. D. A. Bullard, who remembered the old church, and who pronounced it an accurate reproduction. The two rows of

---

[1] See note in first book of post Revolutionary Records of Reformed Church of Schuylerville, pp. 50, 89

windows indicate that the church had galleries on three sides.

From the reminiscences of Mr. J. P. Becker (the Sexagenary), we gather that there was regular worship at the old church before the Revolution; that it was after the Sunday morning service on the 30th of April, 1775, that the people, there assembled, heard of the battle of Lexington from the lips of Gen. Philip Schuyler, and were deeply stirred by the news. He also tells how his father, with two other gentlemen, being desirous to observe at closer range the retreat of Burgoyne and his army, appeared just in the nick of time to save the old church from the torch of a British soldier. He tells of the cannonading it received from the royal batteries during the siege and before the surrender, and how it bore the scars of those iron missiles as long as it stood. It is said to have served as a wayside hospital for the British army during their passage down and up from the battlefield. The late George Strover used to relate the following tragedy, said to have been enacted in that church. A young lady seated at a north window eating an apple was instantly killed by a rifle shot, fired by an American sharpshooter, the ball cutting her throat. She was buried within the church under the spot where she was killed. Mr. Strover himself saw the blood stains on the wainscoting and floor, and also the bones when they were exhumed at the demolition of the building. The church was afterward used as a depot for commissary stores during the unsettled years between the surrender of Burgoyne and the proclamation of peace in the year 1783.[1]

Reorganization After the Revolution. The resources of the society had been so crippled by the war

---

[1] In the Chapter of Anecdotes see The Saving of the Old Dutch Church, Cannonading of Same, and Saratoga after Departure of the British.

DUTCH REFORMED CHURCH OF REVOLUTIONARY DAYS

that several years elapsed ere they felt able to settle a pastor. Preliminary steps, however, had been taken to this end in 1785 by Gen. Philip Schuyler, Cornelius Van Veghten, Killaen De Ridder, James Brisbin and A. McNiel, as trustees. The permanent reorganization took place in 1789 under the supervision of Dominie Eilardus Westerlo, the zealous patriot, who had for years so efficiently served the First Reformed Church of Albany. July 10th of that year a meeting was held in which twenty male members took part and elected Col. Cornelius Van Veghten and Peter Becker, father of the Sexagenary, as elders, and Jesse Toll and James Abeel as deacons. They also resolved that the services of the church should be conducted in the English language, and extended a call to the Rev. Samuel Smith, a young man who had just completed his studies. He accepted the call, arrived on the ground the 9th of December, 1789, and was ordained the 17th of January, 1790.

The reorganization of this impoverished church and the support of a pastor required the assistance of the sister churches in the denomination, which fact became the occasion for the creation of the Board of Domestic Missions of that denomination.[2]

In 1822 the congregation built a new house of worship on the site occupied by the present Reformed Church in the village of Schuylerville.

Post Revolutionary Settlement. When, in 1783, England and the United States concluded to cease fighting, the people had an opportunity to turn their attention once again to the more congenial arts of peace. The militiamen from the sterile hills of New England, and from down the Hudson valley having caught a glimpse of this beautiful country during the campaigns of the Revolution, thought it a veritable land of promise,

---

[2] Corwin's Manual of the Dutch Reformed Churches, third edition, p. 269

and many of them marched away with a secret resolve to see more of it when once the desperate scrimmage with old England was well over. No sooner was peace declared than some of them put their resolves into execution. The tide of immigration set in this direction so strongly and steadily that, at the end of the century, most of the available land in this township was taken up, though by no means cleared. The farms were sometimes purchased outright, but generally they were taken on long leases from the Patentees, such as Gen. Philip Schuyler. For example, the lease of Thomas Jordan was to run through the life of himself, wife and one John Ballard, who lived with him. It was, however, purchased before the expiration of the lease.

Attempt at the capture of Gen. Schuyler. The story of the way in which three settlers in this town obtained their farms is worthy of perpetuation here. We have elsewhere spoken of the raids of the Indians and Tories from the north, and their persistent efforts at kidnapping prominent citizens and carrying them to Canada.

On the 7th of August, 1781, seven men, sent from Canada, came to Albany and in the evening of that day made an attack upon the town-house of General Schuyler, who chanced to be there at the time with his family, instead of Saratoga (Schuylerville), as was his custom in the summer time. Their object was to kill or capture the General. There were in the house with the General at the time John Ward and John Cokely, two of his life guards, and also John Tubbs, an army courier, in his service. These three men made a gallant fight with the seven assassins, who had effected an entrance into the hall. John Tubbs, as his grandchildren now relate it, had a personal struggle with one of them. He pressed him down behind an old oaken chest, then, after getting the mastery he, with his hands on his throat, tried to draw a knife to finish him, but the knife was gone, and so Tubbs was obliged to let him up. Meanwhile General Schuyler had, from the windows above, aroused the town, and the seven men left suddenly, carrying off Tubbs and Cokely with them as prisoners, together with a goodly amount of the General's silver plate as proof that they had actually penetrated into Schuyler's house and made an attempt to execute their appointed task. The prisoners were kept nineteen months on an island in the St. Lawrence. Returning home about the time peace was declared, General Schuyler presented the three men with a deed of two hundred and seventy-five acres of land. The deed is still in possession of the descendants of John Tubbs, and recites that "In consideration of five shillings, and that John Cokely, John Ward and John Tubbs did gallantly defend the said Philip Schuyler when attacked in his own house near the city of Albany, on the 7th day of August, 1781, by a party of the enemy in the late war, sent expressly to kill or make prisoner of the said Philip Schuyler," the party of the first part hath granted and sold to the said Ward, Cokely and Tubbs all that tract and parcel of land "in the Saratoga patent, known and distinguished as the westernmost farm of the south half of lot No. 20, in the grand division of the Saratoga patent made by John B. Bleecker, surveyor, in 1750, containing about two hundred and seventy acres of land."

 The land was first divided into three parts, and the men drew for their respective portions. John Cokely's share ultimately came into possession of John Tubbs' descendants, who held the property until 1894, when it was purchased by Eugene Rogers.

 A compilation of the hundreds of names of those who settled in this vicinity after the Revolution is apart from the scope and purpose of this book, such being of little interest to the general reader. We would therefore refer those interested in that subject to Sylvester's History of Saratoga County, also to the town and church records.

Early Roads. After the settler has once established himself in his new home, about the first thing he must turn his attention to is the means of communication between himself and his neighbors and the markets beyond; he must address himself to the interminable task of road building.

The first roads in a new country are necessarily very crude and rough affairs. The bicycle and automobile could not have flourished here in those pioneer days. For many years after the settlement of the country the only vehicles that could stand the strain were the wood-sled and lumber wagon.

Naturally the first highway built in this section was the river road. But this, unlike any of its successors, was at the outset mainly built at government expense for the transportation of armies and munitions of war. It was generally supposed that the present road coincides nearly with the original one, and that followed mainly the old Indian trail. The canal, however, has in many places supplanted the old road. Some old maps and other documents prove pretty conclusively that much of the way, at least between Schuylerville and Stillwater, there were two roads, one near the river bank and the other along the foot of the bluffs; the latter was used in time of high water. Such was the case between Wilbur's Basin and Bemis Heights at the time of the Revolution,[3] and also just below Schuylerville.[4] Tradition says this

---
[3] See Burgoyne's map, in Public Papers of George Clinton. Vol. II, p. 430. Also the Sexagenary, pp. 70, 72.

[4] Journal of La Corne St. Luc's Expedition against Fort Clinton, p. 53, *ante*, and the Sexagenary, p. 140.

river road forded the Fish creek a few rods above the canal aqueduct, ascended its south bank back of Mr. Lowber's barn (some say where the canal bridge is) and then passed east of the original Schuyler mansion about where the canal is now. This is altogether probable. The writer has found a tradition which says that north of the creek the road struck through where the canal basin is and ran along the low terrace seen in the meadow north of the Ferry street road, and just east of the canal, thence north through Seeleyville, following the present line of North Broadway. It is not probable that there was a bridge across Fish creek till about 1770. As there was a military road cut on the east side in 1709 from the Battenkill to Fort Edward, the old ford across the river just north of the island, over which the road to Greenwich now passes, must have figured as part of that route. In all probability the fort built by Peter Schuyler in 1709 was for the purpose of guarding that ford, and stood on the flats instead of the hill, as has been by some supposed.

Lateral Roads. At the time of the Revolution there was a road running west from Bemis Heights; one west from Swart's house which General Fraser used in his flank movement on the morning of the 19th of September, 1777, the same which now runs west from Searle's ferry. Another road ran west from Coveville, starting just south of Van Veghten's mill. The earliest road to the westward from Old Saratoga (Schuylerville) started at the Horicon mill, ran up the south bank of the creek and followed the line of the present footpath to Smithville.[5] From that point there has been no change in the old line. Then, as now, it crossed the creek just west of Mr. Frank Marshall's, thence southwest past Mr. Charles Cramer's. The present road from Smithville to the

---

See old document copied in Sylvester's Hist. of Saratoga County, p. 269.

river road is very old and antedates the Revolution. We have elsewhere spoken of the road to Saratoga Springs, through Grangerville, built by General Schuyler in 1783. This road originally passed to the north of the creek at Grangerville and so avoided bridge building. The ford across the river at Schuylerville being available only at low water, a ferry was started very early by the De Ridders. This crossed below the island; its western landing place was on the angle just north of the mouth of Fish creek, its eastern landing was fifteen or twenty rods below the bridge. Many old residents of Schuylerville can still remember De Ridder's ferry, it was propelled by horse power, and hence was known as a horse boat. The great increase in travel and traffic which followed on the opening of the canal, made possible the bridging of the Hudson at this point to accommodate the country to the east of the river. This was done by a private company in 1836, and it has ever since remained a toll bridge.

Partition of Saratoga. As we have stated in an earlier part of this work, Saratoga was a name originally given by the Indians to a district of country with indefinite boundaries stretching from perhaps Waterford to the State dam at Northumberland. Then came the Saratoga Patent of 1684, which took in six miles on each side of the river, from Mechanicville north to the mouth of the Battenkill.

March 24, 1772, the New York Colonial Legislature passed the first act which organized this territory into a legal entity. What has since become Saratoga County was then divided into two districts—Half Moon and "Saraghtoga." As there were no towns organized here at that time, the district of "Saraghtoga" included Easton, now in the County of Washington, and nearly all the present County of Saratoga north of Anthony's-kill, which enters the Hudson at Mechanicville, and it so continued until April 1, 1775, when the west part of the county was organized into a separate district called Ballstown. Gen. E. F. Bullard, in his historical address, says very happily: "As Virginia was called the mother of States, so Old Saratoga may be called the mother of towns." First Ballston, as we have just seen, was taken from it. Then, after New York burst the Provincial bud and blossomed into a State, and the machinery of a State government was set running, on the 7th of March, 1788, an act was passed organizing towns in the place of districts. By that act Stillwater, including Malta, was taken off from the Saratoga district, thus making what afterward became Saratoga County into four towns, viz.: Halfmoon, Saratoga, Ballston and Stillwater, all of which were yet a part of Albany County. On the 3d of March, 1789, that part of Saratoga township lying on the east of the Hudson was erected into a township and called East Town. In 1791, this was set off to form part of Washington County. On the 7th of February, 1791, these four towns were separated from Albany County and erected into an independent county, and appropriately named Saratoga.

How Saratoga Springs got its Name. In 1798 this old township was shorn of more of her territory by the organization of Northumberland, which took off all now included in Moreau and Wilton, and the east part of Corinth and Greenfield. The fame of the Springs having drawn to that part of the township many settlers, a petition was granted them in 1819 which resulted in another division of Old Saratoga and the erection of the town of Saratoga Springs. This left to the town its present area of about seven miles square. After this division Saratoga numbered 2,233 inhabitants, and Saratoga Springs 1,909. Here we discover why the Springs came to be called SARATOGA SPRINGS. For the first thirty years of their history they were located within the limits of the town of Saratoga, and when the new town was set off its inhabitants insisted on the retention of the name under which their district had become famous.[6]

[6] Most of the above facts concerning the divisions of the district, and later the town, of Saratoga were taken from Gen. E. F. Bullard's Centennial 4th of July address.

CHAPTER IX

VILLAGES

AFTER the destruction of Old Saratoga, in 1745, eighty years elapsed before another village of equal size grew up within the bounds of this township. Of course it possessed more inhabitants at the end of the eighteenth century than at that epoch, but no villages. These, however, were sure to appear in time.

The first store in town of which we have been able to find any record was opened by Herman Van Veghten some time before 1800.[1] It is, however, probable that supplies had been kept at Schuyler's mills before this. A store was also kept by one John Douglas on the place now owned by Charles Cramer at an early day, just when we have not discovered. The Hill at Cramer's was certainly once quite a business place before the opening of the canal and the subsequent growth of Schuylerville. Besides the store, there was an ashery for the manufacture of potash, the old Baptist church, a school house and one or two mechanic shops. But Schuylerville's "boom" put an end to the aspirations of Dunham's Hill, as it was then called.

Dean's Corners, in the western part of the town, was named from Dr. Dean, who lived at that point and practiced medicine for many years, though he was not the first settler. It contains a store, post office and school house, and numbers about fifty inhabitants.

Quaker Springs derived its name from the conjunction of two important facts. First, because the Society of Friends, or Quakers, were the most numerous among the first settlers, and built a meeting house in that locality,

---
[1] Old Records of the Reformed Church of Schuylerville, p. 88.

where they have worshipped for a hundred years and more; and second, because two very fine mineral springs exist there. The village numbers about 150 inhabitants; it contains a large store of general merchandise, a post-office, a school house, a saw mill, and a Methodist Episcopal church.

The water of the springs is charged with natural gas, and is of very fine quality. One reminds the visitor of those more renowned at Saratoga Springs, and the other bubbling up within twenty-five feet of it, is strongly impregnated with sulphur. Both of them are equal in medicinal properties to those at the great Spa. Were these springs situated say 300 miles from their present location they would be immensely valuable.

Grangerville. Grangerville is a hamlet of fifteen or twenty houses, about two miles west of Schuylerville. The occasion for a village there is a mill privilege on Fish creek. The first mill here was a grist mill, erected by Jesse Toll, before 1800; but the name of one Harvey Granger, who owned and ran the mills for many years, became attached to the hamlet that grew up around him. Besides the grist mill, there is a saw mill on the opposite side of the creek. There, too, are the inevitable village store, blacksmith shop and school house, which also serves the purpose of a church. Here a harvest that is unusual and unique is gathered yearly by the enterprising miller, Mr. Elmer E. Baker. In the month of September great quantities of eels run down the creek into the river. A weir has been so constructed at the dam as to catch the larger eels, and as high as thirty-three barrels, or three tons, of this wriggling. and toothsome product have been shipped to market in a season.

Coveville. Situated three miles south of Schuylerville, on the river road, is another hamlet known as Coveville. This name has supplanted that of Dovegat, which was originally given to the locality. Here General Burgoyne and his army camped for several days on his way down and up from the scene of his defeat. Here Cornelius Van Veghten had a mill as early as 1784. The remains of the dam are still to be seen on the west side of the highway as you cross the creek. Here Herman Van Veghten opened what was, perhaps, the first store in the town. There was a tavern here for many years, but now long since discontinued. Here is a store and a school house.

Victory. This village is mainly the creation of the Victory Manufacturing Company. Before its advent an unbroken woods stretched from above the mills to Schuylerville. It derived its name entirely from the fancy of some patriotic member of the company, who suggested it as the title for their organization in allusion to the victory of the Americans over the British won in the immediate vicinity. It is very pleasantly situated on the north, or left, bank of Fish creek, one and one-half miles above its confluence with the river. The one great industry here is the manufacture of cotton goods.

The village has an unusually spruce and well-kept appearance. Besides the pretty cottages of the operatives, many citizens have built for themselves substantial and beautiful homes along the well shaded streets. In addition to the attractions about the homes the company, with a true public and altruistic spirit, maintains a small park adjoining the mills with beautiful lawn and a profusion of magnificent flowering plants, which afford a pleasant outlook from the mill windows for their employees. This company donated the ground and contributed largely for the erection of a new church edifice. This the company generously keeps in repair.

Victory Mills was incorporated in 1849. The village has an ample supply of hotels, several stores of general merchandise, a post-office, markets, and an excellent graded school.

Schuylerville. At the opening of the 19th century there was no such place as Schuylerville in existence. Broadway was then an open country road. South of the creek then stood the old Dutch Reformed church, of historic memory, with the sexton's house, the Schuyler mansion and several mills, with perhaps several tenement houses. On the north side of the creek there was a distillery, a fulling mill, a grist mill, and a blacksmith shop which stood then, and for a number of years, where the alley, opposite Bullard's paper mill, enters Broadway; just north of the shop was a house. The next building to the north was an old government storehouse or barrack, where the house of James E. McEckron now stands, 191 Broadway; above this there was a log house standing on the northwest corner of Broadway and Spring street, with some old Revolutionary barracks standing a few rods to the northwest. The next house to the north was the parsonage of the Dutch Reformed church, still standing, 265 Broadway, and north of this was the historic Bushee house (since called the Marshall house).

From the recollections of old inhabitants, preserved in Sylvester's "History of Saratoga County" and Gen. E. F. Bullard's historical address, we learn that in 1812 a Mr. Daggett ran the aforementioned blacksmith shop, that a Widow Taylor was running a tavern where the house No. 187 Broadway stands, now owned by Napoleon Gravelle. Just to the north of this, in the old government storehouse, Alpheus Bullard opened a store that same year; Stephen Welsh was then living in a log house on the corner of Broadway and Spring street. North of him a Mr. Peacock lived, and between him and the old Dutch parsonage lived a Mr. Van Tassel. Soon afterwards

Alpheus Bullard gave up store-keeping and built the Mansion House on the southwest corner of Broadway and Spring street, no doubt to accommodate the travel to and from Saratoga Springs, most of which had to go this way at that time. A stage route from Boston to the Springs ran this way until after 1830. The tavern was afterward turned into a dwelling house and is now occupied by Mrs. R. D. Lewis. About the same time (1813 or 1814), Daniel Patterson built a tavern, which still stands, and bears the name of the Schuylerville House. Soon after the war of 1812 Abraham Van Deusen opened a store on the site of the present Bullard block; his house stood where the bank now is, 98 Broadway.

At this time the ancient woods still covered most of the hillside to the west of Broadway, and indeed they were not fully cleared till after 1840; and the earthworks thrown up by Burgoyne thirty-five years before still remained untouched, except by the elements. Wild game of every kind yet roamed the forests all about, tempting the hunter forth to try his skill.

The Effect of the Canal on Schuylerville's Growth. The growth of Schuylerville was very slow till after the opening of the Champlain canal in 1822. Through the influence of Philip Schuyler, 2d, with the State authorities, and as part payment for the right of way through his extensive estates, a commodious basin, with ample dockage, was built at this point. Now a basin in a canal is equivalent to a bay along the sea-coast, a boat can turn around, as well as load and unload at its docks. Possessed of this boon, Schuylerville was at once raised from the obscurity of a wayside hamlet to the dignity of an open port and an important shipping point.

Before the opening of the canal the farmers, as far north as Lakes George and Champlain, had to draw their produce in wagons or sleighs down to Waterford. Judge then what a boom the opening of this waterway gave to the farming interests everywhere within reach of it. Whitehall, Fort Edward, Schuylerville and Stillwater at once became shipping points and depots for supplies. Schuylerville rapidly sprang into importance and became the most important place between Whitehall and Waterford, and the outlet for a large district of country both to the east and west of the Hudson. Large warehouses were built for the storage of grain and mercantile goods, many of which are yet standing as reminders of the epoch when the packet boat was queen.

Besides the vast quantity of grain shipped from here in those early days, when later Washington and Saratoga counties became great potato producing sections, as many as sixty and seventy canal boat loads of this product have left these docks for market in the fall of the year. This means a great deal when one considers that each boat load was equal to a train load of freight cars of the size in vogue at that time. Of course all this business centering here made an opening for merchants and mechanics and innkeepers and laborers, which they were not slow in entering. Stores and shops, hotels and residences rapidly multiplied, and soon the citizens began to talk of incorporating their thriving village. This was done by special act of Legislature in 1831.

Mr. Albert Clemments in his reminiscences, published in Sylvester's History of Saratoga County, says that he was the engineer who laid out the village, and that Philip Schuyler, 2d, and a Mr. G. C. Bedell carried the chain for him. Mr. Schuyler at that time owned practically the entire site of Schuylerville. Mr. Bedell kept a store at 122 Broadway, owned at present by Philip Kahn. We have not discovered the date of the laying out of the town site, but in all probability it was done soon after the opening of the canal, and before much building had been done, certainly before the incorporation according to the village records. The system of alleys between the streets, quite unusual in New York villages, was an excellent idea.

The canal had not been running for many years before a company of citizens thought they would be warranted in building a toll bridge across the river to accommodate the constantly increasing traffic from the east. This important piece of engineering was completed and opened in 1836. And then passed for ever the old "horse-boat" which for so many years had ferried the multitudes across the brimming river.

The Advent of Railroads. After the people began to build railroads, and they became assured of their practicability, every town of size in the State fondly hoped that it would soon be provided with this marvelous means of communication. The first railroad built to carry passengers in the United States was from Albany to Schenectady in 1831; the next year one was completed from Schenectady to Saratoga Springs. That same year, 1832, a company was incorporated to build a road from the Springs to Schuylerville, but of course it was not built, and Schuylerville had to be content with the canal packet and stage coach. In 1869 the town bonded itself for $100,000 to aid in the construction of a road from Mechanicville to Fort Edward. This is the natural route for a railroad to the north from Albany, as it was at first of the Indian trail, the military road and the canal. A few sections of the road were graded, and those long ridges of earth south of the village are all that the town has to show for its ambitious generosity

In 1870, Greenwich, five miles to the east, got a railroad, and in 1882, the Fitchburg Railroad Company ran in, a branch from Saratoga Springs to Schuylerville which has been of inestimable service to the business and manufacturing interests of the town, as well as an accommodation to the traveling public. The Fitchburg Railroad, with its branches, has this year (1900) become part of the system of the Boston & Maine railroad.

These railroads effectually tapped the country to the east and west, diverting both transportation and travel and, hence, practically ruined Schuylerville's prestige as the great shipping point and depot for this section. But its loss, in this particular, has never interfered with the real growth or importance of the place. The canal still remained and has continued to do a great deal of transportation to and from this point; and it still found itself the center of a remarkable series of water-powers which had never yet been properly developed. These were first, the Fish creek, a large stream which falls a hundred feet within a mile from the canal; second, the Battenkill, just across the river, a stream of equal size and possibilities; and thirdly, the Hudson itself, with its rapids a mile or two above. Soon its enterprising citizenship, together with capital seeking investment from without, transformed Schuylerville from a distributing and shipping mart to a manufacturing center. But this characteristic was the "image and superscription" stamped upon it at the first by Gen. Philip Schuyler. Yes, from its earliest history, as we have already seen, Old Saratoga has been known as the place of great mills.

CHAPTER X

THE SARATOGA MONUMENT

"National monuments not only mark, but make, the civilization of a people."—Horatio Seymour.

SARATOGA MONUMENT, like the Bunker Hill, and Washington, and Bennington, and Oriskany monuments, is founded on and reared by sentiment. "A rather unsubstantial basis for such substantial structures," says one. Yes, but substantial and puissant enough to have placed every course of those granite blocks from bed rock to apex. The sentiment that wrought this miracle in stone and bronze was pride in the deeds of the fathers, and reverence for their characters. Lord Macaulay in his remarks on the siege of Londonderry said: "A people which take no pride in the noble achievements of remote ancestors, will never achieve anything worthy to be remembered with pride by remote descendants."

Whether we have done anything worthy to be remembered by our descendants they alone will be competent to judge, but of one thing we are certain, that we are proud of the American forefathers. And we want the world to know it; hence, these noble monuments.

The Monument Association. The Saratoga Monument was conceived, and prophesied long years before it became a reality. But the first time that men of the right timber and enthusiasm got together to consider what steps should be taken to incarnate their dream was on October 17, 1856. That first meeting was held in the Schuyler mansion, here at old Saratoga; a fitting place for launching so noble an enterprise. There were present Judge John A. Corey of Saratoga Springs, George Strover and several other patriotic gentlemen. Alfred B. Street was also present and read a poem written for the occasion.

The result of this meeting was the organization in 1859 of the Saratoga Monument Association, under a perpetual charter of the State of New York. After the Association was incorporated the organization was perfected by the selection of the following

Officers

Hamilton Fish	President
New York City	
Philip Schuyler	Vice-President
Pelham-on-Sound, N. Y.	
James M. Marvin	Treasurer
Saratoga Springs	
John A. Corey	Secretary
Saratoga Springs	
James Romeyn Brodhead,	Corresponding Secretary
New York City	

Trustees

Horatio Seymour	Utica, N. Y.
Benson J. Lossing	Poughkeepsie, N. Y.
Peter Gansevoort	Albany, N. Y.
James M. Cook	Ballston Spa, N. Y.
Edward C. Delavan	Ballston Center, N. Y.
William Wilcox and George Strover	Schuylerville, N. Y.
Henry Holmes	Corinth, N. Y.
Asa C. Tefft	Fort Miller, N. Y.
Leroy Mowry	Greenwich, N. Y.

The trustees held several meetings and had agreed upon the location of the future monument when the outbreak of the Civil War, in 1861, completely diverted the thought and energies of the people to the saving of the Union, which the fathers had formed at such costly sacrifice. The work thus suspended was not resumed till the autumn of 1872. A reorganization then became necessary, as several of the trustees had died.

Soon the representatives of the new organization began to besiege the State and National legislatures for appropriations with which to begin the work. The original intention was to build a plain obelisk of the Bunker Hill order, 300 feet high and to cost $500,000. But soon they found that they had set their mark too high, as the funds were not forthcoming, hence were compelled to modify their plans, and finally decided upon a less lofty structure, and one that should combine sculpture with architecture.

The Association met with numberless embarrassments and discouragements at the hands of apathetic legislatures and unsympathetic governors. Finally by an appeal to patriotic persons throughout the State they succeeded in obtaining sufficient money to purchase the lot, lay the foundation and construct enough of the base to enable them to lay the cornerstone, which was done on the centennial anniversary of the surrender of Burgoyne, October 17, 1877.

Laying the Cornerstone. Elaborate preparations were made for the proper celebration of that event, both by the citizens of Schuylerville and the Monument Association. As a result the town witnessed the most imposing patriotic celebration in all its history, yes, and in the history of northern New York. The Masonic fraternity was gathered here from every quarter, military organizations from all over the State and New England were massed here by the thousands, and multitudes of civilians, statesmen, etc., prominent in the public eye, were here from all the States. A grand procession was formed, two miles in length, which marched through the streets and then to the monument, where the cornerstone was laid in "due and ancient form" by the Grand Master Mason in the presence of 30,000 people.

Orations and addresses were then delivered and original poems read from two grandstands, one located at the monument and the other on the then open flats south of the Church of the Visitation (Catholic). All the literary exercises were of an exceptionally high order, and to this day thrill the heart of the patriotic reader with their eloquence. The orations of Horatio Seymour and George William Curtis are not only eloquent, but display a remarkable grasp of the philosophy of our history. The entire program, including the speeches, historical addresses, and poems, were collected and published by the Association in a memorial volume.

But grand civic pageants and orations, and poems, by no means piled the granite and laid the capstone of the monument that day, though they helped amazingly in firing the hearts of the people to the point where they were willing to have their representatives appropriate the necessary means. The Association now addressed themselves to the great task before them with renewed zeal. Being composed of men of wide influence, they used it all, and needed it all, to accomplish their high purpose. The recital of the harassments, and annoyances, and disappointments they met with by the way, and the wellnigh insuperable obstacles they overcame makes a long story, and one often wonders, as he reads the account, why they did not abandon the whole thing in disgust. As it is, the completed structure is as truly a monument to the indomitable perseverance, and patience, and resourcefulness, of the members of that Association and the victory they won over the opposition of narrow-minded legislators, as it is to the victory of American arms and ideas over British pride and tyranny.

Description of the Monument. The hill on which the monument stands is 240 feet above the river, and was known in the Revolution as the Heights of Saratoga.

Here Burgoyne had his intrenched camp. The plinth or base of the monument is forty feet square. The shaft is twenty feet square at its base. Its height is 155 feet. The monument is a combination of the Egypian obelisk, with Gothic features in the first stories. It is ascended by 189 steps. The architect who designed it was Mr. Jared C. Markham of New York City. Morgan's statue was executed by W. R. O'Donovan; Gates' by Geo. E. Bissell, and Schuyler's by Messrs. Moffett and Doyle. The historic tablets were designed by J. C. Markham; eight of them were executed by J. E. Kelly, and eight by J. S. Hartley. The cost of the monument was $105,000. Private individuals gave $10,000; the State of New York, $25,000, and the United States Government $70,-000. It is not yet finished according to the original designs. Twenty tablets remain to be inserted in the three upper stories. The names of Schuyler, Morgan, Gates and Arnold have not yet been cut beneath their niches, and the several captured cannon are not yet secured and mounted. This is because the Association lacked the means to transport them hither and properly mount them. Steps are again being taken to secure them, with good hope of success. Twice the monument has been struck by lightning, which badly shattered the apex, necessitating costly repairs.

For the first few years the visitors to the monument were few and far between, but now their numbers mount into the thousands each month during the season of touring.

View from Monument. The view from the monument is superb. Nowhere else can one obtain so extensive and gratifying a view from so slight an elevation. At your feet lies the pretty village of Schuylerville, embowered in trees; just beyond flows the matchless Hudson, gleaming in the sun. On every side within the radius of a few miles are scenes of Colonial and Revolutionary events, of surpassing historic interest. To the north on a clear day one can see the villages of Glens Falls, Hudson Falls, Fort Edward, and Fort Miller; to the east Greenwich and North Easton, and to the west Saratoga Springs, and the entire picture is enframed in magnificent mountains. To the north are the mountains round about Lakes George and Champlain, and peeping over their tops are the peaks of Marcy and McIntyre, and other monarchs of the Adirondacks, eighty miles away; to the east are the Green Mountains of Vermont, with Mounts Equinox and Saddleback right abreast of you; to the south are the Catskills, seventy-five miles distant, with Black Head, Black Dome and Thomas Cole Mountains looming up, three in a row, making saw teeth with the horizon; and to the west are the Palmertown and Kayadrosseras ranges, foothills of the Adirondacks. "But it is not because of the scenery —hill and dale, sparkling water, beauteous wood, ethereal vault of blue, and misty mountains of enchantment— that this locality allures and holds the vagrant vision. This monument is the cynosure of patriotism."[1]

---

[1] Hon. S. S. Cox, in the U. S. Senate, 1884.
"The above facts concerning the Monument, were mainly gleaned from Mrs. E. H. Walworth's Battles of Saratoga, and Saratoga Monument Association."

Yours Sincerely

John H. Brandow

BOOK III

New York's Share in The Revolution

BY

JOHN H. BRANDOW, A. M.

BOOK III

NEW YORK'S SHARE IN THE REVOLUTION

CHAPTER I

ONE would naturally think that at this late day there could be no occasion for writing a serious chapter under the above title. For if New York really had a place, or took any worthy part in the Revolution, it would have been measured and assessed long ere this, and her rightful position assigned her. But students of her history have latterly been more and more impressed with the fact that New York, as well as other States, has never been granted her rightful share of space in our current histories, nor designated her legitimate place on the roll of honor. This is mainly due to the fact that the most widely read histories of the United States have been written in one section of the country, i. e. New England. Endowed with literary genius of a high order, men of New England gave us during the first hundred years of our national existence the major share of America's literary productions, and for this her full meed of praise we freely grant her. Indeed we, as a nation, would be vastly poorer in this respect without her contributions.

But in the sphere of history there is a certain element demanded that is not so essential in poetry and fiction, and that is truth, or the correspondence between statements and occurrences. Of late years this has been more and more insistently called for. Men are demanding to know the authority for all the statements of the historian that they may be in a position to verify them. Truth in history also demands that men and events should receive treatment proportionate to their relative merits. As a result of much painstaking investigation, and a careful appraisal of values, it has been discovered that our New England historians have often unduly magnified the importance of New England men and events and have slighted other contributions, fully as valuable, to the cause of Independence.

This, we feel sure, has not been due to any set purpose to deceive, but mainly to other causes. First among these was an inherited prejudice against the people of other commonwealths, especially if those neighbors, over the line, spoke another language, and their social customs were somewhat different. Such differences were especially marked between New York and New England in Colonial days. All New Yorkers were reckoned as Dutchmen, and at that time, and long afterwards, Dutchmen were held in contempt by all New Englanders. Secondly, there is that inveterate human tendency for men to magnify the doings of their own people or family to the belittlement of others. The third cause for such unfairness was a failure to search carefully the records of the various States. This, again, was owing to the lack of ability on the part of the average historian of those days to put himself in touch with the many unpublished, and unedited, records to be found outside of New England. While this was unquestionably true of the early writers it affords no excuse for those who have wrought within the last seventy years.

In his "Discovery of America" (Vol. I-443), John Fiske characterizes the tendency of historians to exalt the doings of their own people and province to the neglect and disparagement of their neighbors over the border as "ancestor worship." The appropriateness of the

THE STORY OF OLD SARATOGA 391

term will, we think, become quite obvious to the reader of the succeeding pages.[1]

The above paragraphs are presented as our excuse for writing the following chapters. A full and adequate treatment of what they suggest would require a volume. But our space will permit a presentation of only a bare outline of what ought to be said, but enough, we hope, to inspire some better equipped and more facile writer to handle the subject as it deserves; or better still to write a history of the United States wherein the events that gave the set to the currents of our civilization, and the men who did things that have endured, will be given their proper place and true appraisement. For sure it is that as a result of their leadership in American literature, one finds that to all questions regarding the origin of our civil and religious institutions, and the source of those ideas which have fructified in our national independence, the stock answer is returned that they were invented by the brilliant and prescient founders of Massachusetts.

In what we are about to say we know that we are laying ourself open to the criticism we have just made of others. We repeat, therefore, by way of emphasis, that we are not here attempting a full orbed history, but would call special attention to what New York did, and compare her, not with all the States, but chiefly with Massachusetts, who, in writing our histories, is more particularly chargeable with self or "ancestor worship."

But no true New Yorker is open to the charge that we would claim everything in sight. No. We do claim, how-

---

[1] "Of this small company who called themselves Pilgrims—the proudest pedigree in Massachusetts, *or* AMERICA." Geo. L. Austin's History of Mass., p. 3.

"Massachusetts has a history which both she and her sister States may well regard with pride. Within her borders were sown the seeds which have given birth to a great people. . . . Here American freedom raised its first voice." Preface to the above.

ever, what rightly belongs to us, no more, and no less. And we cheerfully accord the same right to others, because being Americans first and New Yorkers second, we do glory in everything noble that bears upon it the image and superscription of America. As Americans we are proud of Concord and Bunker Hill, of Trenton and the Cowpens, and of Yorktown, but we are equally as proud of Oriskany, and Bennington, of Saratoga and Stony Point. As true born Americans we are amazingly proud of James Otis and the Adamses, of Jonathan Trumbull, of Jefferson, and Madison, and Franklin, of Generals Greene and Knox, of Washington, and Morgan; but we are quite as proud of Generals Schuyler, Montgomery, and Herkimer, and Col. Gansevoort, of William, and Robert R. Livingston, of Gouverneur Morris, of Hamilton and Jay.

New York from the Beginning Cosmopolitan. In order to understand New York's position in the Revolution one should know the character and number of her populace, as compared with the other Colonies, her social and religious conditions, the attitude of her people toward all attempts to abridge their liberties, and the relative number of patriots and loyalists within her borders.

It is well known that the Hudson and lower Mohawk valleys were settled by Hollanders who held the country for sixty years. During that period a goodly number of Walloons and French Huguenots settled among the Dutch. There was also quite an immigration from Massachusetts of Quakers, Baptists, and others escaping from religious persecution.[2] Then when England acquired control here there naturally came with the royal Governors, and other officials, quite a following of Englishmen, such as merchants and traders. In 1708 and later came that large body of Germans who settled along

---
[2] Brodhead's Hist. of New York, Vol. I, 332-3.

the middle Hudson, in the Schoharie, and upper Mohawk valleys. These were followed by many of the Scotch Irish driven from northern Ireland by English tyranny and persecution. And finally we note that body of Scotch Highlanders induced by Sir William Johnson to migrate and settle on his ample estates west of Schenectady. The outcome was that at about 1770 New York had the most heterogeneous or mixed population of any of the Colonies, though New Jersey and Pennsylvania were not far behind in this respect. Gov. Horatio Seymour once illustrated in a speech New York's unique position in this particular by giving the racial origin of nine of her leading men in the Revolution. Philip Schuyler was Dutch. Gen. Montgomery was Irish, Herkimer was German, Gen. A. McDougall was Scotch, Robert R. Livingston was Scotch-Dutch, Gov. Clinton was Scotch-Irish, John Jay was French-Dutch, Gouverneur Morris was Welsh-French, and Alexander Hamilton was Scotch-French. Thus instead of being pronouncedly English it is found that from the beginning our population has been surprisingly cosmopolitan.

As germane to the above we quote the following from a speech delivered by Woodrow Wilson in Charlotte, N. C., in May, 1916. Now Mr. Wilson was a recognized authority in American history before he became President of the United States. Said he: "America did not come out of the south, nor did it come out of New England. The characteristic part of America originated in the Middle States of New York, and New Jersey, and Pennsylvania, because there from the first was that mixture of populations, that mixture of racial stocks, that mixture of antecedents which is the most singular and distinguished mark of the United States."

The people who first settled within the bounds of New York came from the Dutch Republic, a country which, at that time was the freest and most civilized under the sun. To the Netherlands fled the persecuted religionists of England and France, who found there a refuge and a welcome. And it should never be forgotten that the civil institutions of Holland were established here from the first; e. g. the citizen's right of sharing in the government, an elective judiciary, and religious liberty. The church and school were everywhere set up as soon as the settlement was established. Thus New York was not settled by men seeking for broader liberties, but by those who wanted more room, and better opportunities, for becoming men of independent means.

New Netherland Wrested from Holland. But England had long looked with covetous eyes on New Netherland with its splendid bay and beautiful river. So one day King Charles II intimated to his brother James, Duke of York and Albany, that if he could capture the prize it should be his. Not long thereafter, in 1664, a British fleet swooped down on unsuspecting New Amsterdam and compelled its surrender, and soon Fort Orange followed. Now all this occurred while Holland and England were supposed to be at peace. But soon this, and other aggressive acts on the part of England, resulted in war between the two countries. In 1674, or after the war, New Netherland was confirmed to England by Holland. New Amsterdam and Fort Orange were renamed New York and Albany after the Ducal titles of the new lord of the Province.

James appointed Richard Nichols as the first Governor of New York, and invested him with regal authority, and thus he was endowed with all the legal attributes of a perfect Despot. The articles of surrender included the reservation of certain ancient rights of the Dutch settlers, among which were religious liberty, and "a voice in public matters." But Gov. Nichols proceeded to ignore the agreement, and when, two months later, he called the people together to swear allegiance to the King of England, they refused till he ratified, over his own signature, the articles of surrender. And this was a sample of the spirit exhibited by New Yorkers toward many a royal Governor way through till we saw the last of them.

New York in a Class by Herself. New York being a conquered province it was put in another class and treated quite differently from the other Colonies. She was henceforth regarded as a private perquisite of the Crown. Other Colonies were granted charters in which their rights and liberties were clearly defined. But New York was never granted a charter, though, at one time, James had one drawn, and promised to sign it, but never did. She was left largely to the personal whim of Governors, many of whom were incompetent, greedy, and conscienceless. Such rights and liberties as the people enjoyed were secured by eternal vigilance, and by taking advantage of favoring conditions through which they wrung desirable concessions from reluctant and hard pressed Governors.

During most of the period of England's control New York was ruled by a Governor appointed by the King, a Council appointed by the Governor, and an Assembly elected by the freeholders; the latter to hold for a term of seven years, or during the King's pleasure. Massachusetts had a Governor appointed by the King, but a Council elected by her citizens, and an annually elected House of Representatives. Another outstanding fact should be stated here; viz. that those English Governors did what they could to discourage general education in this colony, and this doubtless on the ground that despots do not want their people to know too much. In this they were lamentably successful. But Massachusetts, possessed of ampler chartered rights, and being a homogeneous people, speaking one language instead of a dozen, was enabled, during this while, to maintain her schools at a higher state of efficiency. The result was that the percentage of illiterates in New York, at the time of the Revolution, was higher than in Massachusetts.[3]

Some of New York's Early Contributions to Our Civilization. Though the principal events provocative of the war occurred after 1760 yet there were certain things accomplished in New York before that date which in the later period proved so generally useful and permanently efficacious that we feel constrained to allot a little space to them.

We would first call attention to the establishment of religious liberty. Peter Minuit, one of the earliest Dutch Governors, proclaimed freedom of worship in this Colony in 1626. But this was simply an importation from the Dutch republic. Rhode Island, Pennsylvania, and Maryland, later gave to their citizens this precious boon, but in a limited degree. The Episcopal church, through the English Governors, strove to revoke this privilege, granted by the Dutch, but were defeated in their efforts. Massachusetts on the contrary established a State Church. From 1630 onward a freeman in that Colony was one who was a member of the Congregational Church. Such only could vote or hold office. But every property holder, whether a church member or not, was taxed for the support of the church.[4]

To say that the Puritans came to America to establish religious liberty is contrary to fact. They came here first that they might escape the persecution of the State Church, and secondly, to set up their own ideals of

---
[3] See Sherman William's N. Y. in History, p. 343.
[4] Hildreth's United States, I, 190.

church and state. Then they proceeded to visit on those who dared to disagree with the tenets of Congregationalism all that they had suffered from Episcopacy in old England.

For more than a hundred years Massachusetts was as intolerant religiously as Spain at her worst. In Spain it was the dungeon, the rack, or the faggot. In Massachusetts it was banishment, the whip, or the gibbet. It was not till 1833 that complete religious liberty was established by statute law in that State.[5] E. g. In 1631 those who were heard to speak against Massachusetts' Colonial government, or church, or wrote home discouraging letters, were whipped, cropped of their ears, and banished.[6] In 1656 two Quaker women were subjected to the most heartless and revolting forms of persecution. Again, in 1659, several Quakers, including women, were executed in Boston.[7]

The Liberty of the Press. One of the most contemptible and worthless men whom the English Ministry sent over here to recover a wasted fortune by trying to rule, and incidentally rob, the people of this Colony, was William Cosby. He was not here long before the better people felt themselves outraged by his pernicious activities. The only newspaper published in New York city at that time was under government control, hence, in order that selfrespecting and orderly people might openly advertise and protest against his iniquities, a new sheet was started named the New York Weekly Journal. This was published by John Peter Zenger, a Palatine, who, as an orphan, had been bound out to, and learned his trade of William Bradford, the Government printer. Articles appeared in the new paper exposing the knavery

---

[5] C. Francis Adams' Mass., Its Historians and Its History, p. 9.
[6] Story's Miscellanies, 66. Hildreth's United States, I, 194.
[7] Ditto, 408.

and venality of the men in power. Squibs, satires, ballads, and witticisms, were emitted lampooning the Governor and his satellites, till driven to madness Cosby procured the arrest of Zenger and an indictment against him for publishing "a false, scandalous, malicious, and seditious libel."

On the day of the first hearing the unscrupulous judge arbitrarily disbarred the two eminent lawyers, James Alexander and William Smith, retained by Zenger to defend him. This left him without counsel. But on the day of the trial there appeared in his defense, through the agency of the disbarred lawyers, and the Sons of Liberty, Andrew Hamilton, a great Philadelphia advocate, then nearly fourscore years of age, a brilliant, fearless, and noble man. To the surprise of the Court, and of all others, Hamilton acknowledged that his client had published the alleged libels, but insisted that the statements were all true and he would prove it; hence, if true, they could not be libellous. This proposition was wholly contrary to practice and precedent, for, up to that time, the accepted legal maxim was: "The greater the truth the greater the libel." The outcome, contrary to the instructions of the court, was that the jury brought in a verdict of *not guilty*. And thus for the first time in history the liberty of the press was asserted and established.

This verdict and the reasons for it were published everywhere, but naturally were not accepted everywhere. They were, however, gradually adopted and acted upon. For in those exciting days, preliminary to the crucial struggle, we find that many a printer was emboldened by that verdict to dedicate his printing outfit to the cause of truth and liberty. As a result we can affirm without fear of contradiction that the press, thus Providentially set free, did far more in the way of educating and arousing the Colonies to action than did the fiery appeals of a

James Otis or a Patrick Henry apart from the press. The freedom of the press is now everywhere acknowledged to be one of the chiefest bulwarks of liberty. So put it down that this is one of New York's, or rather Pennsylvania's and New York's contributions to humane progress.[8]

Gouverneur Morris said: "The trial of Zenger was the germ of American freedom—the morning star of that liberty which subsequently revolutionized America."

New York should rear a monument to John Peter Zenger, and that jury of brave men who, in acquitting him, proclaimed to the world THE FREEDOM OF THE PRESS.

The Sons of Liberty. And here in this connection, we find ourselves in touch with another valuable contribution of New York to the consummation of national independence. It was in connection with the maladministration of Governor Cosby, and the outrages connected with the arrest and trial of J. P. Zenger, that the organization known as the Sons of Liberty appeared. Soon after the Zenger incident had closed Governor Cosby died. Conditions improved under the next Governor so there seemed to be no occasion for their peculiar activities, they therefore remained in a comparatively quiescent state till the aggressions of Parliament, in connection with the Stamp Act, threatened our liberties. These aroused them to renewed activity. Then, quickly, other Colonies caught the idea, and copied it from New York, and not from New England as has been claimed.[9]

The Sons of Liberty were regarded as radicals, visionary and fanatical, by the conservatives of that day. But the unfolding years have revealed the fact that they were the men of vision, of resolution, and tireless perseverance,

---

[8] J. R. Brodhead's Hist. of N. Y., Vol. I, 459.

[9] See H, B, Dawson's Sons of Liberty, where this is fully discussed. Also Prentice's Hist. of N. Y.

who, as watchmen on the towers of the sanctuary of human rights, maintained a sleepless vigilance against the encroachments of the insidious and artful enemy of their liberties. They were the men who, for the good of humanity, braved the jeers and contempt of the aristocrats and men in power, and dared social ostracism, imprisonment, outlawry, and the gibbet, if, by so doing, they could defeat the aims of heartless and greedy tyrants. They were the heralds of the men who wielded the sword and carried the musket and, hence, really prepared the way for independence.

The American Revolution not an Accident in History. The average reader of the history of our Revolution is apt to regard that occurrence, with its outcome, the American nation, as a sort of prodigy, an event in history that appears suddenly, like a mushroom that comes up and perfects itself in a night. But not so. It was instead the fruitage of a long period of quiet and unobtrusive growth. The germs of it appeared in far earlier times, and came from other lands, but they found here a congenial soil and a favoring clime. Here, under the rough tillage and somewhat violent pruning of unfriendly husbandmen, these unpromising and wayward plants brought to perfection a product which has since been the astonishment and joy of the whole earth. Nor should one think that the Revolution comprises only the events that occurred between the battle of Lexington in 1775, and the evacuation of New York by the British army in 1783. By rights the story of it should include a rehearsal of the irritating acts which precipitated the struggle, and also the product, or permanent effects of that war. Otherwise it would have to be classed with the aimless and resultless revolutions that have, for so long, been a curse to Mexico and Latin America.

Where the Blame for the War Rests. The American Revolution was the result, first, of a failure of the two peoples involved to understand each other, and second, a determination on the part of King George the Third to establish personal rule in his realm, as did later the Hohenzollern dynasty in Germany.

The vast distances both in time and space which then separated England from America, making intercourse and interchange of ideas very difficult, the novel conditions incident to the conquest of a wilderness, the intermingling here of peoples from countries and races heretofore hostile, and the very liberal first charters, that granted to most of the colonies self government, served to generate political ideas and methods suited to the new situation. The outcome of this really unconscious schooling was that, at the end of the French and Indian war, the Colonies had so far outstripped England in political evolution that neither the people nor government of England could understand conditions in America.

To the people of England representative government meant representation by, and for, the upper classes only. Representation according to the population of a district or province was unknown in the British Isles. It is said that of the 8,000,000 population in Great Britain at that time, only about 200,000 had any choice as to who should represent them in Parliament.[10] The colonists believed in, and generally practised, government by, not all, but most of, the people; the English were accustomed to, and quite content with, government by a class. Thus the colonial idea of home government was widely different from the system then in vogue in England. "Taxation

---

[10] Goodrich's British Eloquence, pp. 148, 151. Howard's Preliminaries of the Revolution, pp. 4, 10, 14, 15, 17.

without representation" was not violated in respect to Americans as it was then understood and practised by Englishmen in England.

The main responsibility for the American revolt lies at the door of George the Third, and "the King's Friends" who deliberately aimed at autocratic or irresponsible rule, and not here alone but in England as well. Unfair reports, sent by petty, narrow minded, Colonial governors, and other agents, concerning the stubborn wilfulness of the colonists, prejudiced the administration against them. The King and his ministers therefore resolved that these disorderly subjects must be properly tamed. Unwise and vexatious acts were then passed that served only to create open discontent and finally alienate them from a government they much preferred to remain subject to, and hold in reverence. Few Americans thought of separation from England till after the war was already under way.

The King's arbitrariness had produced similar effects in England. For example we read that "in 1775 John Wesley solemnly warned Lord North that the bulk of the population were effectually cured of all love and reverence for the King and his Ministry, that they were ripe for rebellion, and that they wanted nothing but a leader."[11] It is also fair to recall that the wisest English statesmen of the time, who though knowing they were cordially hated by the King, were in thorough sympathy with the great political principles for which the colonists contended. Pitt, Fox, Burke, and Walpole were, in spirit, the allies of Jay, Adams, Franklin, and Washington. Said Pitt in Parliament, after hearing of the first Congress: "Sir, I rejoice that America has resisted. Three millions of people so dead to all the feelings of

---

[11] Trevelyan's Am. Revolution, Part 2d, Vol. I, p. 9.

liberty as to voluntarily submit to be slaves would have been fit instruments to make slaves of the rest of us."[12]

In view of these facts it is hardly fair for us Americans to keep on fostering our old prejudices against the English people, for, as a whole, they were in no way responsible for that war. Indeed so unpopular was it that King George had to hire Germans, Hessians, and Brunswickers, to fill the ranks of the armies he would send against us.

---

[12] Green's Hist. of the English People, IV, p. 227.

CHAPTER II

Causes Provocative of the Revolution

The close of the French and Indian war left England badly in debt. Much of this had been incurred in the defense of her American colonies. Having received such timely and effectual assistance she concluded that they ought to, and hence must, help her to foot the bills. This she did without reflecting upon what that war had already cost them, in men and money,[1] and also without asking their consent. Having expelled the French from Canada, and thus being relieved of the menace of interference from that quarter, she now resolved to go a step farther and check the growth of the spirit of independency among the colonists by withdrawing certain privileges granted in their charters, etc.

Unjust Navigation Acts. First she decided to enforce the Navigation Acts, previously enacted, which closed our ports to all but English vessels, and limited the exportation of American products to England alone. But up to this time England had not been over strict about these laws, hence smuggling and illicit commerce had been more or less winked at by officials. But now she drew the reins more tightly. The first example of this more rigorous enforcement occurred in Boston. In 1760 Justice Hutchinson, a native of Massachusetts, began to issue "writs of assistance," or search warrants, authorizing the sheriff, or his deputies, to enter buildings indiscriminately in search of smuggled goods.

Naturally this unwonted procedure awakened hot resentment, and aroused vigorous opposition on the part

---

[1] In the French and Indian war the Colonies lost 13,000 men, and were left with a debt of £13,000,000, or $65,000,000. Booth's Hist. N. Y. City, p. 407.

of the populace. The legality of it was argued before the Massachusetts Court in February, 1761. James Otis then made a telling speech in which he argued against the "writs of assistance" on the ground that they annuled the natural rights of the colonists, and were likewise unconstitutional. On this ground he challenged the right of Parliament to make a law permitting a public official, or his deputy, to enter buildings without leave of the owner. "I am determined," he said, "to sacrifice estate, ease, health, applause, and even life to the sacred calls of my country, in opposition to a kind of power, the exercise of which cost one king his head and another his throne." His speech was published by a "free press" and went forth with amazing power. Bancroft, quoting John Adams, claims that this speech "was the opening scene of American resistance." We cheerfully admit this, but Boston happened to be the first and only place where the like of it was attempted. And the offensive act was done, not by an Englishman, but a native of Massachuetts.

New and Vexatious Rules as to Judges and Other Officials. In this connection it is interesting to note that in this same year, 1761, the royal Governor of New York appointed one Benjamin Pratt, of Boston, to the supreme Judgeship of this Colony. The fact that he was an outsider, and was to hold office "at the king's pleasure," instead of "during good behavior," as had ever been the rule, greatly exasperated the people. To show their resentment the New York Assembly absolutely refused to pay his salary, and, as a consequence, he was obliged after a season to resign and go home. A judge holding his office "at the pleasure of the king" instead of "during good behavior" made him a tool of the Crown, and took away his sense of independence. The people clearly understood its implications, and saw that in many cases their property and personal liberty would be jeopardised. This act of resistance, nearly coincident with and involving a principle quite as fundamental as the above, is rarely mentioned in the histories though Bancroft does so in Vol. IV-427. In this incident we see that New York, like Massachusetts, accepted with alacrity the first challenge to stand for her rights.

On this subject of the Crown's appointment of judges "during the king's pleasure" another has well said: "The New York Assembly began early in 1762 a series of addresses to the King which were the most elaborate and courageous state papers that had, up to that time, emanated from any legislative body on this continent."[2]

At the beginning of the year 1763 Parliament decreed that all royal officers in America, including the judges, should be independent of the colonial Assemblies, and receive their appointment and salaries directly from the Crown. It was, of course, plain to all that this would make the more important officers wholly subservient to the throne. It aroused opposition everywhere, but the first vigorous protest sent to Parliament against the measure was from New York, and this was in February of the same year, 1763.

"The People" a Source of Authority. As tending to show that all original thinking in the field of politics was not done in Boston in those days we quote the following from a letter of Governor Colden to the Board of Trade in London. It was written in January, 1762. In it he reports the activities of three lawyers in his Council who "get the applause of the mob by propagating the doctrine that all authority is derived from the people." These objectionable men were William Livingston, John Morin Scott, and William Smith. This obnoxious doctrine about "all authority being derived from the people" smacks strongly of the Declaration of Independence,

---
[2] See Am. Historical Rev., Vol. I, 245.

though the world had to wait fourteen years for the publication of that immortal document. But did this idea originate with those noble spirited New York lawyers at that time? Let us see.

In the Charter of Liberties and Privileges promised to the people of New York by James, Duke of York, in 1683, it was declared that "The supreme legislative authority shall be vested in a Governor, a Council, and in the People met in general Assembly." This is the first instance in American history where "the people"· are acknowledged and declared *in a public document* to be a source of authority. When James became king he revoked his promise because, as he said, he did not like the looks of "The People" in a state paper of that character. Here are his words as used in the so called Revocation of the Duke's laws: "The words, The People met in General Assembly are not used in any other Constitution in America, but only the words General Assembly."[3] Such a proposition was utterly abhorrent to English statecraft then and for many a year thereafter. But the people of New York never forgot that declaration in their promised Charter. Hence those lawyers, in their writings, were simply restoring and retouching a doctrine long since formulated in New York and in the Netherlands, and deeply cherished by our citizens of Dutch descent.

NOTE.—Our friends in Connecticut have been accustomed to claim that the idea and affirmation that "The People are the source of all authority," originated with them, and also that the first written constitution in all history appeared in connection with the founding of that Colony in 1636-39.[4]

We cheerfully acknowledge that the Rev. Thomas Hooker, the founder of the Hartford colony, a born statesman and leader

---
[3] N. Y. Colonial Hist., Vol. III, 358.
[4] Read, e.g., "The First American Democrat," in Founders and Patriots, Publication, 1-13.

of men, a sagacious thinker, did, in a remarkable sermon, say, among other things, "The foundation of authority is laid in the free consent of the people." We also agree that the constitution, adopted by the several Connecticut settlements in 1639, was a most notable document, in certain particulars surpassing any instrument of like character that had yet appeared. But we cannot agree that the concept that "the people are the true source of authority in civil government" originated with Thomas Hooker, or that Connecticut's constitution of 1639 was the first one that ever appeared in history.

The Provinces of the Netherlands, from the 14th century, contained many free cities which were ruled by magistrates chosen by the votes of the citizens.[5] During their great struggle for independence from Spain several of those Provinces drew up and agreed to what is known as The Union of Utrecht. This historic document was signed Jan. 23, 1579, and it became the foundation of the Dutch Republic. It contained twenty-six articles. Naturally it was somewhat crude and tentative in its character, but despite that fact it proved to be the stock whence all modern constitutions have grown.[6]

Says a deep student of those people: "The Dutch were the first to stand for the principle, and fight for it, viz.: No taxation without consent of the taxed. They were the first to teach by revolt against despotism, that power, under God, originates with the people; that government exists for nations and not nations for government."[7] "No taxation without consent" had maintained in the Province of Holland since 1477.[8]

Driven out of England by persecution Thomas Hooker fled to Holland in 1630, then the only country in the world that granted religious liberty. There he spent three years before coming to America. Having suffered so much from a despotic government in his homeland it is fair to presume that he proved an apt pupil in the free cities of the Dutch Republic. The same may be said with equal truth of the Pilgrims and their leaders who, for like reasons, spent eleven years in Holland before starting for New England.

---

[5] Motley's Dutch Republic, Vol. I, 37 flg.

[6] Ditto, Vol. III, 411 flg. Also Brodhead's Hist. of New York, Vol. I, 445 flg. Brodhead cites original sources.

[7] See W. E. Griffis' Influence of the Netherlands on the English Commonwealth; the American Republic. Also his Brave Little Holland.

[8] Brodhead's Hist. of N. Y., p. 473.

As agreeing with the foregoing and confirmatory of other previous statements we would add that in 1639, the year of the Connecticut constitution, at the instance of Director Kieft of New Netherland, twelve Selectmen were chosen by the people to aid and advise him in dealing with the Indians. This was again done in 1643. In 1647 Director Stuyvesant needed money for public works and to make possible the administration of public affairs, so he asked the people to elect men who should have power to levy taxes, and administer the proceeds. In these cases those New York Dutchmen were simply using the civil methods which had long been in vogue in the Netherlands, their native country. The seats of authority in the England of that day recognized no such principles of government.[9]

To show that this idea, about the people being the fount of authority, is not a modern discovery, and that it did not even originate with the Dutch, we will here quote Marsiglio of Padua, who in his Defensor Pacis, published in 1324, says: "The true legislator is *the people*, or community of citizens, or the majority of them, determining by their choice or will, expressed by vote in a general assembly, that anything should be done or omitted regarding man's civil acts, under pain of temporal punishment."[10]

That affirmation was given to the world more than three centuries before Thomas Hooker preached his historic sermon. And now after nearly six centuries of civic development it would be hard to improve upon Marsiglio's definition. This mediaeval scholar studied the writings of Aristotle, the Greek philosopher of the fourth century B. C., who in his Politica enumerates 158 constitutions that had already appeared, among which was the constitution of Sparta, written by Lycurgus, about 800 B. C. Marsiglio emphasized the importance of the individual man in matters civil and religious, and denied all coercive and especially any civil authority to the ministers of religion, i.e., he argued for religious liberty, and the separation of Church and State.

An original and clear visioned thinker, he was, of course, far in advance of his time, but subsequent thinkers and leaders, under more favorable conditions, set forth to embody the principles of Marsiglio in the democracies of later times. Govern-

---

[9] Brodhead's Hist. of N. Y., Vol. I, pp. 317, 327, 364, 474. Also E. H. Robert's Hist. N. Y., pp. 566-574.

[10] Marsiglio's Defensor Pacis, Part I, Chap. XII. See also Creighton's Hist. of the Papacy, Vol. I, 43.

ment by the people, as we know it, is the fruitage of ages of political evolution.

The Stamp Act. The next move made by England to prove her right to interfere in the internal affairs of her colonies was the passage of the Stamp Act. Henceforth no legal or commercial paper would be valid, nor could a newspaper be sold, unless properly decorated with a government stamp, duly paid for. In March, 1764, Grenville the Premier introduced the Act in Parliament where it was discussed for a little, and then laid on the table for future action. It was finally passed in March, 1765.

But the mind of the average colonist, at that period, was exceeding sensitive about anything that touched his rights, hence, the news of this proposed Act aroused a storm of protest throughout the country. John Fiske in his History of the Revolution says: "The first deliberate action with reference to the proposed Stamp Act was taken at a Boston town meeting in May, 1764. There Samuel Adams drew up a series of resolutions which contained the first formal public denial of the right of Parliament to tax the Colonies without their consent. Others followed."

We will agree with Fiske that this was the first protest against the Stamp Act uttered by a represenative body[11] in this country, but we seriously doubt the truth of his second claim. For, apart from what the other Colonies might present in rebuttal, we find in the records of New York the following "denials of the right of Parliament to tax a Colony without its consent."

First in The Charter of Liberties and Privileges, before alluded to, as promised to New York in 1683, it was

---

[11] This representative body was the Boston Town Meeting, not the Mass. House of Representatives, and the protest was evidently designed for home consumption, as it was never officially sent to Parliament.

declared that "No tax shall be assessed on any pretext whatever but *by consent of the Assembly*" who represented the people. Italics ours. Second. When in 1708 it was found that the Governor, Lord Cornbury, was appropriating public funds to his own use, the New York Assembly decided to collect and disburse their own taxes. In connection with this they passed certain resolutions among which was the following: "Resolved, that the imposing and levying of Monies upon his Majestie's Subjects of this Colony .... without Consent of the General Assembly, is a Grievance, and a violation of the People's Property."[12] Again in September, 1762, the General Assembly of New York presented an address to Parliament through Governor Colden, in which these words appear: "We hope your Honor will join in an endeavor to secure that great badge of English liberty of *being taxed only with our consent.*" This referred to the so called "Sugar Act," and was a year and eight months before Samuel Adams' resolutions.

We should add that in that set of resolutions, composed by Adams, he suggests the expediency of a union of all the Colonies for the defense of the common interests. This was a most timely suggestion, and the first one uttered having *union for defense* in view.

In June, 1764, the Massachusetts House of Representatives resolved "That the Impositions of duties and Taxes by the Parliament of Great Britain upon a people not represented in the House of Commons is absolutely irreconcilable with their rights." This Massachusetts resolution gave birth to the phrase, so popular at that time, "No taxation without representation."

Pamphlets were published in Massachusetts, during this year, protesting against Parliamentary taxation, but advocating patient submission till that body should de-

---
[12] Journal of the General Assembly, August, 1708.

velop a better state of mind. James Otis of Massachusetts, Franklin of Pennsylvania, and Governor Fitch of Connecticut, at this time, believed the Colonies would patiently accept the situation.

Massachusetts in November, 1764, sent a mild remonstrance to Parliament against their taxation schemes, but New York had already, in October, adopted and sent one so vigorous and peppery that no member of that body could be induced to present it, and compared with which that of Massachusetts seemed tame indeed. But these were not the only protests sent. Connecticut, Pennsylvania, Virginia, and South Carolina, all were heard from in stentorian notes. But Bancroft admits, in Vol. V-215, that "At that moment [Sept., '64] the spirit of resistance was nowhere so strong as in New York." And in Parliament New York was classed with Massachusetts in its open antagonism to the acts of Government. The Board of Trade represented to the King that the Legislature of Massachusetts by its vote in June, 1764, and that of New York, in its address to Governor Colden in September, had been guilty "of the most indecent disrespect to the Legislature of Great Britain."[13]

Despite the pleas and protests of the Colonies the Stamp Act became a law in March, 1765. In order to soothe and mollify their victims, native Americans were appointed as stamp distributors. But the colonists were proof against such tempting bait. The House of Burgesses of Virginia was in session when the news about the passage of the Act arrived. That was in May. At once a vigorous declaration of rights, drawn up by Patrick Henry, was adopted, and resolutions counseling resistance, if this menace to our rights were persisted in. Thus, after the obnoxious Act became a law, Virginia

---

[13] Bancroft's United States, Vol. V, 226.

issued the first official challenge to England. These were published and sent broadcast over the land, and were very influential in promoting unity of purpose.

In all the Colonies the stamp officers were either persuaded, or compelled by mob violence, to resign. E. g. Massachusetts hung their man Oliver in effigy and threatened his life. In New York, not only did her man find it wise to resign, but the citizenry succeeded in so intimidating the royal Governor Colden that when the stamps arrived he dared not attempt their distribution. And here is one of the placards posted by the Sons of Liberty, the day before the stamps were to be issued, which speaks for itself concerning the spirit then dominant in New York:

" PRO PATRIA.
The first Man that either distributes, or makes use of Stamped Paper, let him take care of his House, Person, and Effects.
Vox Populi.
We Dare." [14]

As an illustration of our contention that New York, and the other Colonies, have not received an equitable share of credit for their achievements, in the chronicles of the past, we notice that Bancroft, a typical New England historian, devotes ten and one-half pages to a description of the Stamp Act disturbances in New England, and but one page to all the rest of the Colonies. Now it is certain that what was done elsewhere was just as interesting and quite as effectual as the aforesaid in arousing the people, and stiffening their resolution to fight for their rights. But more of this anon.

The First Colonial Congress. Massachusetts through James Otis was the first to suggest the calling

[14] Dawson's Sons of Liberty, p. 82.

together of an American Congress to consider the recent acts of Parliament, and what the attitude of the Colonies should be toward them. The first cordial response came from South Carolina. This first gathering of the representatives of the Colonies met in New York city on the 7th of October, 1765. The Assemblies of Virginia and North Carolina, having adjourned before the call from Massachusetts came, were, therefore, not represented. New York was in the same predicament, but she was represented, though not officially, by her Committee of Correspondence.

There were many able men in that Congress, and three strong state papers were issued embodying the thought of that assemblage. Two of the three were the work of New Yorkers. One of these, John Cruger, was deputed to write a Declaration of Rights; the other, Robert R. Livingston, prepared the Petition to the King; and James Otis of Massachusetts, wrote a memorial to both Houses of Parliament. These set forth in clearest phrase the principles that governed the men of the Revolution which broke out ten years later.

The Nonimportation Compact. Another occurrence tending to show that in those critical days New York did not always have to wait for inspiration, or novel ideas, from the other Colonies, was the launching of the nonimportation league. The expediency of striking a body blow in retaliation for the Stamp Act, and the proper place to land it, occurred to some New York merchants.

These men, the leaders of whom were Sons of Liberty, called a meeting on the 31st of October, 1765. This was a week after the adjournment of the Colonial Congress. At that meeting they proposed to discontinue the importation from England of all the taxed articles after the first of January, 1766. This suggestion met with the enthusiastic approval of all present, and was put in writing and signed. A gathering of patriotic citizens, afterward, improved on this by adding a non-consumption agreement, and thus they cooperated heartily with the merchants. Because of the situation thus created domestic manufactures were started in almost every Whig family, and ultimately throughout the Colonies.

Next a committee was appointed to confer with other Colonies upon this line of policy. The result was that they all quickly entered the league. But pause for a moment and reflect! Was not that a high keyed proof of courage and character when those merchants of New York resolved to sacrifice their commercial interests to the cause of liberty? And their act looms still more grandly when one considers that at the time New York's trade was greater than all of New England's combined, and many of her citizenship depended solely upon commerce for their livelihood.

It is easy to make such an agreement, but quite another thing to keep it. Did New York stick to her text? John Fiske says that she was the only one of the Colonies that proved untrue to her promise. George Bancroft says, (Vol. VI.-308) "The agreement of non-importation originated in New York, where it was rigidly carried into effect." Which of these historians is right? Fiske, no doubt, has in mind New York's conduct after the repeal of the Revenue Act, in 1770, which relinquished the tax on all commodities except tea. In response to that the New York merchants decided, on July 9th, to resume the importation of all articles, tea excepted. Massachusetts and Pennsylvania remonstrated strongly, as did the New York Sons of Liberty, but to no avail.

Now what reason, if any, did New York have for her course in this matter? In the first place Bancroft justifies his declaration by a quotation from a letter from W. S. Johnson, afterwards President of Columbia College, to Gov. Trumbull, dated March 6th, 1770. In this it appears that during the five years of the league's existence "New England and Pennsylvania had imported nearly one-half as much as usual; New York alone had been perfectly true to its engagement, for its importations had fallen off more than 5 parts in 6."[15] Evidently those New York merchants having become certified by the results that their scheme had been measurably effectual in bringing England to her senses, they would be equally generous and meet her advances by the resumption of the importation of the exempted articles. Then, too, they must have sorely felt the financial loss and personal discomforts to which they had freely subjected themselves during those five years. Question! In view of New England's and Pennsylvania's record, the former two sacrificing three-sixths and New York five-sixths of her commerce, is Fiske justified in his declaration? And furthermore, three months later, on October 11th, Boston resolved to follow New York's example in this matter of importations.[16]

The Committee of Correspondence. Among the instrumentalities devised in those stirring days to keep their neighbors informed of the state of the political thermometer in each Colony, and secure unity of action, were the Committees of Correspondence. They proved themselves remarkably efficient and influential. Indeed the ultimate harmony of those dissonant Commonwealths of which the Continental Congress and the Continental Army were the first fruitage, would have been impossible without their tireless and judicious labors. Because of the important work they did the historians of a number of the States have labored to prove that the honor of this invention belongs to their Commonwealth. Massachu-

---
[15] Bancroft, VI, 365. Sons of Liberty, p. 87.
[16] Leake's Life of Gen. Lamb, p. 70.

setts and Virginia have each claimed the precedence in this creation.

As a result of a somewhat extended research we found the first reference to such a committee was in connection with the issuance of the Massachusetts protest against the proposed Stamp Act. A committee to correspond with other Colonies was then appointed. That was about July 1st, 1764. Rhode Island appointed one soon afterward, July 30th, the same year. The New York Assembly, after it had completed its vigorous protest to Parliament, on October 18th, appointed such a committee "to write to and correspond with the several Assemblies, or committees of Assemblies, of this Continent . . . on the subject of the impending dangers which threaten the Colonies of being taxed by laws to be passed in Great Britain."[17] So the honor of first employing this organism, which proved so efficient in massing resistance to tyranny, and promoting independence, evidently belongs to Massachusetts.

New York Punished for Contumacy. One reason given by the Colonial Governors for their failure to enforce the Stamp Act was their lack of an adequate military backing. The home Government saw the point and decided to increase the standing army in America and insist upon the Colonies housing and feeding it. The ostensible reason given for thus strengthening the army was that it should act as a police force for the maintenance of order, and as a defense against sudden attacks from without. But the knowing ones were not deceived by this.

New York having been especially bold and defiant in its resistance to the exactions of the Crown, and this in face of the fact that her chief city was, at the time, the

---
[17] Journal of the General Assembly of New York, Oct. 18, '64.

headquarters of the army in America, the Ministry, therefore, decided to send the first addition to the larger army here. So in December, 1765, New York was required to provide quarters, and certain specified necessaries, for as many soldiers as England should choose to place here. But the Assembly resolutely refused to care for more than they had been accustomed to, which was two battalions of about 500 men each. It also insisted on appointing its own Commissary to look after the expenditure of the funds appropriated. This was a wise precaution, but hurt the feelings of the expectant profiteers and extortioners. Therefore, because this New York Assembly dared to exhibit such insolence and open rebellion, it was decreed, on June 7th, 1767, that its power to legislate should be suspended till such time as it should be ready to yield proper obedience to the royal mandate. All this, evidently, was intended to serve as a warning to the other Colonial legislatures.

Now observe that in this matter New York stood stark alone, just as Boston stood alone three years later in the matter of the Port Bill. Moreover that was a remarkably bold and risky thing to do, to array herself openly against the military power of Great Britain, which was already posted on her territory. And the doing of it at that particular juncture created a great stir on every side, and wrought mightily in encouraging, and strengthening, the resolution of the other Colonies to resist every encroachment on their rights. The Virginia House of Burgesses, and other Assemblies, congratulated New York on the spirit she had shown, and voted remonstrances against closing her Assembly. Now place all this over against the following: During the following year the Massachusetts House of Representatives was dissolved by royal decree for an act of disobedience in refusing to rescind a circular letter which had been inspired by acts of Parliament very obnoxious to the Colonists. These acts were first, the aforesaid dismissal of the New York Assembly; second, the laying an import tax on tea, glass, paints, etc., and third, the increase of the British army in America. This circular letter had been sent to the other Colonial Assemblies acquainting them with the contents of a letter of earnest and respectful protest sent by said House to Parliament through its agent, accompanied by a petition to the King on the same subject, and inviting said Assemblies to stand by Massachusetts in maintaining the liberties of America. Much is made, and very properly, of this brave stand of Massachusetts in our leading histories, but in many of them nothing at all is said about New York's earlier, equally courageous, and fully as influential act.

Truth and fairness, however, demand that we should say that later a more compliant Assembly was elected in New York, by special effort of the royalists who were very powerful here, which made more liberal appropriations to the soldiery, though the Sons of Liberty and other patriots protested against such legislation most vigorously.

Whence the Idea of Political Independence. Another opportunity which came for the exhibition of timely leadership was in the matter of political independence. Who first caught the vision of it as a condition essential or desirable, and therefore to be promoted? John Fiske says that in 1768 "no one as yet, except perhaps Samuel Adams, had begun to think of a political separation from England. Even he did not look upon such a course as desirable."[18] Well, if this is so, all honor to Mr. Adams, for without question he did much statesmanlike thinking. But, was his the only eye in the Colonies that "saw visions," was he the only one who

---
[18] Fiske's Am. Revolution, Vol. I, pp. 46, 52.

"dreamed dreams?" We will not rehearse what Virginians, or North Carolinians, and others thought, and many of them were thinking seriously, constructively, but will cite a few of the cogitations of New Yorkers about that question.

For example: Holt's New York Gazette in its issue of May 24th, 1764, says: "If the colonist is taxed without his consent he will, perhaps, seek a change." That statement has always been regarded as having an evident squint toward independence. And just before the Stamp Act took effect the same paper said: "The Colonies may, from present weakness, submit to the impositions of the Ministerial power, but they will certainly hate that power as tyrannical, and as soon as they are able will throw it off." Again, in May, 1765, John Morin Scott, over the signature "Freeman," argued that "If the interest of the mother country and her colonies cannot be made to coincide, if the same constitution cannot take place in both, if the welfare of the mother country necessarily requires a sacrifice of the most valuable natural rights of the Colonies .... then the connection between them ought to cease, and sooner or later it must inevitably cease."[19] And once more; both Bancroft and Lossing do New York the honor of quoting what follows from a remarkable paper by William Livingston, (as is generally conceded) one of that famous triumvirate of New York lawyers, John Morin Scott and William Smith being the other two: "Courage, Americans; liberty, religion, and science are on the wing to these shores. The finger of God points out a mighty empire to your sons .... The day dawns in which the foundation of this mighty empire is to be laid by the establishment of a regular American Constitution. All that has hitherto been done seems to be little besides a collection of materials for this glor-

---
[19] Holt's N. Y. Gazette, No. 1170.

WILLIAM LIVINGSTON

ious fabric. 'Tis time to put them together. The transfer of the European family is so vast, and our growth so swift, that, before seven years roll over our heads, the first stone must be laid." The time of this remarkable utterance was April, 1768, and its prophecy, as we know, was and is yet being literally fulfilled. One wonders why more has not been made of this amazing production in the histories of that period, especially in our New York histories. Lossing says: "No man held a more trenchant pen than William Livingston." [20]

It would thus appear that New York had it in mind and openly talked independence long before Massachusetts did. Furthermore, it is well known that Otis, Boston's leader and principal writer, during this period, counseled submission to Parliament. But, of course, the honor of moving a Declaration of Independence in the Continental Congress, and of writing that immortal document belongs to Virginia. Bancroft, in summing up the parts taken by the principal actors in this the first Act of the great drama of the Revolution, says: "Virginia marshalled resistance, Massachusetts entreated union, and New York pointed to independence."

Henry Cabot Lodge, in his American Revolution, I-121, says: "In the middle Colonies, where the Loyalists were strong, little was done to hurry on the Revolution." Comment is unnecessary.

The Battle of Golden Hill and the Boston Massacre. Very much has always been made by the New England writers of the so called Boston Massacre. The British government had billeted soldiers upon Boston as a punishment for Massachusetts' disobedience in the matter of the "Circular Letter." These proved themselves a thorn in the flesh and a menace to her citizens. Offensive words and irritating acts were bandied between the

---
[20] Our Country, I, 642.

rougher street elements and the soldiers till finally one day, the 5th of March, 1770, a few soldiers, goaded beyond endurance, opened fire on their persecutors and killed five. Naturally this event caused tremendous excitement in the city. The soldiers were arrested, tried, and acquitted, all, except two who were let off with slight punishment. On the basis of this event Boston has always claimed that the first blood of the Revolution was shed in her streets.

But an event which was almost an exact duplicate of the above occurred in New York city on the 18th of January preceding, which has been called the Battle of Golden Hill. The quarrel in New York was over what had come to be called the Liberty Pole, and which, by the way, was the first one in the country christened by that name when set up. This had been erected after the repeal of the Stamp Act ostensibly in honor of "The King, Pitt, and Liberty." But the soldiery, and in their hearts the citizens, regarded it as really a symbol of the people's victory at that time over the King, and hence it was to the former a most offensive object, an eyesore. This pole the soldiers repeatedly cut down and destroyed, only to see another raised in its stead by the Sons of Liberty. In defense of their pole and of their right to maintain it they got into a fight with the soldiers, in which melee one citizen was killed and several badly wounded. So blood was shed in New York in defense of the people's rights six weeks before the collision at Boston. The Boston scrimmage was provoked by the insulting behavior of the hoodlums. This must have been well nigh outrageous and inexcusable or a Boston jury would not have acquitted the soldiers. But in the New York affray the soldiers were clearly the aggressors.[21]

---

[21] See Hildreth's United States. Leake's Life of Gen. Lamb.

Right here we would call the reader's attention to the fact that Bancroft devotes fifteen pages to the Boston massacre and but one to the battle of Golden Hill. John Fiske also expatiates at length upon the former, but fails even to mention the latter. So far as one can see Golden Hill was just as significant and worthy of note as the Boston massacre, especially since the New Yorkers had a worthier pretext for their fight than did the Bostonians.[22]

The Boston Port Bill with its Results. The refusal of the Colonies to receive any tea so long as Parliament insisted that they pay an import duty on it had brought the great East India Tea Company to the verge of bankruptcy. As a result they besought Parliament to remove this duty so that they could resume their trade. Parliament refused because the question of its right to tax the Colonies without asking their consent was at stake; but early in 1773 it agreed to remove the customary export duty. This would enable the company to undersell all competitors in the American market. Lord North assured the company that the colonists could be depended on to buy their goods in the cheapest market, duty or no duty.

Ships laden with tea were, therefore, sent to Boston, New York, Philadelphia, and Charleston. Tea commissioners were appointed in these cities to receive the tea and collect the duty. So soon as this news reached

---

[22] What one of our New York " Dutch " ministers said about Hollanders in a twenty-fifth anniversary sermon has been equally true of New York writers generally. Said he, D. J. Burrell, D. D.:

" It has never been the custom of our people to speak of their achievements in loud swelling words. The trouble with the Hollanders who came over with Hendrick Hudson in the *Half Moon* was that they were inadequately supplied with wind-instruments. Whether or no " the breaking waves dashed high," when they landed at the Battery, their " mute ignoble Miltons " never sang: and the historiography of their successors has been more honored in the breach than in the observance. But ' blessed are they that do.' "

America it aroused everywhere the old spirit of protest and resistance. The earliest public meeting to consider what sort of reception should be given the expected tea ships was held in the city of New York on October 15th, 1773. It was then resolved that Tea Commissioners and Stamp Distributors were alike obnoxious. On the following day a similar meeting was held in Philadelphia, with like results. The Committees of Correspondence got busy, and in all the Colonies a similar style of reception for the expected ships was agreed upon. Their landing the tea was to be resisted at all hazards. Through these committees it is generally conceded that the noble tribe of white Mohawks appeared simultaneously in New York and Boston, who acted as chief servitors at those historic "Tea Parties."[24] The tea ships destined for Boston arrived first, the one bound for New York having been driven out of its course by a fierce storm, and greatly damaged, did not arrive till much later. To this accident is no doubt due the fact that the first "Tea Party" occurred in Boston the night of December 16th, 1773. New York had hers on the first opportunity, which was the 23d of April following.[25]

As a punishment for her contumacy Parliament declared the port of Boston closed against all shipping till such time as she should resolve humbly to submit to royal authority. The custom house and courts were ordered removed to Salem. It was evidently the purpose of Parliament, in this case, to make an example of Boston as a warning to the other Colonies. In this affair Boston exhibited a spirit which was the admiration and pride of all her sister Colonies, and many of them hastened to offer not only their sympathy but sent her material aid in the distress which naturally followed.

---
[24] Leake's Life of Gen. Lamb, p. 76.
[25] Ditto, p. 82.

For example, the people of Schoharie, N. Y., sent the Bostonians 525 bushels of wheat.[26] But that she was not regarded in England as alone and singular in her resistance to the mandates of the Crown appears very clearly in a speech of Edmund Burke against the proposed port bill in Parliament. He said among other things: "The bill is unjust since it bears upon the city of Boston alone, while it is notorious that all America is in flames; that the cities of Philadelphia, of New York, and all the maritime towns of the continent have exhibited the same disobedience."

The official Port Bill arrived in Boston on the 10th of May, 1774. But a copy of it had already reached New York by another ship. The Sons of Liberty called a meeting on the 14th of May to consider it, with the result that they passed strong resolutions; first, of encouragement to Boston, and, second, that in their judgment the only safeguard for the freedom of the Colonies was in the assembling of a general Congress. These were immediately dispatched to the east by their trusted postrider John Ludlow. Near Providence he met Paul Revere riding post haste to the west and south with a message from the Bostonians invoking sympathy, and asking counsel from the other Colonies in this hour of perplexity and darkness.

This letter on reaching New York was handed to the Committee of Fifty-one, which had just been appointed to deal with the great questions of public policy then demanding study and solution. A sub-committee of five was appointed to draft an answer to Massachusetts' request for advice. This reply was drawn up by John Jay, and it proved to be an embodiment of such sound and timely wisdom, and a document of such far reaching consequences, that we are moved to quote from it liber-

[26] See Lossing's Field Book, Vol. I, p. 511.

ally: "While we think you justly entitled to the Thanks of your Sister Colonies for asking their Advice on a Case of such extensive Consequences, we lament our Inability to relieve your Anxiety by a decisive Opinion. The Cause is general and concerns a whole Continent who are equally interested with you and us; and we foresee that no Remedy can be of avail, unless it proceeds from the joint Act and Approbation of all. From a virtuous and spirited Union much may be expected; while the feeble efforts of a few will only be attended with Mischief and Disappointment to themselves, and Triumph to the Adversaries of our Liberty. Upon these Reasons we conclude that a Congress of Deputies from the Colonies in general is of the utmost Moment; that it ought to be assembled without Delay, and some unanimous resolutions formed in this fatal Emergency, not only respecting your deplorable Circumstances, but for the Security of *our common Rights*. Such being our Sentiments it must be premature to pronounce any judgment on the Expedient which you have suggested. We beg, however, that you will do us the Justice to believe that we shall continue to act with a firm and becoming regard to American Freedom, and to co-operate with our Sister Colonies in every Measure which shall be thought salutary and conducive to the publick Good." The date of the above letter was May 23d, 1774.

Now it would not be fair to claim that New York was the only one that thought of and suggested such a gathering, for on the same day, May 23, a Virginia committee took similar action. Rhode Island had on the 17th suggested the same thing, and S. Adams the preceding year had advocated such an assemblage. But still the important fact stands out that the above quoted answer of New York's Committee of Fifty-one, written by John Jay, was the first serious and authoritative suggestion for a general Congress to consider the "COMMON RIGHTS" of the Colonies, not those of Massachusetts alone. New York's suggestion for such a Congress to meet for such a purpose secured the approval of every Colony, and so Massachusetts appointed the 5th of September for that great historic gathering. But this momentous and epoch making letter of John Jay has rarely seen the light since that day, and hence has been made little of, because apparently unknown to our own historians.

The first Continental Congress met at Philadelphia, as per call, on the 5th of September, 1774. Two of the four great state papers issued by that notable body were the work of New York men: The Address to the People of Great Britain was written by John Jay, and the memorial to The Inhabitants of the several British American Colinies was the work of William Livingston, recently become a citizen of New Jersey, and father-in-law of John Jay. The other two were by John Dickinson of Pennsylvania. Daniel Webster once spoke of the above paper by Jay as "standing at the head of the incomparable productions of the first Congress." Thomas Jefferson, while still ignorant of the authorship of this address, declared it "a production of the finest pen in America."[27] And yet neither Bancroft nor Fiske say aught of John Jay or his work at the first Continental Congress. Well, it is worth noting here that neither at this Congress nor at any later one, that had to do with laying the foundations of this Government, did Massachusetts have any men who distinguished themselves by drafting great state papers, or by really creative statesmanship.

[27] Jefferson's Writings, 7-8.

CHAPTER III

Some Reflections on the Preceding Events. In this hurried glance at the exciting skirmishes preliminary to the great conflict, which is about to open, one fact, at least, must have intruded itself upon the alert reader. He must have noted a remarkable harmony of sentiment on the questions at issue, and a simultaneousness of suggestion, or acts, among the leaders of thought in all the Colonies. For example, the universal revolt against the Stamp Act, the simultaneous rise of the Committees of Correspondence, the synchronous proposals of union and independence, the avidity with which all concerned adopted the non-importation idea, and those suggestions for the several Congresses.

These related facts are all significant of something; they all point in the same direction, toward something. But toward what? To the fact that all the Colonies must have served time in the same training school. The term had been a long one, anywhere from a hundred to one hundred and fifty years, and the tasks most difficult, but they had learned some things well. They had become Masters of Arts in self government, and government building. They had come to know the worth of civil liberty, and what are the inalienable rights of men, and they had acquired the courage and decision of character to stand for their defense. It is evident that all these commonwealths had reached nearly the same plane of civil and intellectual development, so that no one of them could truthfully boast itself as very much above the others in these particulars. But why do we think so?

As the first step toward an answer we will quote an old and accepted maxim, viz.: "Like causes produce like results." That is true provided the materials on which the causes work are alike and happen to be in like conditions, otherwise not. For example, you grasp a hammer with which to drive a nail. You may strike either the board, the nail, or pound your finger. The cause is the same but the results are quite different. Or, here is a man with a whip in hand. He may use it in driving a team of mules, or a gang of slaves. By a timely application of it he will increase the product of their labor. But if, for the same end, he should attempt to use that whip upon a lot of intelligent mechanics in one of our modern factories, instead of increasing their production he would be mobbed, and receive more blows than he gave.

George III tried the whip act, or its equivalent the Stamp Act, upon his colonists, whom he had presumed to class with slaves, but to his astonishment he found them to be self respecting, high spirited men, on a level with himself, and the whole group of them quite ready to strike back at him, and with knock-out blows. We conclude, therefore, that the several Colonies must have attained about the same plane of Christian civilization, i. e. the civil conditions must have been practically alike or they could not have agreed to act together in a matter of such consequence, and in response to the *one exciting cause*. Or to put it differently: We will suppose Massachusetts, Pennsylvania, and Virginia to have been the highly civilized commonwealths which they really were, but the only ones of the whole lot. Connecticut, New York, and New Jersey had attained only the civilization of Mexico. Maryland and Delaware were on the level of the peasantry of Russia, and the Carolinas were as capable of self government as are the Chinese of today. Of what avail would have been the appeals of James Otis against the tyranny of the Port Bill, or the tax on tea addressed to the peons of Connecticut, of New York and the Jerseys? Could the peasants and serfs of Delaware and Maryland have seen and felt the force of the "Pennsylvania Farmer's" argument against "taxation without representation?" Or think you that the splendid ideal of an independent nation, as portrayed in the eloquence of a Patrick Henry, would have aroused the sodden pigtails of the Carolinas to say in response, "Go ahead, we are with you, at the risk of our lives, our fortunes, and our sacred honor?"

In view of these considerations it must be patent to all the fair minded that those thirteen Colonies had all reached practically the same plane of intellectual and political development. Therefore, does it not seem ungenerous, egotistical, narrow-minded for any one, or any group of the original Thirteen to boast that the great ideas connected with the inception of this nation were mainly conceived and born of them, that the deeds done and the words uttered within their borders were, by reason of that fact, the most influential in achieving the final result? It chafes one to hear the historians of those States constantly reiterate: "We made the suggestions, we set the example, others followed." "We were the great kite that mounted the heavenly steeps, toward the fuller and freer civic life; the other Colonies served as the tail, and got up there only because they happened to be joined to us by a common interest."

Massachusetts, and indeed all New England, stood among the giants of those days; they exhibited a truly heroic spirit, set a splendid example, made great sacrifices, and in influence were equal to any other group, but we cannot agree that Massachusetts surpassed Virginia, or the Carolinas, or Pennsylvania, or even New York in these respects. Massachusetts boasts that Samuel Adams was the Father of the Revolution. He was a father of it for Massachusetts, but New York had her fathers of the Revolution in John Morin Scott, William Livingston, and Isaac Sears; Pennsylvania had her Franklin, and John Dickinson; Virginia had her Lee and Henry; and

South Carolina her Gadsden, each as influential in his home Colony and out of it as were Samuel Adams and James Otis. Massachusetts points with pride to Faneuil Hall as the Cradle of Liberty. It truly was for Massachusetts; but New York had her Cradle of Liberty in The Fields, Pennsylvania had her Independence Hall, and Virginia her Raleigh Tavern. Indeed every one of the thirteen had its cradle of liberty, but the average American looks more confidently and tenderly toward old Independence Hall in Philadelphia than to all the others combined. And finally, we should not forget that in those days, before the advent of the steam engine, the telegraph, etc., Massachusetts and Georgia were farther from each other, in time, than is Australia from us today. Hence, a month, or more, must elapse before one could hear about what had been said, or done, in the other Colony or State. Another reason, this, tending to show that those Colonies must have reached about the same plane of civilization, that each was quite sufficient to itself in the domain of political thought, and that all had developed the same spirit of resistance to tyranny, else there could have no spiritual concert, no unity of purpose and action when the hour for the uprising struck.

CHAPTER IV

THE WAR IN NEW YORK

Political and Material Conditions. We have now reached, in the progress of our story, the verge of the arena where the battle royal was to be fought between the advocates of government by the consent of the governed, and the liegemen of one who has arrogated to himself the right to govern others without their consent. It will put us in a position to estimate more justly the importance and nature of New York's share in the Revolution if we could know first, the political situation within her borders at this period, and secondly, the peculiar risks and dangers she would necessarily face should she decide to enter the struggle.

We have already described the somewhat peculiar circumstances of the settling of New York, and have shown how hers was the most cosmopolitan population on the Continent. In the troubles and discussions that prepared the way for the break with England there had existed here, for a while, three parties: First, the radicals, or Sons of Liberty, who had worked openly for greater freedom; the conservatives who counseled submission to the crown on the best terms attainable without resorting to force and arms; and a goodly number of the undecided, or those who held themselves open to conviction. After the rupture came these parties were practically reduced to two: the sworn friends of liberty, and the out and out loyalists, or tories. There were, however, a few who remained strictly neutral. Most of the official class and members of the church of England by natural sympathy were tories, so were many of the large land-holders, and also recent emigrants from Britain, such as the tenantry on the Sir William Johnson estates in the Mohawk valley. To the whigs, or patriots, gathered most of the old Dutch stock, the Germans, the Scotch, and Irish. The merchants in the cities were divided. While in the other Colonies it was reckoned that one-third of the populace were tories, in New York nearly one-half stuck by King George. If the latter had been headed by able and resolute leaders they would have made vastly more trouble than they did. But such an apportionment promised more trouble for New York than would probably befall the others.

A Word More About the Tories. As to the Tories or Loyalists of Revolutionary times it has been the usual custom of our historians to treat them as a perfidious lot of people, unworthy of any sympathy. It would seem that the time has come when we can afford to consider their case fairly.

It is true that there was a plentiful sprinkling of cruel and violent men among the Tories who, during the war, did an infinite amount of harm to their neighbors, but the majority of that faction could not truthfully be classed with the implacables. This majority was largely made up of the wealthy and cultured elements of society, who, by the way, in every age are generally conservative on all questions, social, economic, and political. Many of them, however, prior to the war, were quite in sympathy with the advanced American ideals of civil liberty, and their leaders had signed several of the pleas and protests sent to Parliament asking for more considerate treatment. But they believed that if the Colonies would only exercise sufficient patience, in time the English government would surely grant them all concessions demanded. In their mind it seemed suicidal for these weak discordant Colonies to foment rebellion and make war on so strong a nation. And furthermore, for sentimental reasons, the very thought of breaking with the mother country was most abhorrent to them.

Those Revolutionary Loyalists held the same position as did the so called Unionists in the south during our civil war. These more modern Tories deplored the thought of destroying the union of the States, and therefore refused to fight for the Confederacy; indeed whole regiments of them enlisted and fought with the North for the maintenance of the Union. In the south they were treated with contempt, but we of the north held them as true patriots, worthy of all honor. It is fair to presume that in both cases most of those conservative men were conscientious. But one may be conscientious and yet radically wrong in the position he takes, as we believe those Revolutionary Tories were.

After our Independence had been achieved the Tories were very harshly dealt with. The property of most of them was confiscated, and they with their families were driven from the country, and left to the tender mercies of the Government of their choice.

The Strategic Importance of New York. From the military standpoint, New York was at that time the strategic center of the Continent. As an example of the mind of the British on this point, Daniel Taylor, Sir Henry Clinton's messenger to Burgoyne, said in his confession after capture: "I was likewise to inform Gen. Burgoyne that they had now the key of America," i. e. the Highlands after the fall of Forts Clinton and Montgomery, in October, 1777. Military men were agreed that they who held New York could hold it all.[1]

In the old French and Indian wars New York had been the tramping ground of armies, and this because she possessed the one open door to the north, toward

---

[1] See Washington's opinion. Clinton Papers, II-560.

Canada. Hence, every well read American knew that in the event of war New York must inevitably be the chief bone of contention, the military cockpit of the continent. Then, too, there was the fact that New York had a meagre coast line and only one sea-port, the closure of which would shut her off from commerce with the other Colonies and the rest of the world. And finally there loomed the portentous fact that within the boundaries of New York was that great confederacy of the Six Nations, the most crafty, warlike and formidable of all the native races; infinitely more to be dreaded than the various Algonquin tribes with which the other Colonies had to deal. These had for a long while been in league with the English nation, and the presumption was that they would hold to their old alliance. And this presumption materialized into horrible facts, to the inexpressible misery and cost of the frontiersmen. Thus one can see that for New York to join in the revolt against England was a very risky venture, and yet when the hour struck she unhesitatingly hazarded her all on the side of the right.

The Value and Significance of Lexington and Bunker Hill. The first clash of arms occurred in Massachusetts. The occasion for this event was, first, the massing of British troops in Boston to aid in the enforcement of the decrees of Parliament; second, the cancellation of the charter of Massachusetts; and, third, the placing over her a military Governor. All this was intended as a warning to other Colonies who were equally contumacious. The appointed Governor was General Gage, a man wholly unfit by temperament and training for the task asigned him. Accustomed to have his orders obeyed instantly, unquestioningly, he had no patience with a lot of people who wanted to be shown why before consenting to do as they were told. The result was that Massachusetts saw that she must consent to be ruled by brute force, or fight for liberty. At once she resolved to fight, and then she set herself to prepare for it. Thousands of men were enlisted who began to organize and drill. Skilled mechanics were set to work forging weapons, powder mills were established here and there, and storage magazines were planted at central points. So Massachusetts was the first to make actual preparation for war. But this, we believe, was because she was the first to have occasion for it.

An attempt to seize the contents of one of those newly constructed magazines was the occasion for the so-called battle of Lexington and Concord. It is not our purpose to describe this contest, nor any other, in this connection. Our aim is to estimate the significance and effect of this, and the battle of Bunker Hill, in comparison with some other battles of the Revolution. The average history of the United States devotes a great deal of space to a description of these encounters. They enter into all the minutiae of each affair and tell all about what the most ordinary men did, and where they were throughout the day. Then they elaborate upon the surprising effects these collisions produced in the other Colonies and the rest of the world. This they rarely, if ever, do with the other contests of the Revolution. The natural inference to be drawn is that none of the others are to be compared with Lexington and Bunker Hill in real importance and permanent results, and indeed they leave the impression that our independence was practically won there and then, and that subsequent battles served only to confirm and establish what was there achieved.

Now as to Lexington and Concord we note that this was the first time that a sizable body of Americans seized their arms for the express purpose of defending their rights. It was not a battle in the technical sense but a sort of bushwacking fray between a crowd of unorganized, but fully determined men, and an organized body of disciplined troops, whom they regarded as their oppressors. Bunker Hill was the first conflict of the Revolution between two duly organized bodies of men drawn up in battle array. The significance of these collisions was this: First, they demonstrated that those men of Massachusetts had lost all hope in argument and petitions as a means of redress, and had resolved to appeal to arms; secondly, they proclaimed to the people of England, and the world, and that in no uncertain voice, that these Colonists were not the slaves and cowardly poltroons they had pictured them, but were men of courage, of resolute and knightly spirit, and in short a body of men not to be fooled with. The effect upon their fellow Colonists was electrical. It compelled every man to stand forth and show his colors. It said to all: We have set the pace, now let all men of like spirit catch the step and "fall in." It proved to be a ringing cry "To arms, to arms! the life and death struggle has begun!"

As battles Lexington and Bunker Hill decided nothing except that the time had come to fight, and that they were ready to fight. They in no way resulted in any strategical advantages, their effect was psychological, or moral, and that alone. But that was the one thing needful at the time. The fire had to be kindled by someone, the game had to begin somewhere, and just as well at Boston as anywhere. It only remained to be discovered whether the others were in an inflammable mood, or were ready for the game. If they were not, such resistance, such battles anywhere in the Colonies, would accomplish nothing, and would be of only passing interest to the others. Well, for 1775, that team of Thirteen was a good one and it was found that all the members were ready for the signal shot.

We find an exact counterpart of the above at the beginning of the Civil War in the attack on Fort Sumter, and the battle of Bull Run. The spirit of insurrection had spread and the people of many of the southern states had become defiant of the Government at Washington. Roger A. Pryor, a member of Congress from Virginia, was haranguing a meeting in the streets of Charleston, in April, 1861. In the peroration of his speech he said: "Do not doubt Virginia, strike a blow! The very moment that blood is shed old Virginia will make common cause with her sisters of the south." Fort Sumter fired the heart of the south, welded their union, awakened the north to the imminence of war, and the battle of Bull Run confirmed their fears. But neither of them decided anything from a military point of view, their effect was wholly psychological.

The Effects of Some Other Battles Compared with Lexington and Concord. There were many battles of the Revolution of far greater consequence to the end in view than those we have been considering. For example: the closing days of 1776 saw Washington retreating through the Jerseys, and finally crossing the Delaware with only a skeleton of the army with which he fought the battles of Long Island, and White Plains. That was a moment of utter gloom and despondency throughout the country. But the battle of Trenton changed the whole aspect of affairs. It restored to us nearly all of New Jersey, and put new heart into all the people. That was a great strategical and psychological victory. It was one of the decisive battles of the Revolution, but, for all that, our New England historians give comparatively little space to Trenton.

A like situation was created in New York the following year, in 1777, only on a larger and more determinate scale. After the loss of Ticonderoga to Burgoyne the

THE STORY OF OLD SARATOGA

people everywhere seemed heart sick and well nigh panic stricken. But the two engagements of Oriskany and Bennington, fought by embattled farmers, shattered the plans of the enemy, and like Trenton, secured and held for us valuable territory, revived the courage of the people, and so made possible the great victory at Saratoga. And Saratoga, which, by common consent of disinterested historians, is one of those few battles in all history which have served to give a new set and direction to the currents of a true civilization, Saratoga, fought in New York, ONE of the SIXTEEN DECISIVE BATTLES OF THE WORLD, think of it, only sixteen so classed among the thousands fought, this very exceptional battle has received but scant notice at the hands of our leading historians. For example, Bancroft in his great History of the United States, devotes 22 pages to the skirmish of Lexington and Concord, and 42 pages to the effects of it in America and Europe. To the battle of Bunker Hill he gives 18 pages, and 6 to the results of it. To the two battles fought at Saratoga, and the capitulation of Burgoyne he allows $11\frac{1}{2}$ pages, with no space given to the results. And to the entire Burgoyne campaign, including the advance from Canada, the strategies, its thrilling incidents, and its six battles, he gives 45 pages. Place that over against the 64 devoted to Lexington! John Fiske, one of our fairest historians, requires 10 pages to describe Lexington and Concord, but gives $3\frac{1}{2}$ to Saratoga. Trevelyan, an Engish historian, who evidently sees things from a different standpoint, and in their proper proportions, devotes 5 pages to Lexington, 16 pages to Bunker Hill and 110 to the Burgoyne campaign. Of Lexington and Concord he says: "Pages and pages have been written about the history of each ten minutes of that day, and the name of every Colonist who played a part there is a household word in America."

Another Englishman, M. A. M. Marks, in his "England and America in 1763-1783," gives 4 pages to Lexington, 1 to its results, 4 to Bunker Hill, 18 to Saratoga and the surrender, and 30 pages to its effects in England and France.

Modern historians of the Civil War have comparatively little to say of Fort Sumter and the battle of Bull Run, except as signal guns for starting that struggle, but they do have very much to say about Gettysburg, the decisive battle of that great war. Since then that whole battlefield has become the possession of the United States Government, and is treated as a public park. Moreover, the entire field of Gettysburg has been decorated with costly monuments by nearly every military organization that fought there, and very properly. But mark! If there had been no Saratoga there would have been no French alliance, and without the French alliance there would have been no Yorktown for us, and had there been no Yorktown in 1781 there would have been no Union to fight for in 1861. And yet the field of Saratoga is still in possession of private farmers who quietly till the ground whereon Arnold and Morgan, and Poor, and Learned and Ten Broeck fought against Burgoyne and Fraser, and Riedesel, and Phillips. It is visited by only a very few persons, because known to but a few, and no great monuments adorn that ground made sacred by the blood of patriots, and where was settled the question whether there should be established in the earth "a government of the people, by the people, and for the people." I say no great MONUMENTS. There are on that field a few markers raised by a private association of patriotic men and women. All honor to them for their self-sacrificing devotion.

The American writers above mentioned do say some very handsome things about the spirit shown, and things that happened in other Colonies, or States, but too frequently they limit themselves, in such cases, to mere sentences or paragraphs. Now, we submit, that the average reader who finds several pages devoted to the description of an event which happened in one place, and only a paragraph given to a like event that happened in another place, will naturally conclude that the event to which the larger space is given must surely be the more important. Lossing, e. g., in his "Our Country" allows 6 pages to the Boston Massacre and one paragraph to the battle of Golden Hill. H. C. Lodge in his American Revolution gives 12 pages to the battle of Lexington, and half a page to Sullivan's expedition in western New York.

First Aggressive Acts of the War. We have already stated that in case of war with England New York would probably be a principal sufferer. But that she did not falter because of this, and that she was keyed up to as high a pitch of patriotism as the other Colonies, is clearly demonstrated by her behavior from the beginning to the end of the conflict. For example, the news of the fight at Lexington and Concord reached New York on Sunday morning, April 23d, 1775. The effect was instantaneous. It found the Sons of Liberty apparently expecting something of the sort, and ready for action. Regardless of the sanctity of the day they assembled at the wharves in force, seized a number of vessels laden with supplies for the King's troops at Boston, and straightway unloaded them, and thus £80,000, or $400,-000, worth of provisions were added to the Colonial stores. On the following day, Monday, under the lead of Isaac Sears and Marinus Willet, the custom house was secured, the arsenal was seized, 600 stand of arms were taken, and cannon were hauled up to King's Bridge to defend the pass at that place. These arms were afterward used by Cols. Gansevoort and Willet for the defense of Fort Schuyler (originally Ft. Stanwix, Rome, N. Y.)[2]

Thus the first act of aggression on the part of the Colonists, occurred in New York, and the first spoils of the war were gathered in by those same doughty New Yorkers, on April 23d and 24th, 1775. But a far richer prize, as the fruit of aggressive act number two, was secured within the bounds of New York only a few days later, on the 10th of May, when Ethan Allen and his Green Mountain Boys, accompanied by Benedict Arnold, captured Forts Ticonderoga and Crown Point.

A short while after these events Arnold sailed down lake Champlain with a schooner, which he had armed with cannon seized at "Ti," and with a crew of 50 men attacked the fort at St. John's, captured it, and also a sloop of war, named George III, mounting 16 guns. The first naval battle of the Revolution did not occur on Lake Champlain as has been claimed, but was fought on the 5th of May, 1775, with a vessel fitted out by the people of New Bedford and Dartmouth, Mass. It attacked and recaptured a prize with 15 prisoners, Americans, taken by the Falcon, a British sloop of war. This happened in a harbor of Martha's Vineyard.[3] But the first navy of the United States was built on Lake Champlain. It was placed under the command of Benedict Arnold who, on October 11th and 12th, 1776, fought a remarkable battle against a vastly superior British fleet. Though himself defeated his antagonist was so badly crippled that it is conceded he saved the lake, including Ticonderoga, for us that year.[4]

New York Gets Her First Installment of the War's

---

[2] Dawson's Battles of the U. S. Lossing's Field Book, II, 587. Letters from N. Y., Apr. 24, 1775, in Am. Archives.

[3] Winsor's Nar. and Critical Hist., VI, 564.

[4] See Capt. Mahan's Navy of the Revolution.

Cost. This same year, 1776, occurred the disastrous battles around the city of New York, which resulted in the loss of our one seaport, and the most thickly populated area in our State, including Staten Island, nearly all of Long Island, the city and county of New York, all of which remained in the hands of the enemy for seven years. And furthermore, during that period, the major portion of Westchester county was regarded as anybody's land, or neutral territory, the foraging ground of the so-called Skinners and Cowboys.

1777 was the year of the Burgoyne campaign, already mentioned, with its many battles, which resulted in the devastation of most of the Hudson river country north of Stillwater. The only area not overrun at sometime by an enemy was along the Hudson from Kingston to Stillwater, and from Hoosic on the east to the vicinity of the present city of Amsterdam on the Mohawk; a distance of 75 miles north and south and about 50 miles east and west at the widest point. After the evacuation of Boston in the spring of 1776 Massachusetts saw no more of the devastation of war, nor experienced its more dreadful hardships. Rhode Island suffered vastly more than did Massachusetts, because a large portion of it was, for three years, in the hands of the enemy who exhibited while there a most implacable spirit, and wrought an immense amount of material damage. The coast of Connecticut was harassed from time to time by buccaneering parties, and was twice invaded by the enemy, but she gave them so warm a reception that they beat a hasty retreat. New Hampshire never saw an armed Britisher within her borders. But at no time was any part of New England made the sole aim or coveted prize of a carefully planned campaign like the several fully equipped expeditions, and the vehement attempts made by them at getting possession of the Hudson valley.

New York's Revolutionary Population Compared With the Other States. In comparing New York's contributions and losses with those of the other States during those times that tried men's souls one surely ought to know the comparative number of their populations. The average citizen of today who knows that New York, for many years, has stood at the head of the list of States in point of population is apt to think it has always been so. But that is a great mistake. At the period of the Revolution she ranked number 7 in this respect. At that time the aggregate population of the 13 Colonies was reckoned to be about 3,000,000. It was actually less than that. Today New York alone has over three times that number.

From a census taken in 1771 we learn that New York's population was 168,007, of which 19,833 were blacks. Massachusetts reported none of the latter at that time. Granting that the population increased 10 per cent in the next four years, (there would be no immigration after the war started in 1775) then New York had at that date about 184,800. The population of Kings, Queens, Suffolk, Richmond, New York counties and, say, half of Westchester, then in British hands, numbered 62,400. It was reckoned that one-third of the population in this area were patriots. Suppose that all of these escaped to the north, (which they did not) that would leave 41,600 from whom no recruits could be drawn for the American army. In this estimate we are not counting the several thousands who went to Canada with Sir John Johnson and other Tory leaders. Hence there would be left 143,200 inhabitants in that part of the State unoccupied by the British. From James A. Roberts' "New York in The Revolution" we learn that this State had on her muster rolls 43,645 men "in good standing as soldiers." That would indicate that 30 per cent of her available population had served in the Revolution.

As a help to a fuller comprehension of our general theme, "New York's Share in the Revolution," it will be interesting to look over the following table of the populations of the States at that time and the comparative percentages of soldiers sent into the service:

STATE	Inhabitants	[5]Troops	Approx. Percentage
New York	143,200	43,645	30
Massachusetts	339,000	69,907	21
Connecticut	196,000	31,939	16
New Hampshire	81,000	12,497	15
Rhode Island	55,000	5,908	11
Georgia	26,000	2,679	10
New Jersey	120,000	10,726	9
Pennsylvania	302,000	25,678	9
Delaware	30,000	2,386	8
Maryland	200,000	13,912	7
Virginia	500,000	26,728	6
South Carolina	175,000	6,417	4
North Carolina	260,000	7,263	3

At this point we think the following extract from a speech of Alexander Hamilton fits in admirably. It was delivered before the New York Convention assembled to consider the ratification of the Federal Constitution in 1788.

He said: "How have we seen this State, though most exposed to the calamities of the war, complying in an unexampled manner with the Federal requisitions, [for troops of The Line and provisions] and compelled by the delinquency of others to bear most unusual burdens! Of this truth we have the most solemn proof on our records. .... Gentlemen have said that the non-compliance of the States had been occasioned by their sufferings. This

---

[5] The above table of population is taken mainly from "A Century of Population Growth in the U. S." The table on Troops from Roberts' "N. Y. in the Revolution," and "Carrington's Battles of the Revolution," p. 653.

may be true in part. But has this State been delinquent? Amidst all our distresses *we* have wholly complied.[6] If New York could comply wholly with the requisitions, is it not to be supposed that the other States could in part comply? Certainly every State in the Union might have executed them in some degree. But New Hampshire, which has not suffered at all, is totally delinquent. North Carolina is totally delinquent. Many others have contributed in a very small proportion. And Pennsylvania and New York are the only States which have perfectly discharged their Federal duty."[7] Hamilton spent years as private secretary to Washington, and was unremittingly in correspondence with leading delegates to Congress, hence well knew what he was talking about.

Again look over the following exhibit of the comparative number of battles and bloody encounters fought in the several States from 1775 to 1783:

	1775	1776	1777	1778	1779	1780	1781	1782	
Massachusetts	11	3	0	0	0	0	0	0	=14
New York	2	21	27	6	11	14	10	1	=92
Connecticut	1	0	3	0	6	1	3	0	=14
Rhode Island	1	0	2	2	0	0	0	0	= 5
New Jersey	0	4	10	4	4	8	1	0	=31
Pennsylvania	0	0	0	5	0	0	0	0	= 5
Delaware	0	0	2	0	0	0	0	0	= 2
Virginia	3	1	1	1	1	0	9	0	=16
North Carolina	0	1	0	0	0	4	8	0	=13
South Carolina	2	5	0	0	0	6	35	25	=79
Georgia	0	1	1	3	7	2	4	4	=22

But figures, however accurate, can never adequately portray the miseries due to the dread of terrible things liable to happen any moment. The sight of one's home and property consigned to the flames, the being brutally

---

[6] New York sent her full quota of Continental troops, besides militia for the protection of her own borders. Clinton Papers, VI, pp. 357, 580, 748. Elliot's "Debates on The Federal Constitution," p. 360.

Elliot's "Debates on the Constitution," p. 360.

bereft of loved ones, the horrors of the massacre, and the tortures incident to captivity among savages. The frontiers of New York, including the Rondout, the Schoharie, the Delaware, the Susquehanna, the Mohawk, and the upper Hudson vallies, for five long years served as the arena of "that warfare of arson, massacre and ambush fighting of which the Indians were masters. Those vallies became a land of terror and at last were reduced to a land of silence. Twelve thousand farms ceased to be cultivated in that territory. Quite two-thirds of the population died or fled, and among those who survived were three hundred widows and two thousand orphans.[8]

To this we might add that there were destroyed in Tryon county, in the fall of 1780 alone, 150,000 bushels of wheat, besides other grain, and 200 dwellings. The same fall Sir John Johnson in his raid through the Schoharie valley, destroyed 80,000 bushels of grain. And this loss, as Washington wrote to the Congress, "threatened alarming consequences." For it must be remembered that New York, at the time, was the chief granary of the Continental army. All this was calamitous not only for the army, but for our citizens as well.[9]

Here is a sample of the refinement of cruelty and efficiency to which some of those Indians, in British employ, attained in venting their hatred upon the white men who rebelled against King George. The story is told by Simms, and is quoted in Curtiss' Nat Foster, p. 163. Hess, the Indian, lived near Little Falls, N. Y., and there Nat Foster met him. Foster having unlimbered his tongue by a glass or two of fire water, Hess began to display some tokens of his prowess. "Among others was a tobacco pouch of delicate leather. 'This,' said the crafty warrior, 'me got in war. Me kill white woman, rip open

---

[8] Proceedings of N. Y. Hist. Assn., Vol. III, 37.
[9] See Clinton Papers, VI, 354-6.

belly, find papoose, skin him some and make pouch.' The Indian then opened a box in the breech of his rifle and exhibited evidences he there carried of the number of scalps he had taken in the war. 'The tally,' said Foster afterward, 'ran up to the almost incredible number of forty-five,' and he added, 'I had almost a notion to shoot him on the spot.'"

In addition to the destruction of the homes of many and their means of subsistence there was generally a well nigh total lack of money with which to do ordinary business. In the winter of 1780-'81 the greater part of the Continental army was quartered in New York. That winter Connecticut refused room within her borders for a cantonment of troops, and referred Washington to Massachusetts.[10] At that time the pay of the army was in arrears for more than a year, and much of the time the men were without sufficient provisions. As a result the inhabitants for miles around were living in constant dread of those half starved and mutinous soldiers. The well nigh practical worthlessness of the paper money then current, together with their previous costly experiences, had caused the farmers to refuse to exchange their produce for mere scraps of paper. The Legislature of New York, fearing that financial ruin was impending made a special appeal to the Congress that it would devise some means to meet the emergency. From this appeal we quote these words: "By our exertions, by a series of Compulsory Laws, and by use of the most rigorous Means to execute them, our Inhabitants as a result feel themselves so aggrieved, that Prudence forbids any further attempts on their Patience; new Requisitions upon them, before their demands on the Purchasing Officers are satisfied, would be vain."[11]

---

[10] Ford's Writings of Washington, IX, 62.
[11] Clinton Papers, V I, 582-3.

THE STORY OF OLD SARATOGA 449

And sometime previous to the above, in a letter to Gen. McDougall, Gov. Clinton says: "I need not tell you that this State has suffered more by the enemy than any other on the Continent, and being the principal Seat of the War, the Inhabitants have of course experienced as much Injury from our own Army, which under former Commands was not a little." Here is a sample of what the Governor refers to. "Immediately upon the evacuation of White Plains by the British Army, in November, 1776, a body of Massachusetts militia under command of Major Austin took possession of White Plains and proceeded to rob the defenseless inhabitants, both patriot and Tory, with great impartiality—a thing that even the British had failed to do during their occupancy of the village. Every article that was portable was sent into the homesteads of Connecticut and western Massachusets; and many of the poor sufferers, including both women and children, were left with insufficient clothing, blankets, etc., to keep them comfortable during the rigorous season fast approaching."[12]

And here is another instance: "August 17, [1777] Captain Parker of the 7th Mass. and the officers with him were arrested for pillaging Ballston. [N. Y.] This contrary to strictest orders."[13]

These hardships which the people of this State suffered at the hands of our own armies are seldom referred to in histories of that time, but they were quite as real and vexatious as were the hurts inflicted by the enemy: E. g., the billeting of troops upon the people during the winters, the impressment of forage and teams for public use, often when these were sorely needed by the people for their own maintenance, the seizing of sheep, cattle,

---
[12] Proceedings of N. Y. Hist. Assn., IX, 164.
[13] Diary of Capt. Benj. Warren.

etc., by the soldiers for food, the cutting down private forests for fuel, and in lieu of kindling wood burning up the farmers' fences.[14] For all of which the pay offered by the Commissaries were more scraps of paper, or Continental money, worth at that time 2½ cents on the dollar. Added to all this there were the thousands of refugees from the frontier settlements that had been destroyed by Indian and Tory raids. There too were the friendly Indians who had also been impoverished by the war who required food and shelter. Nor must we forget those other thousands escaped from New York city and vicinity, all of whom had to be succored and cared for, and no one was found offering to aid them but their nearest neighbors, who were New Yorkers, or perhaps some friends in New Jersey.

Of these latter phases of warfare New England had little or no experience. The ambushments, the massacres, the depopulation and devastation of the most fertile areas, and the plundering by our own armies, were unknown east of the Berkshires. For New York, being the buffer State, got most of the bumps and bruises. She, more than any other, was torn and mutilated from top to toe, and when the agony was finally over she was left prostrate and well nigh helpless, both in property and personnel. Afterward, when it came to providing for the payment of the public debt, Congress refused to make any allowance in behalf of those States that had suffered most.[15]

Being thus freed from the worst hardships of the war all of the New England citizenry, except those at the front with the army, or off at sea on profitable privateering ventures, could abide at home and go about their accustomed tasks with "none to molest or make them afraid."

---

[14] Clinton Papers, II, 823-4; V, 479.
[15] Clinton Papers, VIII, 81.

Why New England Excelled New York Educationally. In addition to what we said under this head on a preceding page we here discover a principal reason why New York fell behind her eastern neighbors in the matter of education, with its natural fruitage of literature. During the war, or for eight years, her schools were most of them closed perforce. Then too, with the war, came her tremendous losses in property and personnel. When the day of peace finally dawned she was compelled to repopulate and rebuild vast areas of the desolated regions, and because the most of her people for many years were obliged to bend every energy toward this task of reconstruction, and the procuring the means of bare subsistence, there was but little time, energy, or money left for the support of schools and the building up of educational institutions. It was not till after the beginning of the next century that New York got on her feet again, and was in a position to give the necessary attention to the matter of common schools. But in New England they had little or no interruption in the work of education. Hence, after the war closed they had plenty of men, trained, and equipped with leisure and means, to write and publish the annals of New England connected with the Revolution, in which they describe in detail and glorify home men and events, and slur over the men and deeds of other States, excepting the few which stubborn facts compelled them to regard as of supreme importance. And so these narratives served as the standard histories in our schools for a hundred years or more; all of which helps us to understand why Lexington and Bunker Hill bulk more largely in the minds of our older people than do Oriskany or Saratoga, about which so little was said in the books we read and studied when young. Here then we have a good and sufficient reason why so little is known or uttered about the people who sacrificed and suffered most for the attainment of our liberties.

What Some New Yorkers Did in Three Crises. One of those critical moments in the war of the Revolution when the question of its continuance hung trembling in the balance was during the latter part of the year 1777. This was when that conspiracy was hatching for ousting Washington and substituting Gates as commander-in-Chief. This is known in history as the Conway cabal.

Every biographer of a Revolutionary worthy has been very anxious to shield his hero from the charge of participation in that affair. And the actors themselves, as soon as the matter became public, and they began to hear the deep rumblings of public reprobation, were all of them diligent to cover their tracks. Hence the history of the conspiracy is involved in much obscurity. Still the names of a number of those who were actively or sympathetically mixed up with it are known.

Richard Henry Lee of Virginia is known to have been one of those who openly ascribed to Washington a lack of energy in the prosecution of the war. Dr. Benjamin Rush, of Philadelphia, lent a pliant hand in minimizing the efficiency of the Commander-in-Chief. James Lovell, a delegate to Congress from Massachusetts, was proved to be one of the conspirators. Anonymous letters in his handwriting, comparing Washington's failure in Pennsylvania, during that year, with the success of Gates at Saratoga, were spread abroad and many were won over. Both Samuel and John Adams, though not to be lined up with the conspirators, were openly impatient of Washington. Henry Cabot Lodge, in his life of Washington, writing of Samuel Adams' attitude toward his hero, says of him: "A born agitator, and a trained politician, able, narrow, and coldly fierce, the man of the town meeting and the caucus, had no possibility of intellectual sympathy with the silent, patient, and hard gripping soldier, hemmed with difficulties, but ever moving straight toward his object."

That Samuel Adams was not an accurate judge of men is also shown by his criticism of Schuyler and his estimate of Gates, found in a letter to Richard Henry Lee, a congenial partisan of his, written just after the news came of the fall of Ticonderoga, in July, 1777. Among other things he says: "You have his [Schuyler's] account in the enclosed newspaper, which leaves us to guess what has become of the garrison. It is indeed droll enough to see a General not to know where to find the main body of his army. Gates is the man of my choice. He is honest and true, and has the art of gaining the love of his soldiers, principally because he is always present and shares with them in fatigue and danger"(?) See *ante* pp. 140, 151-3, 208-10.

Julian Hawthorne in his History of the United States, II-517, says: "All the people, all the army, and even the British praised Washington; there was but one body of men who belittled and hampered him, and that was the American Congress led by John Adams. 'I have been distressed,' declared this incorrigible gentleman, 'to see some of our members disposed to idolize an image which their own hands have molten. I speak of the superstitious veneration paid to General Washington. I honor him for his good qualities; but in this house I shall always feel myself his superior.'"

That Congress favored the plotters is proved by the fact that, inspired by them, it reorganized the Board of War making General Gates its President, Gen. Mifflin, openly antagonistic to Washington, a member, and Gen. Thomas Conway, the chief conspirator, after whom the cabal or faction was named, Inspector General of the Army. This Board was given much power that properly belonged to the Commander-in-Chief, clearly with a view to so disgusting him that he would resign. Matters seemed to be moving toward the desired end when suddenly, and prematurely, the secret became known, and the plot went up in smoke.

Now, all the above is offered only as a preface to the following brief story of what New York did to defeat that atrocious plot so full of fateful possibilities: On October 14, 1777, the Congress passed a rule that no State should be represented by more than seven or less than two. Sometime later the Conway Cabal discovered that New York had but two delegates present, viz., Francis Lewis and William Duer, and that one of these, Mr. Duer, was seriously ill. Gouverneur Morris, the third delegate, was absent from town. Taking advantage of this situation the Cabal induced Congress to appoint an early day for the selection of a committee who were to be authorized to proceed to Valley Forge, and arrest Washington. Mr. Lewis thereupon sent post-haste for delegate Morris.[16]

Mr. Duer, learning of the situation, sent for his physician, Dr. John Jones, and demanded to know whether he could be removed to the Court House, where Congress sat. "Yes, but at the risk of your life," replied the doctor. "Do you mean that I would expire before reaching the place?" "No, but I would not answer for your life 24 hours after." "Very well, sir," said Mr. Duer, you have done your duty and I will do mine. Prepare a litter for me; if you do not somebody else will, but I prefer your care in the case." The litter was prepared and the sick man was about to risk his life for his country. But just at this juncture Gouverneur Morris arrived, and the faction knowing that New York's delegates would now make a majority against them gave up the fight, and, in-

---

[16] Francis Lewis was the father of Morgan Lewis, a member of Gates staff at Saratoga, and later Governor of this State.

cidentally, the hazardous venture of Col. Duer was rendered unnecessary.[17]

It is very gratifying to reflect that three high principled New York statesmen were equal to this grave emergency, and were able to save George Washington for the army, our country, and the world. But all honor to the men from other States, whoever they were, that helped to make that opportune majority. But mark, none of that precious and timely majority, so far as this writer can learn, was from the State of Massachusetts. And again, so far as we can discover, no prominent New York man, after once he had shown his colors, ever sided with the enemies of George Washington.

In this connection and under this head, it is fitting that we call to remembrance those three trustworthy and unbribable New York soldiers who in 1780 saved to us the stronghold of West Point, "The Key of America," from the hands of a traitor. Their contribution to the success of our struggle for liberty was quite as worthy as anything done by Paul Revere, that worthy and much belauded Bostonian, but we have yet to see the thrilling ballad that worthily extols the sturdy patriotism of John Paulding, David Williams, and Isaac Van Wart. But at the time of it George Washington evidently realized the value and significance of their exploit; for in a letter to Congress announcing the treason of Arnold, he speaks by name of the captors of Major Andre, Arnold's accomplice, and of them says: "Their conduct merits our warmest esteem; and I beg leave to add that I think the public will do well to make them a handsome gratuity. They have prevented in all probability, our suffering one of the severest strokes that could be meditated against us."[18] In this connection read *ante*, pp. 357-8, about Col. James Livingston, another New Yorker, whose alertness

---

[17] Dunlap's New York, Vol. II, 133. W. A. Duer's Life of William Alexander, Lord Stirling.

and timely action made possible the arrest of Major Andre.

But there was another supreme crisis in that mighty effort to establish in the world the rights of man, when the ability and willingness to continue the struggle was strained to the limit. That was also during the sombre year of 1780. Many patriots were sadly disheartened by defeats in the field, which defeats also served to stir the Tories to renewed activity in aid of King George; moreover, multitudes of the friends of the cause had become heartily tired of the long drawn tussle, and what was quite as material, Congress was wholly lacking in funds with which to continue the war. The army must be fed, and paid, and equipped if it were to hold together and keep the field. But in that year the soldiery found hunger and nakedness a more dangerous foe than British brigades and batteries. The Congress made requisitions on the States for these necessities, but they were shamefully slow in responding, and, as we have seen, some States totally ignored the pleas of Congress and Washington. Hence there were periods when the army had to exist on short rations, and some days they were treated to none at all. The natural results followed: mutinies, as in the Pennsylvania and New Jersey lines. And finally there came a time when the said army must either be provided with food or disband. Washington, seeing the crisis approaching, sent for Governor Clinton that he might be present at a council of war, and at the same time see for himself the situation. And sure enough he was present and saw. He saw that the disbandment of the army was imminent, and that such a catastrophe meant the collapse of the people's hopes of liberty and independence. But let the Governor tell in his own words how New York sprang into "the imminent deadly

---

[18] Ford's Writings of Washington, VIII, 474.

GOV. GEORGE CLINTON

breach" at this critical moment. It was at one of the sessions of the New York Convention for ratifying the Federal Constitution, already mentioned. James Duane, one of the members of that historic body, at a certain juncture, arose and propounded a question:

"As I am sensible the gentleman last on the floor [George Clinton] was in the confidence of the Commander-in-Chief, I would wish to ask if he did not at different times, receive communications from his Excellency, expressive of this idea—that, if this State did not furnish supplies to the army it would be disbanded?

"Governor Clinton. It is true, sir, I have received such communications more than once.[19] I have been sent for to attend councils of war where the state of the army was laid before me; and it was melancholy indeed. I believe that at one time the exertions of this State in impressing flour saved the army from dissolution."[20]

Thus three decisive battles were fought and won by patriotic New Yorkers who unfalteringly threw their might on the side of right when the fate of this great American essay for the world's betterment hung trembling in the balances. These battles were fought, not on a material field, as at Saratoga, but upon one just as real, viz.: the field of morals. They were victories won by principle over prejudice, by character over cupidity, and by self devotement over supineness. They are worth recording, they are worth acclaiming, because they attest the incomparable value of sturdy character in times of testing, and certify the truth of the Bible precept: "That which is altogether just shalt thou follow, that thou mayest live, and inherit the land which Jehovah thy God giveth thee." Deut. 16-20. A rule as applicable today as when first uttered.

[19] Clinton Papers, VI, pp. 270, 273, 284, 286, 298, 441, 485, 597. See also Writings of Washington, VII, p. 228.

Elliot's "Debates on the Constitution," p. 232.

CHAPTER V

THE TREATY OF PEACE WITH ENGLAND

THE surrender of an army, as at Saratoga, was an un-unprecedented event in English history. But later when the news came that Lord Cornwallis had surrendered a second army to those beggarly colonists the English were utterly confounded. Lord George Germaine was the first to break the news to Lord North 'at his office in Downing street, London. "And how did he take it?" said an inquirer. "As he would have taken a bullet in his breast," replied Lord George, "for he threw up his arms, exclaiming wildly, as he paced up and down the apartment, 'O God, it is all over, it is all over.'" And that expressed the sentiments of well informed and influential Englishmen generally, when they heard it, or we would better say, all except the stubborn George, who sat on the throne, and tried to be the sort of king his mother had exhorted him to be.

The Rockingham ministry which soon succeeded the downfall of Lord North let it be known that they were ready to talk peace with men properly accredited by the Americans. The Commission, appointed by Congress to arrange and execute a treaty of peace with England, consisted of Benjamin Franklin, John Jay, Thomas Jefferson, John Adams, and Henry Laurens. It happened that Jefferson was detained in America, Adams was held in Holland on important diplomatic business, Laurens was a prisoner on parole in London, and Jay was in Madrid vainly trying to induce the Spanish court to acknowledge our independence. Rockingham was quite ready to acknowledge the independence of the Colonies, as demanded by Franklin who opened the negotiations for

America, and for awhile acted alone. But the early death of Lord Rockingham forced another change in the ministry, and Lord Shelburne was called to the place. About this time Franklin sent for Jay to come to his assistance. Franklin, though a born diplomat, was quite ignorant of the legal side of treaty making. John Jay was a learned and level headed lawyer, and a keen judge of character.

Jay Becomes the Leader in This Business. Jay arrived in Paris June 23d, 1782. The next day in company with Dr. Franklin they waited on Vergennes, the Premier of France, the France which had befriended us in the hour of need. Franklin confided in the integrity and open mindedness of Vergennes. But after a few conferences, and a study of the situation, Jay detected that both Vergennes and D'Aranda, the Spanish minister also present, were typical diplomats of the old school, and were not playing the game in our behalf purely for benevolence. D'Aranda was there because Spain would have a word to say about the proposed treaty when it came to the subject of boundaries.

Lord Shelburne was not disposed to be as liberal in his dealing with the revolted Colonies as was Rockingham. He commissioned his agent Oswald to make the proposed peace treaty, not with the United States of America, but with the "Colonies and Plantations." Though Franklin in the beginning, as we have seen, exacted the acknowledgment of our independence as a preliminary to treaty making he, after the announcement of the Shelburne program, receded from his original position, and was inclined to agree with Vergennes that national independence should be the consequence of the treaty rather than a preliminary to it. Mr. Franklin fell sick about this time and was incapacitated for work from September 8th to October 25th. From henceforth Mr. Jay assumed the leadership in the negotiations. When Jay learned from Franklin Shelburne's plan of procedure he opposed it strenuously, and argued that we should be recognized by England as a separate and independent nation before we could begin to do business with her, otherwise we would be classed as a nondescript sort of people. With true legal acumen he clearly saw that colonies like serfs, or bankrupts, were not competent to make bargains that would bind their overlords, or creditors. Hence, he clearly perceived that other nations, like France, or Spain, or even England, later on, could easily take advantage of such a situation.

Not long thereafter Jay discovered that Vergennes had sent a secret agent to confer with Lord Shelburne in London, and, if possible, agree with him on some line of procedure, in their dealings with the Americans, mutually beneficial to themselves. About the same time he got hold of a dispatch from Marbois, Secretary of the French legation in Philadelphia, intended for Vergennes, opposing the American claim to fishing rights in Newfoundland. At once, without consulting Franklin, he sent his friend Dr. Vaughn to London to suggest to Lord Shelburne that on certain points it would be well that they treat directly without referring to France. The hope of separating France and America caught Shelburne's fancy and he decided to act on Jay's suggestion.

This proposal of Jay was in direct violation of the explicit instructions of Congress, which charged the Commissioners "to undertake nothing without the knowledge and concurrence of the French cabinet." Jay refused to be governed by such a rule because it compromised the dignity and independence of the nation which they, the Commissioners, represented. In this attitude of Jay's, Mr. Adams heartily agreed when he got to know the situation. On August 12th Jay had a conversation with Mr. Oswald, the English agent, in which he insisted on England acknowledging our independence as a necessary preliminary to further negotiation. On the 13th, or the following day, John Adams wrote him from Holland, insisting that England shall first acknowledge us as the United States of America. September 1st, Jay replying to Adams, says: "My opinion coincides with yours as to the impropriety of treating with our enemies on any other than an equal footing. We have told Mr. Oswald so, and he has sent to London to require further instruction." September 27th Oswald received a new commission which instructed him to "treat with the thirteen United States of America."

The Subject Matter of the Treaty. This fundamental concern being settled they were ready to proceed with the main business of treaty making. The principal matters to be settled were 1st, the subject of boundaries, for the United States was a new creation under the sun, and the question was how much room on the map shall it be allowed. 2d, there was the matter of our rights in the Newfoundland fisheries. 3d, the question of private debts as between Englishmen and Americans. 4th, the treatment of the Loyalists.

First, as to boundaries. Spain at that time had possession of the Floridas, the mouth of the Mississippi, and all the territory west of that river. France joined her in the set purpose of making the Alleghany Mountains the western boundary of the United States. The secret of this was their clear apprehension of the future growth and power of this budding nation, if allowed too large a place in the sun. As to the fisheries, France, in an adroit and quiet way, strove to shut us out of them. Her real reasons for this, though not the published ones, were 1st, we might interfere in certain rights she possessed in them. 2d, she saw that if we were allowed to engage in those fisheries the business would prove a training school for a navy which might, ere long, prove a menace to the rest of the world. The matter of debts and the treatment of the Loyalists called for the most delicate tact, and far seeing diplomacy, but after a number of conferences these questions were finally settled satisfactorily.

John Adams, detained in Holland, had succeeded in consummating a treaty of amity and commerce with that nation, and, moreover, had secured from her a large and much needed loan. He did not reach Paris till October 28th. Jay rehearsed the state of the negotiations up to date, and having given him his views on the attitude of France and Spain in the efforts at treaty making, says: "He [Adams] concurred with me on all these points." In connection with this treaty it has been well said that "Adams' temperament was that of a fighter, and not that of a diplomat." For example, he failed to exhibit ordinary diplomatic courtesy by neglecting to call on Vergennes after his arrival in Paris, or notifying him of his presence. This gave serious offense. He was very suspicious of Frenchmen generally, and showed it in some of the conferences. Hence, he became *persona non grata* to Vergennes and his coadjutors.

But despite every barrier and marplot the outcome of the business was that we obtained all that we could rightly claim, and far more than France or Spain expected we could get, or were willing should be granted us. Indeed when Vergennes learned that the major part of the treaty had been wrought out without consultation with him, or his agents, he felt much aggrieved, and claimed that France had been unjustly dealt with. And it required all the tact and suave diplomacy of Franklin to prevent a break with her.

Our histories of the Revolution have uniformly left the impression on us Americans that France was influenced by purely benevolent motives when she loaned us treasure, and sent armies and fleets to our aid in the war for independence, and therefore we owe her unqualified praise and gratitude. Indeed, we have always been and still should be very grateful to her. But the fact remains that we owed France no more gratitude for siding with us than she owed us for affording her a rare chance to strike back at, and humiliate, England, her ancient adversary and rival. France wished America to be independent of England, sure enough, but she was equally anxious to keep the new nation so dependent that she would need a protector, and manager, and France had evidently planned to serve us in that capacity. Our true policy was very finely summed up by John Jay, at the time, in a letter to Robert R. Livingston: "Let us be honest and grateful to France, but let us think for ourselves. . . . . Since we have assumed a place in the political firmament, let us move like a primary and not a secondary planet." The treaty was signed by the contracting parties November 30th, 1782. The definitive treaty, which included France, was not signed till September 3d, 1783.

An Estimate of Jay's Part in the Treaty of 1782. Now it will be worth our while to know what competent judges have thought of this treaty, and the part taken by a New York man in its execution. Henry Cabot Lodge, a Massachusetts man, in his American Revolution, accords Mr. Jay a decidedly subordinate part in this diplomatic triumph. With him Franklin was the man. We think well to leave the assignment of his proper place in this achievement to those of his contemporaries who were in a position to know about, and able to assess the value of, his services.

Thomas Jefferson, in a letter to Jay dated April 11th, 1783, says: "I cannot avoid paying to yourself, and to your worthy colleagues, my homage for the good work you have completed for us, and congratulate you on the singular happiness of having borne so distinguished a part both in earliest and latest transactions of this Revolution. The terms obtained for us are indeed great, and are so deemed by your countrymen."

John Adams said: "A man and his office were never better united than Mr. Jay and the commission for peace. Had he been detained in Madrid as I was in Holland, and all left to Franklin, as was wished, all would have been lost."[1]

Alexander Hamilton said in a letter to Mr. Jay: "The peace, which exceeds in the goodness of its terms the expectations of the most sanguine, does the highest honor to those who made it. . . . . The people of New England talk of making you an annual fish offering as an acknowledgment of your exertions for our participation in the fisheries."

Fitzherbert, afterward known as Lord St. Helens, the English peace agent to the French Court, present at the time our Commission was in Paris, in a letter to William Jay, 1838, said: "It was not only chiefly, but solely, through his [Jay's] means that the negotiations of that period, between England and the United States, were brought to a successful conclusion."

Over against the judgment of Mr. Lodge we place that of another modern, Theodore Roosevelt, who in his life of Gouverneur Morris says: "It was a great triumph—greater than had been won by our soldiers. Franklin had a comparatively small share in gaining it. The glory of carrying through the most important treaty

---
[1] John Adams' Works, IX, 516.

JOHN JAY

THE STORY OF OLD SARATOGA   465

we ever negotiated belongs to Jay and Adams, but especially to Jay."[2]

Now after the above appraisement of the services of John Jay, world-wide and permanent in their effects, done at an acutely critical period in our nation's history, indeed in the world's history, read the following by that influential New England historian, George Bancroft: "His [Jay's] superior endowments, his activity and zeal for liberty, tempered by a love for order, made him, *for a quarter of a century, distinguished in his native State."!!*[3] Italics our own. The natural inference from the above is that John Jay was a man little known beyond the bounds of "his native State," and short lived was his renown.

The signing of this treaty of course put an end to the long wearisome war. And here it should be noted that in the providence of God it has turned out that in that war Americans were as truly fighting for the liberties of Englishmen as for their own. Also, as a result of that conflict, England learned a lesson in the treatment of her colonies which she has never forgotten. Since that very costly experience she has freely granted to all her colonies the right of home rule, with the result that all of them have held true to the mother country, and even mustered large armies for her in the great war of 1914-19.

A Word about Gouverneur Morris. In this list of New York's contributions to the founding of our nation we should not fail to mention Gouverneur Morris, another of those farseeing and constructive statesmen, fitted by Providence to aid in completing the great world

---

[2] The authority for such statements as have not been given can be found in Life and Correspondence of John Jay, by Wm. Jay. Life of Jay, by Wm. Whitelock, and Winsor's Narrative and Critical History, Vol. VII, Chap. II.

[3] Bancroft's United States, Vol. VII, p. 78.

task of that day. Though not as well poised or evenly balanced a character as, perhaps, Jay or Hamilton, yet the part rendered by him in laying the foundations has proved of permanent value.

For several years he represented New York in the Continental Congress. In this capacity he proved himself one of the most broad minded and clear visioned members of that body, especially in the sphere of finance. His unusual talents in that direction were recognized by Robert Morris, the great financier of the Revolution, who, in 1781, called Gouverneur Morris to be his assistant, and then after the war retained him as a business partner. In that great struggle, as in every war, ready money was quite as essential to ultimate success as were men in the field, even though its deeds are not so spectacular. Hence that war could not have been won without Robert and Gouverneur Morris any more than without George Washington.

Few of us average Americans know who was the inventor of our very familiar and most admirable national currency. Well, it was while serving as assistant minister of finance that this same Gouverneur Morris conceived and outlined our still popular decimal system of coinage. Afterwards it was modified somewhat by Jefferson, and then adopted by Congress. As soon as introduced it brought order out of horrible chaos in both state and national exchange.

In 1787 Mr. Morris was chosen by Pennsylvania as one of her delegates to the Convention that created our Federal Constitution. It is conceded by historians that he showed himself to be one of the more influential and useful factors in that most remarkable body of men. That great instrument having been completed in the rough, a committee was appointed to put it in proper linguistic shape. Of that committee Gouverneur Morris was chosen a member. History tells us that because of

GOUVERNEUR MORRIS

his well known and exceptionally fine literary taste the other members gave over the task mainly into his hands, just as, previously, did that Committee, appointed to draft the Declaration of Independence, put their task mainly into the hands of Thomas Jefferson. And so that great and incomparable charter of civil liberty, as to its arrangement and literary style, is principally the work of Gouverneur Morris.

A Note about Philip Schuyler. The very prominent and effective part taken by General Philip Schuyler in the Revolution; how he created and organized the Northern Department, assembled and equipped the forces that met and vanquished the armies of Burgoyne, how he labored and sacrificed to sustain the courage and keep up the morale of our people here in the North, has been told at length in the section of this book devoted to military history; which see.

CHAPTER VI

Origin of the Federal Constitution

Chaotic Conditions Following the War. The period of the Revolutionary war has been aptly called "the time that tried men's souls." But the five years that followed the close of that war was a period that tried men's patience and principles, and tested their resourcefulness. The prolonged strain of the war was followed by a remarkable reaction. Those newly created States straightway proceeded to forget that very important adjective, "United," which they had so religiously applied to themselves during the war, and had insisted on in the treaty with England, and quickly relapsed into the old colonial attitude of mutual jealousy and suspicion. Each began to behave as if it were in no way obligated to the rest. They all practically, though not formally, repudiated the confederation through which they had won their independence from England, and proceeded to act as if each, being sufficient to itself, would establish a separate government.

The Congress had been constituted by the States mainly for the prosecution of the war, and now, that being over, it found itself only a government in name. The Continental armies having been disbanded, and there being no United States courts of justice, it could neither enforce its enactments at home, nor defend its citizens abroad. Its function, therefore, was chiefly advisory. It lacked all coercive power. Foreign nations having assumed it to be a responsible government had consummated treaties with it; e. g., in the treaty with England Congress had agreed that private debts to Englishmen should be paid, and that it would advise the States to deal gently with the Loyalists. But in many cases the States totally ignored these agreements and that body could not help itself. Hence, when European governments discovered the weakness of our supposed central government they proceeded to treat us with contempt.

When the Continental armies disbanded they were obliged to trudge their way homeward without pay because Congress had no money to hand them. But what made a bad matter worse was the fact that Congress had no authority to levy taxes, either to run the national business, or to pay its debts. Here then was a so-called government, without an army, without a navy, without credit, and lacking the respect of its constituent parts. No wonder that foreign nations shrugged their shoulders at us.

But why was not Congress clothed with the necessary power? Because the Americans of those days had a mortal dread of centralized rule. They could not forget the injustices they had suffered from such a power located in London, which had tyrannized over them so long, and was accountable to no one but itself. So they feared that if they created a government endued with real authority it would soon, and surely, be usurping powers never granted it, hence, they "would rather suffer the ills they had than fly to others that they knew not of."

The war left the people and the nation badly in debt, and everywhere there was a dearth of cash with which to transact business. Paper, or fiat, money was everywhere tried with the usual disastrous effects. Coins of all nations, and most of them mutilated, or clipped, circulated, and these with the paper money made confusion worse confounded, through lack of any standard medium.

Then, too, the several States began to discriminate against each other in the matter of domestic commerce. Massachusetts compelled Rhode Island, and others, to pay port fees and imposts on entering her territory. New York made the Connecticut and New Jersey farmers pay duties on all articles of traffic, and so on throughout the whole Thirteen. In some States, as Massachusetts and Rhode Island, the efforts of creditors to enforce payment of debts, or of debtors to compel the acceptance of paper money for goods purchased, or for cancelling old debts, caused insurrections and riots, culminating in the formidable Shays rebellion in Massachusetts. The increase of lawlessness breaking out in so many places thoroughly frightened the people, because they saw themselves drifting toward anarchy.

During this while a quarrel arose with Spain over the navigation of the lower Mississippi. New York and New England were willing, for peace sake, to give up its navigation for a period of twenty-five years. But the States to the south of New York would not yield, and threatened to secede and form a Union of their own. This meant two confederacies instead of one, a most ominous outlook for the future.

Finally in order to secure means with which to conduct the national government, and meet its obligations, Congress advised a scheme of imposts, or customs dues, similar to what we have today. After much wrangling twelve of the States agreed to submit to it, but the thirteenth State, which proved to be New York, stood out, and refused to listen to pleas and arguments, and so defeated this plan which promised so much for giving strength and tone to the confederacy. This last event occurred early in 1787, and seemed to fill to overflowing the cup of bitterness, precipitated the disruption of the States, and forced the country to choose between anarchy or a Union constructed on a wholly different basis.

So then here was a government in the last stages of decrepitude; a nation of men without a recognized and ample standard currency with which to do business; armies of debtors and creditors forever haggling and wrangling; thirteen States each trying to make game of the other, and at the same time torn with internal strife and riots; then too there loomed the threats of disunion and rival confederacies. And added to all this discerning people became aware that the nations of Europe stood around, like hungry vultures, waiting the dissolution of this moribund republic, and impatient to pounce upon and devour the remains. Here are some facts which should be emphasized and remembered; that those were the most critical and perilous years in our history, that all of the States were guilty of acts and policies of which none of us today are proud, and that New York stood abreast but not ahead of the worst of them.[1] In this situation thoughtful men felt that something must be quickly done to avert approaching disintegration, or the achievements of those eight sacrificial years would vanish in smoke; and slavery, or serfdom, would after all be their fate.

Here is an instance where religious people see clearly the hand of God guiding in the affairs of men and nations. In the esteem of contemporary European statesmen there was no future for this newborn republic, because plainly it was verging toward anarchy and consequent disruption. All the precedents of history pointed that way, and many wise ones in our own land saw nothing roseate ahead. But the gracious God had long before determined that a new nation, under a more liberal and humane government, should be established in the world, and on this continent, which would prove itself an uplifting force, an inspiring exemplar, and a blessing to the rest of mankind. Hence, under His direction, the harsh and bitter experiences of those five years had

---
[1] Read John Fiske's Critical Period of American History.

served effectively to school many selfish, stubborn, and narrow minded men to long for something more stable, and prepare them to readily submit to the strong and beneficent constitutional government which He had been quietly evolving. And furthermore, under the same beneficent hand, concurrent with the war and the crucial years that followed, a number of remarkably wise and far sighted men had been in training "for such a time as this," so that, when the hour struck, they stepped forth ready for the work needing to be done.

Beginning with Pharaoh's cruel treatment of the Hebrews as a necessary inducement to their exodus from Egypt, and escape from slavery, the history of human progress is replete with like occurrences. Only after bitterest experiences will men consent to exchange the passably good for the manifestly better. E. g., the Magna Charta in old England would never have become an historic fact had not the people been persistently outraged by the brutal tyrannies of King John. And, the heartless despotism of the Stuart kings forced the revolution of 1688, with its fruitage of larger liberties. The fierce religious persecution, instigated by Philip II. of Spain, aroused the Netherlands to fight for and win the boon of civil and religious liberty, the latter a new thing in the world at that time. And it required the mighty convulsion of the civil war to cure our nation of the heresy of State rights and rid us of the vampire of human slavery. Thus, in the end, God makes "the wrath of men to praise Him, and the remainder of wrath He restrains."

The Rise of Political Parties. It seems that during this period there had sprung up two political parties in the nation; the Federalists, who labored for a stronger and more efficient central government, and the State's Rights men, then in the majority, who would make the States paramount, and leave the national government subservient to them in most things. In Massachusetts the State's Rights leaders were Samuel Adams and John Hancock, and of the Federalists, Fischer Ames and James Bowdoin. In New York George Clinton was an uncompromising leader of the State's Rights men, while General Schuyler, John Jay, and Alexander Hamilton were leaders of the Federalists. In Virginia the State's Rights leaders were Richard Henry Lee and Patrick Henry, while Washington, James Madison, and John Marshall labored for a closer union and a stronger government. Indeed each State had its rabid representatives of both parties.

During all this while the broad minded and far sighted men of the country were doing a deal of thinking on the factious conditions looming everywhere so ominously. These leaders of thought began to exchange ideas through correspondence. For example, George Washington opened an extended correspondence with men in whose wisdom and judgment he had confidence. It is gratifying to know that several New Yorkers were in this select company, among whom were John Jay and Alexander Hamilton. Also among them were General Knox of Massachusetts, and James Madison of Virginia, but neither of the Adamses or Hancock, or Gerry, of Massachusetts was appealed to. Washington found himself in thorough agreement with these men as to the secret of our troubles and the remedy for the same, which was a strong central government capable of enforcing its mandates, paying its debts and protecting its citizens. But on a certain day when the outlook for the republic seemed especially hopeless to Washington he unbosomed himself to John Jay in a letter, in which he expressed his belief that "virtue had in a great degree taken its departure from the land, and considered the lack of disposition to do justice to be the source of the national troubles." But Jay was not ready to despair. With a deep religious reliance on Providence he replied that he "could not believe that such a variety of circumstances had combined, almost miraculously, to make us a nation for transient and unimportant purposes."

The Dawning of a Brighter Day. An effectual movement toward better things, if ever realized, must needs start from some influential source and what place more fitting than Mount Vernon, and who among Americans so influential as George Washington? And sure enough, now as before, he proved himself the man for the hour. With prescient mind he saw a great future for the lands beyond the Alleghanies. He had visions of an empire in the Mississippi valley. To retain that empire he felt that the east and the west must be held together by oneness of aim and union of sentiment. The most efficient means to this end was the maintenance of commercial intercourse. Just before resigning his commission in 1783 he had explored the Mohawk valley, saw its marvelous possibilities as an open door to the west, and prophesied its wondrous commercial future. The nearest counterpart to this at the south was the Potomac valley. He persistently advocated the use of this river so far as navigable, to be supplemented the rest of the way by a canal competent to transport the products, and serve the needs of the growing west. The people of that region listened and began to act. In order to carry out the enterprise it became necessary for the two States of Virginia and Maryland to act in concert. So, early in 1785, a joint commission of the two States met in consultation at Washington's home in Mount Vernon. An agreement insuring harmonious cooperation was prepared by the commissioners; and then, as Washington's scheme involved connecting the headwaters of the Potomac with those of the Ohio, it was found necessary to invite Pennsylvania to become a party to the compact.

From such a modest beginning there finally developed a demand for a gathering of commissioners from the Thirteen States to meet at Annapolis, Md., in September, 1786, to discuss the best method of securing a uniform scheme of duties, and some balanced and nation wide system of legislation on the subject of trade. The invitations were issued by the Governor of Virginia, but when the Convention assembled it was found that only five States were represented. Others had appointed commissioners, but they were not there. The result was that nothing authoritative could be done. But before separating they decided to issue an address drawn up by Alexander Hamilton, of New York, calling another Convention to which the delegates should come clothed with ampler powers. In simple but energetic language the address set forth the chaotic condition of the country, the evils and dangers that threatened it, and the grave need for a complete reorganization of the government. Between the proclamation of this address and the time suggested for the proposed convention occurred an aggregation of the most startling events, including the Shays rebellion in Massachusetts, which created a fear of anarchy among the people, greater, by far, than any they had ever harbored against a centralized government.

By way of encouraging the assembling of the wished for Convention Virginia led off by choosing her most distinguished citizen, George Washington, as one of her delegates. As soon as this became known there was an outburst of joy throughout the land. With Washington in the Convention the people felt that such a body might be trusted to act sanely, and do something dependable for the common good. Not long thereafter all the States, save Rhode Island, had chosen delegates to the Convention.

The Birth of the Federal Constitution. On the 25th of May, 1787, delegates from nine States assembled at Philadelphia, organized themselves, and selected George Washington to preside over their deliberations. That body was composed of choice men from all the States represented. Few of them were of mediocre ability. Gladstone once said: "It is no extravagance to say that, although there were only 3,000,000 people in the thirteen States at the time of the Revolution, the group of statesmen that proceeded from them were a match for any in the whole history of the world, and were superior to those of any other one epoch."[2] In that body of fifty-five delegates there appeared four men of the first order of ability, men of prescient mind, who thought continentally. These were Washington, Franklin, Hamilton, and Madison. The average nation rarely produces more than one or two of this type of statesmen in a generation. Then there were a number of men whom we must rank as second in that remarkable body, but who would stand among the first in ordinary times; such as John Dickinson, Robert Morris, Oliver Ellsworth, Gouverneur Morris, William Livingston, and James Wilson. Thomas Jefferson, then in Paris, characterized the Federal Convention "an assembly of demigods."

Many of the delegates came to the convention with the thought that its sole business was to patch up and in some way improve the old Articles of Confederation. But a number of the leading men counselled against such a proposal from the beginning, and argued for some essential changes in the basic principles of the government. After

---

[2] D. Campbell's Puritans in England, Holland, etc., p. 5.

some days had been spent in listening to the various plans proposed for improvement, Hamilton arose and plead for the utter abandonment of the old, and the establishment of a strong and thoroughly organized central government. In his speech he exhibited the utter weakness of the existing Articles of Confederation, the folly of continuing it, and the necessity of something stable embodying elements that had proven workable in the older types of governments then existent. This speech occupied five or six hours, and Gouverneur Morris described it as the ablest and most impressive he had ever heard, embodying all the accumulated knowledge and reflection of years. Although Hamilton's plan for a stronger government was not, in several respects, the one finally adopted, yet he quite convinced the delegates, by the light of recent experience, that any attempt to improve that which clearly lacked the first elements of virility, and had proved itself a conspicuous failure, would be folly, and he furthermore braced their resolution to attempt that which was ultimately created: our Federal Constitution.

We think we are justified at this point in emphasizing the fact that John Jay was one of the very few men in the country who had a clear vision of the type of government which ought to supersede the inefficient Federal Congress then in control, and from the start was in substantial agreement with Hamilton. In a letter to Jefferson, dated August 8th, 1786, he says: "To vest legislative, judicial, and executive powers in one and the same body of men, and that too in a body daily changing its members, can never be wise. In my opinion those three great departments of sovercignty should be forever separated, and so distributed as to serve as checks on each other."[3] And, as we shall see, what Jay suggested was accomplished by

---
[3] Jay's Jay, Vol. I, 256.

that historic Convention. His attitude being widely known doubtless yields the reason why he was not sent to that assemblage. The State's Rights men being in control in New York would naturally see to it that a majority of their representation in the Convention should be of their party.

New York had comparatively little to do with the work of constructing the Constitution for the simple reason that two of her three delegates, Robert Yates and John Lansing, were out and out State's Rights men, and as above suggested, could be depended on to vote against everything looking toward a strong central government. Hamilton seeing that the vote of his State would be cast against anything he might advocate felt that it would be useless and unwise for him to have much to say on the floor of the Convention, so he absented himself part of the time, frequently returning, however, and devoting himself, while there, mainly to personal conferences with the constructive leaders. James Madison of Virginia has been called the "Father of the Constitution," and it is true that the Constitution under which we live is more his work than that of any other one man, though other members of the Convention had not a little to do with its moulding.

After three and one-half months of arduous toil the time was come for the members to set the seal of their approval on their great work by appending their names to the document. But concerning this there was much hesitation in certain quarters. A majority of the members wished it to go forth to the people, not only as the act of the Convention, but as the act of every member thereof. Some who had not been able to agree to all its parts objected seriously to approving the whole of it now by such an act. Here again was a grave crisis in our affairs, for unless practically the whole Convention should sign it there would be but little chance for its approval by the people, and so all their work and trouble would go for naught. In this emergency Alexander Hamilton stepped to the front, and in a thrilling speech plead for united action, saying that the Constitution as formulated would not establish as strong a government as he had hoped for, and further, quoting him: "No man's ideas are more remote from this plan than my own; but is it possible to deliberate between anarchy and convulsion on one side, and the chance of good on the other?" His vigorous appeal, and a similar one by Benjamin Franklin, caused every member present to sign, excepting Mason and Randolph of Virginia, and Gerry of Massachusetts. Yates and Lansing of New York, disgusted with the way things were going, had long since gone home.

Thus our Federal Constitution is the fruitage of many compromises, and much yielding, on the part of the several members of that epochal assembly. But this is a sample of how things have been done on the line of humane progress from the beginning. Coincident with every notable step forward in civilization three classes of men become prominent. First, the reactionaries who are ever afraid of progress, and have a mortal dread of experiments. They remind one of the old couple who always rode backwards in their one horse shay. They never caught sight of what was ahead, they could see only what was behind. Second, that type of visionaries who will consent to nothing short of their full orbed ideal. Say they, "the space between us and the goal must be leaped at one bound or there is no use to try." Third, the wise men of vision; such, though eager to attain the perfect, are content to take a step at a time, make the most of what they have in hand, or is within their reach, never forgetting the ideal, these are the ones who ultimately reach the higher levels and take humanity with them.

CHAPTER VII

Adoption of the Constitution and Launching of the Government

The New Constitution Strongly Opposed. Simultaneously with the submission of the proposed new charter of government by Congress to the States a storm of opposition arose among conservative thinkers; so different was it from what they had in mind when the delegates were sent to the Convention. It also resulted in a more rigid alignment of political party divisions, and gave a new name to one of those parties. Those who favored the new Constitution retained the name of Federalists, while those who opposed its adoption called themselves Antifederalists. Here in New York the contest had an early beginning. Yates and Lansing, having quit the Convention in a huff before it adjourned, came home and did all in their power to bring its proceedings into ill repute. Pamphlets, broadsides, caricatures, and stump speeches were the weapons used against the dangerous document. And this was a sample of what happened in most of the States. But coincident with these there appeared in every State a host of able defenders of this novel instrument of government. Chiefest among these was a New Yorker, in the person of Alexander Hamilton. Fond of debate these opposition essays and pamphlets were a challenge quite to his taste. And though, as he said in the Convention, the Constitution in many respects was not at all to his liking, yet it was vastly better than anarchy, which was the sole and only alternative left for the people. So he seized his pen, which proved itself in his hand to be mightier than the sword, in its defense. He resolved to explain the meaning of all parts of the Constitution in a series of short incisive essays. He announced his purpose to two kindred spirits, men whom he considered best equipped for the task, James Madison and John Jay. Madison was a member of Congress, which, at that time, was holding its sessions in New York City. These men cordially joined in the work, and the result was "The Federalist," perhaps the most famous of American books, and undoubtedly the most profound and suggestive treatise on Federal government ever written. And to this day, apart from judicial interpretation, it is reckoned the best explication of the Constitution extant. Indeed, it was turned to as an authority by the leading minds of Germany when they were intent on the formation of the Germanic Empire.[4] Of the 85 papers of this profound treatise Hamilton wrote the major part. These essays, sent everywhere and republished throughout the country, were acknowledged to have surpassed any other means used in winning votes for the new scheme of government.

John Fiske in his Critical Period of American History says: "Among political writers Alexander Hamilton and James Madison must be ranked in the same order with Aristotle, Montesquieu, and Locke; and The Federalist, their joint production, [including John Jay] is the greatest treatise on government ever written." And right here we would insert the estimate of John Adams as to the value of John Jay's services to the country in that time of testing. In a letter to James Lloyd, in 1815, about the early Federalists, Adams said: "I forebore to mention one of more importance than any of the rest, indeed of almost as much weight as all the rest. I mean Mr. Jay. That gentleman had as much influence in the

---

[4] Lodge's Life of Hamilton, p. 68.

preparatory measures, in digesting the Constitution, and obtaining its adoption, as any man in the nation."[5]

The principal contests over the adoption of the Constitution took place in the States of Virginia, Pennsylvania, Massachusetts, and New York. In their Conventions weeks were spent in dissecting and weighing every section and paragraph of the document. In every State there were strong men who fought against its adoption. It is interesting to recall that in Massachusetts Samuel Adams, the home christened "Father of the Revolution,'' John Hancock, and Elbridge Gerry, acted as leaders of the Antifederalists. They felt sure that a government on the model of the proposed Constitution would seriously interfere with State rights, and lead to tyranny. In New York the great leader of the Antifederalists was Governor George Clinton. He had done a great work during the war in raising and feeding armies, and in keeping New York headed for Independence, but like his Massachusetts compeers, above mentioned, he lacked the continental vision. He became uncompromising in his hostility to the proposed new plan of government, and furthermore, he was a born politician, who, by skillful manipulation, had gained control of the State, and his partisans were wondrously well organized. He would prefer to establish New York as an independent republic rather than allow her to lose her individuality by acknowledging the overlordship of a great central government, which he was sure would legislate against her interests.

The New York Constitutional Convention met at Poughkeepsie on the 19th of June, 1788. There were 65 delegates in attendance. Of this number 46 were against and 19 in favor of the adoption of the Constitution. The

---
[5] John Adams' Works, Vol. X, 115.

leader of the opposition was Melancthon Smith, a man of learning, and one of the ablest debaters in the country. His aides were Yates and Lansing, above mentioned. The leader of the minority was Alexander Hamilton, ably seconded by John Jay and Robert R. Livingston. The outlook for ratification was very doubtful. That majority was too big to be wheedled, or bought, or reduced by political finesse. The average man would have said: "It is no use to tackle the case with such odds against us." But not so Hamilton and his aides. They were ready and eager for the fray. The job before them was to convert this hostile majority by sheer force of argument into a friendly majority, and this labor of Hercules fell chiefly on one man, Hamilton. Day after day he was on his feet meeting their objections with convincing logic, rugged facts, or historical precedents. The enemy then changed their tactics and made personal attacks, treating him as if he were himself the odious Constitution incarnated. But keeping his temper well under control he parried all these vicious thrusts, and forced the opposition to face the great question before them, viz.: The ratification of this Constitution or a plunge into anarchy. So cogent were his arguments and so resistless his eloquence that finally Melancthon Smith, Clinton's great champion, openly acknowledged himself convinced by Hamilton, and declared that he would vote for the Constitution. The result was that the Convention ratified it by a small majority, and so New York decided to join her fortunes with the rest in the great experiment.

Now this victory of Hamilton's has ever since been regarded by competent judges as one of the most remarkable achievements of forensic debate on record. Henry Cabot Lodge, himself a U. S. Senator of recognized ability, and wide experience, says, in his Life of Hamilton: "Tried by the severest test, that of winning votes,

ALEXANDER HAMILTON

Hamilton's victory is of the highest rank in the annals of oratory."

In this connection we would call attention to another illustration of our contention in the first chapter, that New York and other States have not been given the space and consideration fairly due them in our popular histories. E. g. John Fiske in his Critical Period &c., previously mentioned, devotes 33 pages to a sketch of the State Conventions called to ratify or reject the Constitution. Of these 33 pages, 3½ are given to the contest in Virginia, 6 to Pennsylvania, 2½ to New York, and 15 to Massachusetts. The space given to Pennsylvania seems fair and equitable, but Virginia's consent was more essential to the end desired than that of Massachusetts, first, because of her geographical position, and second, because she was the most populous of the thirteen. Then, too, the forces for and against the proposition were so evenly divided in Virginia that no one at the beginning dare predict the outcome, and this mainly because such giants in debate were there arrayed against each other. E. g., Patrick Henry and George Mason against James Madison and John Marshall. Query: In a matter so vital and interesting to the issues at stake why so little attention given to Virginia?

And, as to New York, though ranking 7th in population, Fiske acknowledges that commercially and geographically she was the center of the Union, because of which he says: "It was rightly felt that the union could never be cemented without this central State." With Massachusetts located on the north eastern end of the line a union composed of the remaining 11 or 12 could easily succeed, but a confederacy made up of two clusters of commonwealths separated from each other by a foreign and hostile state was manifestly impossible. Hence, one wonders why Fiske should devote, in his story of the

Massachusetts Convention, two pages to the speech of one Jonathan Smith, a farmer from Lanesboro, and not quote a sentence from the speeches of Hamilton or Madison who did more than all the farmers of Massachusetts, or any other two men in the country, to secure the adoption of the Federal Constitution, and hence, the launching of the United States government.

The Constitution, even after its ratification, was as a ship on the ways. It still had to be launched, its motive power and steering gear installed, and its captain with crew selected and commissioned. As per the rules laid down in the new organic law, the members of the Senate and House of Representatives were duly chosen, and also the electors of the President. George Washington was by them unanimously chosen as the first President of the Republic, the wisest possible choice for the difficult and delicate work to be done. He was inaugurated in New York city on the 30th of April, 1789. Robert R. Livingston, first Chancellor of the State of New York, administered the oath of office.

After the new Federal Congress had assembled and thoroughly organized itself for business, one of its first acts was the creation of three executive departments of government. These were the Department of State, the Treasury, and War Departments. An important piece of legislation this, but a matter of higher importance, just then, was who should be chosen to head those departments, especially the second one. For this was another very critical juncture in our history, the trial of a brand new scheme of government. The choice of the heads of Departments fell upon Washington, and here again he proved himself the man for the hour. Now Washington was a remarkably accurate judge of men; rarely did he make a mistake. Hence, would one assess the value of any man conspicuous in the civil or military service of that time, he would do well first to learn what George Washington thought of him, or what was his attitude toward him; for be it known that the men whom he chose as aides or advisers have, with few exceptions, received the approval of history.

For Secretary of State he chose Thomas Jefferson, of Virginia. This position was first offered to John Jay, but since he was given the choice of either this or that of Chief Justice of the Supreme Court, he chose the latter. General Knox of Massachusetts, whom Washington, during the late prolonged struggle had learned to respect and trust, was chosen Secretary of War. The situation of the newly organized government at that time was such that the Treasury Dept. was, by far, the most important of the three. Great debts were owing both to foreign and domestic creditors; over against these were an empty treasury and no revenue. Now, a nation is much like an individual, it cannot get very far in this world without paying its way and meeting its obligations. The United States at that juncture had no credit in the markets of the world; no one would trust it. The first task of the new Secretary would be to establish the public credit, or create something where nothing existed before. To do this for a nation, where so many diverse interests were involved, would require genius of the highest and rarest kind. The man chosen by Washington for this tremendous task was Alexander Hamilton and it proved to be a choice of the highest wisdom.

Our space will not permit us to enter into the details of the system he created, but suffice it to say that he quickly reported to Congress a practical scheme for raising a public revenue, for funding the national debts, and, furthermore, he devised a workable system for the conduct of the financial business of the nation. These were adopted by Congress, and put in practice, with the result that in a remarkably brief space of time the government of the United States was on its feet financially, with its credit and self-respect established before the world. It is fitting to add that most of his schemes were strenuously opposed at every step, and that his road to success was an exceedingly rugged one, and studded with many thorns. The above noted work of Alexander Hamilton has always been regarded as phenomenal, unique. And be it also remembered that what he then did was not just for the passing moment, or to meet a transient emergency, but permanent in its nature. The finances of our government are still mainly conducted on the principles laid down by Hamilton. Thus he proved himself to be a constructive statesman of the first order of merit, and one of the chiefest founders of our Government. When he addressed himself to his great work our Government was much like a watch with all its parts assembled except the mainspring. All else, however perfect in their adjustments, were of no avail without that member. He fabricated and introduced that essential part, and straightway the machine began to move smoothly and efficiently.

As we have already seen, Hamilton had comparatively little to do with the moulding of our national Constitution, but it developed later, as we have endeavored to show, that he did more than any other man to make it a workable scheme of government. A somewhat startling assertion this, but by way of substantiating our claim, we would say that in addition to calling into being our national system of finance, it was he who first affirmed the presence of powers latent in the Constitution, and which, as yet, had been unsuspected by its original draughtsmen. This remarkable assertion appeared in connection with his efforts to create a United States Bank as part of his scheme to establish the public credit. His opponents declared that the Constitution granted Congress no powers to authorize such an institution, and hence he was asking the impossible. Hamilton replied that the Constitution, by implication, granted Congress power to do anything that is clearly for the public good. After much heated discussion this was finally conceded, and the bank was authorized. This great principle, afterward adopted by Chief Justice Marshall, that great expounder of the Constitution, as a leading canon of interpretation, because it embodies the tenet of liberal construction, has become the most formidable weapon in the armory of the Constitution. And thus this great document, regarded by many, at the first, as a stiff and rigid charter of government, impossible of adjustment to new and unlooked for conditions, has become, by the application of Hamilton's doctrine of "the implied powers," a flexible and supple instrument that can be easily adapted to a majority of cases liable to arise.

It is sometimes pleasant to have our judgments confirmed by the unsolicited opinion of a disinterested party. Here is one on Hamilton. Talleyrand, that exceedingly shrewd and elusive French diplomat, when visiting New York in 1794, happening to see Hamilton at work late at night in his law office, said of him: "I have seen one of the wonders of the world. I have seen a man laboring all night to support his family, who has made the fortune of a nation." Again he said: "I consider Napoleon, Fox, and Hamilton the three greatest men of our epoch, and without hesitation I award the first place to Hamilton." But this was before Napoleon became ruler of France, and Talleyrand his counsellor.

In the opinion of most political writers Hamilton stood next to Washington among the statesmen of the period immediately following the war of the Revolution. Some have pronounced him "the brains of the first Administration." Jefferson was great, but he excelled Hamilton neither in patriotism nor ability. They came to differ widely, but their differences were mainly in their attitude toward democracy, or in their beliefs regarding the ability of the people to rule themselves. In this respect Jefferson was a little ahead of his time. At the close of that war many people had not yet broken with the idea of subserviency to the rule of the aristocracy, or of the wealthy and cultured class. Hence, at the time of the formation of the Federal Constitution and the organization of our Government, a conservative of Hamilton's type was better adapted for the work of the hour than a radical democrat, as Jefferson was then considered. The experiences of the next 20 years brought the people nearer to Jefferson's position. But Jefferson was not by nature fitted for the kind of foundation work done by Hamilton, nor for the times when it was done.

We have now seen the new ship of state safely launched, and auspiciously started on her remarkable career, and so have reached the *terminus ad quem* of the story which we set for ourselves at the beginning, i. e., the end of the Revolutionary period. Whether our recital of New York's share in that great drama, as compared with that of Massachusetts', has in any way tended to augment New York's glory we will leave the patient reader to judge.

We think it proper that we should here reassert our belief that in a regulation history of the United States, or of a State, the ideal historian should exhibit no unfair prejudice in favor of any event, person, or locality. He should strive to state with judicial fairness the true values of deeds and events, by whomsoever wrought and wheresoever done.

In the face of such a statement this writer, a New Yorker, dealing with her history, may be charged with stultifying himself by an exhibition of rank prejudice as against Massachusetts. In reply to such a challenge we would say that we were moved to the treatment of this phase of New York's history, and the compilation of the above chapters, only after a careful study of Revolutionary events, especially those which occurred here in the North. As we said at the beginning we discovered that most of our histories have been the work of Massachusetts men. One cannot read these histories without receiving the impression that the men of Massachusetts stood preeminent for vision and initiative, and that, with few honorable exceptions, the leaders of other States were merely their echoes, and that the deeds done elsewhere were mainly the fruits of the seed sowing and tillage begun in Massachusetts. Reflecting that the aforesaid histories have set the key, and served as exemplars for most of those written since and elsewhere, we felt moved to prove our contention by a deliberate comparison of each State's contribution, using therefor the parallel column method. Knowing how hard it is for truth to catch up with and supplant a lie, in such a case as this, we have been at pains to keep to the fore and specially emphasize what New York did and suffered, lest the reader straightway forget and lapse into his old attitude. Therefore what we have written has been wholly in the interest of truth, and as a protest against such partial treatment as New York and other States have thus far received. Moreover, so long as one presents the truth equitably in dealing with similar and synchronous events he cannot be fairly charged with prejudice. Because of the above cited facts, and, as aforesaid, through lack of space, we have limited our comparisons to New York and Massachusetts, and have rarely mentioned the deeds done in and by other States, most of which stood quite abreast of any other one.

Guide to the Saratoga Battle Field

Guide to Revolutionary and Colonial Sites at Schuylerville

GUIDE TO THE SARATOGA BATTLE FIELD

How to Get There. From Schuylerville. If you are a good walker go first by electric car to Wilbur's Basin. From there walk to Freeman's Farm, one and one-half miles to the west. After starting take first left hand road up the hill. From there it is a straight road to the battlefield. After crossing the ravine turn in at the first house on the left. You are then at the place.

If you are not a walker, then take a carriage at Schuylerville. Perhaps it were better to go by Quaker Springs and return by the River road. The scenery from Quaker Springs to the battle field is superb. After leaving Quaker Springs, up the second road to your left came General Fraser on the morning of the 19th of September, 1777, on his way to the battle. Near here he turned southward. After passing the Quaker meeting house, a half mile farther on at a fork in the roads, you keep to the left; then take second road to the left and turn in at the first house you come to on the right. You are then at the Freeman's Farm House (now Esmond's).

From Saratoga Springs. It is nine miles to the battle field. You will need to take a carriage, and a lunch, as it will be quite late before you get back. Drive out Union Avenue to Moon's; then down the hill back of his place, cross the trestle bridge over the foot of the lake; then along the shore of the lake for a mile and a half to the Cedar Bluff house. Take first left hand road beyond this up the hill. On top of the hill turn to the right, a little farther on turn to the left, then southwest for half a mile till you meet a road running directly east, take this over hill and dale for three miles, passing three cross roads from the north, till you come to a school house and the Quaker meeting house. Arrived at this turn you are on historic ground. It was near here that General Fraser with his brigade, coming up from the river on the morning of the 19th of September, 1777, turned to the south on his way to the battlefield. Now turn up the hill to the right past the school house and church. About half a mile south of the church at a fork in the roads, you keep to the left; then take second road down the hill to your left, turn in at the first house you come to on your right; this is Freeman's farm (now Esmond's).

From Mechanicville and the south. Take electric car to Stillwater or Bemis Heights; there get a carriage to the battlefield. Turn up the hill at Bemis Heights. About a mile up the hill another road comes in from the north. Follow this road for a mile and a half turning to the right at the second cross road, then down the hill, and turn in to the right at the first house you come to; this is Freeman's farm.

Arrived at Freeman's farm, first obtain permission to look over the grounds. Then as you stand at the front of the house facing the west you are looking out on the field of the first day's battle; but remember that all the land in sight was then covered with dense forests except about 15 acres around and west of the house, and a few clearings on and about the low hills to the west. The original Freeman cottage stood to your left near the west line of the barnyard. It was at and about this cottage that Morgan met the British scouts under Major Forbes. He drove them back into the woods just north of the road, and was there in turn driven back and scattered by Burgoyne's main body. Burgoyne formed his line of battle just south of the ravine which runs parallel with and a little to the north of the road. Then he advanced and the battle raged for four hours back and forth across the open clearing both to the east and west of the cottage, but principally to the west. The battle ended when the

SOME MARKERS ON THE BATTLEFIELD

Germans coming up from the river occupied the knoll to the south of the barns with reinforcements and turned the American right wing, just at dark.

After the battle the British held the field and fortified themselves. See map for location and direction of their lines. Here they remained for seventeen days. Let us now look over the grounds a bit.

The Old Battle Well. 1st: In the hollow just beyond the barnyard at the south you see the old battle well. About this well many poor fellows were found dead after the battle, who in their last moments had dragged themselves here to quench their raging thirst, a condition which always follows loss of blood.

The Great Redoubt. 2nd: From the well, climb the knoll and pass to the southwest till you come to the fence. It was on this knoll that Riedesel posted his infantry and cannon whose attack decided the battle of the 19th of September, 1777, for the British. About the knoll the British built a strong redoubt, also breastworks which served as the southwest defense of their camp. Against this redoubt Arnold led the ineffectual charge after the retreat of the British on the 7th of October. On the little rocky knoll, a few rods to the west of you, the British had an outwork.

Remains of Burgoyne's Camp Defenses. 3d: Should you wish to see the only remains of Burgoyne's camp defenses, take the road one-half mile to the east to Mr. E. R. Wilbur's. The ravine you cross on the way was the line between Hamilton's and Fraser's camps. About a half mile from Mr. Wilbur's to the south, in the bushes, are some well preserved breastworks. Their location and form are marked on the map, as is also the location of Burgoyne's headquarters tent. When there, look for remains of old camp well over the fence to the west.

THE STORY OF OLD SARATOGA 499

These are on the land of Mr. Eugene Curtis, and it is hoped that they may be preserved intact, as relics of the historic past are becoming more scarce and more interesting as the years go by.

Breyman's Hill. 4th: About sixty rods to the northwest of Freeman's farm, and north of the road, is Breyman's hill, called by the residents Burgoyne's hill, a misnomer. This defended the extreme right of the British camp, and was held by the Germans under Colonel Breyman. The capture of this strong position by Arnold ended the second day's battle, and forced Burgoyne to retreat. Arnold broke through the breastworks between the road and the first clump of trees. Once within the works, he quickly compelled the defenders to retreat. In the contest which followed his entrance he was wounded, and Colonel Breyman was killed. The tablet is placed on the line of the works, while Arnold was doubtless wounded a little to the rear, to the east. Hardly a suggestion of the old earthworks remains here.

Where General Fraser was Shot. 5th: Returning to the road, pass up the hill to the west and turn to the left. It was this high ground, over which the road runs, that Fraser occupied and held during the first day's battle. Just after you have passed three houses, look on the right side of the road for the tablet which marks the place where General Fraser was shot. The basswood tree over the tablet grew out of the stump of the original one, under which the tragedy occurred. The man who shot him, Timothy Murphy, doubtless stood some eight hundred or a thousand feet to the west or south-west of this point.

Scene of Second Day's Battle. 6th: Passing on you will notice, as you descend the hill, a tablet on the right of the road, against the fence. This is about on the line where Burgoyne posted his forces before the second battle. The British grenadiers, under Major Ackland, were posted from near this point around the base of the hill to the left. The British light infantry, with one cannon, occupied the hill over to the right and also a part of the plain this side of the hill. The Germans held the center. The artillery was posted at intervals from the right of Ackland's grenadiers to the center of the German lines. The twelve-pounders, over which there was such a stubborn fight, were posted in the rear of the German left, a little up the hill.

The battle opened with an attack by the Americans under General Poor on the grenadiers at the extreme left; at nearly the same time Dearborn and Learned struck both the British and German lines in front, while Morgan charged up the hill at the rear of the British extreme right, and forced them to retire. Soon Arnold compelled the Germans to give way when, after fifty-two minutes of fiercest fighting the entire force of the British were compelled to hurry back to their camp, which was stormed by Arnold and their right defense taken, as previously stated.

The Middle Ravine and Observation Hill. 7th: Leaving the second day's battle ground, you pass toward the south, over a stone bridge. This bridge spans the Middle ravine, which figures so prominently in the history of the hostile camps, and the two battles. Passing on you soon come to an isolated hill crowned with farm buildings. From the top of the log house, which then stood there, Colonel Wilkinson observed the British army deploying into line and apparently offering battle, which fact he reported to General Gates, who at once ordered the attack. At the foot of this hill stands a tablet whose inscription gives the impression that from here General Fraser was shot. This could not be for two reasons: first, because Morgan and his men were not here, but were engaged with the British right, half a mile and more to the northwest; and second, because the shoulder of the hill would prevent seeing General Fraser from here, or if not the hill, the trees, and also the smoke of battle would screen him at this distance.

Fort Neilson. 8th: Passing on three-fourths of a mile toward the southeast, and climbing the hill, we come to the site of Fort Neilson, which defended the northwest angle of the American camp. The barns stand on the site of the old log barn about which the ramparts were thrown up. The wing to the rear of the main house is the identical one occupied by Morgan and Poor as their quarters. The interior has been kept intact. From this point Arnold no doubt mounted his horse and rushed into battle without orders. For the location and direction of the American works, and the point of departure of the divisions into battle, see map.

Gates' Headquarters. 9th: After leaving Fort Neilson, as you continue down the road toward the south, somewhere down in the field to the left stood the ammunition magazine of the Americans. At the intersection of the roads, as you turn to the left, you will observe a tablet. A little way back of this in the field was Gates' headquarters, and up to the right of it was the hospital. Here Gates stayed during the second day's battle, and here he had the heated argument with Sir Francis Clerke, a wounded prisoner, over the merits of the questions at issue between the Americans and British, apparently more anxious to win in the battle of words than in the life and death struggle waging beyond the sally port of his camp.

Bemis' Tavern and River Defenses. 10th: When you reach the foot of the hill at the river, you will see on your left, next the fence, a tablet marked Bemis' tavern. Fothem Bemis kept a tavern here, and owned part of the heights to the west. Hence the name, Bemis Heights. The old tavern stood over in the fields a little way to the north. Now turning northward, you will soon see another tablet in front of a house to your left. From here ran strong entrenchments to the river, where a floating bridge spanned that stream. Note here the narrowness of the passage between the hill and river It was a veritable Thermopylæ. Burgoyne acknowledged in his testimony before the court of inquiry that he dare not attempt to force it. The crest of the hills, as you pass northward, were crowned with strong breastworks and batteries. Three-fourths of a mile to the north of Bemis', you will see another tablet on the right side of the road in front of a barn. This marks the site of the advance works of the Americans. Those entrenchments, however, were near the river to the south-east. See the map. A little farther on you will notice two houses, some distance off to your right, next the river. The lower farm was Vandenburgh's, and served as a stopping place over night for the frightened inhabitants on their way from the north to a place of safety. The highway ran along the river till after the Revolution.

Burgoyne's River Defenses. Fraser's Grave. 11th: Two miles to the north of Bemis Heights we come to Wilbur's basin. Here just to the north of the buildings Burgoyne had his hospital, his park of artillery, and its magazines. At the river bank were tied his transportation boats, and thrown across the river was a pontoon bridge. Up to the left you will notice three hills. On each of these was placed a battery for the defense of his camp and stores. On the middle one General Fraser was buried, and his body was never removed, so far as is known. Consult map for locations. The fourth house to the north along the river is Ensign's, where Neilson had his struggle with the big Indian described in the chapter of anecdotes.

Swart's House. 12th: Nearly two miles north of Wilbur's basin you come to Searle's ferry. Forty rods above the ferry is a farm house. Turn to the west just north of the barns, pass over the canal bridge, and a few rods to the west of the bridge, on a rise of ground, and a little to your left, you will see a depression in the ground. That marks the cellar of Swart's house, which Burgoyne occupied two days as headquarters, and in the vicinity of which his army was encamped.

Willard's Mountain. 13th: Throughout the day you have noticed a high mountain on the east side of the river, about six miles away. That is Willard's mountain, so called from the fact that a Mr. Willard posted himself on that mountain during the latter days of Burgoyne's advance and signaled his observations to General Gates.

GUIDE TO REVOLUTIONARY AND COLONIAL SITES AT SCHUYLERVILLE

Schuylerville is connected by rail with Saratoga Springs, thirteen miles; Fort Edward, twelve miles; Greenwich, six miles; Mechanicville, sixteen miles.

As many are curious to know whether there are yet any relics at Schuylerville left from Revolutionary and Colonial days, we will give for their information the following list with their location, together with the location of historic sites. This guide is a condensation of the detailed descriptions found in the preceding pages.

As the multitudes of tourists who visit this hallowed spot naturally turn their steps toward the monument first, we will begin our tour at that point.

The Monument. FIRST: The monument stands within the lines of Burgoyne's fortified camp. This camp took in the buildings just north of the monument, extended diagonally southeast down the hill across the road to near Chestnut street, thence south along the crest of the terrace into the Victory woods; thence west just over the brow of the hill to a point south of the cemetery; thence north along the western slope of the cemetery ridge to the place of beginning.

Morgan's Breastworks. SECOND: About sixty rods northwest of the monument on a knoll covered with small trees, and now known as the Finch burying ground, but owned by James H. Carscadden, are to be seen remains of earthworks thrown up by Morgan's men. This place can be seen from the monument. Look for them on the east side of burying-ground and also in the bushes.

British Earthworks. THIRD: In the Victory woods, south of the monument, there are hundreds of feet of the British breastworks in an excellent state of preservation.

THE STORY OF OLD SARATOGA 505

The ground never having been permanently cleared nor plowed, these earthworks remain as the British left them, except that the logs, which may have entered into their construction, are rotted away. To find them, look for two pine trees near the northern end of the woods; between these trees you will find an angle in the woods running south and west. At the upper end of the northern leg of this angle are some rifle pits, plainly discernible; there are also some in front and south of it. Next, about 125 feet to the southwest, you will find another angle running west and then south; walk on the crest of these works till you come to an obtuse angle which veers to the southwest; near this some breastworks run directly south on the edge of a clearing. You can follow these easily for several hundred feet. Near the southern end of these turn to the left down into the woods and you will find a line of breastworks running from the swampy place through the woods to the crest of the ridge on the east. These two latter works were doubtless intended to cover their outposts, or advanced pickets.

The writer asked Mr. J. J. Perkins, then custodian of the monument, who was in the artillery service several years during the civil war, to go over the ground with him, and he declares that there is no doubt of their genuineness.

These being the only relics of Burgoyne's defensive works remaining on this side of the river, at Schuylerville, it is earnestly hoped that they may be preserved intact. They will doubtless remain undisturbed so long as they continue in the hands of the Victory Manufacturing Company. These woods ought to be owned by the village, or State.

American Earthworks. FOURTH: Back of the Victory schoolhouse, on a knoll covered with pines, may be seen remains of earthworks thrown up by the Americans. These are in a good state of preservation. This site is visible from the windows of the fourth and fifth stories of the monument.

Other American Earthworks. FIFTH: Above the Victory Mills, on the south side of the creek, is a clump of pines against a hill. On the top of the hill back of those pines are remains of Gates' works, where he had a battery posted. This site is also visible from the monument. Just below the Victory stone bridge, on the right bank of the creek, is the site of Schuyler's upper sawmill, the only building spared to him by Burgoyne. That mill sawed the timber in the present Schuyler mansion.

Camp Grounds. SIXTH: Going down Burgoyne street from the monument, after you cross the railroad, the next street you come to is Pearl street. On either side of this street as you look northward you see the camp ground of several companies of British troops and some Germans who tented in the woods. A few of the ancient oaks may yet be seen in the Reformed Church yard.

The Surrender Elm. SEVENTH: A few rods north of the foot of Burgoyne street, on the east side of Broadway, between the blacksmith shop and the brick store, stood the old elm under which, tradition says, Burgoyne signed the agreement to surrender, or "Convention," as he loved to call it. The tablet which hung on the old elm is now attached to the brick wall.

Fort Hardy. EIGHTH: Old Fort Hardy was located in the angle of Fish creek and the river. The road to Greenwich crosses its site. It was built in 1757 under the supervision of Colonel Montressor, a royal engineer, and it covered about fifteen acres. It supplanted a wooden or blockhouse fort which stood in the same angle, but the latter was, of course, a much smaller structure.

Burgoyne's Artillery. NINTH: On the continuation of Spring street, east of Broadway, is the place where Burgoyne had his artillery parked behind strong entrenchments. Directly opposite this on the other side of the river, on the high bluff, now void of trees, is the place where General Fellows had his battery posted, which so seriously annoyed the British. On the wooded bluff just to the north of this stood a Colonial fort built in 1721 (?).

German Camp Ground. TENTH: On the northwest angle of Spring street and Broadway, and on the high ground west of Broadway, as you go to the north, was the camp ground of the Germans ("Hessians"), under General Riedesel. A few rods northwest of the house on the corner, now owned by Mr. P. McNamara, were the barracks, built before the Revolution, burned by the British, and then rebuilt and occupied at one time by General Stark. Here no doubt the noted spy, Lovelass, was tried and condemned.

The Marshall House. ELEVENTH: The Marshall house is the one in whose cellar the Baroness Riedesel (pronounced Re-dáy-zel), with her children, and the wounded officers, found refuge during the six days' siege of Burgoyne. This is located about a mile north of Fish creek and on high ground to the left of the road. It can be reached by electric cars. An iron sign marks the place. This house was built by Peter Lansing of Albany in 1773, as a farm house. In 1785 it came into the possession of Samuel Bushee, who in turn, sold it to his brother-in-law, Samuel Marshall, in 1817. His son, William B. Marshall, repaired and altered it somewhat about 1868. He, however, had the good taste to leave the lower rooms and cellar, the really interesting portions, as they were.

The Marshalls relate the visit of an old man to the house in the early part of the nineteenth century. He had not been here since the Revolutionary war, but always wanted to come and visit that house. He said that he was the gunner that leveled the cannon that bombarded the house, that they shot several times before they got the range; finally they saw the shingles fly, and then they kept it warm for that house and its occupants, as well as other points, till Burgoyne showed the white flag. On being asked why they fired on women and wounded soldiers, he replied that they supposed it to be Burgoyne's headquarters.

Approach to Burgoyne's Pontoon Bridge. TWELFTH: A little to the north of the Marshall house, take the road to the east across the Canal bridge to the iron bridge that crosses the Hudson to Clark's Mills. Stop in the middle of the bridge and a little way to the north, on the east side in the rear of Mr. John A. Dix's house, you will see a road running diagonally down the bank. This was cut by the British as an approach to their pontoon bridge, there anchored. This road, together with the cut through the bank on the opposite side, locates the exact point where Burgoyne and his army crossed the Hudson September 13-15, 1777.

Burgoyne's Breastworks. THIRTEENTH: Remains of the breastworks thrown up by Burgoyne to defend the bridge are to be seen just north of Mr. Dix's house, and the board fence which starts from the bridge, and runs north to the barn, is built on the crest of a portion of those old defenses.

Furnival's Battery. FOURTEENTH: Looking east from this bridge, and a little to the left, are two rounded and bare knolls or hills. On the crest of the eastern one Captain Furnival posted his battery from which he began the cannonade of the Marshall house.

The Fords and Old Mill Sites. FIFTEENTH: Returning to and through Schuylerville, place yourself on the bridge that crosses Fish creek, near the south end. The stream which this bridge spans figures largely in both Colonial and Revolutionary history. It was the south line between the British and American armies during the siege of Burgoyne. Looking down stream the old ford crossed just this side the canal aqueduct, or about opposite the Schuyler mansion. There the French and Indians crossed on the night of November 27, 1745, to the massacre of Saratoga. There the armies in Colonial times crossed on their expeditions into Canada. There the British army crossed before and after the battles, and again after the surrender on October 17, 1777. A few rods below the bridge on the right side of the stream, in a recess in the bank, is the probable site of the early sawmill mentioned by the French in their story of the massacre of Saratoga, and also the site of one of General Schuyler's sawmills burned by Burgoyne. On the opposite side or left bank of the creek, just this side of the brick grist mill, stood General Schuyler's grist mill, also burned by Burgoyne. Turning around to your right you observe some cotton mills just above the bridge, and to the south of the creek. There stood several of the mills of General Schuyler burned by Burgoyne. Here was erected the first flax or linen mill in America, put up and run by General Schuyler. The tall mill nearest you and covered with vines, is the oldest cotton mill in New York State. It was erected by Philip Schuyler, 2d, in 1828.

The Several Schuyler Mansions. SIXTEENTH: Leaving the bridge we come next to the Schuyler mansion, embowered in its grove of ancient trees. This was erected by Gen. Philip Schuyler in the month of November, 1777. The main house was put up in seventeen days by the artisans of Gates' army. This house has sheltered as guests, Washington, Alexander Hamilton, Gov. George Clinton, and Lafayette, and many other notables of our country. It remains substantially as General Schuyler left it. Its predecessor was burned by General Burgoyne on the 11th of October, 1777. That house stood about twelve rods southeast of the present one. The lilac bushes at the bottom of the excavation are the descendants of the ones that stood in the garden of mansion No. 2.

The original house, the one burned by the French and Indians at the time of the massacre, stood twenty rods directly east of the present one on the bank of the canal. That one was built of brick. In it Capt. Philip Schuyler, uncle of the general, was shot and a number of other occupants perished in the flames. To the east of the canal on the flats were the wheat fields set on fire by Mrs. General Schuyler to prevent them becoming forage for the British army.

Where Lovelass, the Spy, was Executed. SEVENTEENTH: Retracing your steps to the road near the bridge, and looking south you see at a little distance a brick house. Back of this house is a gravel hill which originally extended to the east across the road. On the eastern brink of that hill, as it then was, the noted spy Lovelass was hung, on the limb of an oak tree. He was buried underneath it in a sitting posture; John Strover saw him hung and buried, and told his son George all about it. When the Waterford and Whitehall turnpike was built this gravel hill was partially dug away. George Strover was present and waited until Lovelass' remains were unearthed, when he appropriated the skull. This gruesome relic is still kept in the Schuyler mansion.

The Old Dutch Reformed Church. EIGHTEENTH: About one-third of a mile south of the creek, and in the fork of the River and Victory roads, stood the old Dutch Reformed Church. It was built in 1771. Here after service on the 30th of April, 1775, the people of this neighborhood heard the news of Lexington and Concord from the lips of General Schuyler. That church was used by the British for a hospital. A young woman while sitting at one of the north windows was shot by an American sharpshooter, and her blood stained the floor as long as the building stood. The church was damaged a few days later by several cannon balls shot from the British batteries. It was afterwards used by the Americans as a commissary depot. This church was taken down in 1822.

Forts Saratoga and Clinton. NINETEENTH: Pass down the road a few rods till you stand under the rocks, and in front of a small house on the hill. Right east of you on the river bank you see the site of two, and perhaps four Colonial forts. The last two which stood there were the only ones of the eight, built in this vicinity, that saw any fighting. The first of the two was known as "the fort at Saratoga," and was burned by the French on the night of the massacre in 1745. Without the walls of the last one, or Fort Clinton, several bloody and disastrous encounters took place with the French and Indians. This fort experienced at least one successful mutiny. It was soon after dismantled and burned by orders of Gov. George Clinton in October, 1747. The location of these interesting forts was lost for many years, but was discovered by the writer of this book in the spring of 1900. Loose stones and brick-bats covered the site of the forts.

Where Burgoyne Delivered His Sword. TWENTIETH: Somewhere between the above mentioned house and the canal bridge, and south of where you stand, is the place where Burgoyne went through the formal act of surrender by drawing his sword and delivering it to General Gates.

The exact location has been irretrievably lost. The tablet that purports to mark the place should probably stand several rods to the north. The old road is said to have run where the canal now is.

The Tory and Colonel Van Vechten. TWENTY-FIRST: About ten rods below the canal bridge is a little ravine where a Tory waylaid Colonel Van Vechten, of Coveville. Screened by some trees he waited till the Colonel passed along a-horseback on his way up to visit General Schuyler. The Tory had his rifle leveled at him, and was about to pull the trigger, when his nerve failed him and he allowed the Colonel to pass unharmed. He related this incident after the Revolution.

Remains of Revolutionary Earthworks. TWENTY-SECOND: On the east side of the river, a mile or more south of the bridge, on the edge of a high bluff facing the south and overlooking a ravine, are some breastworks thrown up by the Green Mountain boys during the siege of Burgoyne. They are in an almost perfect state of preservation, still being breast high. They are on the farm now owned by Nathan Corliss. These were identified as Revolutionary remains by the writer during the summer of 1900, after his attention had been called to them by Mr. Robert Coffin, who lives in the neighborhood.

Gates' Headquarters. TWENTY-THIRD: About one and one-third miles below Fish creek, on the east side of the road, stands the house which was probably used by General Gates as his headquarters from the 10th to the 15th of October, 1777, and again used by him after the surrender. On the 14th or 15th of October he moved up to the place south of the old Dutch Church, where the formal surrender occurred on the 17th. The house was enlarged after the Revolution and is now owned and occupied by Edward Dwyer, who has the good taste to keep the house in its ancient form.

Willard's Mountain. TWENTY-FOURTH : Looking off to the southeast from almost any point in or about Schuylerville one sees a mountain about ten miles away. That is Willard's Mountain; so called from the fact that a Mr. Willard posted himself on its top during the advance of Burgoyne, and signaled his observations to General Gates. This mountain is about 1,400 feet above sea level, and affords the finest and most extensive view to be had from any point within thirty miles from here.

First Village of Saratoga. Old Saratoga, destroyed by the French and Indians in 1745, was situated, mainly, just below the fort marked No. 17 on the map.

Schuylerville is well supplied with excellent hotels and well-equipped liveries and garages. Carriage drives hereabouts are unusually numerous and attractive: To the battle-field, two ways, 9 miles; to Saratoga Lake, 9 miles; to Fort Miller, 5 miles; to Cossayuna Lake, 12 miles; to the magnificent Dianondahowa Falls, 3 miles; to Greenwich, 5 miles; to Bald Mountain, the deserted village, 4 miles, and to the top of Willard's Mountain, 12 miles. The roads are unusually good.

Sources and Literature

We subjoin herewith a list of the authorities which we found especially useful in the preparation of this work:

Documents Relating to the Colonial History of New York, 10 Vols. Folio.
Documentary History of New York, 4 Vols. Folio. E. B. O'Calligan.
The Sir Wm. Johnson MSS. State Library. Story's Life of Sir Wm. Johnson.
Journal of the Legislative Council of N. Y. in MSS. State Library.
Manuscripts in the Albany Co. Clerk's Office, Albany.
Colonial New York. Geo. W. Schuyler.
Jesuits of North America. Francis Parkman.
Travels in North America. Peter Kalm.
The Colonial Laws of New York.
Montressor's Journal. N. Y. Historical Society's Col's. Vol. 14.
The American Lady. Mrs. Grant of Laggan.
History of Saratoga Co., both editions. N. B. Sylvester.
History of Washington Co., N. Y. Johnson.
Burgoyne's State of the Expedition from Canada. Edition of 1780.
Lieut. Hadden's Journal, annotated by Rogers.
Lieut. Digby's Journal.
Lieut. Anburey's Travels.
Capt. Pausch's Journal, annotated by Stone.
Memoirs, by Gen. James Wilkinson.
Diary of Baroness Riedesel. W. L. Stone.
The Sexagenary, J. P. Becker, edited by D. C. Bloodgood.
The Clinton Papers. Hugh Hastings.
Revolutionary Letters. W. L. Stone.
Field Book of the Revolution. Lossing.
Travels in North America. Marquis de Chastellux.
Burgoyne's Campaign and St. Leger's Expedition. W. L. Stone.
Winsor's Narrative and Critical History.

Our Country. Lossing.
The American Revolution. John Fiske.
History of Lake Champlain. Palmer.
The Burgoyne Campaign. Charles Neilson.
Battles of Saratoga and History of Saratoga Monument Ass'n. Mrs. E. H. Walworth.
Schuyler MSS. loaned by Miss Fanny Schuyler of Pelham-on-Sound, N. Y.
Schuyler Papers. N. Y. Historical Society Collections, Vol. 12.
History of Maj. Gen. Philip Schuyler. Lossing.
Tuckerman's Life of Gen. Philip Schuyler.
Major Gen. Philip Schuyler and the Burgoyne Campaign. By Gen. J. Watts De Peyster.
Justice to Schuyler. De Peyster.
Schuyler and Practical Strategy. De Peyster.
Border Wars of New York. J. R. Simms.
A Godchild of Washington. Mrs. C. S. Baxter.
Reminiscences of Saratoga. W. L. Stone.
Centennial Fourth of July Oration. Gen. E. F. Bullard.
Memoir of the Centennial Celebration of Burgoyne's Surrender, Stone.
Records of the Dutch Reformed Church of Saratoga (Schuylerville).
Records of the Village of Schuylerville.
Drake's French and Indian Wars.
Journal of the General Assembly of N. Y.
Council Minutes.
Soldier's Minutes.
Jones' New York in the Revolution.
German Allies in the Revolution.
Col. John Trumbull's Reminiscences of his Own Times.
Trevelyan's American Revolution.
Belcher's First American Civil War.
Collections of the New York Historical Society.
New York Historical Society Magazine.
Fonblanque's Burgoyne.
Magazine of American History.
Hough's Northern Invasion.
Watson's Men and Times of The Revolution.

THE STORY OF OLD SARATOGA 517

In addition to certain of the above the following were especially useful in preparing New York's Share in the Revolution.

J. R. Brodhead's History of New York.
Hildreth's United States.
H. B. Dawson's Sons of Liberty.
W. E. Griffis' Influence of the Netherlands on the English Commonwealth and the American Republic.
Motley's Dutch Republic.
George Bancroft's History of United States.
Leake's Life of Gen. Lamb.
Ford's Writings of Washington.
Robert's New York in the Revolution.
Proceedings of the New York State Historical Association.
Elliot's Debates on the Federal Constitution.
Wm. Jay's Life of John Jay.
Wm. Whitelock's Life of John Jay.
John Fiske's Critical Period of American History.
D. Campbell's Puritans in England, Holland, etc.
H. C. Lodge's Life of Alexander Hamilton.

INDEX

A — PAGE

Abercrombie, Gen. Jas., leads against "Ti." 74
Ackland, Maj. John Dyke, wounded 144
saved from being shot........ 148
Ackland, Lady, bravely seeks her husband, the Major.......... 159
Adams, John, belittles Washington 453
his share in peace treaty with England 460
consummates a treaty with Holland 462
his estimate of John Jay's services 482
Adams, Samuel, impatient of Schuyler, favored Gates...... 452
States' Rights leader in Mass... 483
Aggressive acts of Revolution, the first occurred in New York.. 441
Algonquin Indians, with Champlain 1
guide Courcelle against the Mohawks 9
Amherst, Gen., captures Ticonderoga 75
Andre, Major, captured by New Yorkers 356, 455
Anecdotes of Revolutionary period, 2 chapters 235-271
Anne, Ft., built................. 25
battle at 86
Arnold, Gen. Benedict.
fights naval battle on Lake Champlain 81
is sent to Schuyler's aid....... 102
is sent to Gansevoort's aid..... 107
reports to Gates............... 123
advises Gates where to make his stand 124
given command of left wing.... 125
advises Gates to attack Burgoyne 129
leads in the first battle........ 130
breaks with Gates............ 140
rushes into second battle without orders 145
wounded 148

PAGE

Association, The Saratoga Monument, first officers and Trustees of 378

B

Ballston, raided by Tories........ 221
Battles, three decisive, won by New Yorkers 451
Baume, Col., starts for Bennington 108
killed at Bennington........... 111
Bemis Heights, where Gates made his stand 124
Bennington, Vt., threatened by Baume 109
battle of 111
battle of, its moral effect...... 439
Boston massacre 421
tea party 424
port of closed by Act of Parliament 424
Boundary disputes, explained..... 87
Brant, Indian chief, leads attack at Canajoharie 219
Breyman, Col., sent to Baume's aid 110
aids Fraser at Saratoga battle.. 130
killed in second battle of Saratoga 148
British officers, their snobbery.... 74
Brudenell, Chaplain, his burial of Gen. Fraser described........ 157
bravely accompanies Lady Ackland 160
Bunker Hill, battle of, its value and significance 435
Burgoyne, Gen. John, at Boston and in Canada.............. 82
commissioned for campaign of 1777 83
size of his army.............. 84
appoints thanksgiving service... 97
his advance impeded by Schuyler 98
at Fort Edward............... 108
delayed by Bennington......... 119
crosses the Hudson.......... 120

	PAGE
advances to first battle	128
fortifies at Freeman's Farm	136
and Gates compared as to courage	151
describes Gen. Fraser's burial	151
orders retreat	157
occupies the Schuyler mansion	163
fortifies Saratoga heights	166
orders burning of Schuyler's buildings	169
agrees to surrender his army	186
the formal surrender	194
army conducted to Boston	205
returns to England	206
about two of his messengers	252

C

Canada, invaded by Indians	3, 10
by New Yorkers	18, 19
Canal, the Champlain, when built, its effect on growth of Schuylerville	374
Champlain, Samuel de, discovers the lake and defeats the Iroquois	1
Champlain and Hudson valleys, strategic value of	xi
Cherry Valley, massacre of	213
Chew, Capt., sent on scout from Ft. Clinton	50
Church, old Dutch, saved from burning	256
cannonaded	258
people in attendance hear news of Lexington, etc.	302
sketch of its founding and Revolutionary experiences	359
Civil war, about the	272
Clements, Albert, laid out Schuylerville	375
Clinton, George, Colonial Governor, reports to the Lords of Trade	30
reports on Saratoga massacre	40
characterized	41
orders burning of Ft. Clinton	62
Clinton, Gov. George, begs Gates to fortify the Highlands	209
heads troops from Saratoga against John Johnson	219
trys to buy Saratoga Springs	334

	PAGE
quoted on war's cost to New York	447
how he saved Washington's army from disbandment	456
State's Rights leader of, in New York party	473
Clinton, Sir Henry, sends dispatches to Burgoyne	134
Cobleskill, destroyed by Indians and Tories	213
Cokely, John, fights to save Gen. Schuyler	363
Gen. Schuyler gives him a farm	364
Congress, the, deaf to Schuyler's appeals for aid	101
Connecticut refuses Washington room for his army	448
Constitutional Convention, the, meets in Philadelphia	476
Continental Congress meets at Philadelphia	427
its lack of power and money	469
its abortive efforts to raise money	470
Conway Cabal, the	208, 452
Cornbury, Gov., Lord, builds fort at Saratoga	24
Coveville, Burgoyne encamped at	122
Burgoyne retreats to	158
described	371
Courcelle, Samuel de Remi, leads an attack against the Iroquois	9
Cowpens, battle of the, mentioned	225
Cramer, John, his escape with his family	307
Crown Point, fortified by the French	28

D

Dean's Corners, whence its name, etc.	376
Dearborn, Major, in command of riflemen	124
his experience while in command at Saratoga	233
Denonville, Gov. of Canada, starts trouble with the Iroquois	10
De Ridder, or De Ruyter, murdered by Indians	70
De Ridder, the family, early settlers	295

INDEX

521

	PAGE
Dickinson, John, prepares two papers for first Constitutional Congress	427
Dieskau, Baron, attacks Johnson, brought a prisoner through Saratoga	66, 71
Digby, Col., tells of depressing effect of Bennington	112
Dix, John A., ex-Governor, preserves historic sites	120
Dovegat (Coveville), Burgoyne at	122
Duer's House, Burgoyne's headquarters	120
Duer, William, sketch of his life and character	352
first Judge of Charlotte (Washington) county	353
risks his life to keep Washington in command	454
Dunham, Hezekiah, captor of Lovelass the spy	268
an early settler	297
Dunham's Hill, an early business center	370
Dutchmen of Albany ransom Father Jogues and pay his passage to France	4

E

Education, general, discouraged in New York by Colonial Governors	395
Edward, Fort, Ft. Nicholson built at	25

F

Federalist, the, a series of papers expounding the Constitution	482
Fellows, Gen., occupies heights of Saratoga	162
crosses and occupies east side of Hudson	163
Ferry, first at Old Saratoga	68
Fiske, John, his estimate of Gen. Schuyler	118
Flag, the American, the first appearance in action	86
first unfurled to grace a victory	198
Ford at Saratoga changed	68
Fort Anne, built	25
surrendered to British	220
Fort Clinton, built at Saratoga	45
various enemy attacks nearby	46-47

	PAGE
La Corne St. Luc's ambush at	52
its location established	53-56
abandoned	60
burned	62
Fort Dayton, same as Herkimer, New York	107
Fort Edward named	66
brick yards at	72
Jane McCrea, killed at	98
Burgoyne at	108
Col. S. Warner and regiment stationed at	214
Fort Hardy, built at Saratoga	70
Fort Independence, evacuated by Gen. St. Clair	85
Fort Miller, Israel Putnam's adventure at	76, 103
Burgoyne's headquarters at	120
William Duer's home at	352
Fort Neilson, Arnold's headquarters	125
Fort at Saratoga, the first	23
the second	25
the third	29
the fourth	30
the fifth	45
Fort Hardy, the sixth	70
Fort St. Frederic, at Crown Point	28
French council at	32
Fort Schuyler, formerly Fort Stanwix	82
Fort Ticonderoga, evacuated by St. Claire	85
Fort William Henry, built by Sir Wm. Johnson	67
captured by Montcalm	69
Fort Winslow at Stillwater	68
Franklin, Benj., his part in peace treaty with England	459
France, about her motives in helping us in the Revolution	463
Fraser, Gen. Simon, encamped at the Battenkill	108
crossed the Hudson, and recrossed	119
bridges the Hudson	120
led Burgoyne's right, both battles	129
shot	146
died, his burial	155
Frontenac, Count de, sends an expedition against Albany	13

INDEX

G

	PAGE
Gansevoort, Col. Peter, at Ft. Schuyler	105, 107
Gates, Gen. Horatio, intrigues against General Schuyler	89, 90, 91
relieves Schuyler for a while, and retires	91
supersedes Schuyler in command	115
starts northward to check Burgoyne	124
orders attack on Burgoyne	129
removes Arnold from command	141
and Burgoyne compared as to courage	151
his argument with Sir Francis Clarke	152
his generalship estimated by Col. Wilkinson	153
protects British sick and wounded	158
sends force to occupy heights opposite Saratoga	165
follows Burgoyne northward	168
makes an abortive attack	169
begins a regulation siege	172
agrees with Burgoyne on articles of surender	186
receives Burgoyne's sword	200
tardily returns troops to Washington	206
ordered by Congress to retake Highlands	208
connection with the Conway Cabal	208
duel with Col. Wilkinson	210
and the expedition against Canada	210
ends his career	211
George's, King, war	30
George, Lake, first discovered	3
George III, his desire for personal rule kindled the Revolution	401
why he hired Hessians, etc.	403
Gettysburg, the field of, becomes a national park	440
Glover, Gen., sent to Schuyler's aid	102
Glover, Gen., commanded a brigade at Saratoga	127
Grangerville, whence its name, described	371
Grant, Mrs., of Lagan, describes Gen. Schuyler's doings, etc., at Saratoga	291
Grants, the Hampshire, described	88
Guide to Colonial and Revolutionary sites at Schuylerville	502
Guide to the Saratoga battlefield	494

H

	PAGE
Haines, Thomas, narrow escape from burial, etc	150
Hamilton, Alexander.	
sent by Washington to hasten return of troops	206
married Elizabeth Schuyler	312
appraises New York's contributions and sufferings	445
formulates paper whose adoption creates the Contitutional Convention	475
argues for a brand new form of government	477
leads in fight for adoption of new constitution	482
what John Fisk thought of him and his work	482
fights for the Constitution in New York Convention	484
chosen first Secretary of Treasury of United States	487
originated the financial system of our government	488
first to assert the "implied powers" of the Constitution	489
and Jefferson compared	490
Hamilton, Andrew, in the fight for the liberty of the press	398
Hendrick, King, quoted	63
with his braves joins Sir Wm. Johnson	65
Herkimer, Gen. Nicholas	105, 106
Hessians desert Burgoyne	138
Histories of United States. Who wrote our first influential	390
Hooker, Rev. Thos., quoted	407
Howe, Lord, reassures Gen. Webb	69
killed at Ticonderoga	75
Howe, Sir William, his movements in New Jersey	83
why he failed Burgoyne	134

INDEX 523

Hubbardton, Vt., battle at mentioned 86
Hudson and Champlain valleys, strategic value of xi
Hudson, Hendrick, discovers river which bears his name 2

I

Indians, Burgoyne's, their atrocities 98, 99, 103, 106, 238, 447
Ingoldsby, Fort, at Stillwater 25
Iroquois Indians, how they became conquerors xii
a party of, defeated by Champlain 2
they capture Father Jogues 3
their expedition against Canada 10
their friendship gained by Peter Schuyler 21

J

Jay, John, writes a great letter to the Bostonians 426
writes the address to the people of Great Britain 227
becomes leader in the peace treaty with England 459
an estimate of his services in the peace treaty 464
outlines the form of government of the United States 477
chosen first chief justice of the United States 487
what John Adams thought of his services 482
Jefferson, Thomas, commends John Jay 464
chosen first Secretary of State. 487
compared with Hamilton 488
Jogues, Father, captured by Iroquois Indians 3
escapes by aid of the Dutch.... 4
returns and starts a mission among the Mohawks 5
is murdered 6
Johnson, Sir William, warns Fort Clinton 50
appointed leader against Crown Point 65
would relieve Fort William Henry 69

Johnson, Sir John, leads a destructive raid up the Mohawk.... 217
leads an attack on Schoharie... 220
Journals of soldiers, extracts from 77-79

K

Kalm, Peter, naturalist, describes fort at Saratoga 54
version of attack on Fort Clinton 58
more about his visit 288
Kayadrosseras trail described 8
de Tracy takes it against Mohawks 10
Kieft, Gov., charitable to Father Jogues 4
Knox, Colonel and General, removes cannon from Ticonderoga 305
chosen first Secretary of War. 487
Kosciusko, Polish engineer... 102, 124

L

Lafayette, Marquis de, in command of expedition against Canada 210
visits Schuylerville 346
Lake George receives its name... 66
Learned, Gen., commanded a brigade at Saratoga battle 144
Leisler, Jacob, becomes Governor of New York 15
Lexington and Concord, battle of, its value and significance..... 435
Liberty, religious, New York's contribution 396
in Holland since 1477 408
Sons of, originated in New York 399
Lincoln, Gen., sent to Schuyler's aid 102
on his way to reinforce Schuyler 116
commands right wing at second battle 138
is wounded 155
Livingston, Henry, commandant at Saratoga 46, 49
Livingston, Col. James 107, 127
sketch of his life 354
drove off the Vulture, Maj. Andre's ship 356

524 INDEX

died and is buried at Schuylerville 358
Livingston, Phillip, builds fort at Saratoga 29
Livingston, William, prophesies American independence 420
prepares a paper for First Continental Congress 427
Lovelass, the spy, his capture, and execution 268
Lydius, John H., first settler of Fort Edward 32
his house used as jail by the French 33

M

McCrea, Jane, her murder, its result 98
Mansions, the Schuyler 309
Marin, M., leader in Saratoga massacre 32
Marshall house cannonaded 165
Baroness Riedesel at 176
Marshall family, experiences of.. 241
Marshall, John, used Hamilton's "implied powers" in expounding the Constitution 489
Marsiglio of Padua, quoted on rights of the people 409
Massachusetts, people homogeneous 396
allowed her citizens no religious liberty 397
Justice Hutchinson, a native of, issued the "Writs of Assistance" 404
rebels at "Writs of Assistance" 405
taxation without consent opposed by 410
"no taxation without representation" suggested by 411
Committees of Correspondence originated in 416
Bostonians resisted landing of tea 424
refuses Washington room for an army camp 448
militia loot White Plains, and Ballston, N. Y 449
Middle Ravine, described 125
mentioned 142, 143
Mohawk Indians, defeat Courcelle 9

aid Pieter Schuyler in raid on Canada 20
Frontenac's punishment of 21
Montcalm, Gen., captures Fort William Henry 69
defeats Gen. Abercrombie 75
Montgomery, Gen. James, invades Canada 81
Montressor, Col. James, builds Fort Hardy 71
Monument, The Saratoga, the story of its building 378
Morgan, Col. Daniel, sent north by Washington 116
his corps placed in advance.... 123
bags a lot of prisoners 126
in first battle of Saratoga 130
in second battle of Saratoga...
.... 144, 146
how he came to Cambridge, Mass. 157
with his corps joins Washington 206
wins battle of the Cowpens.... 225
Morris, Gouverneur, quoted on Zenger and liberty of press.. 399
helps to save Washington from Conway Cabal 454
becomes assistant to Robert Morris as financier of the Revolution 466
the inventor of our decimal currency 466
put the Federal Constitution in literary shape 467
Morris, Lewis. quotation from his will 103
Mount Defiance, captured by British 85
Moses creek, Gen. Schuyler halts army at 102

N

Nicholson, Gen. Francis 25
Fort, built 25
Neilson's encounter with big Indian 248
New Netherland, wrested from Holland and renamed 394
New York State, from the beginning cosmopolitan 392
allowed no charter by England. 395

INDEX 525

granted religious liberty to her citizens 396
first to grant liberty of the press 396
Sons of Liberty originated in.. 399
repudiates a king appointed judge 405
protests against Crown appointed officials 406
protests against taxation without consent 410
first Colonial Congress meets in New York city.............. 412
non-importation compact originated in 414
refuses to house and feed an army and is punished by Parliament 417
first in advocating Independence 419
battle of Golden Hill in.:..... 421
had her Tea Party............. 224
political and material situation in, at start of Revolution.... 432
strategic importance of........ 434
first aggressive acts of Revolution occurred in........... 441
how much of it devastated by the enemy 443
how she ranked in population.. 444
compared as to soldiers in service 445
compared as to battles fought on her territory 446
how she suffered from American soldiers 448
how her delegates to Congress saved Washington 454
three decisive battles fought in 451

O
Orange, Fort, a trading post...... 2
Otis, James, of Mass., quoted..... 405
Oriskany, battle of.............. 105
Oriskany, battle of, its moral effect 439

P
Peace Commission to Paris, its personnel 458
People, the, the true source of authority, whence the idea..... 406
Peters, Col., defends Canadian Provincials 112

Phillips, Maj. General........85. 131
Picquet, Abbe, Chaplain to M. Marin 32
Pitt, William, English statesman. quoted 402
Poor, Gen. in command of a brigade, under Arnold.... 127. 143
Political parties, the rise of...... 472
Providence, band of seen in Burgoyne campaign 135
exhibited in National affairs... 471
Putnam, Israel, adventure at Fort Miller 76

Q
Quaker Springs, whence its name. etc. 370

R
Railroad, its coming to Schuylerville 376
first passenger railroad in the United States 376
Regiment, the 77th, of Civil war. about it 275
Revolution, American, causes of.. ....80. 301
where the blame for rests...... 401
chaotic conditions that followed 468
Riedesel, Baroness, relates experiences on the retreat......... 164
relates her experiences at the Marshall house 176
kindly treated by Gen. Schuyler 175
Riedesel, Gen., crosses the Hudson 121
rescues Burgoyne 131
Road, first military built......... 25
Schuyler builds the first to Saratoga Springs 331
Roads built in Saratoga Township 365
Rogers family, experiences of.... 242

S
Sacrament, Lac St., first name for Lake George 3
Salt, a famine of in New York State 214
Saratoga, battle of, its effect compared with Lexington and Bunker Hill 439
Lake, by whom discovered...... 4

INDEX

	PAGE
Old, first settlers at	284
first mills at	286
settlement after massacre	288
Mrs. Grant of Lagan writes about	291
first permanent settlers at	295
partition of the township	367
significance of word	280
different spellings, the name first of a district	7
basis of its historic importance	7
trail	8
Gov. Lord Cornbury recommends fort at	24
Pieter Schuyler builds fort at	25
third fort built at	29
massacre of	36
experiences of Saratoga captives	42
first battle of	129
second battle	144
Burgoyne retreats to Old Saratoga	157
Burgoyne surrendered at Old Saratoga	172
a decisive battle, why?	201
Col. Seth Warner ordered to occupy	211
people need salt	214
Gen. Stark in command at	226
Lord Sterling at	229
Gen. Stark gives dark picture, conditions at	230
the Saratoga patent	281
Saratoga Springs, Gen. Schuyler builds first road to	331
Washington visits	334
Col. Dearborn visits	233
how it got its name	368
Schaghticoke Indians, at Saratoga	23
captured by M. Marin	33
Schenectady, massacre of	13
Washington visits	333
first railroad built to	376
Schoharie, devastated by John Johnson, Tories and Indians	220
Schuyler, Capt. Abram, sent on scout	17
Schuyler, Capt. Johannes, leads first armed force into Canada	18
furnishes material for fort at Saratoga	29
begins settlement at Saratoga	285

	PAGE
Schuyler, Catherine, Mrs., her family connections	311
burns the wheat fields	316
Schuyler, John Bradstreet, to him, his father, the Gen., gives Saratoga property	336
death of	341
Schuyler, Pieter, leads second expedition into Canada	19
commended to English government	20
leads pioneer force, builds forts, etc.	25
Schuyler, Col. Peter, of N. J., Commandant at Saratoga	49
suppresses a mutiny at Saratoga	59
Schuyler, Phillip, uncle of the General	34
killed at Saratoga	37
Schuyler, Gen. Phillip, at battle of Lake George	67
quits Gen. Winslow for Col. John Bradstreet	69
takes body of Lord Howe to Albany	75
learns through spy the aims of Burgoyne	83
removes garrison, artillery, etc., from Fort Orange	86
his connection with "The Grants" dispute	88
his blame for loss of Ticonderoga considered	89
vindicated by Congress	91
obstructs Burgoyne's advance	93
letter about quoted	100
asks Washington for aid	101
reinforces Gansevoort	107
withdraws to "sprouts of Mohawk"	108
relieved of his command	114
estimates of his character	117
present at the surrender	195
receives Burgoyne's apology and entertains him in Albany	200
supplies Saratoga garrison with food	221, 225
wins Gen. Stark's good will	227
Mrs. Grant of Lagan writes about	291
the Schuyler mansions	309

INDEX

	PAGE
sketch of family	311
distinguished guests of	314
attempt on his life	315
makes a record in housebuilding	323
builds first road to Saratoga Springs	331
attempted capture of	363
Schuyler, Phillip, 2d, inherits Saratoga estate	343
erects second cotton mill in New York State	344
Schuylerville, strategic position of.	xi
whence its name, etc	281
first settlers at	284
Col. James Livingston, died and is buried at	358
post Revolutionary settlement of	362
second cotton mill in New York built at	344
history of modern village of	373
by whom laid out	375
the coming of the railroad	376
Scott. John Morin, argues for Independence	420
Scott. Gen. Winfield, quoted	108
Capt. messenger of Burgoyne	253
Sexagenary, The, who he was	235
Seymour, Horatio, his estimate of Gen. Schuyler	117
speaks of New York's mixed population	393
Shelburne, Lord, represents England in peace treaty	459
Skenesborough, Americans retire to from "Ti"	86
Burgoyne reaches	97
garrison at	214
attacked by Tories	217
St. Clair, General, commandant at Ticonderoga	84
evacuates Ticonderoga	85
was he to blame for loss of "Ti"?	89
joins Schuyler at Fort Edward.	100
St. Leger, Col., would capture the Mohawk valley	82
besieges Fort Schuyler. 105, 106.	107
leads an expedition from Canada	228
St. Luc. La Corne. expedition against Saratoga	50
deserts Burgoyne	112

	PAGE
Stamp Act, The, how received in New York and Massachusetts	410
Stampede of inhabitants of the upper Hudson 95,	238
Stark, Gen. John, accepts command of N. H. troops	109
assembles forces at Bennington.	110
fights battle at Bennington	111
reinforces Gates	126
at Saratoga	174
and expedition against Canada.	210
in command of Northern Dept.	213
ordered to Saratoga by Washington	226
speaks highly of Gen. Schuyler.	227
Sterling, Lord, given command of Northern Dept.	228
celebrates surrender of Yorktown at Saratoga	230
Stillwater, fort built at	25
Fort Winslow built at	68
Dirck Swart's house at	104
Gen. Schuyler's headquarters at.	104
Tories at	240
Col. Jas. Livingston settled at.	357
Strover, Col. George, becomes owner of Schuyler property.	350
Sullivan expedition against the Indians referred to	216
Swart, Dirck, his house Schuyler's headquarters	104
Sword's, (Swart's) House, Burgoyne at	123

T

Talleyrand, C. M. de, his opinion of A. Hamilton	489
Taxation without consent, opposed by Massachusetts and New York	410
Tenbroeck, Gen., at Gates' first war council	116
in second battle	146
Thirteen, about the number	270
Ticonderoga, its capture purposed.	66
Tories, The, an appeal to fairness concerning	433
Tory women stranded at Saratoga.	222
Tracy, Marquis de, leads a successful foray against the Mohawks	10
Trails, the Saratoga and Kayadrosseras	8

528 INDEX

Treaty of Peace with England, the story of it 458
Trenton, battle of, its effect sized up 438
Trumbull, Col. John, exonerates St. Clair 89
Tubbs, John, fights to save Gen. Schuyler from capture 363
Schuyler gives him a farm 364

U

Union of Utrecht, referred to 408

V

Van Veghten, Col. has narrow escape 267, 298
kept the first store in Old Saratoga 370
Vergennes, Compt de, French minister, his part in peace treaty. 459
Victory Mills, an account of the village of 372
Virginia, makes first official protest against Stamp Act 411
Vrooman, Bartel, first settler at Old Saratoga, murdered 16
more about him 285
War, King George's 30
William's, King, what it cost Albany county and the Iroquois. 22
Ward, John, fights to save Gen. Schuyler 363
Schuyler gives him a farm 364
Warner, Col. Seth, arrives at Bennington 110
aids Gen. Stark at Bennington.. 111
ordered to occupy Saratoga 211
garrisons Fort Edward 214
Washington, George, leader against the French 65
successes and defeats in 1775, '76 81-2
cheerfully backed Schuyler 101
begs Gates to return troops 206
orders Gen. Stark to Saratoga.. 226
receives surrender of Yorktown 230
twice visits Old Saratoga 332
tried to buy Saratoga Springs... 334
the Conway Cabal and 208, 452
corresponds with Hamilton and Jay about factious conditions 473
promotes commerce with Mississippi valley 474
chosen first President of United States 486
Webb, Gen. Daniel, a coward.... 69
Webster, Daniel, his estimate of Gen. Schuyler 117
his estimate of John Jay 427
Week's William, letter on soldier's experiences quoted 104
Welch, Joseph, had a narrow escape 244
Wilbur's Basin, Burgoyne establishes himself at 136
Wilkinson, Col. James, estimate of Schuyler 117
advises Gates to attack, second battle 143
saves Maj. Ackland 149
his estimate of Gates' generalship 153
saves Gates from a disaster.... 170
and the Conway Cabal 210
Willet, Col. M., defeats Col. Ross near Johnstown 229
Wilson, Woodrow, quoted on New York's mixed population 393
Winslow, Gen., John, leader against Crown Point in 1756. 68
Winthrop, Fitz John, Gen 17
Wolves disturb Burgoyne's camp. 139

Y

Yankee Doodle, first played as an American air 197

Z

Zenger, Peter, who fought and won liberty of the press 397

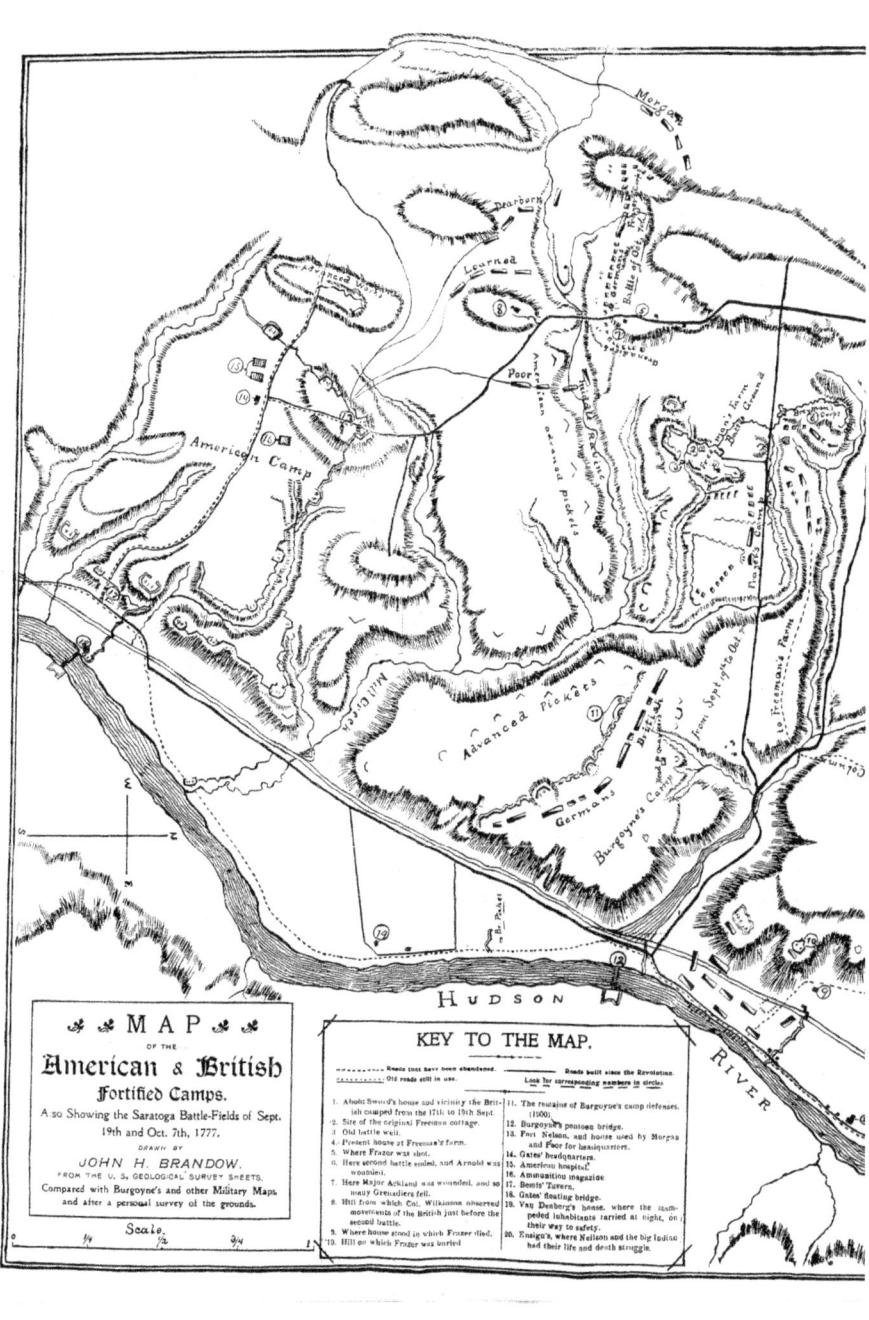

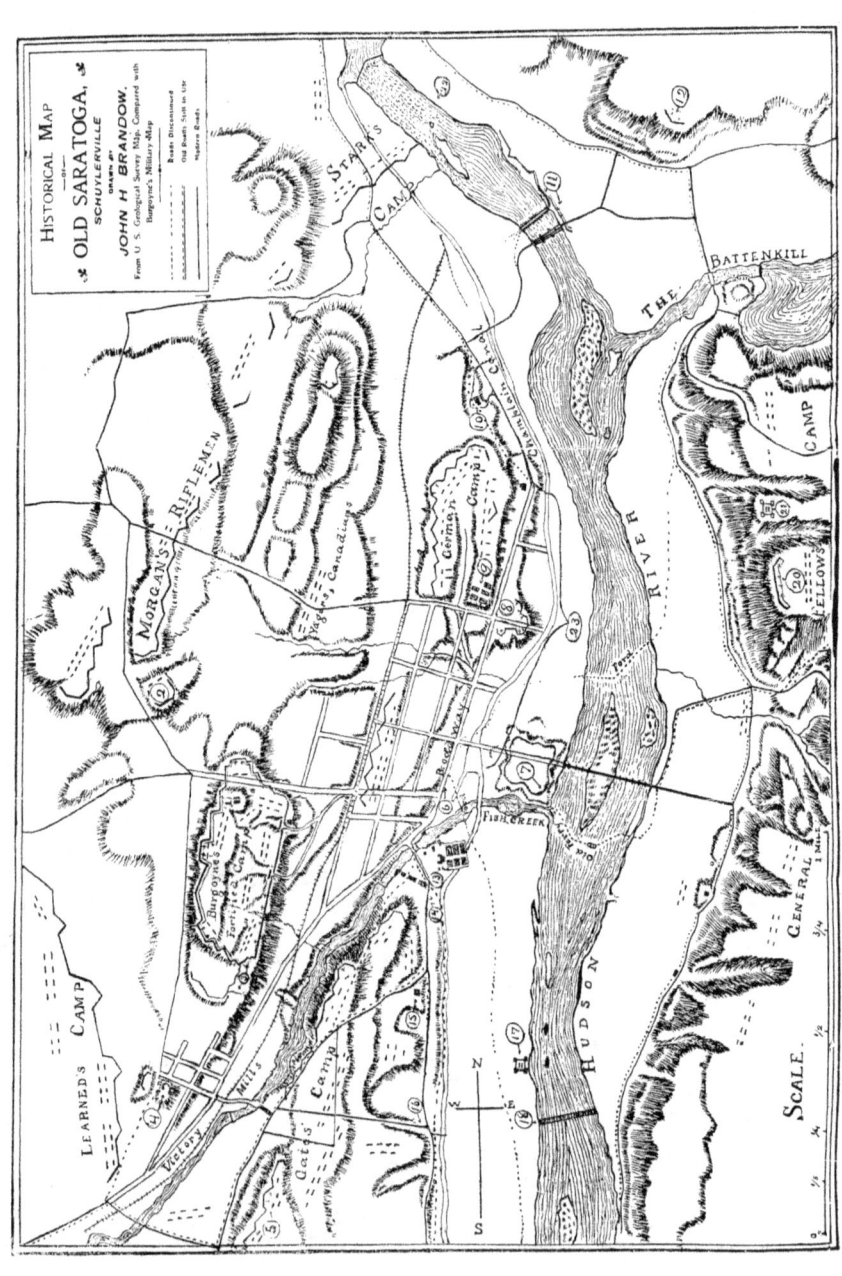

www.ingramcontent.com/pod-product-compliance
Lightning Source LLC
Chambersburg PA
CBHW071712300426
44115CB000108/1396